*SAT Math FOR DUMMIES®

by Mark Zegarelli

WILEY

Wiley Publishing, Inc.

***SAT Math For Dummies®**

Published by
Wiley Publishing, Inc.
111 River St.
Hoboken, NJ 07030-5774
www.wiley.com

For general information on our other products and services, please contact our Customer Care Department within the U.S. at 877-762-2974, outside the U.S. at 317-572-3993, or fax 317-572-4002.

For technical support, please visit www.wiley.com/techsupport.

Wiley also publishes its books in a variety of electronic formats. Some content that appears in print may not be available in electronic books.

Library of Congress Control Number: 2010929312

ISBN: 978-0-470-62085-4

Manufactured in the United States of America

10 9 8 7 6 5 4

WILEY

About the Author

Mark Zegarelli is the author of *LSAT Logic Games For Dummies* (Wiley) plus four other *For Dummies* books on basic math and pre-algebra, Calculus II, and logic. He holds degrees in both English and math from Rutgers University and is an SAT teacher and tutor.

Mark lives in Long Branch, New Jersey, and San Francisco, California.

Dedication

This is for my dear friend Simon Stanley Marcus, with much gratitude for your boundless wisdom and presence.

Author's Acknowledgments

This is my sixth *For Dummies* book, and again I enjoy the privilege of working with an editorial team that continues to inspire and call me to my best. Thank you to my Wiley editors: Chrissy Guthrie, Danielle Voirol, and Lindsay Lefevere. More thanks for my technical editors, Amy Nicklin and Benjamin Wyss, for setting me on a better course whenever 2 + 2 = 5.

I really don't know how to express proper gratitude for all of the wonderful people in my life who surround me with constant love, support, encouragement, and joy. But I want you to know that I feel truly blessed and fortunate to make my home here on Earth with all of you. So a very deep thank you to my family: Alan and Mary Lou Cary, Joe, Jasmine, and Jacob Cianflone, Deseret Moctezuma, Janet Rackham, Anthony and Christine Zegarelli, and Tami Zegarelli. And one more to my family of friends: Pete Apito, Bradley Averill, Joel Cohen, Chip DeCraene, Mark Dembrowski, Chris Demers, David Feaster, Rick Kawala, Michael Konopko, Al LeGoff, Brian London, Stephen McAllister, Lou Natale, Tom Nicola, Mark O'Malley, Tim O'Rourke, Christian Romo, Robert Rubin, Alison Sigethy, Rachel Silber, and Ken Wolfe.

And again, I must pay tribute to the kind folks at Maxfield's House of Caffeine for providing a seemingly endless supply of coffee, bagels, bananas, and carrot juice.

Publisher's Acknowledgments

We're proud of this book; please send us your comments at `http://dummies.custhelp.com`. For other comments, please contact our Customer Care Department within the U.S. at 877-762-2974, outside the U.S. at 317-572-3993, or fax 317-572-4002.

Some of the people who helped bring this book to market include the following:

Acquisitions, Editorial, and Media Development

Senior Project Editor: Christina Guthrie

Senior Acquisitions Editor: Lindsay Lefevere

Senior Copy Editor: Danielle Voirol

Assistant Editor: Erin Calligan Mooney

Senior Editorial Assistant: David Lutton

Technical Editors: Amy L. Nicklin, Benjamin Wyss

Editorial Manager: Christine Meloy Beck

Editorial Assistants: Rachelle Amick, Jennette ElNaggar

Cover Photos: © iStock / Keith Bishop

Cartoons: Rich Tennant (`www.the5thwave.com`)

Composition Services

Project Coordinator: Patrick Redmond

Layout and Graphics: Carrie A. Cesavice, Nikki Gately, Erin Zeltner

Proofreader: Henry Lazarek

Indexer: BIM Indexing & Proofreading Services

Publishing and Editorial for Consumer Dummies

Diane Graves Steele, Vice President and Publisher, Consumer Dummies

Kristin Ferguson-Wagstaffe, Product Development Director, Consumer Dummies

Ensley Eikenburg, Associate Publisher, Travel

Kelly Regan, Editorial Director, Travel

Publishing for Technology Dummies

Andy Cummings, Vice President and Publisher, Dummies Technology/General User

Composition Services

Debbie Stailey, Director of Composition Services

Contents at a Glance

Table of Contents

Part II: Did They Really Cover This Stuff in School? A Review of Math Skills ... 33

Introduction

Just like the senior prom or getting a driver's license, the SAT is one of those milestones in the life of a high school student. I wish I could say it was as much *fun* as those other things, but if I did, you probably wouldn't believe anything else I say in the rest of the book.

But any way you slice it, the SAT is still there, scheduled for some Saturday morning a few weeks or months from now. Most colleges require you to submit an SAT score as part of your application process. So because there's no getting around it and it's not going away, your best bet is to do some preparation and get the best possible SAT score you can.

That's where this book comes in. The entire book you have in your hot little hands right now is devoted to refining the math skills you need most to succeed on that all-important SATurday.

About This Book

A lot of SAT prep books divide their attention among all three sections of the SAT: critical reading, writing, and mathematics. This is fine as far as it goes, because you probably want to boost all three scores. But in this book, I focus exclusively on math, math, and more math to help you achieve the best score you can on this — what can I say? — most often dreaded part of the test.

The SAT covers a variety of areas, including arithmetic, algebra, geometry, functions and graphs, and statistics and probability. But it doesn't require the quadratic formula or anything you'd cover after that in an algebra class, so you don't need to know trig or calculus. This book focuses on SAT topics and helps you get used to problem-solving so that you can turn facts and formulas into useful tools.

I wrote this book to give you the best possible advantage at achieving a good score on the math portion of your SAT. There's no shortcut, but most of what you need to work on comes down to four key factors:

- Know the basics inside and out.
- Get comfortable using your calculator.
- Strengthen SAT-specific math skills.
- Practice answering SAT questions.

For that last point, *every* example and problem here is written in SAT format — either as a multiple-choice question or as a student-produced grid-in question. From Chapter 3 to Chapter 8, every chapter contains math skills that are essential to the SAT, with dozens of SAT examples followed by a set of 20 practice problems. And to give you that test-day experience, this book also includes three practice tests. That's hundreds and hundreds of questions designed to strengthen your "SAT muscle," so to speak.

Conventions Used in This Book

Following are a few conventions to keep in mind:

- New terms introduced in a chapter, as well as variables, are in *italics.*
- Keywords in lists and numbered steps are in **boldface.**
- Any Web sites appear in `monofont`.
- The final answers to problems appear in **bold.** For multiple-choice questions, that's a letter from **(A)** to **(E).** For grid-in questions, I write the answer as you'd fill it in on the test. So as a test answer, I give $\frac{7}{9}$ as **7/9** or **.777** or **.778**, which are all acceptable ways to write it on your answer sheet.

Foolish Assumptions

This is an SAT prep book, so my first assumption is that you or someone you love (your son or daughter, mom or granddad, or perhaps your cat) is thinking about taking the SAT sometime in the future. If not, you're still welcome to buy the book.

My second assumption is that you're currently taking or have in your life at some point taken an algebra course, even if you feel like it's all a blur. Now, I *wish* I could tell you that algebra isn't very important on the SAT — oh, a mere trifle, hardly a thought. But this would be like saying you can play NFL football without getting rushed at by a bunch of 250-pound guys trying to pulverize you. It just ain't so.

But don't worry — this book is all about the blur and, more importantly, what lies beyond it. Read on, walk through the examples, and then try out the practice problems at the end of each chapter. I can virtually guarantee that if you do this, the stuff will start to make sense.

How This Book Is Organized

This book is organized into five parts, taking you from an overview of SAT math through the nitty-gritty skills you need to get the best possible score. Here's a look at what's waiting for you in these chapters.

Part I: Making Plans for This SATurday: An Overview of SAT Math

Part I introduces you to the SAT in general and the math sections in particular. Chapter 1 provides you with the most basic and important information about SAT math. You see the general areas of math that you need to focus on: arithmetic, algebra, geometry, coordinate geometry, plus a few additional scattered topics.

In Chapter 2, I talk about the two types of questions you face on the SAT: multiple-choice questions and grid-in questions. I go over some of the "fine print" information that the test-makers, in their infinite wisdom, provide to make the test fair. I also touch upon the list of formulas that you don't have to memorize because you'll have them on the test. I discuss when and how to use your calculator, and I provide some advice on strengthening a few mental math skills so you can answer questions quickly and confidently.

Part II: Did They Really Cover This Stuff in School? A Review of Math Skills

In Part II, I review the basic skills you need to remember from your math classes before sitting for your SAT. I also provide lots of practice problems in SAT style so that you can strengthen these skills.

In Chapter 3, I discuss topics in arithmetic, such as integers, digits, the number line, divisibility, percents, ratios, and more. Chapter 4 covers algebra, from simplifying and factoring to solving systems of equations, working with inequalities, and answering SAT questions that give you new, unfamiliar notations to work with. In Chapter 5, the focus is on geometry, including the basics about lines, angles, circles, and the ever-important right triangle. To finish up, I give you a few important formulas in solid geometry and tips on questions that test your geometric perception. In Chapter 6, you look at functions and coordinate geometry, which is geometry on the *xy*-plane.

Chapter 7 is a grab bag of topics you'll probably see on your SAT but that don't fit neatly into any of the other chapters. It includes number sequences, set theory, statistics, graphs of data, and more.

Part III: Your Problems Are Solved! SAT Problem-Solving Techniques

Part III takes a step forward, showing you how to pull together the set of skills from Part II to answer more-complicated SAT questions. In Chapter 8, you concentrate on word problems.

Chapter 9 takes a wide view of SAT strategy, giving you a few perspectives on how to approach the questions. I discuss how problems are arranged by difficulty and show you how to match the skills in your math toolbox to each question as you face it. I also show you how to read a question and anticipate the formulas that may be helpful to answer it.

Part IV: Practice Makes Perfect: SAT Math Practice Tests

Part IV gives you three opportunities to practice your SAT skills under timed conditions. Each practice test also comes with an accompanying chapter that provides the answers to the questions, along with explanations to help you understand why the correct answers are correct.

Part V: The Part of Tens

In this part, I give you the best ways to utilize your study time between now and the big day. I also identify ten smart but simple things you can do just before the test to help boost your score.

Icons Used in This Book

In this book, I use these four icons to signal what's most important along the way:

REMEMBER: This icon points out important information that you need to focus on. Make sure you understand this information fully before moving on. You can skim through these icons when reading a chapter to make sure you remember the highlights.

TIP: Tips are hints that can help speed you along when answering a question. See whether you find them useful when working on practice problems.

WARNING!: This icon flags common mistakes that students make if they're not careful. Take note and proceed with caution!

EXAMPLE: Each example is a formal SAT-style question followed by a step-by-step solution. Work through these examples and then refer to them to help you solve the practice problems at the end of the chapter.

Where to Go from Here

This book is organized so that you can safely jump around and dip into every chapter in whatever order you like. You can strengthen skills you feel confident in or work on those that need some attention.

If this is your first introduction to SAT math, I strongly recommend that you start out by reading Chapters 1 and 2. There, you find some simple but vital SAT-specific information that you need to know before you sit down with pencil in hand to take the test.

If it's been a while since you've taken a math course, read the math-skills chapters (Chapter 3 to Chapter 7) in order. Chapter 3, which focuses on arithmetic, can get your math brain moving again, and you may find that a lot of this stuff looks familiar as you go along.

Finally, if you read through a few chapters and feel that the book is moving more quickly than you'd like, go ahead and pick up my earlier book, *Basic Math & Pre-Algebra For Dummies* (Wiley). There, I adopt a more leisurely pace and spend more time filling in any gaps in understanding you may find along the way.

Part I

Making Plans for This SATurday: An Overview of SAT Math

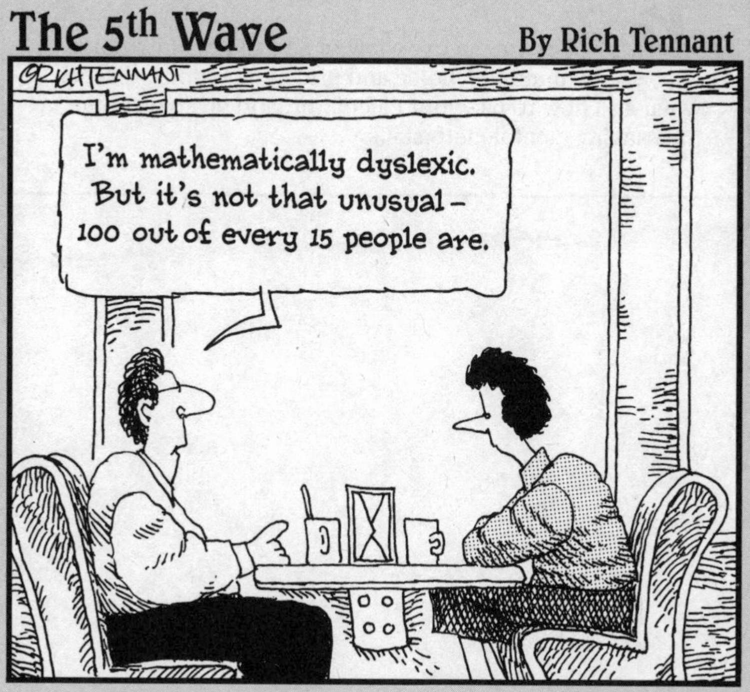
The 5th Wave
By Rich Tennant
I'm mathematically dyslexic. But it's not that unusual – 100 out of every 15 people are.

In this part . . .

Part I gives you an overview of SAT math. I introduce you to multiple-choice and grid-in questions, discuss when and how to use your calculator, and give you some time-saving mental math skills.

Chapter 1

SAT Math Basics

In This Chapter

- Overviewing the three SAT math sections
- Knowing what's covered and what's not covered on the SAT
- Understanding some basic SAT problem-solving skills

SAT math — what joy, what utter bliss! Well, all right — back on Earth you probably have some work to do before you reach that stage. I promise to do everything in my power to make your study time as painless and productive as possible. All I ask is that you trust in yourself: You already know more than you think you do.

If you've taken algebra in school, much of this book may seem like review. The task at hand is to focus your work on the skills you need to get the best SAT score you can. So in this chapter, I give you a road map to rediscovering the math you know, getting clear on the math you're sketchy on, and preparing to take on some new and useful skills in time for the test.

I start off with an overview of the SAT math sections. I then go over the specific math skills you need to focus on, which I cover in detail in Part II. Then I set your mind at ease by mentioning a few areas of math that you don't have to worry about because they're *not* on the test. Finally, I talk a bit about problem-solving and applying all those math skills.

Getting an Overview of the SAT Math Sections

Your total SAT *composite score* is a number from a lowest possible score of 600 to a highest possible score of 2,400. Out of that, your mathematics score ranges from 200 to 800, based on your performance on the three mathematics sections of the test.

Here's an overview of the three math sections of the SAT:

- A 25-minute section containing 20 multiple-choice questions, which require you to choose the right answer among five choices, (A) through (E)
- A 25-minute section containing 18 questions: 8 multiple-choice questions and 10 grid-in questions (also called *student-produced response questions*), which require you to record the right answer into a special grid
- A 20-minute section containing 16 multiple-choice questions

Generally speaking, questions within each section of the SAT get progressively more difficult. Early questions usually test you on a single basic skill. In the middle of the section, the questions get a bit more complicated. By the end of the test, you usually need a variety of math skills to answer a question.

In Chapter 2, I discuss the two types of questions (multiple-choice and grid-in) in more detail. I also give you some guidelines on writing your answers for grid-in questions. Later, each of the three practice tests in Part IV (Chapters 10 through 15) gives you three math sections that mirror the ones you'll face when you sit for your SAT.

Knowing What's In: The Math You Need for the SAT

The SAT covers math up to and including the first semester of Algebra II. A good rule of thumb is that SAT math

- Includes the quadratic *equation* ($ax^2 + bx + c = 0$) and everything covered before it
- Excludes the quadratic *formula* ($x = \frac{-b \pm \sqrt{b^2 - 4ac}}{2a}$) and everything covered after it

In this section, I give you an overview of some important math topics that are part of the SAT, in each case focusing on the specific skills I cover in each chapter.

Calculating with arithmetic questions

In this section, I cover the arithmetic skills you need most on the SAT. You can flip to Chapter 3 for more detail.

Digital computing

The number system uses ten digits — 0, 1, 2, 3, 4, 5, 6, 7, 8, and 9 — from which all other numbers are built. Some SAT questions require you to figure out the value of a number based on the values of its digits. For example, you may be asked to find the value of four-digit number *ABCD* based on clues about its individual digits, *A*, *B*, *C*, and *D*.

Number lines

A *number line* is a visual representation of a set of numbers. For example,

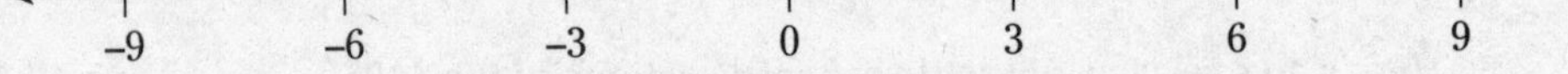

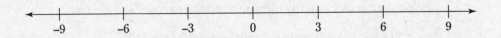

The number line here is labeled with seven *tick marks,* each labeled with a number. On this number line, the *interval* between each pair of tick marks is 3. An SAT question may ask you to figure out the value at a given point or the distance between two points on a number line. In some cases, drawing your own number line can help you solve word problems, as I show you in Chapter 8.

Divisibility, factors, and multiples

When one number is *divisible* by another, you can divide the first number by the second number without leaving a remainder. For example, 10 is divisible by 5, because $10 \div 5 = 2$. Two other important words to describe divisibility are *factor* and *multiple*. Here's how you use these words to describe the fact that 10 is divisible by 5:

5 is a *factor* of 10

10 is a *multiple* of 5

Some SAT questions ask you directly about divisibility, factors, and multiples. Other times, knowing about divisibility can help you cross off wrong answers if, for example, you're dividing and looking for an answer that's an integer (a positive or negative whole number).

Percents

A *percent* is a fractional portion of a whole amount. For example, 50% of 22 is 11, because half of 22 is 11. In this example, you start with the whole amount 22 and then take half of it (because 50% means *half*), which gives you 11. In Chapter 3, I show you some useful ways to work with percents, including problems in percent increase and percent decrease.

Ratios and proportions

A *ratio* is a mathematical comparison of two quantities, based on the operation of division. For example, if a family has 3 girls and 4 boys, you can express the ratio of girls to boys in any of the following ways:

$3{:}4 \quad 3 \text{ to } 4 \quad \frac{3}{4}$

A *proportion* is an equation based on two ratios set equal to each other. For example, you can set up the following equation, which pairs words and numbers:

$$\frac{\text{Girls}}{\text{Boys}} = \frac{3}{4}$$

SAT questions may give you ratios outright, or you may find that setting up a proportion is a useful way to think of a problem that deals with comparisons. For example, a problem may tell you that a club has the same ratio of girls to boys and ask you to figure out how many boys are in the club, given the number of girls. You can set the ratios equal to each other and find the number of boys by using cross-multiplication, as I show you in Chapter 3.

Powers and roots (radicals)

Raising a number to a *power* means multiplying it by itself a specified number of times. For example, $3^4 = 3 \times 3 \times 3 \times 3 = 81$. In the expression 3^4, the number 3 is the *base* — the number being multiplied — and the number 4 is the *exponent* — the number of times the base is multiplied by itself.

The most common exponent is 2, and raising a number to a power of 2 is called *squaring* that number. When you find the *square root* of a number (also called a *radical*), you reverse this process by discovering a value that, when multiplied by itself, gives the number you started with. For example, $\sqrt{49} = 7$, because $7^2 = 49$.

Doing the algebra shuffle

This section begins with a review of basic algebra concepts and terminology. In Chapter 4, I discuss the basic algebra concepts you need for the SAT.

Evaluating, simplifying, and factoring expressions

An *algebraic expression* is any string of mathematical symbols that makes sense and has at least one variable (such as x). For example,

$$3x + 2 + x$$

You can *evaluate* this expression by substituting a number for x and then finding the resulting value. For example, here's how you evaluate the expression if $x = 5$:

$$3(5) + 2 + 5 = 15 + 2 + 5 = 22$$

You can *simplify* an expression by combining *like terms,* which are parts of the expression that have the same variables. For example,

$$3x + 2 + x = 4x + 2$$

And you can *factor* an expression by separating out a common factor in the terms. For example, in the expression $4x + 2$, both terms ($4x$ and 2) are divisible by 2, so you can factor out a 2:

$$4x + 2 = 2(2x + 1)$$

Evaluating, simplifying, and factoring are important tools that give you the flexibility you need to solve equations using algebra. In turn, solving equations (which I discuss in the next section) is the central skill that makes algebra vital for answering questions on the SAT.

Solving an equation for a variable

The main event in algebra is solving an equation that has one variable (such as x) to discover the value of that variable. The most common way to do this is to *isolate the variable* — that is, get the variable alone on one side of the equal sign and a number on the other side.

Each step along the way, you must keep the equation *balanced* — that is, you have to perform the same operation on both sides of the equation. For example, you solve the following equation by subtracting 7 from both sides of the equation and then dividing both sides by 3:

$$3x + 7 = 13$$

$$3x = 6$$

$$x = 2$$

Solving an equation in terms of other variables

When an equation has more than one variable, finding the value of any variable may be impossible. You can, however, find the value of any variable *in terms of* the other variables in the equation. For example, suppose you want to solve the following equation for b in terms of the variables a, c, and d:

$$a + bc = d$$

To do this, use algebra to isolate b on one side of the equation. Begin by subtracting a from both sides; then divide both sides by c:

$$bc = d - a$$

$$b = \frac{d - a}{c}$$

Solving an equation for an expression

Sometimes, you can solve an equation that has more than one variable to find the numerical value of an expression that contains both variables. For example, look at the following:

$$7p = 3q$$

Suppose you want to solve this equation for the value of p/q. To do this, use algebra to isolate p/q on one side of the equation. Begin by dividing both sides by 7 and then divide both sides by q:

$$p = \frac{3q}{7}$$

$$\frac{p}{q} = \frac{3}{7}$$

Solving a system of equations

A *system of equations* is a set of algebraic equations that are simultaneously true. Because a system of equations contains the same number of equations as variables, you can find the value of both (or all) variables. You first solve for one variable; then you plug that value into one of the original equations and solve for the other variable. For example, suppose you have these equations:

$$x + y = 3$$

$$x - y = 1$$

To begin, first add the two equations. Because the y values cancel each other out, you're left with an equation that you can solve easily:

$$2x = 4$$

$$x = 2$$

Now substitute 2 for x back into either equation and solve for y:

$$2 + y = 3$$

$$y = 1$$

Thus, in the original system of equations, $x = 2$ and $y = 1$. I show you how to apply this skill to SAT questions in Chapter 4.

Solving an inequality

An *inequality* is a math statement that uses a symbol other than an equal sign — most commonly $<$, $>$, $\leq$, or $\geq$. Solving an inequality is similar to solving an equation, with one key difference: When you multiply or divide an inequality by a negative number, you have to reverse the direction of the sign. For example, to solve the inequality $-4x < 12$, isolate x by dividing both sides by -4 *and* changing the $<$ to a $>$:

$$\frac{-4x}{-4} > \frac{12}{-4}$$

Now simplify both sides of the equation:

$$x > -3$$

You get to practice this skill on SAT questions in Chapter 4.

Working with new notations

A common SAT question presents you with the definition of a new mathematical notation and then requires you to use it to solve a problem. For example,

Let $x@y = x^2 - y^2$

Now you can use this definition to evaluate an expression that uses the new notation. For example, here's how you find 5@3 (which tells you that $x = 5$ and $y = 3$):

$5@3 = 5^2 - 3^2 = 25 - 9 = 16$

Therefore, 5@3 = 16.

Go figure: Doing geometry

If you've taken a geometry class, you probably spent a lot of time on geometric proofs. Although the SAT doesn't test proofs directly, it does include lots of questions where a strong knowledge of geometric theorems is indispensable. In this section, I outline a few of the main topics that are covered in greater depth in Chapter 5.

Measuring angles

Geometry provides some important theorems for measuring angles. You're virtually guaranteed to see one or more questions on the SAT that require you to know these basic theorems. For instance, when two lines cross each other, any two adjacent angles are *supplementary angles*, which means that they add up to 180°. Furthermore, angles opposite each other are *vertical angles*, which means that they're equal to each other. For example, in the following figure, $a + b = 180°$ and $a = c$.

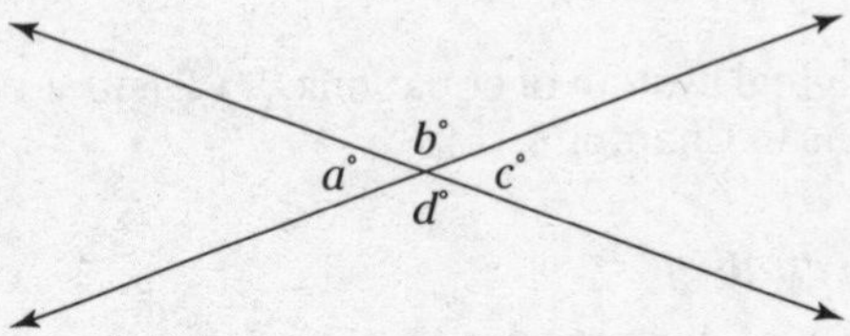

When a line crosses a pair of parallel lines, any two alternate angles on the same side of the line are called *corresponding angles*, which means that they're equal to each other. For example, in this next figure, $j = k$:

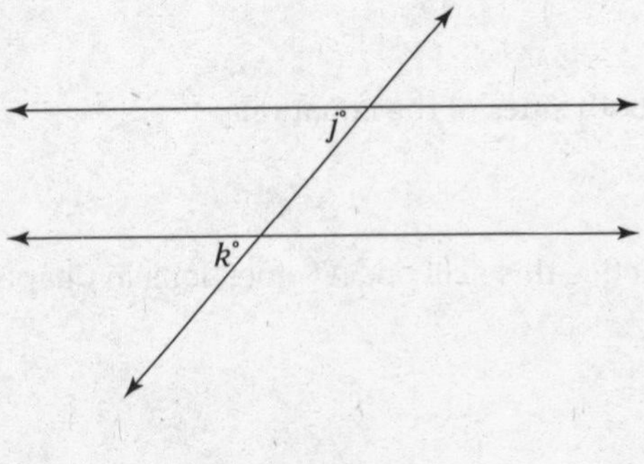

Finding angles and sides of triangles

Geometry includes many theorems about triangles, and some of these are pivotal to answering SAT questions. For instance, the three angles in a triangle always add up to 180°. In the following triangle, $p + q + r = 180°$:

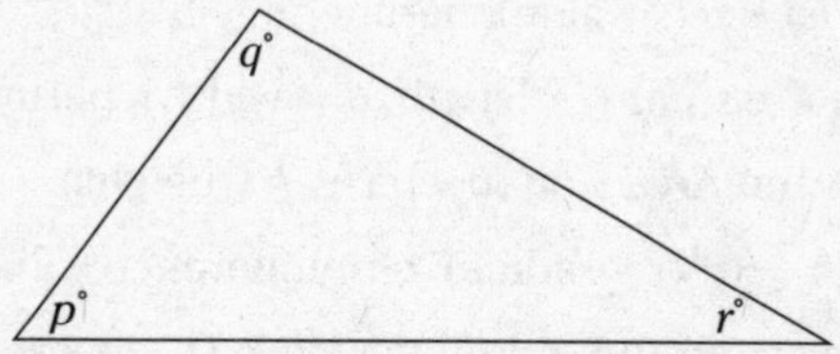

Right triangles also play a big role on the SAT. Every triangle with a right angle (90° angle) is a *right triangle*. The two short sides of a right triangle are called *legs,* and the long side is called the *hypotenuse*. As the following figure shows, the Pythagorean theorem always holds true for a right triangle with legs a and b and a hypotenuse of c:

$$a^2 + b^2 = c^2$$

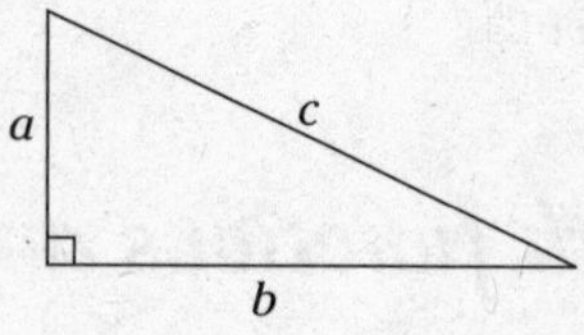

One common right triangle is the 3-4-5 triangle, which has legs of lengths 3 and 4 and a hypotenuse of length 5.

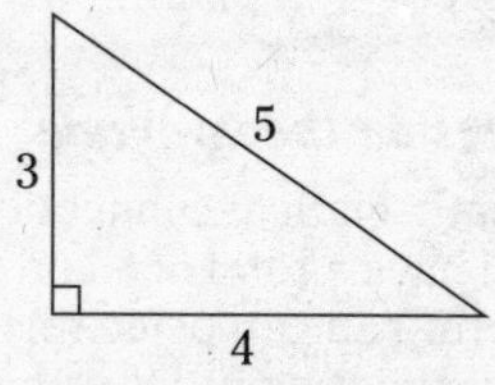

Two other important right triangles are the 45-45-90 triangle and the 30-60-90 triangle, which are named by their angles and have sides in set ratios:

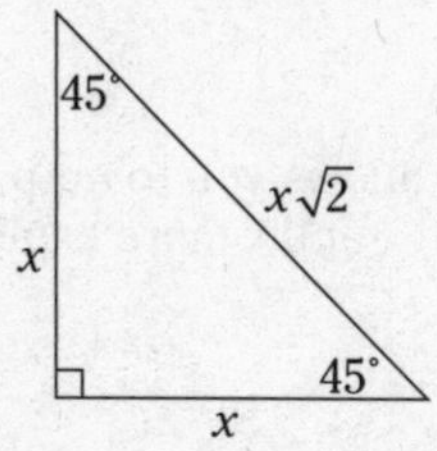

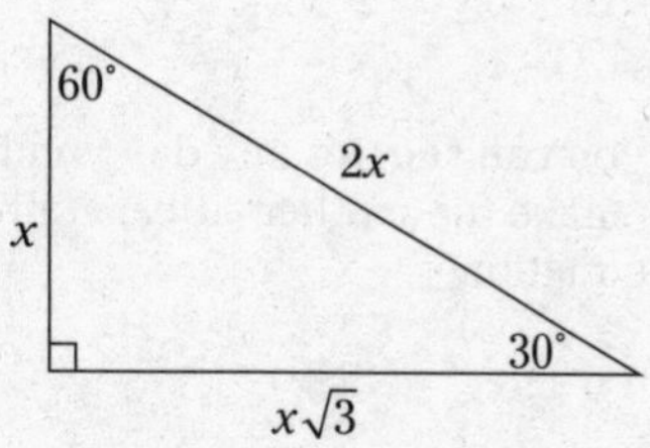

Finding area, perimeter, and volume, and more

Geometry provides a bunch of useful formulas for measuring a variety of shapes and solids. Here are a few important formulas that you need to know how to use to do well on the SAT:

- **Triangle:** Area = $\frac{1}{2}bh$ (b = base, h = height)
- **Square:** Area = s^2 (s = side), perimeter = $4s$
- **Rectangle:** Area = lw (l = length, w = width), perimeter = $2l + 2w$
- **Parallelogram:** Area = bh (b = base, h = height)
- **Circle:** Area = πr^2 (r = radius), circumference = $2\pi r$, diameter = $2r$
- **Rectangular solid (box):** Volume = lwh (l = length, w = width, h = height)
- **Cylinder:** Volume = $\pi r^2 h$ (r = radius, h = height)

Geometric perception

Geometric perception is the ability to imagine a geometric object when it's turned around and viewed from a different perspective. SAT questions typically test geometric perception in a few different ways. In some cases, a two-dimensional shape is rotated on the plane. In others, a solid is turned around in space. And another common question type requires you to imagine folding a two-dimensional shape into a solid. You see how to handle these types of questions in Chapter 5.

Working with functions and coordinate geometry

Functions and coordinate geometry are usually the focus of the second half of Algebra I and a starting point for most of Algebra II, so they play a big role on the SAT. A *function* is an equation linking an input variable (usually x) and an output variable (usually y) so that any value of x produces no more than one value of y. *Coordinate geometry* brings together concepts from algebra and geometry by graphing equations on the xy-plane. In this section, you get an overview of what I cover in Chapter 6.

Modeling with functions on the xy-plane

A function is simply a mathematical connection between two values. For example, if you save $5 every day, you'll have a total of $5 on the first day, $10 on the second day, $15 on the third day, and so forth. You can place this information into an *input-output table*, with the input x being the day and the output y being the amount saved:

x = day	1	2	3	4	5	...	10	...	100
y = amount	$5	$10	$15	$20	$25	...	$50	...	$500

As you can see, for any day you input, the table allows you to output a dollar amount. You can make the mathematical connection between x and y more explicit by representing it as an equation:

$$y = 5x$$

In this equation, y is determined by x — that is, for any value of x, you always know the value of y. Another way of saying this is that "y is a *function of* x." You can write this statement mathematically as follows:

$$y = f(x)$$

Every point in the function corresponds to a *coordinate pair* (x, y) on the *xy*-plane, connecting a value of x with a value of y. The *xy*-plane provides a setting to connect two important branches of math — algebra and geometry — allowing you to plot algebraic equations containing x and y. For example, to plot the equation $y = 5x$, plot the points from the table, and then draw a line connecting them:

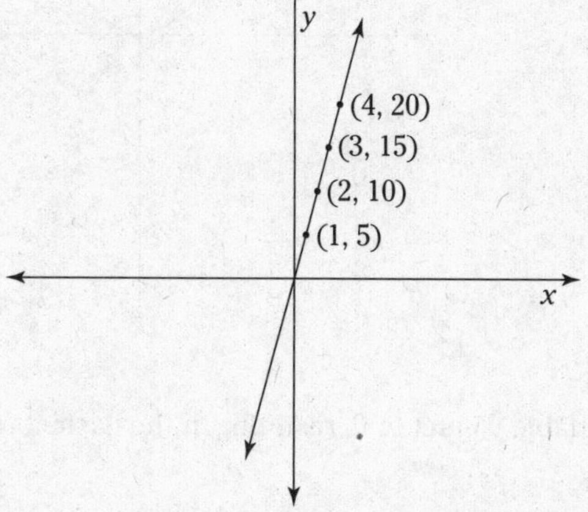

I discuss functions on the *xy*-plane in greater detail in Chapter 6.

Looking at common functions: Linear and quadratic functions

The most common functions on the SAT are linear and quadratic functions. The most basic function on the *xy*-plane is the *linear function*, which produces a straight line. The basic form of the linear function is the *slope-intercept form:*

$$y = mx + b$$

In this function, m represents the slope (steepness) of the line and b represents the *y-intercept* (the point where the line crosses the *y*-axis). You can find the slope of a line passing through any two points (x_1, y_1) and (x_2, y_2) using the *two-point slope formula*:

$$\text{Slope} = \frac{y_2 - y_1}{x_2 - x_1}$$

You can also find the equation of a line that has a slope m and includes point (x_1, y_1) using the *point-slope form* for a linear equation:

$$y - y_1 = m(x - x_1)$$

Quadratic functions are also common on the test. A *quadratic* function contains a term whose variable x is squared:

$$f(x) = ax^2 + bx + c$$

For graphing, the $f(x)$ is usually replaced by y, so $y = ax^2 + bx + c$. The graph of a quadratic function is a *parabola* — a bullet-shaped figure as shown here:

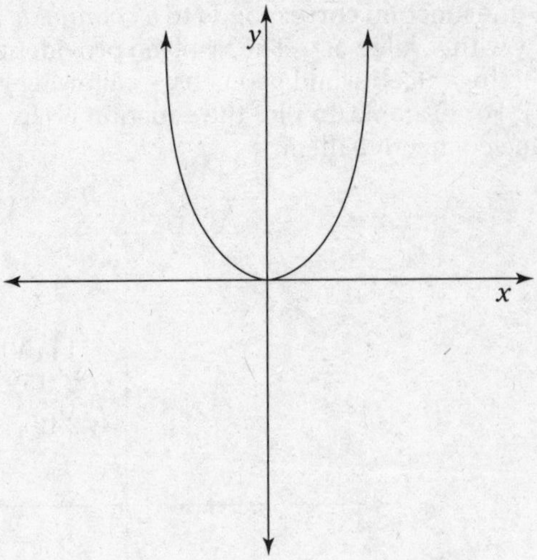

Often, the variable y is set to 0, resulting in the basic form of the *quadratic equation*:

$$ax^2 + bx + c = 0$$

You often have to factor this equation and solve for x. I show you how to handle linear and quadratic functions on the SAT in Chapter 6.

Transforming functions

A small change to a function can cause a predictable change in the graph of that function. The result is the *transformation* of that function. Two common transformations are

- **Reflection:** Changing a function to its mirror image along either the x-axis or y-axis
- **Shift:** Displacing a function up, down, left, or right

In Chapter 6, I discuss both of these types of transformations and how to apply them on the SAT.

Rounding up some grab-bag skills

Some SAT math questions are drawn from a variety of math sources that I collect in Chapter 7 under the loose category "grab-bag skills." In this section, I give you a quick introduction to this variety of problems.

Number sequences

A *sequence* is a list of numbers following a pattern or rule. For example,

1, 4, 7, 10, 13, 16, …

In this sequence, adding 3 to a number gives you the next number in the list. Most SAT questions about number sequences require you to figure out the rule that generates the sequence and then apply it.

Set theory and Venn diagrams

A *set* is a collection of things, typically listed inside a pair of braces. For example,

set $A = \{1, 2, 3\}$

set $B = \{1, 3, 5, 7, 9\}$

The things in a set are called *elements* of the set. For example, set *A* has three elements: the numbers 1, 2, and 3. The *union* of two sets is the set of every element that appears in either set. For example, the union of set *A* and set *B* is $\{1, 2, 3, 5, 7, 9\}$. The *intersection* of two sets is the set of every element that appears in both sets. For example, the intersection of set *A* and set *B* is $\{1, 3\}$.

A *Venn diagram* is a visual representation of two or more sets as a group of interlocking circles, as you see here:

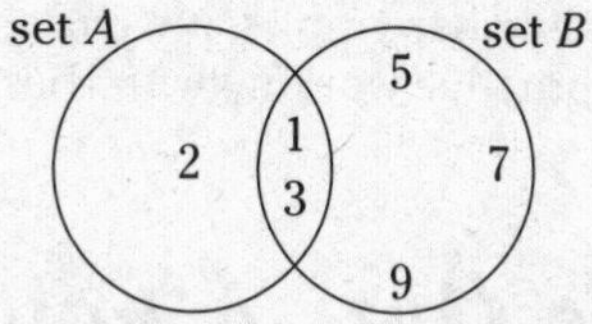

In Chapter 7, you discover how to answer SAT questions that focus on set theory and Venn diagrams.

Logic

A *logic question* provides you with a collection of statements and requires you to make logical deductions to answer the question. In some questions, you may need to place a group of people or events in order from first to last. In others, you may be asked to deduce which statement must be true, given a set of facts. Chapter 7 gives you a good look at how to answer logic questions.

Statistics

Statistics is the mathematical analysis of data — that is, making sense of numbers compiled through measuring real-world phenomena. On the SAT, you need to know the formula for the *average* (*arithmetic mean*) of a set of numbers:

$$\text{Mean} = \frac{\text{Sum of values}}{\text{Number of values}}$$

You also need to know how to find the *median* of a set of numbers — that is, the middle number in the set (or the arithmetic mean of the two middle numbers). You may have to identify the *mode* of a set of numbers, which is the most frequently repeated number in the set. SAT questions may also ask you to determine a *weighted average,* which is the mean average of a set of mean values. You get solid on these skills in Chapter 7.

Probability

Probability is the mathematical likelihood that a specified outcome will occur. Probability questions may focus on flipping a coin, rolling dice, or selecting items at random. The formula for the probability is

$$\text{Probability} = \frac{\text{Target outcomes}}{\text{Total outcomes}}$$

In this formula, *target outcomes* means the number of ways in which the outcome you're measuring can happen, and *total outcomes* means the total number of outcomes that can occur. For example, suppose you want to measure the probability of rolling the number 5 on a six-sided die. The number of target outcomes is 1 (rolling a 5), and the total number of outcomes is 6 (rolling 1, 2, 3, 4, 5, or 6). Thus, you can calculate the probability of this outcome as follows:

$$\text{Probability} = \frac{\text{Target outcomes}}{\text{Total outcomes}} = \frac{1}{6}$$

Therefore, the probability of rolling a 5 on a six-sided die is $\frac{1}{6}$. You discover more about calculating probability and its close cousin, geometric probability, in Chapter 7.

Graphs of data

A *graph* provides visual representations of data. The most common type of graph is the *xy*-graph, which I cover in Chapter 6. Additionally, the SAT may include a variety of other types of graphs, including bar graphs, pie charts, line graphs, pictograms, and scatterplots. In Chapter 7, you get practice working with these types of graphs.

Knowing What's Out: A Few Topics Not Covered on the SAT

Almost as important as knowing what math topics are covered on the SAT (which I discuss in the preceding sections) is knowing the topics you can safely avoid. Here, I put your mind at rest with a list of math skills that you don't need to do well on the SAT:

- **No big number crunching:** SAT math questions are designed to be relatively quick to answer if you approach them right. Although you can use a calculator on the SAT, you don't need to worry about big, unwieldy numbers or endless calculations. In fact, if you find that your calculations for a problem are resulting in surprisingly long numbers, take a step back and look again: You may find that you've made a mistake and that the numbers don't turn out to be as awkward as you thought.

- **Nothing to prove (geometrically speaking):** A typical geometry course focuses a vast quantity of time on Euclidean proofs: beginning with five assumptions called *postulates*, showing how more-complex *theorems* follow logically, and then using these theorems to prove even more-complex theorems. On the SAT, you can forget everything you know (or don't know) about doing proofs.

  WARNING! Even though you don't have to know how to write proofs, you're not completely off the hook. You still need to know some basic theorems — that is, the bottom-line results of proofs, such as the idea that two angles are equal — and how to apply them. You just don't have to *prove* them on the SAT.

- **Avoiding the quadratic quagmire:** At some point in Algebra II, most students commit the quadratic formula to memory. And here it is:

  $$x = \frac{-b \pm \sqrt{b^2 - 4ac}}{2a}$$

  Isn't that just a sight to behold? Truly a work of art. Now forget about it — at least for the SAT — because you don't need to know it. You can solve any quadratic equation on the SAT by gentler means, such as factoring (see Chapter 6).

- **Getting real (numbers):** The SAT includes only the set of real numbers — that is, numbers that you can find on the number line. The number line includes positive and negative whole numbers (and of course, zero) and rational numbers (that is, fractions). It also includes irrational numbers like π and $\sqrt{2}$.

  In contrast, imaginary numbers are *not* found on the number line. (In fact, they have their own number line — but that's neither here nor there.) Imaginary numbers are numbers that contain a multiple of $\sqrt{-1}$, which is represented by the symbol *i* (for *imaginary*). You may have studied imaginary numbers and *complex numbers* — which are the sum of an imaginary number and a real number — in one of your math classes. They're very interesting and useful (or from another perspective, totally boring and useless). But for the purposes of the SAT, you don't have to worry about them.

  WARNING!

  The square root of any negative number is imaginary, so if you find that any question leads to the square root of a negative number, there must be a mistake somewhere. Step back and look for where you went wrong in the calculations.

- **No sines of trigonometry:** *Trigonometry* is the study of triangles, specifically right triangles. You can usually spot trig problems because they contain notation not found in other problems: sine (sin), cosine (cos), tangent (tan), and so forth. Although right triangles are important on the SAT (see Chapter 5 for details), you can safely skip the trig.

Furthermore, any math topic introduced in a trigonometry, pre-calculus, or calculus class is excluded from the SAT.

Building Your Problem-Solving Skills

In Part III of this book, the focus is on important *problem-solving skills* — the application of what you know about math to a specific problem. In this section, I give you an overview of what awaits.

Solving word problems

Word problems (also called *story problems*) require you to apply your math skills to a problem expressed in words rather than symbols. To solve a word problem, you usually need to translate the statements in the problem into one or more equations and then solve for a variable.

Students often find word problems tricky, but they're sometimes easier to solve than other types of problems. After you translate the words into an equation, you may find that the equation is relatively simple. In Chapter 8, I show you how to approach a variety of common SAT word problems.

Figuring out which tools to use

In a typical math class, you practice one set of skills before moving on to the next unit. So even a final exam gives you a big advantage you may not be aware of: The test contains relatively few types of problems, so you don't have to spend a lot of time figuring out what you need to remember before answering each question.

On the SAT, however, each question has no relationship to the previous question, so you have to be able to identify the type of math you need to answer the question as quickly as possible. Instead of testing you on a specific math topic, the SAT has the more general goal of testing your ability to *solve problems* — that is, how well you apply the math you know in new ways.

That's why practice focusing specifically on SAT problems is so important. Frequently, SAT questions (especially the tough ones) respond well to a variety of approaches. Depending upon your strengths, the way you like to think, and the stuff you remember from your classes, you and a friend could arrive at the right answer in two completely different ways. You need to practice finding your own smart ways to cut through to the heart of a problem and arrive at the solution.

TIP

Just as in sports, the most important thing for the SAT is to play game after game after game to find your own unique rhythm. What works best for you? Does drawing a picture help you see better or just confuse you? Should you try to solve an equation or instead try to plug in numbers until one works? Do you do your best work when you spend a few moments thinking about a question until you know which direction to go? Or do you tend to get the right answer when you dive in and start calculating, knowing that the numbers will take you where you need to go? The only way to find out what kind of SAT player you are and improve your performance is to get in the game and play.

In Part IV, I give you three practice SAT math tests. Each test contains three sections with a total of 54 questions — 44 multiple-choice and 10 grid-in — just like the real SAT. Doing practice tests with the clock running is the best way to hammer down the individual math skills you practice in Parts II and III.

Chapter 2

Testing 1-2-3: SAT Math Test-Taking Skills

In This Chapter

- Understanding multiple-choice and grid-in questions
- Focusing on the *Notes* and *Reference Information* at the top of each math section
- Managing your time
- Using your calculator to your best advantage
- Knowing the mental math skills that you need for the SAT

In this chapter, you discover some important information that relates to the math sections of the SAT. First, I focus on the two main categories of SAT questions: *multiple-choice questions*, which ask you to pick the right answer from among five choices, (A) through (E), and *grid-in questions*, which require you to find the answer and fill it into a special grid. I include a set of guidelines on filling in grid-in questions.

After that, I discuss the *Notes* and *Reference Information* that start each math section of the test, and I give you some guidelines on managing your time. Next, you discover what you need to know how to do on your calculator, as well as a few skills you may want to attain to improve your score. Finally, I list a set of basic math calculations you should be able to do quickly in your head. I also suggest some flash cards that can help you strengthen these skills.

Knowing Both Types of SAT Math Questions

Out of the 54 math questions you face on your SAT, 44 are multiple-choice questions; 10 are grid-in questions, which means you have to come up with an answer on your own. In this section, I discuss both types of questions.

Answering multiple-choice questions

Every *multiple-choice question* on the three math sections of the SAT provides you with five possible answers, (A) through (E). You receive one point for each right answer and no points for every answer you leave blank. Additionally (or should I say *subtractionally?*), one-quarter ($\frac{1}{4}$) of a point is deducted for every incorrect answer. This penalty is to discourage wild guessing when you have no idea what the answer is.

TIP

The common wisdom on multiple-choice questions is that you shouldn't guess unless you can confidently rule out at least one wrong answer.

A particular type of multiple-choice question gives you three options, listed as roman numerals I, II, and III, and asks you which among these is correct — Choice (A) may be

"I only," Choice (B) may be "I and II only," and so forth. This type of question often provides an opportunity to take an educated guess if you're running out of time. For example, if you know that III is definitely correct, you can rule out all the answers that exclude this choice and guess one of the remaining answers.

Some multiple-choice questions may be easier to answer by working backwards: Look at the five answer choices and try plugging them in or otherwise using them to get clues about the right answer. Depending on the question, this approach may be more or less helpful, but keep it in mind.

Responding to grid-in questions

Grid-in questions — also called *student-produced response* questions — require you to come up with your own answer to the question instead of picking the right one from among five possible choices. Here's what the grid for a grid-in question looks like:

I'm going to level with you: I don't like grid-in questions. Not one bit. I think they're an interesting idea gone terribly wrong. In my opinion, their potential for confusion far outweighs their usefulness. It pains me to think that smart students are doing good math and then losing points for making minor clerical errors while recording their answers in these stupid little grids. If I were Emperor of the World, my third official proclamation would be to ban grid-in questions from the SAT. (First and second proclamations would be getting rid of four-way stop signs and making it illegal to order hot chocolate *without* whipped cream on top.) Unfortunately, that's not likely in the near future, so you have to deal with the reality of grid-in questions.

In this section, I show you what you need to know to get your right answer recorded correctly into the grid.

Even if you're not sure about your grid-in answer, go ahead and record it. Unlike multiple-choice questions, there's no penalty for wrong answers to grid-in questions.

Lining up and recording your answer

You can record an answer in any way that fits in the grid. For example, here are three equally good ways to align the answer **29**:

2	9		

	2	9	

		2	9

As with multiple-choice questions, grid-in questions provide you with ovals that you *must* fill in to receive points, so don't leave all the ovals blank. The boxes above the ovals are mere window dressing. As you answer each grid-in question, I recommend that you first write your answer in the boxes and then fill in the ovals. Because the boxes are easier to read than the ovals, the boxes may come in handy if you want to go back and check your answers.

Don't place unnecessary zeros into the grid, even if they don't change the value of the answer — leave those ovals blank. For their own special reasons, the SAT folks dislike unnecessary zeros. In fact, they downright *hate* them so much that a single unnecessary zero recorded as part of a grid-in answer will get your otherwise correct answer marked wrong! For example, if you write the number **29** as 029, you won't get credit. This may sound like making a big deal over nothing, but that's how it is.

Gridding in decimal answers

The answer grid contains decimal points (.), so you can record decimal answers. For example, here's how you write the answer **7.23**:

7	.	2	3

When a decimal answer contains fewer than four characters, you can record it in whatever way fits the grid. For example, here are three great ways to align the answer **.3**:

.	3		

	.	3	

		.	3

As always, including unnecessary zeros in a decimal answer will cause your answer to be marked wrong. Unnecessary zeros come in two varieties:

- **Trailing:** A *trailing zero* appears to the right of all nonzero digits in a decimal. For example, if you record the decimal **7.4** as 7.40, your answer will be marked wrong.
- **Leading:** A *leading zero* appears to the left of all nonzero digits in a number. If you write the decimal **.8** as 0.8, you won't get credit for your answer.

If the answer is a repeating decimal, you can cut it off, round it, or write it as its fractional equivalent — see the next section for details.

Writing fractional answers

The answer grid contains fraction slashes, so you can record answers as fractions. Fractions must be in lowest terms. As with whole-number answers, you can record a fraction any way that fits in the grid. For example, here are two valid ways to write the fraction **3/7**:

3	/	7	

	3	/	7

Improper fractions — fractions with a numerator greater than the denominator — are also allowed in the grid. For example, here's how you can record the answer **51/4**:

5	1	/	4

WARNING!

Mixed numbers are *not* allowed in the grid. To see why, notice that if you try to record the mixed number $5\frac{1}{4}$, it's identical to 51/4. So if your answer is a mixed number, you can turn it into either a decimal or an improper fraction:

$$5\frac{1}{4} = 5.25 \qquad 5\frac{1}{4} = \frac{21}{4}$$

Now you can record this answer as either **5.25** or **21/4**:

5	.	2	5

2	1	/	4

Some fractions are equivalent to decimals that have more than three digits. These include repeating decimals that never end. For example,

$$\frac{2}{3} = 0.6666\ldots$$

You can enter this answer as the fraction **2/3** in two separate ways. You can also enter it as **.666**, a repeating decimal taken to the maximum number of places that fit in the grid. Or you can enter it as **.667**, a decimal taken to the maximum number of places that fit in the grid and then rounded up. When entering a repeating decimal, you *must* drop the leading zero in front of the decimal point to make room for the maximum number of decimal places. Here are four ways to record this answer:

2	/	3	

	2	/	3

.	6	6	6

.	6	6	7

TIP

Getting answers that don't fit the grid

After working out a problem, you may find that your answer doesn't fit in the grid because of how the grid is set up. Here are a couple of clues that you should give the problem another try:

- **The answer has more than four digits.** The answer grid contains room for four characters at most — four digits, or three digits and a fraction slash or decimal point. So if your answer to a grid-in question has five or more digits (that aren't just a continuation of a decimal), check it again and find the error that's lurking someplace.
- **The answer is negative.** The answer grid contains no minus sign, so the right answer to a grid-in question is *never* negative. Thus, if your answer to a grid-in question is a negative number, check again and find out where you went wrong.

Focusing on the Fine Print

In the spirit of fair play, every math section of the SAT begins with what I call the "fine print": some legalistic-looking information you'll be tempted to just blow past without reading. In this section, you get a sneak peek at this info so that you know what it covers. This information includes the following:

- **Notes:** Assumptions you can make about the questions
- **Reference Information:** A set of useful formulas and other math facts you can use on the test

Taking note of the Notes: General assumptions

At the start of each math section on the SAT, the *Notes* provide information about the test. This may seem like rather unimportant technical stuff, but it's worth spending a few minutes on so that you're clear about what it means (and so you don't have to sort it out during the test). In this section, I briefly discuss each of the four notes.

Using a calculator

The first SAT note reads as follows:

1. The use of a calculator is permitted.

This is big news — really big. Calculators, which were once forbidden on the SAT, are now allowed. This is both a blessing and a curse. The blessing, of course, is that you can reduce time by using your calculator to crunch numbers that you can't do quickly and accurately in your head. The curse is that everyone else — your competition on the test — has the same advantage.

So a calculator isn't just optional; it's essential. If you don't bring one, or you don't know how to use it, or — horrors! — you find that the batteries run out of juice halfway through the test, you'll have a distinct disadvantage. Later in this chapter, I discuss what you need to know about your calculator to bring the advantage back around to you.

Keeping it real: Using real numbers

Here's what the second SAT note says:

2. All numbers used are real numbers.

All SAT answers and calculations use *real numbers* — that is, numbers that you find on the real number line.

You may be wondering where *else* you'd expect to find numbers other than the real number line. The answer is that imaginary numbers are found on — where do you think? — the *imaginary* number line. An *imaginary number* is the square root of a negative number, such as $\sqrt{-1}$, represented by the symbol *i*. You may or may not have studied imaginary numbers in one of your math courses. In any case, you don't have to worry about them for the SAT.

Figuring out the figures

The third SAT note is long and eye-glazing, but the information it provides is important:

3. Figures that accompany problems in this test are intended to provide information useful in solving the problems. They are drawn as accurately as possible EXCEPT when it is stated in a specific problem that the figure is not drawn to scale. All figures lie in a plane unless otherwise indicated.

Many figures on the SAT are drawn to scale. Some, however, are labeled as follows:

Note: Figure not drawn to scale.

TIP

When a figure is drawn to scale, you can use it to get an intuitive sense of whether an answer looks right. For example, check out the following figure:

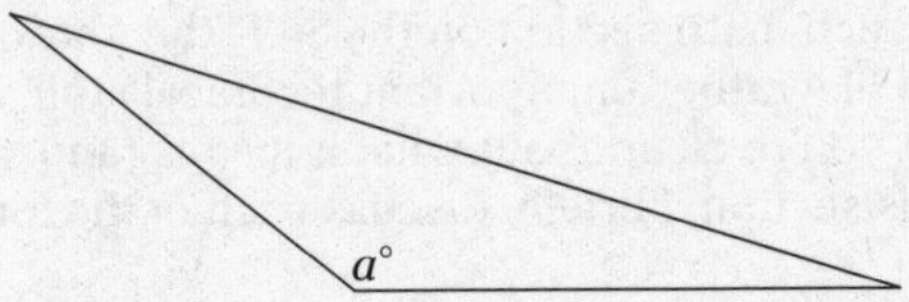

In this figure, angle *a* looks like it's greater than 90°. Because the figure isn't labeled with a warning that it's not drawn to scale, you can assume that it *is* drawn to scale. Therefore, angle *a is* greater than 90°. This information may help you answer the question.

When a figure *isn't* drawn to scale, however, looks may be deceiving. For example, look at this next figure:

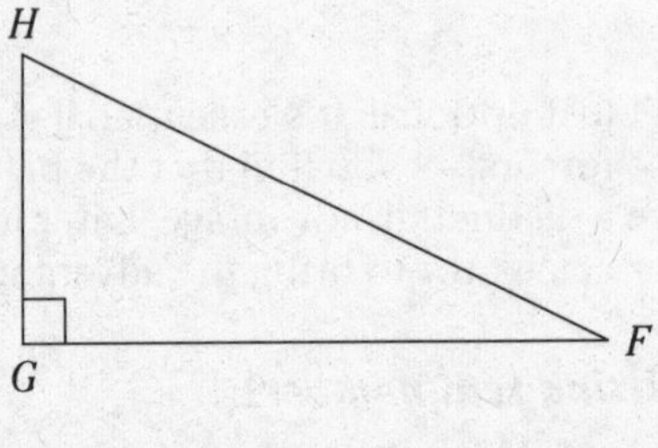

Note: Figure not drawn to scale.

In this figure, *FG* sure does look longer than *GH*. But the figure is specifically labeled as *not* to scale, so be careful! Don't make any assumptions about this triangle other than those that are explicitly indicated — for example, that it's a right triangle.

As an additional point, all figures lie in a plane, which simply means that all the usual theorems that you know from your geometry class apply on the SAT. If a drawing is intended to be a three-dimensional object such as a cube, the question lets you know that.

Digging into the domain: Acceptable numbers to plug in

Here's the fourth and final note that appears at the start of every math section of the SAT:

4. Unless otherwise specified, the domain of any function *f* is assumed to be the set of all real numbers *x* for which *f*(*x*) is a real number.

This is pretty arcane stuff. All it means is that as a rule, you can plug any value of x that you like into a function $f(x)$. And when a function is drawn on a graph, you can assume that it extends infinitely in both the positive and negative directions without any gaps.

Regarding the Reference Information: Facts and formulas

The *Reference Information* is a set of geometric diagrams, formulas, and facts provided on each math section of the SAT. There, you see area and volume formulas, the number of degrees in a triangle, and more. The inclusion of this information allows you to focus on applying these formulas rather just than memorizing them, so don't worry too much about knowing that the volume of a cylinder is $V = \pi r^2 h$. Just make sure you know how to use this formula when you need it!

In Chapter 5, you answer a wide variety of geometry questions that draw from this information. And in Chapter 9, I give you tips on how to make the best use of these formulas and others that aren't included in the *Reference Information.*

Getting the Timing Right

TIP

Students often ask how to budget their time on the SAT. Here are a few tips for pacing yourself as you prepare for the big day:

- **Don't sacrifice accuracy for speed.** This rule is all-important. Don't rush so fast that you start making mistakes that cost you points. You'll get a better score if you answer half the questions correctly than if you rush and answer most of the questions incorrectly. The early, easier questions are worth the same as the later ones, so make sure that you get them right.
- **Allow more time for later problems.** The three math sections of the SAT are timed as follows, which works out to a little more than a minute for each question:
  - 25 minutes for 20 questions
  - 25 minutes for 18 questions
  - 20 minutes for 16 questions

  However, in each section, earlier questions tend to be easier, and later questions, tougher. So you need to answer the early questions as quickly as you can without sacrificing accuracy. Every second you save on the easier questions may help you answer one of the tougher questions later on.
- **Skip over questions that don't make sense to you.** If you find an early question to be confusing or difficult, go to the next question.
- **When the going gets tough, circle back to answer the questions you skipped.** Sooner or later, the questions in each section begin to get difficult enough that in order to keep pace, you may be skipping over more questions than you're answering. At this point, circle back to work on the early questions you skipped. You may find they're not as bad as you thought, and they're probably easier than the questions that await at the end of the section.

TIP

Here's an idea for pacing yourself while taking practice tests: See whether you can complete six easy questions in four minutes. The point is to push yourself to work faster at the beginning in order to save up time for the end. If four minutes seems impossible, set a goal of five minutes and try to attain it. And if four minutes starts to get easy — that is, if you get all six questions right in four minutes without trouble — see whether you can push it to three minutes and still get all correct answers.

Calculating Your Way to Success: Calculators and the SAT

The very idea that students could use a calculator on the SAT was at one time unthinkable. Well, actually, it was unthinkable because the calculator hadn't been invented yet. Soon after its invention in the early 1970s, however, the calculator became the source of a great controversy among math teachers. At one end of the spectrum, some bitterly opposed the introduction of the calculator into the classroom, arguing that this would send math education one giant step down a slippery slope to, well, not a very nice place at all. At the other end were those who believed the calculator should be welcomed into the math curriculum as a drudgery-saving device that could help propel their students into new frontiers of discovery.

In the end, the silent majority of folks who prefer punching a few numbers to doing long division by hand has won out. Like it or not — and most students like it just fine — the calculator is here to stay on the SAT. So the question before you today is not *whether* to use a calculator on your SAT but rather *what kind*, *how*, and *when*.

Choosing an acceptable calculator

Obviously, you want to choose a calculator that you're allowed to use on the SAT. What kind of calculator can you use? The short answer is that you can use a calculator that, strictly speaking, *calculates*. Calculating includes the following:

- **Number-crunching:** Operations on integers, decimals, and fractions; finding an arithmetic mean (average); square roots and π keys; and so forth
- **Algebraic features:** Graphing, solving equations, creating input-output tables, and so on
- **Upper-level math features:** Trigonometric functions; *e* and logarithm keys; calculus functions (you don't need any of these features, but if your calculator includes them, you can still use it on the SAT)

WARNING!

Calculators that do more than just calculate aren't allowed on the SAT. For example,

- Calculators with enhanced input features (keypads with letters as well as numbers — such as QWERTY keypads — or stylus, pen, or touch-screen input)
- Calculators with enhanced output features (printed, audio, video, or Bluetooth output)
- Calculators with enhanced access features (Internet or cellphone access)
- Calculators with audio or video recording capabilities
- Calculators that require a power cord

Given those limitations, you're probably choosing among a four-function calculator (which does addition, subtraction, multiplication, and division), a scientific calculator (which includes roots, powers, and negative numbers), and a fancy graphing calculator. Here's what I recommend:

- If you're not very adept with a calculator or don't plan to do the fancy stuff, get a non-graphing calculator that has the features I list in the next section. That's probably a standard scientific calculator, which has a bit more muscle than a cheap four-function calculator you might bring to the supermarket. (This is the SAT, after all, not the cereal aisle!) Then spend enough time with it that you're comfortable using it to perform basic functions.
- Graphing calculators are expensive, but if you want a competitive edge, buy a graphing calculator and put in the time necessary to use it to full advantage. Some students prefer graphing calculators even for basic operations because the larger screen shows more lines of calculations at once. I discuss what you should explore later in "Considering other things that are good to know how to do on your calculator."

Whichever calculator you choose, make sure you have at least a few weeks to practice and play with it before you take the test. I recommend using the calculator that you plan to use for at least one practice test.

Reviewing what you should absolutely, positively know how to do on your calculator

Before you sit down to take the SAT, make sure you're proficient in the following calculator skills (check out your calculator's manual or reference card if you're having trouble):

- **Performing basic numerical operations:** Make sure you feel very comfortable doing basic addition, subtraction, multiplication, and division on your calculator before sitting for your SAT.
- **Working with decimals:** Locate the decimal point key and make sure you know how to use it.
- **Making numbers negative:** Many calculators have a key for negating a number that's distinct from the key for subtraction. To make sure you know how to use this key, calculate $-4 - 6$. If you get the answer -10, you're good to go.
- **Finding a square root:** Locate the square-root key and make sure you can find the square root of 10,000 (the answer is 100). If you can do this, you're set.
- **Squaring a number:** Your calculator probably has a key that looks something like x^2, used for squaring a number. Make sure you can find the value of 17^2 (the answer is 289).
- **Raising a number to the power of another number:** Your calculator may have a key that looks something like ^ or x^y, which allows you to raise a number to the power of another number. See whether you can use it to find 4^5 (the answer is 1,024).

Considering other things that are good to know how to do on your calculator

Following are a few other skills that are likely to come in handy:

- **Higher-order roots (radicals):** Some calculators have a key that allows you to find higher-order radicals such as cube roots, fourth roots, and so on. But many calculators require you to calculate higher-order roots as powers of a fraction. For example, you may need to calculate $\sqrt[3]{64}$ as $64^{1/3}$. Find out how to do this calculation (the answer is 4) so you can repeat it on the test if needed.
- **Fractions:** Some calculators allow you to perform operations on fractions, providing answers that are also fractions. This feature can be very useful when a multiple-choice

question provides one or more fractional answers. If your calculator has this feature, try it by adding $\frac{1}{5}+\frac{1}{10}$ (the answer is $\frac{3}{10}$).

- **Graphing functions:** If your calculator has a graphing capability and you get good at it, feel free to use it on the SAT. In some cases, you may find graphing a function helpful for answering a question. For example, if you're having trouble solving for x in a quadratic equation ($ax^2 + bx + c = 0$), graphing on your calculator can save time: You can just graph the function and zoom in to figure out where the graph crosses the x-axis.
- **Using input-output tables:** Graphing calculators usually have a feature allowing you to make an input-output table for a function. These tables show you which y values you get for various x values. This feature may come in handy on the SAT, so check it out.
- **Solving equations:** The equations that you need to solve on the SAT aren't designed to be too complex, but if your calculator can solve an equation for a variable, you may find this feature useful.

If you have a TI-83 graphing calculator, you may want to pick up *TI-83 Plus Calculator For Dummies,* by C. C. Edwards (Wiley), for more calculator tips.

Taking calculations step by step

TIP

Some calculations can be done either in a single step or broken into several steps. My recommendation is to break down complicated calculations into several steps whenever possible. The more complicated a single calculation is, the more likely you are to enter it incorrectly. Another advantage to using your calculator for isolated calculations is that you make sure the answer you get is in the ballpark. For example, if you're dividing 2,160 by 60, you should expect the answer to have fewer than four digits. So if the answer you get is 129,600, you probably hit the key for multiplication rather than division.

WARNING!

Be especially careful about making sure you (and your calculator) do operations in the right order, especially with fractions. For example, suppose you want to find the average of 36 and 88. The formula is

$$\text{Mean} = \frac{36+88}{2}$$

When you're rushed on the SAT, you may enter this into your calculator as follows:

36 + 88 / 2 = 80 Wrong!

Most calculators will impose the standard order of operations (order of precedence) and calculate 88/2 *first* (that is, 44) and then add 36, giving you an answer of 80. Clearly, 80 is too big to be the average of 36 and 88, but you may not notice and get the answer wrong, especially on a grid-in question. The best way to handle this problem is in two steps. First, find the sum of 36 + 88:

36 + 88 = 124

Now divide this value by 2:

/ 2 = 62

Alternatively, you can do it all in one step by using parentheses if you're very careful:

(36 + 88) / 2 = 62

Either way, 62 is the right answer.

Knowing the right time to use your calculator

Your calculator is a great tool when you use it just the right amount. If you forget it's there or don't know how to use it, you may make mistakes or lose time trying to do number-crunching on paper. On the other hand, if you use your calculator for every little calculation, you're just as likely to lose time and make mistakes keying in easy problems that you could do just as easily without it. A problem may even be more difficult if you plug in numbers before you try to simplify an equation.

Even if you're timid about your math ability, trust yourself to do small calculations like 3×4 or $10 \div 2$ in your head. And even if you're confident, don't get cocky and avoid using your calculator when it can save you time and avoid errors — for example, finding $1{,}440 \div 8$ or $\sqrt{576}$.

REMEMBER

The ideal rhythm is a good interplay between doing simple calculations in your head and on paper, then using the calculator to help you through the tedious work of dividing large numbers or taking a square root. That's why I recommend that you get comfortable doing basic multiplication, operations with negative numbers, and basic fraction/decimal conversions in your head. I discuss this idea more in the next section.

Putting the Flash Back in Flash Cards

I know some people make the case that knowing stuff like the multiplication tables or conversions from fractions to decimals just isn't necessary anymore. In an age where calculators are cheap and easily available, so the argument goes, why clutter your brain with useless information — especially when you can use a calculator on the SAT?

Of course, your calculator is your friend on the SAT, and you should know how to use it. But if you waste precious time using a calculator to do every little calculation, you're going to be at a distinct disadvantage. So in this section, I provide you with a list of items to place on flash cards so you can drill your way to success.

Using flash cards effectively

I know that flash cards seem like a quaint, outdated learning tool, but I like them. They're easy to make and tailor to your exact needs — all you need is a pack of index cards and a pen or marker. You can carry them with you and practice whenever you have a few spare moments. And when you know the information on them inside and out, just chuck them in a drawer or toss them in the recycle bin.

TIP

Here are the rules for using flash cards effectively:

1. **When you reveal a flash card, respond *immediately* and *out loud*.**

   For example, when you reveal the flash card $5 \times 2 =$, say "Ten" instantly. Saying the answer out loud reinforces your knowledge. (If you're someplace where loud talk would be rude, speak the answer quietly under your breath.)

2. **Turn the card over to check the answer; then place the card back in the stack.**

   - If your answer is right, place the card on the bottom of the stack.
   - If your answer is wrong, take a moment to notice the right answer, and then slide the card into the stack about 8 to 12 cards from the top.

   This procedure ensures that the flash cards you've memorized come up less often than those that you're working to remember.

When you can go through the stack of cards quickly and efficiently, with virtually no errors, consider yourself done. If you use this procedure as outlined, I promise you that you'll find the information on the cards begins to stick to your brain.

Deciding what to put on flash cards

TIP

Here, I present a few mental math calculations that you should be able to do in your head before sitting for your SAT. If you aren't really quick with these calculations, a good way to build up speed is by using flash cards. Even the process of writing out flash cards can be helpful for remembering their content. Here are some topics you may want to include:

- Multiplication tables
- Square numbers, from 1^2 to 12^2
- Square roots, from $\sqrt{1}$ to $\sqrt{144}$
- Basic fraction-to-decimal conversions, including halves, thirds, quarters, fifths, tenths, $\frac{1}{20}$, $\frac{1}{25}$, $\frac{1}{100}$, and so on
- Basic percent-to-decimal conversions, including 75%, 50%, 25%, 20%, 10%, 5%, 1%, and so on
- Multiplying and dividing negative numbers (aim for a nice variety of numbers, including positive/negative, negative/positive, and negative/negative combinations)
- Adding and subtracting negative numbers (again, try a variety that includes positive/negative, negative/positive, and negative/negative combinations)

And if you really want to go all out, try making flash cards with this information:

- **Common denominators:** For example, write a pair of numbers (such as 6 and 10) on one side and their common denominator (30) on the other
- **Decompositions to prime factors:** For example, write the number 12 on one side and its prime factors ($2 \times 2 \times 3$) on the other. If a number is prime, such as 17, write "prime" on the back of the card. (See Chapter 3 for more on prime factors.)
- **Algebra:** Lots of possibilities here! For example, write "Simplify $2x + 3y + 4x$" on one side and "$6x + 3y$" on the back.

Part II
Did They Really Cover This Stuff in School? A Review of Math Skills

In this part . . .

In Part II, the focus is on core math skills necessary to succeed on the SAT — arithmetic, algebra, geometry, and coordinate geometry — plus a variety of grab-bag topics such as graphs, sets, logic, probability, and statistics.

Chapter 3

The Numbers Game: Arithmetic Review

In This Chapter

- Defining integers
- Solving problems based on digits
- Working with number lines
- Getting clear on divisibility, factors, and multiples
- Understanding percents and ratios
- Discovering how to work with powers and roots

Your first stop on the way to developing a good arsenal of SAT tactics is a thorough review of arithmetic. In this chapter, I focus on a variety of topics that appear frequently in SAT questions. First, I discuss integers, which include all positive and negative whole numbers, plus zero. I also show you how to approach and answer questions that involve unknown digits. You then spend some time reviewing the basic number line, with an eye on solving the kinds of problems that you typically see on the SAT.

After that, the focus is on questions about divisibility, factors, and multiples. In the process, you also look at prime and composite numbers. I show you how to work with a variety of common questions that focus on percents and ratios. Next, I discuss square numbers and square roots and then give you the basics in understanding exponents.

To finish up, you have the opportunity to try out 20 SAT questions focusing on these topics. If you have trouble on any of the problems, don't despair. I thoroughly explain how to answer every question in the last section of this chapter.

TIP

If you feel that you need a bit more explanation of any of these topics before moving on, pick up a copy of *Basic Math & Pre-Algebra For Dummies* (Wiley). This book focuses on every aspect of arithmetic at a slower pace and with even more detailed explanations. And for a ton of practice problems, all fully explained, I also recommend *Basic Math & Pre-Algebra Workbook For Dummies* (Wiley).

Maintaining Your Integrity with Integers

REMEMBER

An *integer* is any positive or negative whole number, including zero (okay, technically zero is neither positive nor negative, but you get the idea):

{..., –3, –2, –1, 0, 1, 2, 3, ...}

Some SAT questions specify that an answer has to be an integer. This information is usually necessary to answer the question. Check out the following examples:

The sum of a sequence of five consecutive integers is 5. What is the greatest number in this sequence?

At first glance, this question may seem impossible. But remember that the integers include negative numbers. A little trial and error reveals the five consecutive integers to be $-1 + 0 + 1 + 2 + 3 = 5$. The greatest number in this sequence is **3**, so this is the right answer.

If n is an integer, which of the following could be the value of $3n + 1$?

(A) –12

(B) –8

(C) 0

(D) 8

(E) 12

You can save some time on this problem by noticing that if n is an integer, then $3n + 1$ cannot be divisible by 3. So you can rule out answers (A), (C), and (E). But even if you don't notice this, you can solve problem by setting $3n + 1$ equal to each of the five answers to see which results in a integer value of n. Begin with –12:

$$3n+1=-12$$
$$3n=-13$$
$$n=-\frac{13}{3}$$

The value of n isn't an integer, so you can rule out (A). Now try –8:

$$3n+1=-8$$
$$3n=-9$$
$$n=-3$$

This time, the value of n is an integer — remember, a negative whole number is an integer! — so the right answer is **(B).**

Doing Some Digital Computing

Some SAT questions focus on the ten digits 0, 1, 2, 3, 4, 5, 6, 7, 8, and 9. Many of these questions respond well to some simple trial and error. You can usually find a trick that allows you to constrain the values of the digits to find the answer.

A, B, and C are digits in the positive three-digit number ABC. If A is half of B and B is one-third of C, which of the following inequalities is true?

(A) $ABC < 100$

(B) $100 < ABC < 200$

(C) $200 < ABC < 300$

(D) $300 < ABC < 400$

(E) $ABC > 400$

You know that A is the lowest of the three digits. But A doesn't equal 0, because then B and C would both equal 0; then ABC would equal 0, which isn't a positive number.

If A is 1, then B is 2 and C is 6, so $ABC = 126$, which looks good. Now try a higher value for A. If A is 2, then B is 4 and C is 12, which isn't a digit. A must be less than 2, so the value $ABC = 126$ is the only one that works. Thus, ABC is between 100 and 200, so the right answer is **(B)**.

J, K, L, and M are four digits in the positive four-digit number $JKLM$. J is two greater than K, K is twice L, and M is an even number that is one less than L. If none of the digits equals 0, what is the value of $JKLM$?

The lowest of the four digits is M, which is an even number but not 0, so try $M = 2$. Then, $L = 3$, $K = 6$, and $J = 8$. This works. Starting with $M = 4$ instead would make the values of J and K greater than 9, so you know M does equal 2. Thus, $JKLM = 8{,}632$, which you write as **8632** in the answer grid.

The Space Between: Using Number Lines

A *number line* is a visual representation of a set of numbers. You probably saw your first number line as a child when you were learning to count. Unlike your first number line, however, those you see on the SAT may contain negative numbers or *rational numbers* (fractions or decimals).

Each point on a number line represents a different number. Some of these points are labeled with *tick marks* separated from each other by constant intervals. A *length* on a number line is the distance between two points.

When calculating length on a number line, always measure the intervals between two points rather than counting the tick marks between them.

Number lines on the SAT are *always* drawn to scale — that is, each interval always represents the same length on a single number line. In some cases, the question requires you to figure out what that interval is.

On the number line below, what is the distance between P and Q?

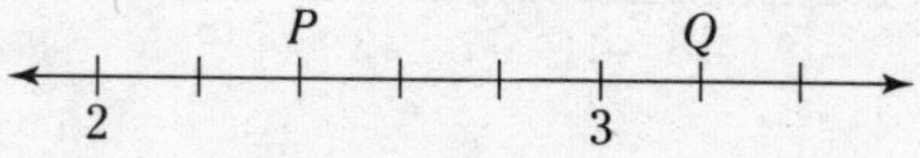

(A) 0.2

(B) 0.8

(C) 1.0

(D) 1.2

(E) 3.2

Two tick marks are labeled with the numbers 2 and 3. You see five intervals between these two tick marks, so each interval represents $\frac{1}{5}$ of the distance from 2 to 3. In decimals, this interval is 0.2.

The distance between P and Q is four intervals, so multiply the length of an interval by 4:

$$0.2(4) = 0.8$$

Therefore, the right answer is **(B).**

EXAMPLE

Another common type of SAT question asks you to label a point on a number line.

On the number line below, what is the value at point P?

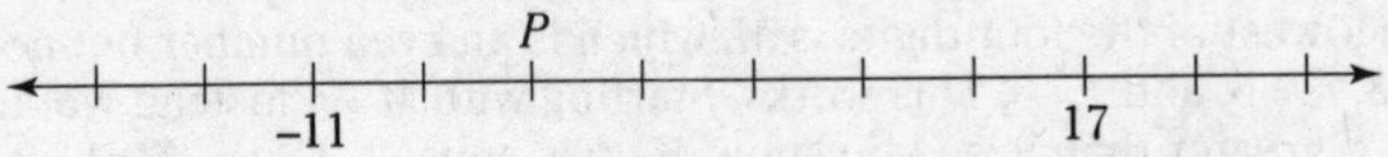

(A) –9

(B) –5

(C) –3

(D) 0

(E) 13

First, calculate the distance between the two values –11 and 17 by subtracting the lower number (farthest left on the number line) from the higher number (farthest right on the number line):

$$17 - (-11) = 17 + 11 = 28$$

These two points are separated by seven intervals, so divide the total by the number of intervals:

$$28 \div 7 = 4$$

Thus, each interval equals 4, so you can label every tick mark on the number line as follows:

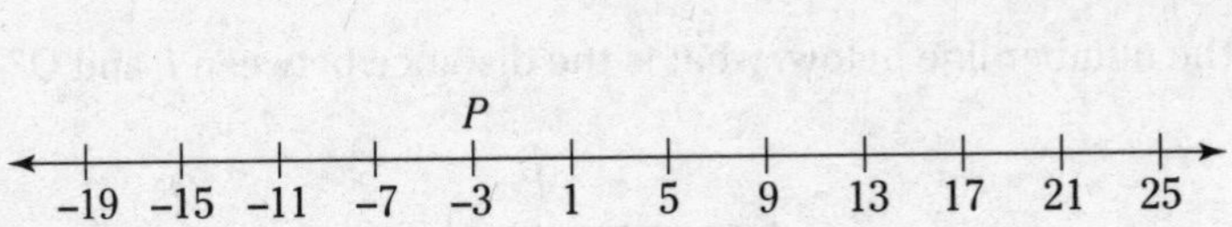

Therefore, the value at point P is –3, so the right answer is **(C).**

Dividing and Conquering: Understanding Divisibility, Factors, and Multiples

An important concept in arithmetic is divisibility. One integer is *divisible* by another if you can divide the first by the second without leaving a remainder. For example,

8 is *divisible* by 4, because $8 \div 4 = 2$ (with no remainder)

8 is *not divisible* by 5, because $8 \div 5 = 1$ r 3 (1 with a remainder of 3)

Another way to describe divisibility is using the words *factor* and *multiple*. For example, when you know that 6 is divisible by 3, you also know the following:

- 3 is a *factor* of 6
- 6 is a *multiple* of 3

Most SAT questions that ask you about factors and multiples focus only on positive integers. However, negative numbers can be factors and multiples, too. In this section, you explore what you need to know about factors and multiples to answer SAT questions.

Testing for divisibility

TIP

Here are a few tricks for testing whether a number is divisible by another number without actually doing the division on your calculator:

- **By 2:** Every number that's divisible by 2 (that is, every even number) ends with 2, 4, 6, 8, or 0.
- **By 3:** Every number that's divisible by 3 has the property that if you add up its digits, the result is also divisible by 3. For example: 444 is divisible by 3 because 4 + 4 + 4 = 12, which is divisible by 3.
- **By 4:** Every number that's divisible by 4 (except 4 and 8, of course) ends with a two-digit number that's also divisible by 4. For example, the number 1,716 is divisible by 4 because 16 is divisible by 4.
- **By 5:** Every number that's divisible by 5 ends with 5 or 0.
- **By 6:** Every number that's divisible by 6 is divisible by both 2 and 3, so it passes the two tests that I list earlier.
- **By 7:** Sorry, folks — there's just no good way to test whether a number is divisible by 7.
- **By 8:** Every large number that's divisible by 8 ends with a three-digit number that's also divisible by 8. For example, the number 19,800 is divisible by 8 because 800 is divisible by 8.
- **By 9:** Every number that's divisible by 9 has the property that if you add up its digits, the result is also divisible by 9. For example: 558 is divisible by 9 because 5 + 5 + 8 = 18, which is divisible by 9.
- **By 10:** Every number that's divisible by 10 ends in 0.

In some cases, knowing these tricks can save you a few keystrokes on your calculator. Every second counts!

What is the greatest number less than 500 that is divisible by both 2 and 9?

You're looking for an even number (because it's divisible by 2) that's both less than 500 and divisible by 9. The divisibility test for 9 says that if you add up the digits, the result is also divisible by 9. Start with 498, then try 496, and so forth until you find the highest even number that works:

498: 4 + 9 + 8 = 21

496: 4 + 9 + 6 = 19

494: 4 + 9 + 4 = 17

492: 4 + 9 + 2 = 15

490: 4 + 9 + 0 = 13

488: 4 + 8 + 8 = 20

486: 4 + 8 + 6 = 18 divisible by 9

At last! The number **486** is the highest even number less than 500 that's divisible by 9, so this is the right answer.

Factoring in knowledge of factors

The *factors* of a number are all the numbers that divide evenly into that number. In this section, I discuss a few key points about factors.

Listing the factors of a number

An SAT question may ask you to list all the factors of any integer. To do so, write the number 1, leave a space, and write the number itself. All other numbers on the list fall between these two numbers. So first check whether the number is divisible by 2; if it is, write down 2 and the answer you get when you divide by 2. Next, check 3, 4, and so on until the numbers at the front of the list meet the ones at the end.

How many positive integers are factors of 24?

To answer this question, you need to list all the factors of 24. Write the number 1, leave some space, and write 24:

Factors of 24: 1 24

Proceed by checking 2: 24 is divisible by 2 because 24 ÷ 2 = 12. So 2 and 12 are the next-highest and next-lowest factors of 24:

Factors of 24: 1 2 12 24

All other factors of 24 must fall between 2 and 12. Next, check 3, then 4; 24 is divisible by both of these numbers, so here's your list:

Factors of 24: 1 2 3 4 6 8 12 24

Any other factor of 24 must fall between 4 and 6. However, 5 isn't a factor of 24, because 24 ÷ 5 = 4 r 4 (4 with a remainder of 4). Therefore, 24 has eight factors, so the right answer is **8**.

Knowing what's so great about the greatest common factor (GCF)

The *greatest common factor (GCF)* of two or more numbers is the highest number that both or all of the numbers are divisible by.

What is the greatest common factor of 20, 28, and 44?

To answer this question, list the factors of all the numbers, as I show you in the preceding section:

Factors of 20: 1	2	4	5	10	20
Factors of 28: 1	2	4	7	14	28
Factors of 44: 1	2	4	11	22	44

The highest number in all three lists is **4**, so that's the right answer.

Understanding prime and composite numbers

Every positive integer (except 1) has at least two factors: 1 and the number itself (for info on integers, see the earlier section "Maintaining Your Integrity with Integers"). When a number has only these two factors, that number is a *prime number*. Here is a list of all the prime numbers under 30:

2, 3, 5, 7, 11, 13, 17, 19, 23, 29

Each of these numbers is divisible only by 1 and the number itself. All other positive integers (except 1) have more than two factors. These are called *composite numbers*.

The number 1 is neither prime nor composite. All integers greater than 1 are either prime or composite. No number is both prime and composite.

A number is prime if it can't be divided by any prime number up to its square root on the calculator. This can help you know when to stop checking numbers and just say it's prime. Here's a quick rule of thumb that's easy to remember: Every composite number under 121 is divisible by 2, 3, 5, or 7.

Which of the following integers is a composite number?

(A) 23

(B) 31

(C) 37

(D) 47

(E) 51

Use the divisibility tests (see the earlier section "Testing for divisibility"). You can see that none of these numbers is divisible by 2 or 5, because none of them is even or ends in 5. Any number that's divisible by 3 contains digits that add up to a number that's also divisible by 3. Quickly running down the list, the digits of the first four numbers add up to 5, 4, 10, and 11, so none of them are divisible by 3. However, $5 + 1 = 6$, which is divisible by 3 (and $51 = 3 \times 17$). Thus, 51 is a composite number, so the right answer is **(E)**.

Understanding prime factors

Every number has a unique list of *prime factors* — the prime numbers that equal that number when multiplied together. For example,

$$56 = 2 \times 2 \times 2 \times 7$$

Note that a list of prime factors may include repeated numbers. However, a list of the *distinct prime factors* of a number includes only one of each number, so 56 has two distinct prime factors: 2 and 7.

How many distinct prime factors does the number 120 have?

(A) 1

(B) 2

(C) 3

(D) 4

(E) 5

A quick way to find the nondistinct prime factors of a number is by using a tree. Begin by writing down the number and then breaking it into two numbers that multiply to the number:

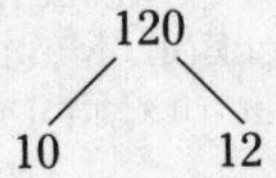

Now break each of these numbers in the same way:

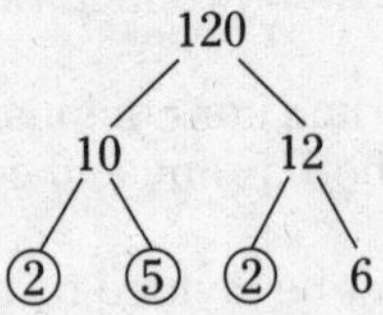

Note that I circle the prime numbers 2 and 5, because these numbers cannot be further broken into factors. To finish, break the number 6 into factors:

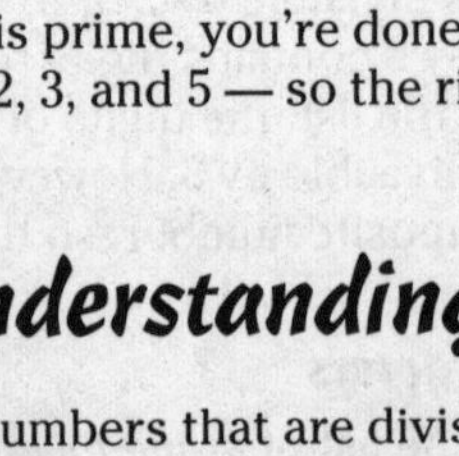

When every number at the bottom is prime, you're done: $120 = 2 \times 2 \times 2 \times 3 \times 5$. Thus, 120 has three distinct prime factors — 2, 3, and 5 — so the right answer is **(C)**.

Multiplying your understanding of multiples

The *multiples* of a number are the numbers that are divisible by that number. In this section, I discuss a few important points about multiples that are useful on the SAT.

Generating a generous supply of multiples

The list of the multiples of a number goes on forever. You can generate this list by adding the number to itself repeatedly. For example,

Multiples of 4: 4, 8, 12, 16, 20, 24, 28, 32, 36, 40, ...

Technically, 0 is a multiple of every number, because 0 is divisible by every number.

Finding the least common multiple (LCM)

The *least common multiple* of two or more numbers is the lowest positive number that is a multiple of both or all of them.

What is the least common multiple of 4, 6, and 10?

To answer this question, generate a list of the multiples of all three numbers until you find the first number that appears on all three lists:

Multiples of 4: 4, 8, 12, 16, 20, 24, 28, 32, 36, 40, 44, 48, 52, 56, 60, ...

Multiples of 6: 6, 12, 18, 24, 30, 36, 42, 48, 54, 60, ...

Multiples of 10: 10, 20, 30, 40, 50, 60, ...

Therefore, the right answer is **60**.

Understanding Percents

Many students feel that they need a refresher on percent problems for the SAT. In this section, I show you the connections between percents and their close cousins, decimals (which are generally easier to work with than percents). Then you see how to answer a variety of percent questions, including percent increase and percent decrease problems.

Converting between percents and decimals

To solve most percent problems, one early step is usually to convert from percents to decimals. At the end of a calculation, you often need to convert a decimal to a percent so you can answer the question. Fortunately, converting between percents and decimals is much easier than converting between fractions and decimals. This section gives you the basics.

Converting percents to decimals

To convert a percent to a decimal, move the decimal point two places to the left and drop the percent sign. For example,

25% = 0.25   36% = 0.36   175% = 1.75

When converting percents that have a 0 at the end, you can drop the trailing zero that results:

10% = 0.10 = 0.1   20% = 0.20 = 0.2   90% = 0.90 = 0.9

Be careful when converting single-digit percents to decimals. Remember to move the decimal point *two* decimal places to the left, placing a 0 after the decimal point. This is a 0 you *cannot* drop:

1% = 0.01   3% = 0.03   5% = 0.05

Converting decimals to percents

To convert a decimal to a percent, move the decimal point two places to the right and add a percent sign. For example,

0.44 = 44%   0.125 = 12.5%   9.99 = 999%

When a conversion results in a leading zero, you can drop it:

0.02 = 02% = 2%   0.06 = 06% = 6%   0.09 = 09% = 9%

Be careful when converting whole numbers and decimals that have only one decimal place. To help you remember to move the decimal point *two* decimal places to the right, you may find it helpful to place a trailing zero at the end of the decimal before you do the conversion:

0.5 = 0.50 = 50%   1.8 = 1.80 = 180%   3 = 3.00 = 300%

Solving basic percent problems

You can solve a wide variety of percent problems using this formula:

Percent × number = result

To see how this formula works, suppose you want to calculate 50% of 40. You can probably do this problem in your head. To use the formula, however, substitute the percent (50% = 0.5) and the number (40) into the formula:

$0.5 \times 40 = 20$

As you can see, the formula gives you the right answer of 20.

Another way to think about percent problems is to translate a sentence involving a percent by changing the word *of* to a multiplication sign (×) and the word *is* to an equal sign. For example,

25% of 60 is 15 *means* $0.25 \times 60 = 15$

If 35% of a number is 140, what is the number?

In this case, the question gives you the percent and the result and asks you to find the number. Write the formula, representing the unknown number as *x*:

$0.35x = 140$

After you have the words expressed as an equation, solve for *x* by dividing both sides by 0.35:

$$x = \frac{140}{0.35} = 400$$

So the right answer is **400**.

What percent of 750 is 105?

(A) 7%

(B) 12%

(C) 14%

(D) 15%

(E) 18%

This time, you're given the number (750) and the result (105) and are asked to find the percent. Represent the unknown number as x in your formula:

$$x(750) = 105$$

To solve, divide both sides by 750:

$$x = \frac{105}{750} = 0.14$$

The question asks for the percent, so convert the decimal to a percent:

$$0.14 = 14\%$$

So the right answer is **(C)**.

An SAT question may require more than one calculation to solve a single problem.

If 85% of a number is 255, what is 40% of that number?

The problem tells you that 85% of a number is 255, so you can use the percent formula to find the number:

$$0.85x = 255$$

$$x = \frac{255}{0.85} = 300$$

Thus, the number is 300. Now use the formula again to find 40% of 300:

$$(0.4)(300) = 120$$

So the right answer is **120**.

Increasing your score (and decreasing your stress) with percent increase/decrease problems

Some of the trickiest SAT problems involve percent increase and decrease. Here, you're dealing with two numbers:

- **Old number:** The number *before* the increase or decrease
- **New number:** The number *after* the increase or decrease

Percent increase and percent decrease problems often give you two numbers and ask you to calculate by what percentage the value has either increased or decreased.

Here's a formula to help you find the change in percent if you know the original old number before the change and the new number after it:

$$\text{Percent increase or decrease} = \frac{\text{Amount of increase or decrease}}{\text{Old number}}$$

In this formula, the *amount of increase or decrease* is just the difference between the old and new numbers, expressed as a positive number. This formula produces a decimal, which you have to convert to a percent.

Martha received a raise, increasing her monthly salary from $3,800 to $4,712. What is the percent increase that she received?

In this problem, the old number (before the raise) is $3,800 and the new number (after the raise) is $4,712. First, subtract to calculate the amount of the increase:

$$4{,}712 - 3{,}800 = 912$$

Now plug the numbers into the percent increase formula:

$$\text{Percent increase} = \frac{912}{3{,}800} = 0.24$$

This result is expressed as a decimal, so convert it to a percent:

$$= 24\%$$

Thus, the right answer is **24**.

To qualify as a welterweight for a boxing match, Antony needs to drop his weight from 150 to 147. What percent decrease in weight does this represent?

(A) 1%

(B) 1.5%

(C) 2%

(D) 2.5%

(E) 3%

In this problem, the old number (before the weight loss) is 150 and the new number (after the weight loss) is 147. Subtract to calculate the amount of the decrease:

$$150 - 147 = 3$$

Now plug in the numbers:

$$\text{Percent decrease} = \frac{3}{150} = 0.02 = 2\%$$

So the right answer is **(C)**.

In some cases, the SAT problem gives you the amount of the increase or decrease, so you don't have to calculate it.

Geoff invested $5,000 and made a $600 profit. What percent increase does this profit represent?

In this example, you're given the amount of the increase, so plug the numbers directly into the formula:

$$\text{Percent increase} = \frac{600}{5{,}000} = 0.12 = 12\%$$

Therefore, the investment yielded a 12% profit, and the answer is **12**.

Jack paid $31.97 to cover the price of a meal plus 15% of the price as a tip for the server. What was the price of the meal without the tip?

(A) $26.60

(B) $27.20

(C) $27.60

(D) $27.80

(E) $28.40

In this problem, you're given the new number ($31.97) and the percent increase (15% = 0.15). You're trying to find the old number, so let *x* equal this number. Here's the formula:

$$\text{Percent increase} = \frac{\text{Amount of increase}}{\text{Old number}}$$

Plug in 0.15 for the percent increase and *x* for the old number. The amount of the increase is 31.97 – *x*, so plug this in as well:

$$0.15 = \frac{31.97 - x}{x}$$

Multiply both sides by *x* to get rid of the fraction and solve for *x*:

$$0.15x = 31.97 - x$$
$$1.15x = 31.97$$
$$x = \frac{31.97}{1.15}$$
$$x = 27.8$$

Therefore, the cost of the meal without the tip was $27.80, so the right answer is **(D)**.

Ratios: Making Comparisons

A *ratio* is a mathematical comparison of two quantities, based on the operation of division. For example, suppose you have two dogs and three cats. Here are a variety of ways to express the ratio of dogs to cats:

2:3 2 to 3 $\frac{2}{3}$

Treating ratios as fractions

TIP

A good way to work with a ratio is to turn it into a fraction. For reference, you may find it helpful to label the ratio by creating a similar "word fraction" that tells you what the numerator and denominator stand for. For example,

$$\frac{\text{Dogs}}{\text{Cats}} = \frac{2}{3}$$

Now you can use what you know about fractions to handle whatever question you need to answer. For instance, you can put a ratio in lowest terms, just as you can reduce a fraction.

EXAMPLE

If a classroom has 12 boys and 15 girls, what is the ratio of boys to girls?

(A) 1:2

(B) 2:3

(C) 3:4

(D) 4:5

(E) 5:6

To solve this problem, turn it into a fraction. Boys are listed first, so they go in the numerator:

$$\frac{\text{Boys}}{\text{Girls}} = \frac{12}{15}$$

You can reduce this fraction by canceling out a factor of 3 from both the numerator and denominator:

$$= \frac{4}{5}$$

The fraction $\frac{4}{5}$ is equivalent to the ratio 4:5, so the right answer is **(D).**

When working with ratios, take a moment to be sure that you're clear exactly which two quantities you're being asked to compare. Look at the following example:

EXAMPLE

Amy and Matt share a bowl of 30 jelly beans. Amy eats 12 jelly beans and Matt eats the rest. Which of the following fractions expresses the ratio of how many jelly beans Matt eats as compared to how many were in the bowl?

(A) $\frac{2}{3}$

(B) $\frac{2}{5}$

(C) $\frac{3}{5}$

(D) $\frac{5}{2}$

(E) $\frac{5}{3}$

The question asks for the following ratio:

$$\frac{\text{Matt's jelly beans}}{\text{Total jelly beans}}$$

Matt eats 30 – 12 = 18 jelly beans, so

$$= \frac{18}{30}$$

You can reduce the fraction by a factor of 6:

$$= \frac{3}{5}$$

Therefore, the right answer is **(C).**

Proportions: Crossing paths with equal ratios

A *proportion* is an equation that uses two ratios set equal to each other. For example, if a club has a 2:1 ratio of boys to girls, you can set up the following proportion:

$$\frac{\text{Boys}}{\text{Girls}} = \frac{2}{1}$$

Depending on the question, you can then plug in information about the number of boys to find the number of girls, or vice versa.

Jake and Keith are both collecting donations for their soccer team. The ratio of Jake's collections to Keith's is 4:7. If Keith has collected \$84, how many dollars has Jake collected?

To begin, set up the ratio as a proportion:

$$\frac{\text{Jake's amount}}{\text{Keith's amount}} = \frac{4}{7}$$

Now replace Keith's amount with the number given in the problem:

$$\frac{\text{Jake's amount}}{84} = \frac{4}{7}$$

You don't know Jake's amount, so replace it with the letter j:

$$\frac{j}{84} = \frac{4}{7}$$

At this point, you can use algebra to solve the problem. First, cross-multiply to clear out any fractions in the equation:

$$j(7) = 4(84)$$

Next, simplify and solve:

$$7j = 336$$

$$j = 48$$

Therefore, the right answer is **48**.

Feeling Powerful with Exponents and Getting Rooted with Roots

In math, raising a number to a *power* means multiplying that number by itself. Raising a number to a power utilizes two different numbers:

- **The base:** The *number* being multiplied by itself
- **The exponent:** The *number of times* the base is to be multiplied

For example, here's how you raise the number 5 to the power of 2:

$$5^2 = 5 \times 5 = 25$$

In this example, the base is 5 and the exponent is 2.

Taking a *root* of a number reverses the process of raising a number to a power. The most common root you see on the SAT is a square root, also called a *radical*. In this section, I show you how to answer a variety of questions that focus on expressions with powers and roots.

Squaring up your knowledge of squares and square roots

Squaring a number means multiplying it by itself — that is, raising it to the power of 2. For example,

$$3^2 = 3 \times 3 = 9$$

Any integer that's the product of an integer multiplied by itself is called a *square number*. For the SAT, knowing the first ten positive square numbers by heart is a good idea:

1^2	2^2	3^2	4^2	5^2	6^2	7^2	8^2	9^2	10^2
1	4	9	16	25	36	49	64	81	100

If the sum of three consecutive square numbers is 149, what is the greatest of these three numbers?

Knowing the first ten square numbers allows you to solve this problem by trial and error:

$$36 + 49 + 64 = 149$$

Therefore, the answer is **64**.

Finding the square root of a number (also called a *radical*) means reversing this process of squaring: Discovering a value that, when multiplied by itself, produces the number you started with.

When you take the square root of a number, you get both a positive and negative answer, because multiplying a negative number by a negative number gives you a positive number. For example, both 3×3 and -3×-3 equal 9. But when you're working with a distance, when the question asks for a positive value, or when the question is a grid-in problem (which doesn't allow negative signs), you only have to use the positive answer.

$\sqrt{1}$	$\sqrt{4}$	$\sqrt{9}$	$\sqrt{16}$	$\sqrt{25}$	$\sqrt{36}$	$\sqrt{49}$	$\sqrt{64}$	$\sqrt{81}$	$\sqrt{100}$
1, –1	2, –2	3, –3	4, –4	5, –5	6, –6	7, –7	8, –8	9, –9	10, –10

On the SAT, you may *not* take the square root of a negative number. The result would be an *imaginary number,* which is outside the set of real numbers. (And yes, "imaginary number" is the official math term.)

The difference between two consecutive square numbers is 19. What is the square root of the greater number?

Again, knowing the first ten square numbers helps solve this problem. Trial and error shows you that the two square numbers are 81 and 100, because $100 - 81 = 19$. The square root of the greater number is $\sqrt{100}$, so the answer is **10**.

Evaluating expressions with exponents and roots

After you understand the basics of square numbers, you can apply this knowledge to higher powers — that is, expressions with an exponent higher than 2. The exponent tells you how many times to multily a number by itself. For example,

$$5^3 = 5 \times 5 \times 5 = 125$$

$$10^4 = 10 \times 10 \times 10 \times 10 = 10{,}000$$

$$2^6 = 2 \times 2 \times 2 \times 2 \times 2 \times 2 = 64$$

Which of the following is correct?

I. $3^4 = 9^2$

II. $4^3 = 8^2$

III. $\sqrt{100} = 10^2$

(A) I only

(B) I and II only

(C) I and III only

(D) II and III only

(E) I, II, and III

Check all three problems by evaluating each side of the equation:

$3^4 = 81$ $9^2 = 81$

$4^3 = 64$ $8^2 = 64$

$\sqrt{100} = 10$ $10^2 = 100$

Thus, I and II are correct, and III is incorrect. Therefore, the right answer is **(B).**

A basic familiarity with square roots can propel your understanding of other roots. For example, a cube root such as $\sqrt[3]{27}$ is a number that you multiply by itself three times to arrive at 27. Here are a few more examples of higher-order roots

$\sqrt[3]{27} = 3$ because $3 \times 3 \times 3 = 27$

$\sqrt[4]{625} = 5$ because $5 \times 5 \times 5 \times 5 = 625$

$\sqrt[6]{1{,}000{,}000} = 10$ because $10 \times 10 \times 10 \times 10 \times 10 \times 10 = 1{,}000{,}000$

Most calculators allow you to find higher-order roots by entering them as exponents that are fractions. For example, if you want to find $\sqrt[3]{27}$, raise 27 to a power of $\frac{1}{3}$. For details, see the later section "Fractional exponents: Combining powers and roots."

You can take roots of negative numbers if the root is an *odd number.* For instance, $(-8)^{1/3}$, the *third* (or cubic) root of –8, is –2, because $-2 \times -2 \times -2 = 4(-2) = -8$.`

If *x* is an integer such that $\sqrt[6]{64} < x < \sqrt[3]{64}$, what is the value of *x?*

(A) 1

(B) 2

(C) 3

(D) 4

(E) 5

Answer this question by evaluating both roots:

$\sqrt[6]{64} = 2$ because $2 \times 2 \times 2 \times 2 \times 2 \times 2 = 64$

$\sqrt[3]{64} = 4$ because $4 \times 4 \times 4 = 64$

Thus, $2 < x < 4$, so $x = 3$ and the right answer is **(C).**

Fractional bases: Raising fractions to powers

An expression with a *fractional base* is one in which a fraction is raised to a power. When working with these expressions, remember that an exponent represents repeated multiplication. To evaluate, first change the power to multiplication and then multiply across:

$$\left(\frac{2}{5}\right)^3 = \frac{2}{5} \times \frac{2}{5} \times \frac{2}{5} = \frac{8}{125}$$

Which of the following expressions equals $\frac{16}{81}$?

I. $\left(\frac{2}{3}\right)^4$

II. $\left(\frac{4}{9}\right)^2$

III. $\left(\frac{16}{81}\right)^1$

(A) III only

(B) I and II only

(C) I and III only

(D) II and III only

(E) I, II, and III

Evaluate all three expressions using fraction multiplication:

$$\left(\frac{2}{3}\right)^4 = \frac{2}{3} \times \frac{2}{3} \times \frac{2}{3} \times \frac{2}{3} = \frac{16}{81}$$

$$\left(\frac{4}{9}\right)^2 = \frac{4}{9} \times \frac{4}{9} = \frac{16}{81}$$

$$\left(\frac{16}{81}\right)^1 = \frac{16}{81}$$

Thus, all three expressions are equal to $\frac{16}{81}$, so the right answer is **(E)**.

Fractional exponents: Combining powers and roots

You can apply your understanding of powers and roots to evaluate expressions that have a *fractional exponent* — that is, expressions with a number raised to a power that's a fraction. When a number is raised to the power of a fraction, the top of the fractional exponent is the power and the bottom is the root.

Fractional exponents with a 1 in the numerator (top number) of the fraction are easy to evaluate as higher-order roots (radicals). For example,

$$16^{1/2} = \sqrt{16} = 4$$

$$125^{1/3} = \sqrt[3]{125} = 5$$

$$128^{1/7} = \sqrt[7]{128} = 2$$

To evaluate an expression with a fractional exponent, rewrite it using a power and a root, according to this formula:

$$n^{x/y} = \sqrt[y]{n^x}$$

For example,

$$27^{2/3} = \sqrt[3]{27^2} = \sqrt[3]{729} = 9$$

Practice Problems for Arithmetic Review

Ready for some practice answering SAT arithmetic questions? The 20 questions in this section include 15 multiple-choice questions and 5 grid-in questions. If you get stuck on a question, flip back through the chapter for ideas on how to proceed. I show you how to work through each problem in the next section.

1. If a school has 60 freshman and 75 seniors, what is the ratio of freshman to seniors?

(A) 2 to 3

(B) 3 to 5

(C) 4 to 5

(D) 5 to 6

(E) 7 to 10

2. The sum of two consecutive square numbers is 145. What is the sum of the positive square roots of these numbers?

(A) 9

(B) 11

(C) 13

(D) 15

(E) 17

3. On the number line below, which of the following has a length of 2.5?

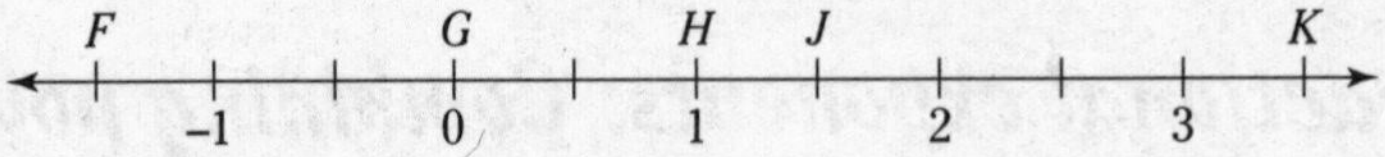

(A) $\overline{FG}$

(B) $\overline{FJ}$

(C) $\overline{GK}$

(D) $\overline{HK}$

(E) $\overline{JK}$

4. T, U, and V are digits in the positive three-digit number TUV, which is divisible by 5. T is three greater than U, and U is three greater than V. What is the value of $T + U + V$?

(A) 9

(B) 12

(C) 15

(D) 18

(E) 21

5. If n is an integer such that $2^6 < n^2 < 1{,}000^{2/3}$, what is the value of n?

(A) 2

(B) 3

(C) 4

(D) 6

(E) 9

6. How many prime numbers are both greater than 50 and less than 60?

(A) 0

(B) 1

(C) 2

(D) 3

(E) 4

7. In two consecutive visits to a veterinarian, a dog weighed in at 48.0 lbs. and 52.8 lbs. What percent increase in weight is this?

(A) 1%

(B) 3%

(C) 9%

(D) 10%

(E) 11%

8. Which of the following integers has exactly the same number of positive factors as 14 does?

(A) 11

(B) 12

(C) 13

(D) 15

(E) 16

9. What percent of 176 is 22?

(A) 8%

(B) 12.5%

(C) 14.4%

(D) 16.5%

(E) 18%

10. How many distinct positive integers are prime factors of both 60 and 66?

(A) 1

(B) 2

(C) 3

(D) 4

(E) 5

11. On the number line below, $S = \left(\frac{1}{2}\right)^3$. What does T equal?

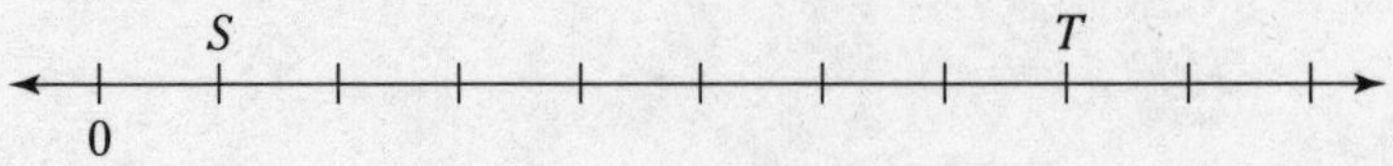

(A) $\frac{1}{2}$

(B) 1

(C) 2

(D) 4

(E) 8

12. X, Y, and Z are digits in the three-digit number ZYX, such that $ZYX > 900$. Additionally, the following conditions apply:

$X + 2 = Y$

$Y + 3 = Z$

Which of the following are square numbers?

(A) Z only

(B) X and Y only

(C) X and Z only

(D) Y and Z only

(E) X, Y, and Z

13. If you bring \$135 on a shopping trip and spend \$99 of it, what percentage of your money have you spent?

(A) 25%

(B) $26\frac{2}{3}\%$

(C) $73\frac{1}{3}\%$

(D) 75%

(E) 99%

14. What is the sum of 19 and the next two prime numbers greater than 19?

(A) 60

(B) 63

(C) 67

(D) 69

(E) 71

15. A gated community has a 7:2 ratio of retirees to nonretirees. If 105 of its residents are retirees, how many people are living in the community all together?

    (A) 115

    (B) 120

    (C) 130

    (D) 135

    (E) 145

16. On the number line below, the tick marks are spaced equally apart. What is the value of *V*?

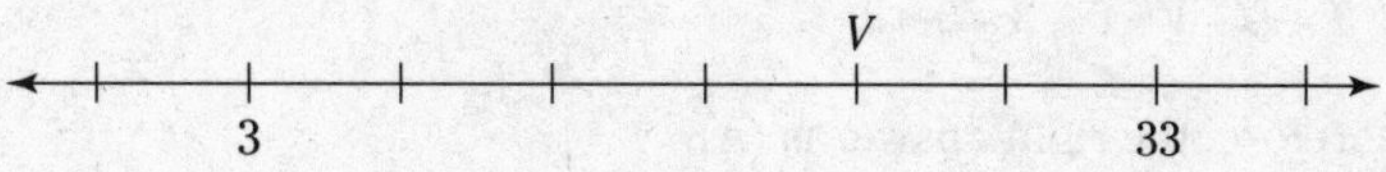

17. What is the sum of the greatest common factor and the least common multiple of 10 and 12?

18. What is the lowest three-digit number that's divisible by both 3 and 5?

19. If 12.5% of a number is 70, what is 55% of that number?

20. Arielle and Mari are both salespeople. Yesterday, the ratio of Arielle's gross sales to Mari's was 5 to 8. If Arielle sold $1,350 in merchandise, what dollar amount of merchandise did Mari sell?

Solutions to Practice Problems

In this section, I provide answers for the practice question from the previous section. In each case, I work through the problem step-by-step so you can see how to get the answer.

1. **C.** To solve this problem, turn it into a fraction:

   $$\frac{\text{Freshmen}}{\text{Seniors}} = \frac{60}{75}$$

   Now reduce the fraction, dividing both the top and bottom by 5:

   $$\frac{12}{15}$$

   You can reduce it still further by dividing the top and bottom by 3:

   $$\frac{4}{5}$$

   Thus, the right answer is 4 to 5, so the answer is (C).

2. **E.** The first ten square numbers are

   1, 4, 9, 16, 25, 36, 49, 64, 81, 100

   The sum of 81 and 100 is 181, which is too big, so the two numbers are within this list. Trial and error shows you that 64 + 81 = 145.

The question asks for the sum of the square roots of these two numbers:

$$\sqrt{64} + \sqrt{81} = 8 + 9 = 17$$

Thus, the right answer is (E).

3. **D.** Every other tick mark is labeled with an integer, so each interval on this number line equals 0.5. Thus, 2.5 = 5 intervals. *H* and *K* are separated by five intervals, so $HK = 2.5$. Thus, the right answer is (D).

4. **A.** The value of *TUV* is divisible by 5, so *V* is either 5 or 0. If $V = 5$, then $U = 8$ and $T = 11$, which is impossible, because *T* is a one-digit number. Thus, $V = 0$, $U = 3$, and $T = 6$, so $TUV = 630$. Find the sum of the digits:

$$T + U + V = 6 + 3 + 0 = 9$$

Therefore, the right answer is (A).

5. **E.** First, evaluate the expressions with exponents:

$$2^6 = 64 \qquad 1{,}000^{2/3} = 100$$

Because *n* is an integer, n^2 is a square number such that

$$64 < n^2 < 100$$

The only square number between 64 and 100 is 81, so:

$$n^2 = 81$$

$$n = 9$$

Thus, the right answer is (E).

6. **C.** You're looking for prime numbers, so you can rule out all composite numbers. Every composite number under 121 is divisible by 2, 3, 5, or 7. All even numbers other than 2 aren't prime, so rule out all even numbers and examine all odd numbers between 50 and 60:

51 53 55 57 59

The number 55 is divisible by 5, so rule it out. Now every number whose digits add up to a multiple of 3 is divisible by 3, so test these four numbers (see the earlier section "Testing for divisibility"):

51: $5 + 1 = 6$ divisible by 3

53: $5 + 3 = 8$

57: $5 + 7 = 12$ divisible by 3

59: $5 + 9 = 14$

So you can rule out 51 and 57. Now test 53 and 59 for divisibility by 7:

53: $53 \div 7 = 7 \text{ r } 4$

59: $59 \div 7 = 8 \text{ r } 3$

Thus, the numbers 53 and 59 aren't divisible by 2, 3, 5, or 7, and they're less than 121, so these are both prime numbers. Therefore, there are two prime numbers between 50 and 60, so the answer is (C).

7. **D.** The old number (before weight gain) is 48.0, and the new number (after weight gain) is 52.8. Begin by finding the amount of the increase:

   $52.8 - 48 = 4.8$

   Now plug the numbers into the formula:

   $$\text{Percent increase} = \frac{\text{Amount of increase}}{\text{Old number}} = \frac{4.8}{48} = 0.1 = 10\%$$

   So the right answer is (D).

8. **D.** First, list the factors of 14:

   Factors of 14: 1 2 7 14

   So 14 has four factors. The right answer has four factors, so you can rule out the prime numbers 11 and 13, because each of these has only two factors. Now factor 12:

   Factors of 12: 1 2 3 4 6 12

   Twelve has six factors, so this is wrong. Next, try 15:

   Factors of 15: 1 3 5 15

   The number 15 has four factors, so the right answer is (D).

9. **B.** Use the percent formula, filling in the number (176) and the result (22) and using *x* for the percent amount:

   $$\text{Percent} \times \text{number} = \text{result}$$
   $$(x)(176) = 22$$
   $$176x = 22$$

   To solve for *x*, divide both sides by 176:

   $$x = \frac{22}{176} = 0.125 = 12.5\%$$

   So the right answer is (B) — 12.5%.

10. **B.** First, find the prime factors of 60:

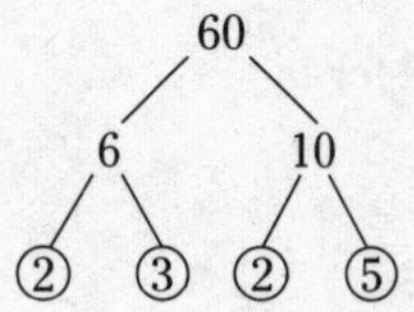

Next, find the prime factors of 66:

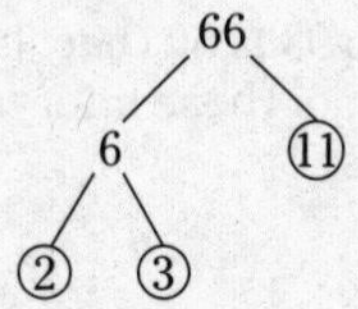

The numbers 60 and 66 have two distinct prime factors in common — 2 and 3 — so the right answer is (B).

11. **B.** To start, evaluate the value of *S*:

$$\left(\frac{1}{2}\right)^3 = \left(\frac{1}{2}\right)\left(\frac{1}{2}\right)\left(\frac{1}{2}\right) = \frac{1}{8}$$

Thus, every interval on the number line equals $\frac{1}{8}$, so you can label the number line as follows:

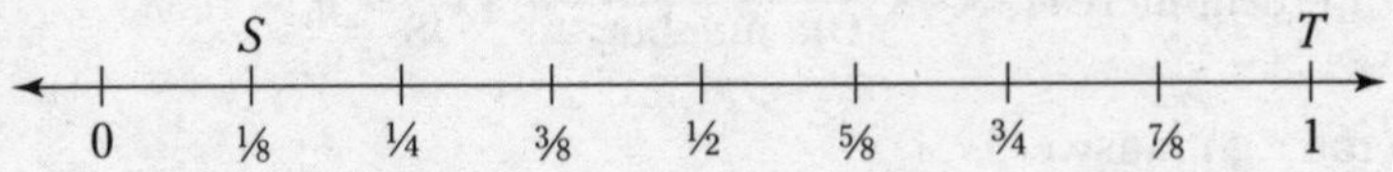

$T = 1$, so the right answer is (B).

12. **C.** $ZYX > 900$, so $Z = 9$. Thus, $Y = 6$ (because $Y + 3 = Z$) and $X = 4$ (because $X + 2 = Y$). Therefore, X and Z are both square numbers and Y isn't, so the right answer is (C).

13. **C.** The question asks by what percent your money has decreased, and it gives you the numbers to plug directly into the formula for percent decrease:

$$\text{Percent decrease} = \frac{\text{Amount of decrease}}{\text{Old number}} = \frac{99}{135} = 0.7333... = 73\frac{1}{3}\%$$

Thus, the right answer is (C).

14. **E.** All prime numbers greater than 2 are odd, so check only odd numbers. Remember that every number under 121 that isn't divisible by 2, 3, 5, or 7 is prime.

The number $21 = 3 \times 7$, so it isn't prime. The number 23 isn't divisible by 2, 3, 5, or 7, so it's prime. The number $25 = 5 \times 5$, so it isn't prime. The number $27 = 3 \times 9$, so it isn't prime. The number 29 isn't divisible by 2, 3, 5, or 7, so it's prime. Thus, $19 + 23 + 29 = 71$, so the right answer is (E).

15. **D.** Set up a proportion using the ratio of retirees to nonretirees:

$$\frac{\text{Retirees}}{\text{Nonretirees}} = \frac{7}{2}$$

The question tells you that 105 residents are retirees, so let n equal the number of nonretirees:

$$\frac{105}{n} = \frac{7}{2}$$

Cross-multiply and solve for n:

$$(105)(2) = 7n$$

$$210 = 7n$$

$$30 = n$$

Thus, there are 30 nonretirees and 105 retirees, so there are 135 residents altogether, and the right answer is (D).

16. **23.** The distance from 3 to 33 is 30 (because $33 - 3 = 30$). The number line has six intervals between 3 and 33, so each of these intervals equals 5 (because $30 \div 6 = 5$). You can label the number line as follows:

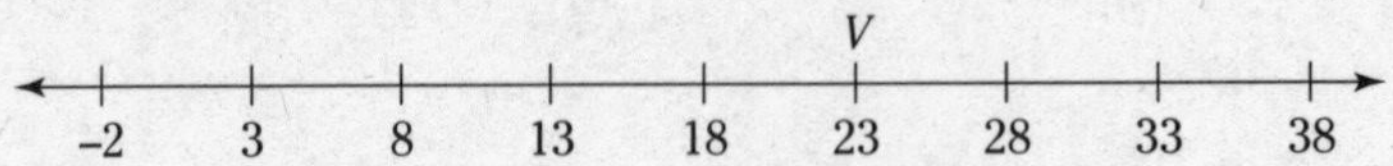

Therefore, the right answer is 23.

17. **62**. To begin, list the factors of 10 and 12:

Factors of 10:	1	2	5	10		
Factors of 12:	1	2	3	4	6	12

So the greatest common factor (GCF) of 10 and 12 is 2. Next, generate lists of multiples of 10 and 12:

Multiples of 10: 10, 20, 30, 40, 50, 60

Multiples of 12: 12, 24, 36, 48, 60

Thus, the least common multiple (LCM) of 10 and 12 is 60. The sum of 60 and 2 is 62, so that's the right answer.

18. **105**. To solve this problem, recall that you can test for divisibility by 3 by adding up the digits of a number. If this sum is divisible by 3, the number is divisible by 3; otherwise, it isn't. The lowest three-digit number is 100. This is divisible by 5 but not by 3, because $1 + 0 + 0 = 1$, which isn't divisible by 3. The next-highest number that's divisible by 5 is 105. It's also divisible by 3, because $1 + 0 + 5 = 6$, which is divisible by 3 (check: $105 \div 3 = 35$). Thus, the right answer is 105.

19. **308**. Use the percent formula, which says that *Percent* × *number* = *result.* You know the result and the percent, so use x as the number you want to find out:

$$0.125x = 70$$

Solve for x:

$$x = \frac{70}{0.125} = 560$$

So the number is 560. Use the percent formula again to find 55% of 560:

$$(0.55)(560) = 308$$

Therefore, the right answer is 308.

20. **2160**. Begin by setting up a proportion using the ratio of Arielle's sales to Mari's sales

$$\frac{\text{Arielle's sales}}{\text{Mari's sales}} = \frac{5}{8}$$

Plug in 1,350 for Arielle's sales and let m equal Mari's sales:

$$\frac{1{,}350}{m} = \frac{5}{8}$$

Cross-multiply and solve for m:

$$1{,}350(8) = 5m$$

$$10{,}800 = 5m$$

$$2{,}160 = m$$

Therefore, the right answer is 2,160.

Chapter 4

Return of the X-Men: Reviewing Algebra

In This Chapter

- Knowing basic algebra vocabulary and skills
- Evaluating, simplifying, and factoring algebraic expressions
- Solving algebraic equations and inequalities
- Working with systems of equations

To many students facing the SAT, algebra resembles a large and hairy beast with multiple heads and thousands of legs (okay, I'm exaggerating — but only by a little). So you may be surprised to find that there's a relatively short list of basic algebra skills, with almost everything else placed in service to one of these skills. From a wide angle, you can divide these skills into four basic categories:

- Working with algebraic expressions
- Working with equations and inequalities
- Graphing (see Chapter 6)
- Solving word problems (see Chapter 8)

In this chapter, I show you what you need to know about the first two categories of algebra skills. First, I give you a refresher on some algebra vocabulary and basic skills. Next, I cover the three basic skills you need when working with algebraic expressions: evaluating, simplifying, and factoring.

After that, you get to the main event: solving algebraic equations. If you've taken a year or two of algebra, you've seen all this stuff before. I divide the skills roughly along lines that will be most useful to you to answer SAT questions. First, I show you how to solve equations that have one variable, such as x. Next, you work with problems that have more than one variable. Then I cover inequalities.

To finish the chapter, I show you how to work with a type of algebra question specific to the SAT: the *new notation question,* in which an unusual symbol or notation is defined and you have to make sense of it. Then you can try your hand at some practice problems.

Knowing the Algebra You Forgot to Remember

Although you've probably taken at least a year of algebra as you prepare for the SAT, you may find that a lot of it looks a little blurry. However, you probably remember a bit more than you think — even if this is a bit less than you'd like!

Not to worry. In this section, I go over some of the basic vocabulary and concepts from algebra. I also provide you with a lot of formulas that you need to know when taking the SAT. Many of these formulas look complicated, but I try to introduce them in an order that makes sense.

Vocab: A few choice words about algebra

The words in this section may not be the ones that you'd pick to describe how you feel in your heart about algebra. They also may not be on your list of vocabulary words for the verbal portions of the SAT. Still, they're worth knowing — in fact, I bet you've heard most of them before.

I admit that this is math jargon, and I prefer to avoid jargon wherever possible. But these words are used so much that avoiding them would be like trying to fix a car without using words like *engine* or *brakes*. (How much confidence would you have in a mechanic who told you, "I think the thingy that makes your car move is all messed up, and the whatsit that stops the car needs fixing, too"?)

Variables and constants

A *variable* is a letter that stands for a number. The most common variable is x, with y a close second. In a single SAT question, a variable always stands for the same number no matter where it appears.

The word *constant* is just another word for *number.* In algebra, this word is usually used in contrast to a variable (and is usually spoken of with disdain, as in "In this problem, x is a beautiful and exalted variable, and 64 is a mere constant"). A constant can be any real number: an integer like 5 or –43, a rational number like $\frac{3}{7}$, or an irrational number like $\sqrt{2}$. Even π, which roughly equals 3.14 but really goes on forever, is a constant.

Algebraic expressions and equations

An *algebraic expression* is any string of mathematical symbols that makes sense when placed on one side of an equal sign. For example, here's an algebraic expression:

$$21\sqrt{2} + \pi + x$$

In this expression, $21\sqrt{2}$ and π are both mere constants. However, the presence of the beautiful and exalted variable x makes this an algebraic expression.

An *algebraic equation* is any string of mathematical symbols that makes sense, has at least one variable, and contains an equal sign. For example,

$$21\sqrt{2} + \pi + x = 100$$

Placing the original algebraic expression on one side of an equal sign and setting it equal to another expression (100) makes this an algebraic equation.

Terms and coefficients

A *term* within an algebraic expression (or equation) is anything that's separated from the rest of the expression by either plus signs or minus signs. For example, look at the expression $3x^2 - 6xy + 5y - 17$. This expression has four terms: three *algebraic terms* ($3x^2$, $-6xy$, and $5y$) and the *constant term* –17. ***Remember:*** Every term includes the plus sign or minus sign that precedes it.

A *coefficient* is the number that appears at the beginning of an algebraic term. For example, take the expression $-7x + y - z$. This expression has three terms. The coefficients of these four terms are, in order, –7, 1, and –1. Notice that *every* term has a coefficient, which includes the sign associated with that term. A coefficient of 1 is typically not shown, but please remember that it's there! A coefficient of zero means the entire term has no value. For example, $0x = 0$, no matter what value x has.

It is written: Knowing some algebra shorthand

In algebra, a variable (such as x) stands for an unknown number. The number that a variable stands for stays the same throughout a single problem. You can work with variables in algebra much as you work with numbers in arithmetic. In this section, you see how algebra shows repeated addition and multiplication, just like the shorthand you use in arithmetic.

Using coefficients to show repeated addition

In arithmetic, you express adding the same number to itself more than once (repeated addition) as multiplication:

$$3 + 3 = 2(3) \qquad 5 + 5 + 5 = 3(5) \qquad 8 + 8 + 8 + 8 + 8 + 8 = 6(8)$$

When you add two or more variables, you can express the result in a single term by attaching a coefficient — that is, a number placed in front of that variable. For example,

$$x + x = 2x \qquad x + x + x = 3x \qquad x + x + x + x + x + x = 6x$$

You can add *like terms* (terms with the same variable) by adding their coefficients:

$$2x + 3x = (2 + 3)x = 5x \qquad \text{because } (x + x) + (x + x + x) = x + x + x + x + x$$

Adding and subtracting coefficients, as well as working with negative coefficients, work according to the rules you already know from arithmetic:

$$8x - 3x = (8 - 3)x = 5x \qquad -7x + 9x = (-7 + 9)x = 2x \qquad -4x - x = (-4 - 1)x = -5x$$

Showing repeated multiplication with powers

In arithmetic, you express multiplying a number by itself more than once (repeated multiplication) by raising that number to a power — that is, by attaching an exponent:

$$(2)(2)(2) = 2^3 \qquad (3)(3)(3)(3) = 3^4 \qquad (10)(10)(10)(10)(10)(10) = 10^6$$

This process works the same in algebra:

$$(x)(x)(x) = x^3 \qquad (x)(x)(x)(x) = x^4 \qquad (x)(x)(x)(x)(x)(x) = x^6$$

When you multiply two (or more) of the same variable raised to a power, you simply add the exponents:

$$(x^2)(x^3) = x^{2+3} = x^5 \qquad \text{because } (x)(x) \cdot (x)(x)(x) = x^5$$

Similarly, when you divide two (or more) of the same variable raised to a power, you simply subtract the exponents:

$$\frac{x^6}{x^4} = x^2 \qquad \text{because } \frac{(x)(x)(x)(x)(x)(x)}{(x)(x)(x)(x)} = x^2$$

When you raise a variable with an exponent to a power, you multiply the exponents:

$$(x^3)^2 = x^{3(2)} = x^6 \qquad \text{because } [(x)(x)(x)]^2 = [(x)(x)(x)][(x)(x)(x)] = x^6$$

These rules help make sense of a convention that many students find confusing: When you raise any number or variable to the power of 0, the result is 1:

$$x^0 = 1 \qquad \text{because } \frac{x^2}{x^2} = x^{2-2} = x^0$$

These rules can also help you understand why raising a variable to a negative power results in a fraction:

$$x^{-1} = \frac{1}{x} \qquad \text{because } \frac{x^2}{x^3} = \frac{(x)(x)}{(x)(x)(x)} = \frac{1}{x}$$

They also show you why raising a variable to the power of ½ gives you a square root:

$$x^{1/2} = \sqrt{x} \qquad \text{because } \left(x^{1/2}\right)\left(x^{1/2}\right) = x = \left(\sqrt{x}\right)\left(\sqrt{x}\right)$$

You can extend this rule to every fractional exponent:

$$x^{5/2} = \sqrt{x^5} \qquad x^{2/3} = \sqrt[3]{x^2} \qquad x^{7/4} = \sqrt[4]{x^7}$$

Expressing Yourself with Algebraic Expressions

Algebraic expressions don't have equal signs, but they still have their uses. You can do three useful things with an algebraic expression (aside from ripping it into tiny pieces and throwing it in the fireplace): Evaluate it, simplify it, or factor it. In this section, I show you how to do all three for the SAT.

Can I get your number? The value of evaluation

When you *evaluate* an expression, you find the numerical *value* of that expression — that is, the number that it equals. To evaluate an algebraic expression, you need to know the value of every variable in that expression. Evaluating turns an algebraic expression into a constant, which is a big step forward no matter which problem you're working on. Check out this problem:

If $x = 2$ and $y = -3$, what is the value of the expression $3xy^3 - x^3$?

(A) 154

(B) 170

(C) –154

(D) –170

(E) It cannot be determined from the information given.

This expression has two variables: x and y. To evaluate this expression, substitute 2 in place of x and –3 in place of y throughout the expression:

$$3xy^3 - x^3$$
$$= 3(2)(-3)^3 - (2)^3$$

You now have an arithmetic expression, which you can evaluate:

$$= 3(2)(-3)(-3)(-3) - (2)(2)(2)$$

$$= -162 - 8 = -170$$

So the right answer is **(D).**

Knowing the simple truth about simplifying

If you don't know the value of one or more variables, you can't evaluate the expression. However, you may be able to simplify it. *Simplify* an expression by removing parentheses, combining like terms, and generally making the expression smaller and easier to work with — you know, simpler.

Combining like terms

Two terms in an expression are *like terms* if the variable parts of both terms are exactly the same. Combine like terms in an expression by adding the coefficients of the two terms and keeping the variable parts. Look at an example:

The expression $x - 2y + 9z - 4x + 10y + 6x$ is equivalent to which one of the following?

(A) $3x + 8y + 9z$

(B) $3x - 8y + 9z$

(C) $3x + 8y - 9z$

(D) $-3x + 8y + 9z$

(E) $-3x + 8y - 9z$

This expression has three x terms (x, $-4x$, and $6x$). Combine these three like terms by adding their coefficients ($1 + -4 + 6 = 3$):

$$\underline{x} - 2y + 9z \underline{- 4x} + 10y \underline{+ 6x}$$

$$= \underline{3x} - 2y + 9z + 10y$$

Now combine the two y terms ($-2 + 10 = 8$):

$$3x \underline{- 2y} + 9z \underline{+ 10y}$$

$$= 3x + 9z \underline{+ 8y}$$

Math folks usually arrange variables in an expression in alphabetical order:

$$= 3x + 8y + 9z$$

Thus, the right answer is **(A).**

Sometimes, you may know the value of some but not all the variables in an algebraic expression. In this case, you can't really evaluate it, but you can find its value *in terms of* the variable(s) whose values you don't know. This is really just another example of simplifying an expression. Look at this next example:

If $x = -5$ and $y = -4$, what is the value of the expression $2xyz + 3xz$ in terms of z?

(A) 25

(B) –25

(C) $25z$

(D) $-25z$

(E) $25z^2$

This expression has three variables: x, y, and z. You're given the values of x and y but not of z, so you can't evaluate the expression as a number. However, you can simplify the expression by plugging in –5 for x and –4 for y:

$$2xyz + 3xz$$

$$= 2(-5)(-4)z + 3(-5)z$$

Simplify further by multiplying the numbers wherever possible:

$$= 40z - 15z$$

These are two like terms, so you can combine them.

$$= 25z$$

Therefore, the right answer is **(C).**

Freeing your expression: Removing parentheses by distributing

Some expressions have parentheses that need to be removed before you can simplify them. This process is called *distributing* — that is, taking what comes right in front of the parentheses and multiplying it by every term inside the parentheses. Here are three basic rules to removing parentheses by distributing:

- When a plus sign (+) immediately precedes a set of parentheses, *remove* the parentheses. (The result is the same as multiplying each term inside the parentheses by 1.) For example,

  $$4x + (3 + y) = 4x + 3 + y$$

- When a minus sign (–) immediately precedes a set of parentheses, *negate* every term inside the parentheses and remove the parentheses. (The result is the same as multiplying each term inside the parentheses by –1.) For example,

  $$2 - (3x - y) = 2 - 3x + y$$

- When a constant (such as –3) or an algebraic term (such as $2x$) immediately precedes a set of parentheses, *multiply* this term by every term inside the parentheses and remove the parentheses. For example,

  $$-3x(4 - xy) = -12x + 3x^2y$$

After you remove the parentheses, you can further simplify an expression by combining like terms, as I show you in the preceding section.

The expression $-6x + 3xy - 4x - (-y + 2xy)$ is equivalent to which one of the following?

(A) $-6xy$

(B) $-8xy$

(C) $-10x + y + xy$

(D) $-10x - y + xy$

(E) $-10x + y + 5xy$

To simplify this expression, first remove the parentheses by distributing the minus sign, flipping the sign of every term inside the parentheses:

$$-6x + 3xy - 4x - (-y + 2xy) = -6x + 3xy - 4x + y - 2xy$$

Now combine like terms:

$$= -10x + y + xy$$

Therefore, the right answer is **(C)**.

Distributing by FOILing: Making sure every term gets its turn

FOIL is an acronym for *First, Outside, Inside, Last.* When you FOIL an expression that has two sets of parentheses, you remove the parentheses by multiplying each term in one set of parentheses by every term in the other. Consider the following example:

The expression $(2x + 3)(5x - 4)$ is equivalent to which one of the following?

(A) $10x - 12$

(B) $10x^2 + 7x - 12$

(C) $10x^2 - 7x - 12$

(D) $10x^2 + 23x - 12$

(E) $10x^2 - 23x - 12$

This expression contains two sets of parentheses immediately next to each other. To simplify it, you need to multiply everything inside the first set of parentheses by everything inside the second. The acronym FOIL helps you keep track of this procedure, reminding you to multiply each of the following pairs of terms:

- **First terms:** $(2x)(5x) = 10x^2$
- **Outside terms:** $(2x)(-4) = -8x$
- **Inside terms:** $(3)(5x) = 15x$
- **Last terms:** $(3)(-4) = -12$

Add the results of these four multiplication problems:

$$(2x + 3)(5x - 4) = 10x^2 - 8x + 15x - 12$$

With the parentheses removed, you can further simplify this expression by combining like terms, $-8x$ and $15x$:

$$= 10x^2 + 7x - 12$$

Thus, the right answer is **(B)**.

Taking the fear out of factoring

In some sense, factoring an expression is the opposite of simplifying it: When you factor an expression, you complicate it with extra parentheses that weren't there from the start. However, sometimes complicating an expression by factoring it is exactly the ticket you need to solve a problem.

Pulling the greatest common factor out of an expression

The simplest type of factoring is to identify and separate out the *greatest common factor* (*GCF*) among the terms in an expression. This type of factoring adds one set of parentheses to the new expression.

When you factor out the GCF of an expression that has two or more terms, you find a single value that divides into both or all of the terms that you're trying to factor. Then you pull it out and divide each term by this value. For example,

$$3x + x^3 = x(3 + x^2)$$

In this example, the GCF of the expression $3x + x^3$ is x. Each term of the expression is divisible by x, so I can pull an x out of each term, set it outside a set of parentheses, and then divide each term by x.

Notice that just as dividing is the reverse of multiplying, factoring is the reverse of distributing, which I discuss in the preceding section. The result of this process is $x(3 + x^2)$, which you can turn back into the original expression, $3x + x^3$, by distributing the x back into $(3 + x^2)$.

EXAMPLE

What is the greatest common factor among the three terms in the expression $8x^4y^3 + 20x^3y^5 + 12x^2y$?

(A) $2x$

(B) $2x^2$

(C) $4x^2$

(D) $4x^2y$

(E) $4x^2y^3$

Begin by factoring out the GCF of the coefficients of all three terms. The GCF of 8, 20, and 24 is 4, so factor out 4 from every term:

$$8x^4y^3 + 20x^3y^5 + 12x^2y$$
$$= 4(2x^4y^3 + 5x^3y^5 + 3x^2y)$$

Now factor out x raised to the greatest exponent shared among the three terms — that is, x^2. To do this, pull x^2 outside the parentheses and divide all three terms by x^2 (by subtracting 2 from the exponent on x in each term):

$$= 4x^2(2x^2y^3 + 5xy^5 + 3y)$$

Finally, factor out y raised to the greatest exponent shared among the three terms — that is, y:

$$= 4x^2y(2x^2y^2 + 5xy^4 + 3)$$

Thus, the greatest common factor is $4x^2y$, so the right answer is **(D).** If you're not sure that this answer is correct, you can check it by reversing the process: Distributing $4x^2y$ into $(2x^2y^2 + 5xy^4 + 3)$, as I show you earlier in this chapter, returns the expression back to its original form of $8x^4y^3 + 20x^3y^5 + 12x^2y$.

Tip: You can answer this question simply by looking at the exponents on the variables, allowing you to skip most of the calculations. The lowest exponent on any of the x's is 2, and the lowest exponent on any of the y's is 1 (it's implied). Therefore, you know the answer has to contain x^2y, and the only answer that fits is Choice (D). You can stop there and mark your answer. Watch for shortcuts like this on the SAT.

Factoring the difference of two squares ($x^2 - y^2$)

Here's a simple rule for factoring the difference of two squares:

$$x^2 - y^2 = (x + y)(x - y)$$

As you can see, this adds two sets of parentheses to an expression. This simple but powerful tool can be very helpful for a variety of SAT questions that don't immediately look like factoring problems. In some cases, factoring the difference of two squares will enable you to cancel out either the $(x + y)$ or $(x - y)$, giving you a much simpler expression to work with. In other cases, you can substitute a number for either $(x + y)$ or $(x - y)$. The next example illustrates this point.

If $x^2 - y^2 = 72$ and $x + y = 12$, what is the value of $x - y$?

(A) 2

(B) 3

(C) 6

(D) 12

(E) It cannot be determined from the information given.

You can solve this problem as a system of equations, as I show you later in this chapter. But factoring the difference of two squares provides a much easier method. Begin by substituting $(x + y)(x - y)$ for $x^2 - y^2$ in the first equation:

$$(x + y)(x - y) = 72$$

Now substitute 12 for $(x + y)$:

$$12(x - y) = 72$$

Divide both sides by 12:

$$x - y = 6$$

So the right answer is **(C).**

Factoring quadratic expressions ($ax^2 + bx + c$)

A quadratic expression is any expression in either of the following two forms:

$$ax^2 + bx + c \qquad ax^2 + bxy + cy^2$$

Here's a bit of good news: The SAT will *not* expect you to remember the long and rather convoluted quadratic formula. However, the SAT-writers do expect you to be able to factor quadratic expressions. This skill is essential for solving quadratic equations, which I discuss in the next section.

In many cases — especially on the SAT — you can factor a quadratic expression into two linear expressions (that is, two expressions whose variables don't have exponents). This process adds two sets of parentheses to an expression. For example, here are two factored quadratic expressions:

$$x^2 + 4x + 3 = (x + 1)(x + 3)$$

$$2x^2 - 7xy - 4y^2 = (2x + y)(x - 4y)$$

Factoring a quadratic is often a matter of trial and error. (For a detailed discussion of factoring quadratic expressions, see *Algebra For Dummies* [Wiley] by Mary Jane Sterling.) Fortunately, the questions on the SAT usually don't require difficult factoring. The main thing is for you to see when factoring is possible and whether it can help you.

EXAMPLE

Which of the following is a factor of the expression $2x^2y + 2xy^2 - 24y^3$?

(A) $4y$

(B) $x + 3y$

(C) $x + 4y$

(D) $x - 4y$

(E) $x^2 + xy - 12y$

Whenever possible, begin by factoring out the greatest common factor (GCF) from every term. In this example, the GCF is $2y$:

$$2x^2y + 2xy - 24y^2 = 2y(x^2 + xy - 12y^2)$$

What's left inside the parentheses is a quadratic expression, so factor it:

$$= 2y(x + 4y)(x - 3y)$$

The second of these factors matches Choice **(C)**, so this is the right answer.

Finding a Balance with Algebraic Equations

Algebra was invented to solve problems that would be difficult or even impossible to solve with arithmetic alone. You can solve algebraic equations in a variety of ways (aside from the option of avoiding them completely — problem solved! — which won't help you much on the SAT).

One key insight makes algebra possible: Making an identical change to both sides of an equation results in another equation. In other words, both sides remain equal. You can think of this as keeping an equation balanced, just as two sides of a scale remain balanced if you add or subtract equivalent weight to both sides. In this section, I show you the basic equation-solving skills you need to answer SAT questions.

A lonely letter: Isolating the variable

To solve most algebraic equations, you need to know the value of all but one of the variables. Solving the equation provides the value of this unknown variable by allowing you to *isolate the variable* — that is, get the variable alone on one side of the equal sign — in a series of steps that don't change the balance of the equation.

In the equation $3x - 8 = x + 14$, what is the value of x?

This equation has one variable, so you can solve it. When solving algebraic equations, it's really helpful to know how to identify terms and coefficients (as I discuss in the previous section titled "Vocab: A few choice words about algebra"). Here's how you solve a basic algebraic equation:

1. **Separate algebraic terms and constant terms, putting them on opposite sides of the equation (either side will do).**

   When you move an algebraic term across the equal sign, negate it (change its sign from plus to minus or from minus to plus). Check out this next equation:

   $$3x - 8 = x + 14$$

   $$3x - x = 14 + 8$$

   What you're really doing here is adding 8 and subtracting x from both sides, which is why the signs change.

2. **Simplify the equation.**

   Combine like algebraic terms on one side and constants on the other side.

   $$2x = 22$$

3. **Divide by the coefficient to isolate the variable.**

   $$\frac{2x}{2} = \frac{22}{2}$$

   $$x = 11$$

   The right answer is **11**.

Doing away with fractions: Cross-multiplying to solve rational equations

A *rational equation* is an algebraic equation in which at least one side of the equation is a fraction. When only one side of an equation is a fraction, you can multiply both sides of the equation by the denominator (bottom number) to remove the fraction. For example, in this next equation, you multiply both sides by 5:

$$\frac{x}{5} = 7$$

$$x = 35$$

A quick way to turn a rational equation in which both sides are fractions into a standard algebraic equation is *cross-multiplication.* This technique simply allows you to multiply by both denominators at once, getting rid of both fractions. Here's how it works:

1. **Multiply the numerator on the left side of the equation by the denominator on the right side.**

2. **Multiply the numerator on the right side of the equation by the denominator on the left side.**

   At this point, you've removed the troublesome fractions from the problem.

3. **Set these two results equal to each other and solve the resulting equation.**

Here's an example that uses cross-multiplication:

In the equation $\frac{6x-1}{3} = \frac{x}{2}$, what is the value of *x*?

This is a rational equation, because both sides of the equation are fractions. To solve it, cross-multiply and simplify:

$$(6x - 1)(2) = (x)(3)$$
$$12x - 2 = 3x$$

At this point, you have an equation that you know how to solve by isolating *x*:

$$-2 = -9x$$
$$\frac{2}{9} = x$$

So the right answer is **2/9**, which you can also grid in as **.222**.

Factoring to solve quadratic equations

The presence of the x^2 term makes isolating the variable in a quadratic equation a bit tricky so that the usual methods don't work. Factoring a quadratic expression (as I show you earlier in "Factoring quadratic expressions [$ax^2 + bx + c$]") is essential for solving quadratic equations.

You can solve every quadratic equation (and many equations where the variable appears with more than one exponent) on the SAT by factoring, *without* resorting to the cumbersome quadratic formula.

If $x = \frac{x^2-3}{2}$ and $x > 0$, what is the value of *x*?

(A) 1

(B) 2

(C) 3

(D) $\frac{2}{3}$

(E) $\frac{3}{2}$

To begin, multiply both sides of this equation by 2 to turn this rational equation into a standard algebraic equation:

$$2x = x^2 - 3$$

Now move *all* terms onto one side of the equation so that the x^2 term remains positive and one side of the equation equals 0:

$$0 = x^2 - 2x - 3$$

Getting 0 on one side of the equation with a quadratic expression on the other side is key to solving the equation, because now you can factor the quadratic expression:

$0 = (x + 1)(x - 3)$

Notice now that you've reached an important crossroads: At least one of the two factors, $(x + 1)$ or $(x - 3)$, *must* equal 0 for the equation to balance properly. You don't know which factor equals 0, however, so break this equation into two separate equations:

$0 = x + 1$ or $0 = x - 3$

Solve both equations for x:

$x = -1$ or $x = 3$

The problem tells you that $x > 0$, so $x = 3$. Therefore, the right answer is **(C)**.

Solving equations that have exponential variables

Equations that have terms with *exponential variables* — for example, 2^x — pose a special challenge. The key strategy to solving equations with exponential variables is to express both sides of the equation using the same *base* (whatever's raised to a power). If the bases on both sides of the equation are equal, the exponents are also equal, so you can throw out the bases and keep the exponents.

As with so many math concepts, this idea makes more sense with an example.

If $3^{x+2} = 81$, what is the value of x?

(A) 0

(B) 1

(C) –1

(D) $\frac{1}{2}$

(E) 2

The left side of the equation has an exponential variable with a base of 3, so express the right side as an exponent with the same base. Because 81 = (9)(9), or (3)(3)(3)(3), it's equal to 3^4:

$3^{x+2} = 3^4$

Now throw out the bases. Set the exponents equal to each other and solve the equation:

$x + 2 = 4$

$x = 2$

Therefore, the right answer is **(E)**.

Solving equations with radicals (roots)

As with other types of equations, solving equations with radicals — that is, with a term that includes a root of x — depends on your skill in isolating the variable. By far, the most common radical on the SAT is the square root. To remove a square root from an equation, you need to get it by itself on one side of the equation and then remove the square root sign by squaring both sides of the equation.

If $\sqrt{4x+5} - 2 = x$ and x is positive, what is the value of x?

(A) 1

(B) $\frac{1}{2}$

(C) $\frac{1}{4}$

(D) $\frac{2}{5}$

(E) $\frac{4}{5}$

First, isolate the radical:

$$\sqrt{4x+5} = x + 2$$

Now square both sides of the equation:

$$\left(\sqrt{4x+5}\right)^2 = (x+2)^2$$

Be sure to square the *whole* left side and the *whole* right side. If you simply square each individual term, your answer will be wrong.

On the left side of the equation, the square root and the square cancel each other out, so you can remove them both. On the right side, remember that squaring means to multiply a value by itself:

$$4x + 5 = (x + 2)(x + 2)$$

Now distribute (FOIL) the right side of the equation (see the earlier section "Distributing by FOILing: Making sure every term gets its turn" for details):

$$4x + 5 = x^2 + 4x + 4$$

Combine like terms:

$$1 = x^2$$

At this point, the equation tells you that x is a number that, when multiplied by itself, equals 1. Only two numbers fit the bill:

$$x = 1, -1$$

The problem states that x is positive, so $x = 1$. Thus, the right answer is **(A)**.

Positive thoughts: Feeling confident with absolute value

The *absolute value* of an expression is the positive value of that expression. For example,

$$|2| = 2 \quad \text{and} \quad |-2| = 2$$

As you can see, two different integers inside absolute value bars have the same value when the bars are removed. This fact has important implications when working with algebraic expressions, because a single equation may have two different solutions.

To find these two solutions, isolate the absolute value expression, remove the bars, and then split the equation into its positive and negative forms. An example can make this process clear.

What positive value of x satisfies the equation $|2x + 7| - 5x = 3$?

Begin by getting the absolute value expression by itself on one side of the equation; simply add $5x$ to both sides:

$$|2x + 7| = 3 + 5x$$

The value $2x + 7$ could be either positive or negative and have the same absolute value, so split the equation to reflect both of these possibilities:

$$2x + 7 = 3 + 5x \quad \text{or} \quad -(2x + 7) = 3 + 5x$$

Solve both equations:

$$4 = 3x \quad \text{or} \quad -2x - 7 = 3 + 5x$$

$$x = \frac{4}{3} \qquad -10 = 7x$$

$$x = -\frac{10}{7}$$

The question asks for a positive value, so the right answer is **4/3**. ***Note:*** If you plug $-10/7$ in for x, you see that it's not a real solution. With absolute values, you sometimes get *extraneous* solutions, which are answers that work in a new form of the equation but not in the original problem. When doing absolute value problems, plug your answers into the original problem to make sure they work.

Solving Problems with More Than One Variable

Algebra becomes a bit more complex when a problem contains more than one variable. In this section, I show you a few ways to approach SAT questions that involve multiple variables.

Solving an equation in terms of other variables

If you don't know the value of two or more variables in an equation, you may be able to solve for one variable *in terms of* the other variables. The goal here is to isolate the variable you're solving for on one side of the equation, with all the other variables on the other side. Check out an example:

What is the value of b in terms of a, c, and d, given that $-3ad - bc = 7$?

(A) $\frac{3ad - 7}{c}$

(B) $\frac{7 + 3ad}{c}$

(C) $\frac{ad - 7}{3c}$

(D) $\frac{3ad + 7}{c}$

(E) $-\frac{3ad + 7}{c}$

You can't find the value of b as a number, because the equation has other variables whose values you don't know. But you can solve for b in terms of the other variables, a, c, and d.

Proceed as if you were solving for a value, separating all terms that have b on one side of the equation and all other terms on the other side:

$$-bc = 3ad + 7$$

Next, divide both sides by $-c$ to get b by itself:

$$b = -\frac{3ad + 7}{c}$$

So the right answer is **(E)**.

Solving equations with extra variables

In most cases, you need at least one equation for every variable you're trying to find. So if you have one equation, you can solve for one variable. Similarly, if you have two variables, you typically need two equations to find the values of two variables.

Some SAT questions, however, give you an equation with more than one variable and ask you to solve it for an *expression* that also includes more than one variable. The trick here is to tweak the equation in order to isolate this expression on one side of the equal sign with a number on the other side.

If $p + 3q = 0$, what is the value $\frac{p}{q}$?

(A) 3

(B) –3

(C) $\frac{1}{3}$

(D) $-\frac{1}{3}$

(E) It cannot be determined from the information given.

The question doesn't give you enough information to solve for either p or q, but that's not what it's asking. To answer it, you need to isolate $\frac{p}{q}$ on one side of the equation. To do this, subtract $3q$ from both sides:

$$p = -3q$$

Now divide both sides by q:

$$\frac{p}{q} = -3$$

So the right answer is **(B)**.

Solving a system of equations

A *system of equations* is a set of two or more equations with two or more variables. Here are the two basic methods for solving a system of two equations:

- **Substitution:** Solving one equation for a variable in terms of the other variable (as I discuss earlier in the aptly named "Solving an equation in terms of other variables") and then substituting the result into the second equation
- **Combining equations:** Adding the two equations together, in some cases after multiplying one or both equations by a constant, so that one variable drops out of the result

These methods allow you to solve for one of the variables. After you know its value, you plug it into one of the original equations and solve for the second variable. Check out an example using substitution:

If $x + 3 = y$ and $3x + 2y = 51$, then $x + y =$

In this problem, y is already isolated in the first equation, so you can plug in $x + 3$ everywhere you see a y in the second equation:

$$3x + 2(x + 3) = 51$$

Now simplify and solve for x:

$$3x + 2x + 6 = 51$$
$$5x + 6 = 51$$
$$5x = 45$$
$$x = 9$$

Now substitute 9 for x back into whichever equation looks easiest to work with — in this case, the first equation:

$$9 + 3 = y$$
$$12 = y$$

Thus, $x = 9$ and $y = 12$, so $x + y =$ **21**.

This next problem uses the combining-equations method to solve the system of equations:

If $6x - 2y = 10$ and $7x + 2y = 29$, then $xy =$

In this problem, neither x nor y is isolated in either equation. Furthermore, if you try to isolate either of them, you're going to find that the equation becomes very complicated. In this case, however, the first equation has the term $-2y$ and the second equation has the term $2y$. Thus, if you combine these two equations by adding them, the y variable drops out because its coefficient becomes 0:

$$\begin{array}{r} 6x - 2y = 10 \\ 7x + 2y = 29 \\ \hline 13x \quad = 39 \end{array}$$

Now you can solve this equation easily by dividing both sides by 13:

$$x = 3$$

You can now substitute 3 for x into whichever equation looks easiest to work with. I use the first equation:

$$6(3) - 2y = 10$$

Simplify and solve for y:

$$18 - 2y = 10$$
$$-2y = -8$$
$$y = 4$$

Thus, $x = 3$ and $y = 4$, so $xy =$ **12**, which is the right answer.

In most cases, you need at least one equation per variable to solve for each variable. But on the SAT, expect the unexpected: A problem may appear to give you less information than you need to solve it. To answer the next question, you need to multiply one of the two equations by a constant so that when you combine them, two variables go away.

If $2a + 3b - 6c = 100$ and $b - 2c = 10$, what is the value of *a?*

To answer this question, you need to find a way to remove both *b* and *c* from an equation. To do this, notice that the first equation includes the expression $3b - 6c$ and the second includes the expression $b - 2c$, which is a factor of $3b - 6c$. So multiply the second equation by –3 and add it to the first:

$$\begin{array}{l} 2a + 3b - 6c = 100 \\ \quad\;\; -3b + 6c = -30 \\ \hline 2a \qquad\qquad\; = 70 \end{array}$$

Now solve for *a* by dividing the resulting equation by 2:

$a = 35$

So the right answer is **35**.

Solving Inequalities

An *inequality* is a mathematical statement telling you that one expression is *not* equal to another. The inequalities that you work with on the SAT fall into four categories: greater than (>), less than (<), greater than or equal to (≥), and less than or equal to (≤).

To keep the direction of the inequality signs clear, remember that < looks like the letter *L*, which stands for *less than.*

In this section, I discuss the ups and downs of solving inequalities.

Solving basic inequalities

The rules for working with algebraic inequalities are virtually identical to those for working with equations, with one key difference: When you multiply or divide an inequality by a negative number, you must *reverse* the direction of the inequality sign.

Look at the following example:

Which one of the following inequalities is equivalent to $4x > 7x + 3$?

(A) $x > 1$

(B) $x > -1$

(C) $x < -1$

(D) $x \geq 1$

(E) $x \leq -1$

To solve this inequality for *x*, first subtract 7*x* from both sides:

$-3x > 3$

To isolate x, you need to divide both sides by –3. Because this is an inequality, you must reverse the direction of the $>$, changing it to $<$:

$$x < -1$$

Therefore, the right answer is **(C).**

Be especially careful when solving an inequality that includes a fraction. The presence of the minus sign in front of the fraction could be trouble. Always move minus signs to the numerator first so you don't have to multiply or divide by a negative number.

Which of the following are possible values of x if $-\frac{x+9}{4} \geq 2x$?

I. 0

II. –1

III. –2

(A) I only

(B) III only

(C) I and II only

(D) II and III only

(E) I, II, and III

This problem has a fraction with a minus sign, so place this in the numerator:

$$\frac{-(x+9)}{4} \geq 2x$$

Now multiply both sides by 4 to remove the fraction:

$$-(x+9) \geq 2x(4)$$

Simplify and solve:

$$-x - 9 \geq 8x$$

$$-9 \geq 9x$$

$$-1 \geq x$$

Note that this last step does *not* require you to change the direction of the $\geq$ sign, because you are dividing both sides by 9. Thus, the value of x is –1 or less, so the right answer is **(D).**

Solving inequalities with absolute value

Solving inequalities that incorporate absolute value is a special challenge. (I introduce absolute value earlier in "Positive thoughts: Feeling confident with absolute value.")

When solving an inequality that involves an absolute value, your first step is to remove the absolute value bars by splitting the inequality into two separate inequalities (just as you do for absolute value equations):

- One of these is a copy of the original inequality without the absolute value bars.
- The other is a copy with the opposite side of the inequality negated. Make sure you reverse the inequality sign on the second inequality.

The following example should help make this clear.

EXAMPLE

Which of the following are possible values of x if $|x + 1| > 2$?

I. 2

II. 0

III. –2

(A) I only

(B) II only

(C) III only

(D) I and III only

(E) II and III only

To begin, remove the absolute value bars by splitting this inequality as follows:

$$x + 1 > 2 \qquad \text{or} \qquad x + 1 < -2$$

As you can see, the first inequality is just a copy of the original without the bars. In the second inequality, I removed the bars, negated the other side (changing 2 to –2), and reversed the inequality sign. Now solve both inequalities:

$$x > 1 \qquad \text{or} \qquad x < -3$$

Therefore, x can equal 2 but cannot equal either 0 or –2, so the right answer is **(A).**

Another approach to this type of problem is to plug in possible answers. Here's how it works:

EXAMPLE

Which of the following are possible x values if $|2x + 1| \geq 3x$?

I. 6

II. 1

III. –5

(A) II only

(B) III only

(C) I and III only

(D) II and III only

(E) I, II, and III

First, plug in 6 for x and see whether the inequality is true:

$$|2(6) + 1| \geq 3(6)$$

$$|12 + 1| \geq 18$$

$$|13| \geq 18$$

$$13 \geq 18 \qquad \text{Wrong!}$$

Thus, 6 isn't a possible value of x, which rules out answers (C) and (E). Next, try plugging in 1 for x:

$$|2(1) + 1| \geq 3(1)$$
$$|2 + 1| \geq 3$$
$$|3| \geq 3$$
$$3 \geq 3 \quad \text{Right!}$$

Thus, 1 is a possible value, which rules out answer (B). Finally, plug in –5:

$$|2(-5) + 1| \geq 3(-5)$$
$$|-10 + 1| \geq -15$$
$$|-9| \geq -15$$
$$9 \geq -15 \quad \text{Right!}$$

Therefore, the right answer is **(D).**

Then again, if you think about what absolute value means, you don't have to do the calculations to check –5 at all. You can instead reason that any negative number will work here, so –5 must be an acceptable answer. Because the left side of the inequality is an absolute value, it can't be negative; but if x is negative, then the right side ($3x$) has to be negative. Finding shortcuts like this can save you time on the test.

Symbol Secrets: Working with New Notations

One common way that the SAT tests your understanding of evaluating expressions is with questions involving a *new notation* — that is, odd-looking math symbols that are defined for the express purpose of making your day more difficult. The good news is that although these questions often look tricky, they're often among the easier types to answer after you know how. Check out the following example:

The notation $x\#y\#z$ is defined as $x^2 + y^2 - z^2$. What is the value of 10#5#6?

This question may throw you because the notation $x\#y\#z$ is something you've never seen before. But all you have to do is just plug in numbers and solve:

$x\#y\#z$ means $x^2 + y^2 - z^2$ so 10#5#6 means $10^2 + 5^2 - 6^2$

Now just crunch the numbers, according to the arithmetic rules you already know and love:

$$10^2 + 5^2 - 6^2 = 100 + 25 - 36 = 89$$

So the right answer is **89**.

Practice Problems for Algebra

Ready to practice the types of questions from this chapter? In this section, I give you 20 practice questions — 15 multiple-choice questions and 5 grid-in questions — on a variety of algebra topics. If you get stuck, flip through this chapter for ideas. I provide a step-by-step solution to each question in the next section.

1. If $f - g = 10$ and $f - g - h = 20$, what is the value of h?

   (A) 10

   (B) –10

   (C) 20

   (D) –20

   (E) 30

2. If $|x - y| = 7$ and $y = -3$, which of the following could be the value of x?

   (A) 0

   (B) 3

   (C) –4

   (D) 7

   (E) –10

3. If $2x = \frac{12 - 10x}{x}$ and x is a positive number, what is the value of x?

   (A) 1

   (B) 2

   (C) 5

   (D) 6

   (E) 12

4. If $mn = k$ and $k = \frac{n}{p}$, where k, m, n, and p are all nonzero numbers, which of the following must be true?

   (A) $m = p$

   (B) $m + p = 0$

   (C) $m + p = 1$

   (D) $mp = 0$

   (E) $mp = 1$

5. If $\sqrt{s + t} = 3$ and $s - t = 3$, what is the value of s?

   (A) 1

   (B) 3

   (C) –3

   (D) 6

   (E) 9

6. Let $a*b*c$ be defined as $\frac{a+b}{a+c}$. Which of the following inequalities is equivalent to $3*x*5 < 2$?

(A) $x < 10$

(B) $x > 13$

(C) $x < 13$

(D) $x > 19$

(E) $x < 19$

7. If $2^{3x-1} = 32$, what is the value of x?

(A) 1

(B) 2

(C) 3

(D) 4

(E) 5

8. If $x + \sqrt{x+5} = 1$ and x is negative, what is the value of x?

(A) –1

(B) –4

(C) –5

(D) –6

(E) –10

9. If $2x + 2y = 16$, what is the value of $\frac{x+y}{2}$?

(A) 1

(B) 2

(C) 4

(D) 8

(E) 16

10. If $\frac{x^2 - y^2}{x - y} = a$, what is the value of x in terms of a and y?

(A) $a + y$

(B) $a - y$

(C) $y - a$

(D) $\frac{a}{y}$

(E) $\frac{y}{a}$

11. If $3x + 2y - 2z = 40$ and $x = y - z$, what is the value of x?

(A) 2

(B) –5

(C) 8

(D) 10

(E) –10

12. If $\sqrt{5} = x - 2$, what is the value of $x^2 - 4x$?

(A) 1

(B) –1

(C) 2

(D) 4

(E) 9

13. If $|16 - 3x| > 5x$, which of the following could be a value of x?

I. 12

II. 1

III. –10

(A) II only

(B) III only

(C) I and II only

(D) II and III only

(E) I, II, and III

14. If $\frac{2x - y}{x} = 7$, what is the value of $\frac{x}{y}$?

(A) –5

(B) 5

(C) $-\frac{1}{5}$

(D) $\frac{1}{5}$

(E) $\frac{7}{2}$

15. The inequality $\frac{x^2 - y^2}{x - y} - x \leq -4$ is equivalent to which of the following?

(A) $y < 4$

(B) $y \leq 4$

(C) $y \geq 4$

(D) $y \leq -4$

(E) $y \geq -4$

16. Let $]x[$ be defined as $x^2 + x$. If the equation $]a - 1[= 30$ is true and a is a positive number, what is the value of a?

17. If $a + 5b - c = -7$ and $a - c = -10$, what is the value of b?

18. If $5^{2x-3} = \sqrt{5}$, what is the value of x?

19. If $7h = 4j$ and $4j = 3k$, what fraction represents the ratio $h:k$?

20. If $|v + 2| = 6$ and $|w + 5| = 4$, with $v < w$, what is the value of vw?

Solutions to Practice Problems

Here are the answers to the 20 practice questions from the last section, complete with worked-out solutions.

1. **B.** Substitute 10 for $f - g$ into the second equation:

   $10 - h = 20$

   Now solve for h:

   $-h = 10$

   $h = -10$

   Therefore, $h = -10$, so the right answer is (B).

2. **E.** Substitute –3 into the equation for y and simplify:

   $|x - (-3)| = 7$

   $|x + 3| = 7$

   Remove the absolute value bars by splitting the equation into two equations:

   $x + 3 = 7$ or $x + 3 = -7$

   $x = 4$ $\quad$ $x = -10$

   Therefore, the right answer is (E).

3. **A.** Begin by multiplying both sides by x to get rid of the fraction:

   $2x^2 = 12 - 10x$

   Simplify the equation by dividing by 2:

   $x^2 = 6 - 5x$

   Move all terms onto the same side of the equation so that the x^2 term is positive:

   $x^2 + 5x - 6 = 0$

   Factor the quadratic expression:

   $(x - 1)(x + 6) = 0$

   Separate into two equations and solve each:

   $x - 1 = 0$ or $x + 6 = 0$

   $x = 1$ $\quad$ $x = -6$

   The answer has to be positive, so $x = 1$. Thus, the right answer is (A).

4. **E.** Substitute mn for k in the second equation:

   $$mn = \frac{n}{p}$$

Multiply both sides by p and simplify:

$$mnp = n$$

$$mp = 1$$

So the right answer is (E).

5. **D.** Square both sides of the first equation to remove the radical:

$$s + t = 9$$

Add this equation to the second equation so you can solve for s:

$$\begin{array}{rl} s + t &= 9 \\ s - t &= 3 \\ \hline 2s \quad &= 12 \end{array}$$

Solve for s:

$$s = 6$$

So the right answer is (D).

6. **C.** The problem defines $a{*}b{*}c$, and you need to find $3{*}x{*}5$. Based on the order of the numbers and variables, $a = 3$, $b = x$, and $c = 5$. Rewrite the inequality as follows, plugging in the values for a, b, and c:

$$\frac{3+x}{3+5} < 2$$

Simplify:

$$\frac{3+x}{8} < 2$$

To remove the fraction, multiply both sides of the inequality by 8. Then solve:

$$3 + x < 2(8)$$

$$3 + x < 16$$

$$x < 13$$

Therefore, the right answer is (C).

7. **B.** Begin by expressing 32 as a power of 2: $32 = 2^5$. Therefore, the following equation is true:

$$2^{3x-1} = 2^5$$

Because the bases are the same on both sides of the equation, the exponents must also be the same, so

$$3x - 1 = 5$$

Solve using algebra:

$$3x = 6$$

$$x = 2$$

So the right answer is (B).

8. **A.** Isolate the square root:

$$\sqrt{x+5} = -x+1$$

Square both sides of the equation:

$$\left(\sqrt{x+5}\right)^2 = (-x+1)^2$$

Remove parentheses, simplify, and set the equation equal to zero by moving all terms to one side of the equal sign:

$$x + 5 = (-x + 1)(-x + 1)$$

$$x + 5 = x^2 - 2x + 1$$

$$0 = x^2 - 3x - 4$$

Factor to solve the quadratic equation:

$$0 = (x + 1)(x - 4)$$

Now split the equation into two separate equations:

$0 = x + 1$ or $0 = x - 4$

$x = -1$ $x = 4$

The problem states that x is negative, so $x = -1$. Thus, the right answer is (A).

9. **C.** Solve for $x + y$ by dividing the equation by 2:

$$x + y = 8$$

Substitute 8 for $x + y$ in the expression:

$$\frac{x+y}{2} = \frac{8}{2} = 4$$

So the right answer is (C).

10. **B.** Begin by factoring the numerator, which is the difference of two squares:

$$\frac{(x+y)(x-y)}{x-y} = a$$

Now cancel out the factor $(x - y)$:

$$x + y = a$$

Now solve for x in terms of a and y:

$$x = a - y$$

So the right answer is (B).

11. **C.** Multiply the second equation by 2:

$$2x = 2y - 2z$$

Substitute $2x$ for $2y - 2z$ in the first equation:

$$3x + 2x = 40$$

Now solve for x:

$5x = 40$

$x = 8$

Therefore, the right answer is (C).

12. **A.** Begin by squaring both sides of the equation:

$$\left(\sqrt{5}\right)^2 = (x-2)^2$$
$$5 = (x-2)(x-2)$$
$$5 = x^2 - 4x + 4$$

You're looking for the value of $x^2 - 4x$, so isolate this expression by subtracting 4 from both sides of the equation:

$1 = x^2 - 4x$

Thus, the right answer is (A).

13. **D.** One way to solve this problem is to split the inequality into two inequalities. However, an easier way is to plug in all three possible answers. First, plug in 12 for x:

$|16 - 3(12)| > 5(12)$

$|16 - 36| > 60$

$|-20| > 60$

$20 > 60$ Wrong!

Thus, 12 isn't a possible value, so you can rule out answers (C) and (E). Next, plug in 1 for x:

$|16 - 3(1)| > 5(1)$

$|16 - 3| > 5$

$|13| > 5$

$13 > 5$ Right!

Thus, 1 is a possible value, so you can rule out answer (B). You can save time by noticing that *any* negative value makes the inequality true, because the left side will then be positive (because it's an absolute value) and the right side will be negative. Thus, –10 is also a possible value, so the right answer is (D).

14. **C.** Multiply both sides of the equation by x to get rid of the fraction:

$2x - y = 7x$

$-y = 5x$

Use algebra to isolate x/y on one side of the equation. First, divide both sides by y:

$$-1 = \frac{5x}{y}$$

Next, divide both sides by 5:

$$-\frac{1}{5} = \frac{x}{y}$$

Therefore, the right answer is (C).

15. **D.** Factor the numerator of the left side as the difference of two squares:

$$\frac{(x+y)(x-y)}{x-y} - x \leq -4$$

Cancel out the $x - y$ factor in the numerator and denominator:

$$(x + y) - x \leq -4$$

Simplify:

$$y \leq -4$$

Thus, the right answer is (D).

16. **6**. First get clear on what the new notation is telling you:

]x[means $x^2 + x$

So just plug in $a - 1$ everywhere you see an x:

]$a - 1$[means $(a - 1)^2 + (a - 1)$

Because you know that]$a - 1$[= 30 is true, you can write the following equation:

$$(a - 1)^2 + (a - 1) = 30$$

Now simplify the equation:

$$(a - 1)(a - 1) + (a - 1) = 30$$

$$a^2 - 2a + 1 + a - 1 = 30$$

$$a^2 - a - 30 = 0$$

This is a quadratic equation, so solve it by factoring:

$$(a + 5)(a - 6) = 0$$

Now split the equation into two separate equations, because one of the values in parentheses has to equal 0:

$a + 5 = 0$ or $a - 6 = 0$

$a = -5$ $\quad$ $a = 6$

The question specifies that a is positive, so the right answer is 6.

17. **3/5** or **.6**. This question provides you with three variables but only two equations. To answer it, you need to find a clever way to isolate b. Do this by substituting –10 for $a - c$ into the first equation. I do this in two steps so that you can clearly see what's happening. First, rearrange the first equation to bring $a - c$ together:

$$\underline{a} + 5b \underline{- c} = -7$$

$$5b + \underline{a - c} = -7$$

Now plug in –10 for $a - c$:

$$5b - 10 = -7$$

Simplify and solve for b:

$$5b = 3$$

$$b = \frac{3}{5}$$

Thus, the right answer is 3/5 or .6.

18. **7/4** or **1.75**. This is an exponential equation, so express both sides as exponents with a base of 5. Recall that $\sqrt{5} = 5^{1/2}$, so

$$5^{2x-3} = 5^{1/2}$$

The bases match, so you can drop the bases and solve. Set the two exponents equal to each other:

$$2x - 3 = \frac{1}{2}$$

$$2x = \frac{1}{2} + 3$$

$$2x = \frac{7}{2}$$

$$x = \frac{7}{4}$$

So you can write the right answer as either 7/4 or 1.75.

19. **3/7** or **.428** or **.429**. The first equation tells you that $7h = 4j$, so substitute $7h$ for $4j$ into the second equation:

$$7h = 3k$$

The ratio $h{:}k$ is represented by the fraction h/k, so solve for this fraction:

$$\frac{7h}{k} = 3$$

$$\frac{h}{k} = \frac{3}{7}$$

So the right answer is 3/7, which you can also write as .428 (cut off decimal) or .429 (rounded).

20. **8**. Remove the absolute value bars in the first equation by separating it into two equations:

$v + 2 = 6$ or $v + 2 = -6$

$v = 4$ $\quad v = -8$

Do the same with the second equation:

$w + 5 = 4$ or $w + 5 = -4$

$w = -1$ $\quad w = -9$

The question states that $v < w$, so $v = -8$ and $w = -1$. Thus, the value of vw is 8, so this is the right answer.

Chapter 5

Picture Perfect: Reviewing Geometry

In This Chapter

- Knowing the basics of lines and angles
- Increasing your understanding of triangles, quadrilaterals, and circles
- Working with solid geometry
- Improving your geometric perception

Although most high school geometry courses focus on geometric proofs, you don't need this skill to succeed on the SAT. What you do need, though, is a general understanding of the main concepts and a working knowledge of basic geometric formulas. So I start this chapter with a review of the basics of geometry: lines and angles. I give you a lot of tips for solving problems of angle measurement, which are common on the SAT.

The next topic is shapes on the plane, starting with triangles. I show you how to calculate the area of a triangle. I also discuss some common types of triangles, including right triangles, with info on the Pythagorean theorem and the ratios of sides in some special right triangles. Then I cover congruent and similar triangles and discuss the triangle inequality. From there, you move on to formulas for measuring the area and perimeter of three common types of quadrilaterals: squares, rectangles, and parallelograms. Beyond that, I show you how to measure the area and circumference of circles. I also discuss arc measurement and lines that are tangent to a circle.

After that, the focus is on key topics in *solid geometry,* the study of objects in three-dimensional (3-D) space. I show you a few formulas for calculating the volume of a variety of objects. Then I show you how to answer questions about *geometric perception* — mental manipulations of geometric objects.

To finish up the chapter, I provide 20 practice questions on the topics I discuss in this chapter, each with a completely worked-out solution.

Working All the Angles

Plane geometry is the study of points, lines, angles, and shapes on the *plane* — an imaginary flat surface that extends infinitely in all directions. In this section, I give you a review of some facts about angles that are useful when answering SAT questions. Angles, which are measured in degrees (not radians) on the SAT, are formed wherever two lines cross in a plane.

Crossing over with vertical angles

REMEMBER

Vertical angles are the opposite angles formed when two lines cross. Vertical angles are always equal to each other. For example, in Figure 5-1, angle a and angle c are vertical angles, so $a = c$; angle b and angle d are also vertical angles, so $b = d$.

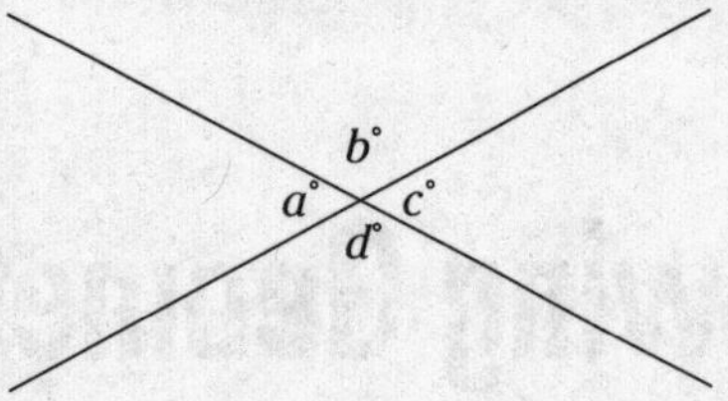

Figure 5-1: Vertical angles are equal.

The following example shows you how to use the fact that vertical angles are equal to set up an equation to answer the question:

In the figure below, angles $3m$ and $4n$ are vertical angles. What is the value of m in terms of n?

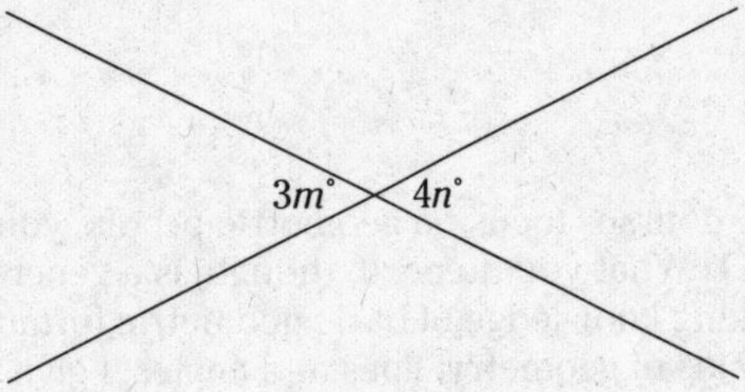

(A) n

(B) $12n$

(C) $\frac{n}{12}$

(D) $\frac{3n}{4}$

(E) $\frac{4n}{3}$

The two angles are vertical angles, so their measures are equal:

$$3m = 4n$$

To solve for m, divide both sides by 3:

$$m = \frac{4n}{3}$$

Thus, the right answer is **(E)**.

Supplementary angles: Doing a one-eighty

When a straight line is split into two angles of any measure, the two resulting angles are *supplementary angles* — that is, their measures add up to 180°. For example, in Figure 5-1, angle a and angle b are supplementary, so $a + b = 180$. The figure also contains three other pairs of supplementary angles: a and d, b and c, and c and d. Thus, $a + d = 180$, $b + c = 180$, and $c + d = 180$.

In the next example, you use the fact that supplementary angles add up to 180° to set up an equation that allows you to answer the question:

In the figure below, $v = 3u$. What is the value of w?

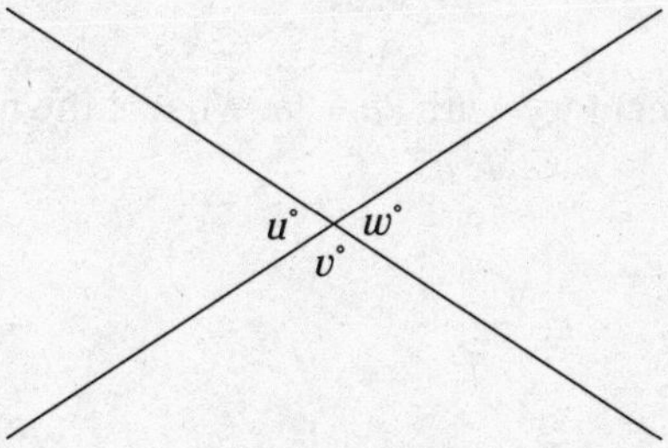

Note: Figure not drawn to scale.

(A) 15

(B) 30

(C) 45

(D) 60

(E) 75

Angles u and v are supplementary angles because they complete a line, so $u + v = 180$. Substitute $3u$ for v into this equation and solve for u:

$$u + 3u = 180$$
$$4u = 180$$
$$u = 45$$

The two angles u and w are vertical angles, so they're equal. Thus, $w = 45$, and the right answer is **(C)**.

Going ninety: Right angles and complementary angles

When two lines are perpendicular, each of the four resulting angles is a *right angle* — that is, an angle that measures 90°. When a right angle is split into two angles of any measure, the result is a pair of *complementary angles* — that is, their measures add up to 90°. For example, in Figure 5-2, $\overline{PR} \perp \overline{QS}$, so angle a and angle b are complementary. Thus, $a + b = 90$.

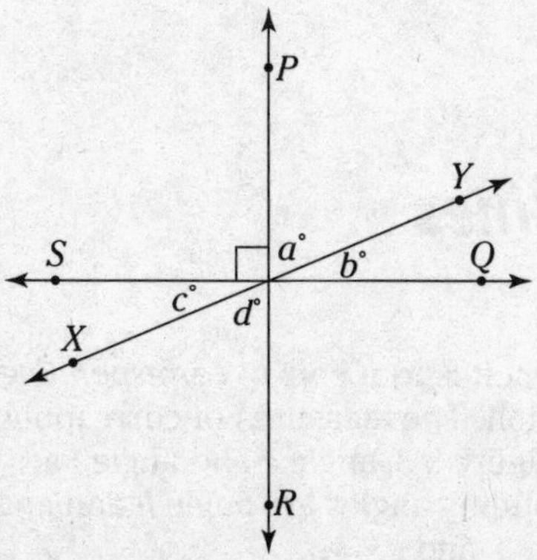

Figure 5-2: Complementary angles form a 90° angle together.

You can use facts about vertical angles to draw additional conclusions. For example, in Figure 5-2, angle b and angle c are vertical angles, as are angle a and angle d, so $b = c$ and $a = d$. Thus, $c + d = 90$, $a + c = 90$, and $b + d = 90$.

In the figure below, angles p and q are complementary, with $2p = 3q$. What is the measure of angle p?

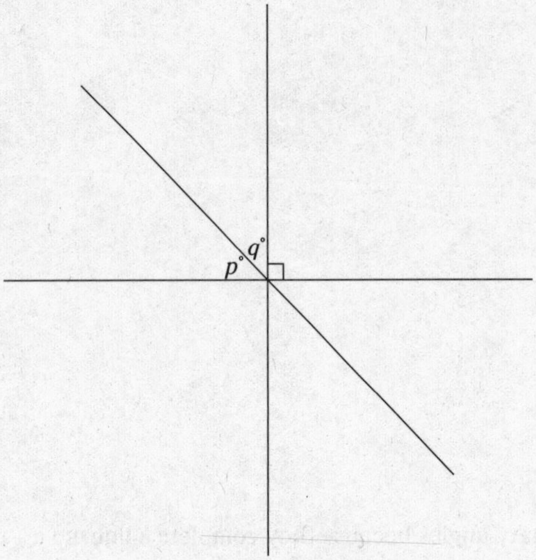

Note: Figure not drawn to scale.

The problem states that angles p and q are complementary, so you have two equations to work with:

$$p + q = 90$$

$$2p = 3q$$

Solve the top equation for q:

$$q = 90 - p$$

Now substitute $90 - p$ for q in the second equation and solve for p:

$$2p = 3(90 - p)$$
$$2p = 270 - 3p$$
$$5p = 270$$
$$p = 54$$

Therefore, the answer is **54**.

Making matches: Parallel lines and corresponding angles

When a line crosses a pair of parallel lines, the result is four sets of *corresponding angles* — pairs of angles that are in the same relative position. The measures of corresponding angles are always equal to each other. For example, in Figure 5-3, angle e and angle i are corresponding angles, so $e = i$. Other pairs of corresponding angles are angle h and angle l, angle f and angle j, and angle g and angle k. Thus, $h = l$, $f = j$, and $g = k$.

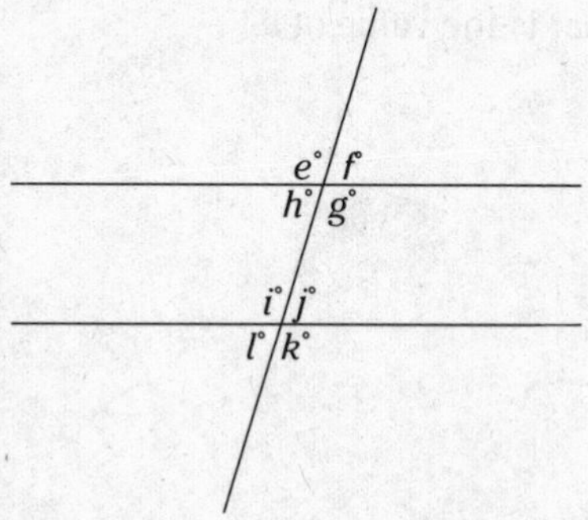

Figure 5-3: When you have parallel lines, corresponding angles are equal.

You can use facts about vertical angles and supplementary angles to draw important additional conclusions about the eight angles in Figure 5-3:

- Because angle e and angle g are vertical angles, $e = g = i = k$. Similarly, angle f and angle h are vertical angles, so $f = h = j = l$.
- Any pair of angles in Figure 5-3 that aren't equal are supplementary. Thus, $e + j = 180$, $h + i = 180$, and so forth.

The following example shows how the SAT may use parallel lines and corresponding angles.

In the figure below, $\overline{EF} \parallel \overline{GH}$. If $t = 4s$, how many degrees is the measure of angle t?

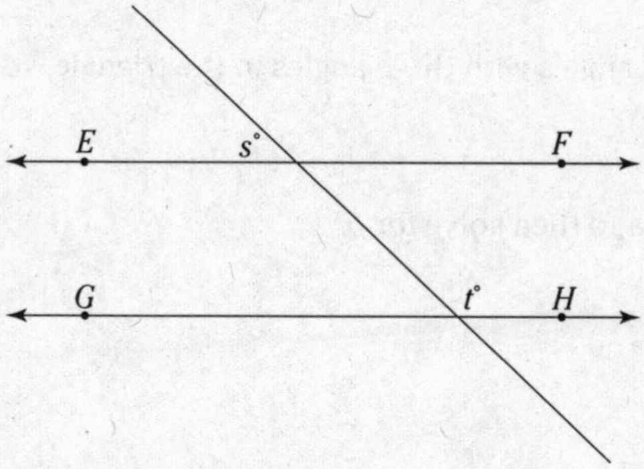

$\overline{EF}$ is parallel to $\overline{GH}$. Thus, angle s and angle t are supplementary, so $s + t = 180$. Substitute $4s$ for t in this equation and solve for s:

$$s + 4s = 180$$
$$5s = 180$$
$$s = 36$$

Thus, angle $s = 36°$, so angle $t = 144°$. Thus, the right answer is **144**.

Sum of the angles in a triangle

As the *Reference Information* at the beginning of every SAT math section tells you, the sum of the three angles in any triangle is 180°. That means that in a right triangle, which has one 90° angle, the sum of the other two angles is also 90°.

The following example question gives you two equations and three variables. Your knowledge of the sum of angles in a triangle enables you to set up a third equation and answer the question.

EXAMPLE EXAM

In the figure below, if $p - 10 = q$ and $p - 20 = r$, what is the value of p?

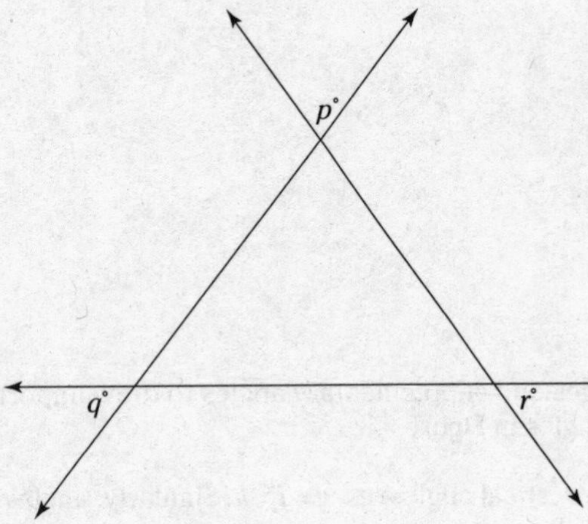

(A) 45

(B) 50

(C) 55

(D) 60

(E) 70

The three angles are paired as vertical angles with three angles in the triangle, so

$$p + q + r = 180$$

Substitute $p - 10$ for q and $p - 20$ for r, and then solve for p:

$$p + (p - 10) + (p - 20) = 180$$
$$3p - 30 = 180$$
$$3p = 210$$
$$p = 70$$

Thus, the right answer is **(E)**.

Putting Triangles to the Test

A *triangle* is a three-sided polygon — that is, a shape with three straight sides and three angles that total 180°. Some common types of triangles are

- **Equilateral triangle:** A triangle with three sides of the same length and three angles that each measure 60°
- **Isosceles triangle:** A triangle with two sides of the same length and two angles that are equivalent
- **Right triangle:** A triangle with one right angle — that is, an angle of 90°

Triangles are important enough that about half the material in the *Reference Information* — formulas and figures that appear at the beginning of every SAT math section — is about triangles. That means you can look up the Pythagorean theorem and the ratio of sides in a special right triangle on the test. But you still need to know how to use this info. In this section, I get you up to speed on what you need to know about triangles to answer the most common types of SAT questions.

Touching base on the area of a triangle

The area of a triangle depends on the measurements of the *base (b)* and *height (h)*. In this formula, the *base* is the length of one side and the *height* is the shortest distance from the base to the opposite corner. Note that the height is perpendicular to the base (see Figure 5-4):

$$A = \frac{1}{2}bh$$

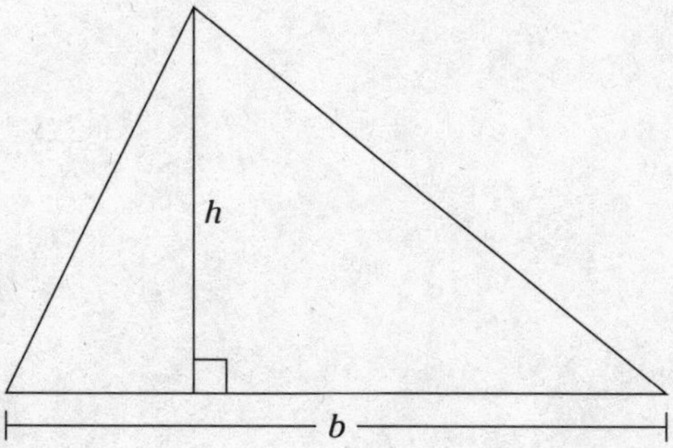

Figure 5-4: The base and height of a triangle.

EXAMPLE

A triangle has a base of 6*x*, a height of 4*x*, and an area of 48. What is the value of *x*?

(A) 1

(B) 2

(C) 3

(D) 4

(E) 8

Plug the base, height, and area into the area formula for a triangle:

$$48 = \frac{1}{2}(6x)(4x)$$

Simplify and solve for *x*:

$$48 = 12x^2$$
$$4 = x^2$$
$$2 = x$$

The value of *x* is 2, so the right answer is **(B)**.

Keeping right triangles cornered

The most important type of triangle is a *right triangle*, which has a right angle (an angle of 90°). In this section, I discuss the ever-popular *Pythagorean theorem*, which allows you to find one side of a right triangle when you know the lengths of the other two sides. I also introduce you to three very common right triangles that you're sure to see on your SAT.

Taking sides with the Pythagorean theorem

The two short sides of a right triangle are called *legs* (a and b). The long side is called the *hypotenuse* (c) — see Figure 5-5. The three sides of a right triangle conform to the famous (or infamous) *Pythagorean theorem:*

$$a^2 + b^2 = c^2$$

TIP

Because the two legs of a right triangle are also the base and height of that triangle, you can plug these two values into the formula for the area of a triangle.

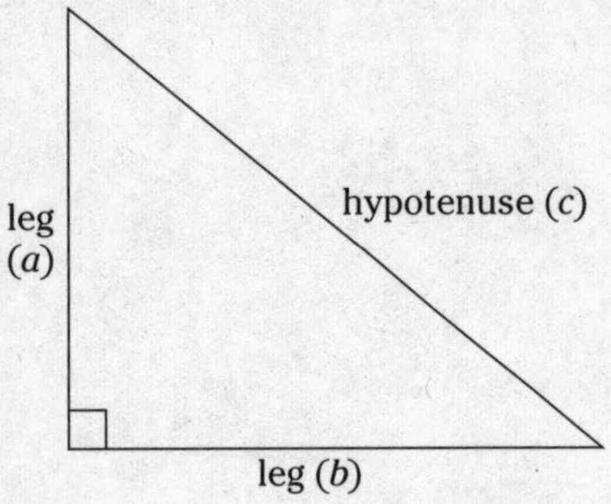

Figure 5-5: The Pythagorean theorem states that $a^2 + b^2 = c^2$ for any right triangle.

EXAMPLE

What is the area of a right triangle with a hypotenuse of 17 inches and one leg of 8 inches?

(A) 60 square inches

(B) 68 square inches

(C) 120 square inches

(D) 136 square inches

(E) 180 square inches

Start by plugging the lengths of the leg and hypotenuse into the Pythagorean theorem. Then solve for b:

$$8^2 + b^2 = 17^2$$

$$64 + b^2 = 289$$

$$b^2 = 225$$

$$b = 15$$

Therefore, the two legs are 8 and 15. In a right triangle, the legs are also the base and height, so plug these two values into the formula for the area of a triangle:

$$A = \frac{1}{2}(8)(15) = 60$$

The area of the triangle is 60 square inches, so the right answer is **(A)**.

Recognizing ratios for three common types of right triangles

TIP

SAT questions often include some common right triangles because they're simple to calculate with. When you spot them, you have a great opportunity to answer questions easily and correctly. Here are three of the most common right triangles on the SAT — the first is named by the lengths of its sides, and the other names deal with angles, but all three triangles have sides that are in specific ratios:

- **3-4-5 triangle:** A right triangle with legs of lengths 3 and 4 and a hypotenuse of length 5 (or a multiple of those lengths)
- **45-45-90 triangle:** A right triangle with two 45° angles
- **30-60-90 triangle:** A right triangle with angles of 30° and 60°

You can usually find side lengths using the Pythagorean theorem, too, but recognizing these ratios allows you to do fewer calculations, which helps you do problems much faster.

3-4-5 triangles

REMEMBER

One common right triangle has legs of length 3 and 4 and a hypotenuse of 5 (see Figure 5-6). A *3-4-5 triangle* is any right triangles whose sides are multiples of 3, 4, and 5 — that is, any triangle with sides $3x$, $4x$, and $5x$. Two common triangles based on multiples of the 3-4-5 triangle are the 6-8-10 and 9-12-15 triangles.

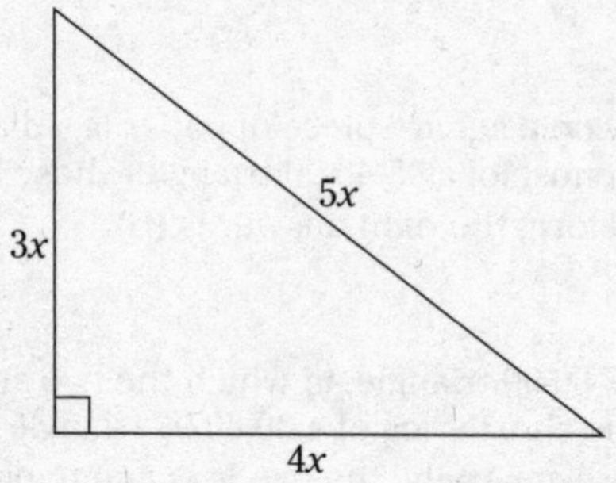

Figure 5-6: A 3-4-5 right triangle.

EXAMPLE

A right triangle has legs of lengths $3n$ and $4n$ and a hypotenuse of 90. What is the value of n?

A right triangle with legs of $3n$ and $4n$ is a 3-4-5 triangle, so its hypotenuse is $5n$. Thus, you can make the following equation:

$$5n = 90$$

$$n = 18$$

Therefore, the right answer is **18**.

45-45-90 triangles

When you cut a square in half diagonally, the two resulting triangles are both 45-45-90 triangles, or *isosceles right triangles*. In a 45-45-90 triangle, you have one right angle, and each of the remaining angles is 45°, as in Figure 5-7.

REMEMBER

When the legs of a 45-45-90 triangle are both 1, the hypotenuse is $\sqrt{2}$. So more generally, the two legs and hypotenuse of a 45-45-90 triangle are in a ratio of $s : s : s\sqrt{2}$.

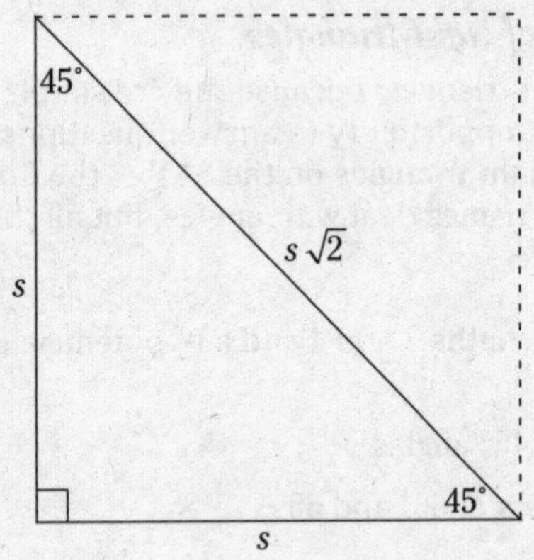

Figure 5-7: A 45-45-90 triangle is half of a square.

EXAMPLE

How many inches is the longest straight line segment that you can draw on an square piece of paper whose side is 8 inches long?

(A) 8

(B) $8\sqrt{2}$

(C) $8\sqrt{3}$

(D) 12

(E) 16

The longest straight line segment you can draw on a square piece of paper is a diagonal from one corner to the other. This is the hypotenuse of a 45-45-90 triangle whose legs are both 8 inches, so its length is $8\sqrt{2}$ inches. Therefore, the right answer is **(B).**

30-60-90 triangles

REMEMBER

Another common type of right triangle is the 30-60-90 triangle, in which the two smaller angles are 30° and 60° (see Figure 5-8). When the shorter leg of a 30-60-90 triangle is 1, the longer leg is $\sqrt{3}$ and the hypotenuse is 2. So more generally, the two legs and hypotenuse of a 30-60-90 triangle are in a ratio of x: $x\sqrt{3}$: $2x$.

TIP

When you cut an equilateral triangle (which has three equal sides and three 60° angles) in half vertically, the two resulting triangles are both 30-60-90 triangles.

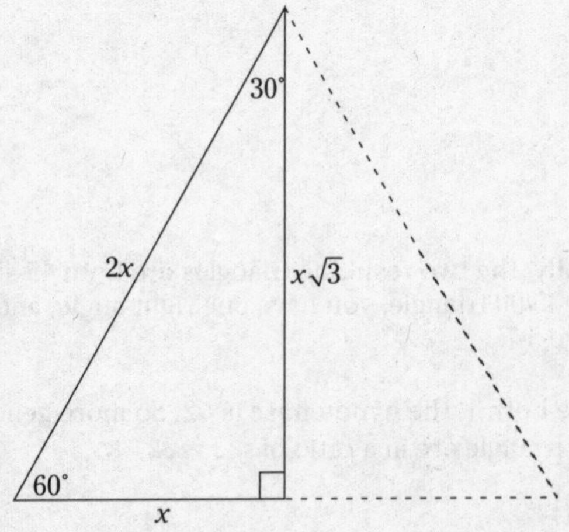

Figure 5-8: A 30-60-90 triangle is half of an equilateral triangle.

What is the area of an equilateral triangle whose side is 10 inches?

(A) $5\sqrt{3}$

(B) 25

(C) $25\sqrt{3}$

(D) 50

(E) $50\sqrt{3}$

To find the area, you need to know the height. You can get the height by splitting the equilateral triangle into two 30-60-90 right triangles:

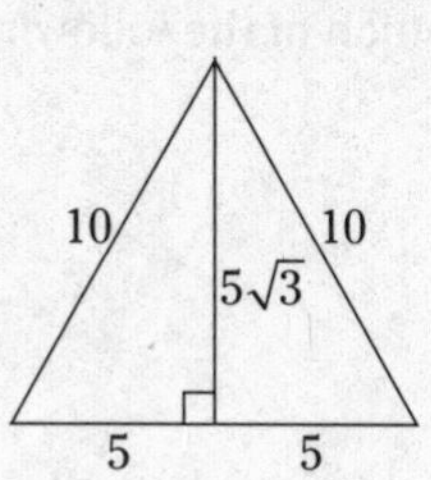

The hypotenuse of this right triangle is 10, so its shorter leg is 5 and its longer leg is $5\sqrt{3}$. In the equilateral triangle, 10 is the base and $5\sqrt{3}$ is the height. Plug this information into the area formula for a triangle:

$$A = \frac{1}{2}bh = \frac{1}{2}(10)\left(5\sqrt{3}\right) = 25\sqrt{3}$$

Therefore, the right answer is **(C)**.

Side shows: The triangle inequality

The *triangle inequality* provides a range of possible lengths of the side of a triangle (c) when you know lengths of the other two sides (a and b, where $a \geq b$):

$$a - b < c < a + b$$

Notice that the inequality gives you a range between the difference on one side and the sum on the other. For example, if two sides of a triangle are 5 and 3, you can plug these numbers into the triangle inequality to find the range of possible lengths for the third side:

$$5 - 3 < c < 5 + 3$$

$$2 < c < 8$$

So the remaining side of this triangle must be greater than 2 and less than 8.

Figure 5-9 shows why the triangle inequality is true. Suppose you tried to make a triangle with sides of 5 and 3 plus a short side of 1: As you can see, the two short sides can't reach each other to close the triangle. Now suppose you tried to make a triangle with sides of 5 and 3, plus a long side of 10: This time, the long side is too long for you to close the triangle.

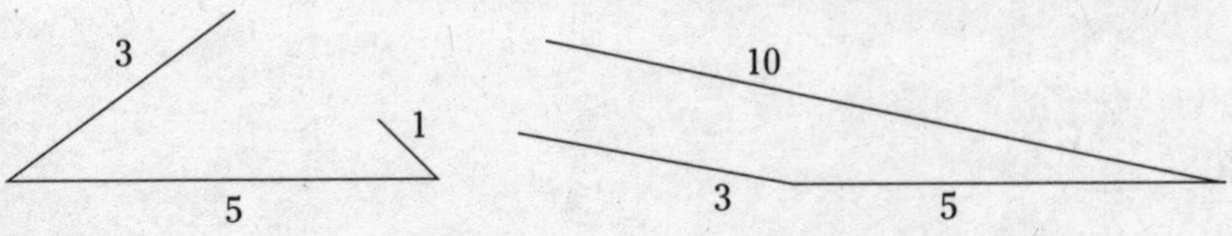

Figure 5-9: For any three sides of a triangle, $a - b < c < a + b$.

In the following example, you apply the triangle inequality to rule out impossible lengths for the third side of a triangle.

EXAMPLE

If x, y, and z are three sides of a triangle, with $x = 4$ and $y = 7$, which of the following could be values of z?

I. 2

II. 7

III. 13

(A) II only

(B) I and II only

(C) III and III only

(D) I, II, and III

(E) None of the above

According to the triangle inequality, $7 - 4 < z < 7 + 4$. Thus,

$$3 < z < 11$$

Therefore, z cannot equal 2 or 13, but z could equal 7, so the right answer is **(A)**.

Getting familiar looks: Congruent and similar triangles

Many proofs in geometry are designed to show that a pair of triangles are either *congruent* (identical in size and shape) or *similar* (proportional to each other). On the SAT, you don't have to worry about doing geometric proofs. But knowing when two triangles are congruent or similar to each other is important. In this section, I skip the proofs but show you the highlights of congruence and similarity.

Congruent triangles

When a pair of triangles are *congruent*, they're identical in size and shape. This means that

- All three pairs of *corresponding angles* are equivalent.
- All three pairs of *corresponding sides* are equal in length.

Figure 5-10 shows a pair of congruent triangles. As you can see, both triangles have sides that have lengths of a, b, and c, and both have angles that measure $x°$, $y°$, and $z°$.

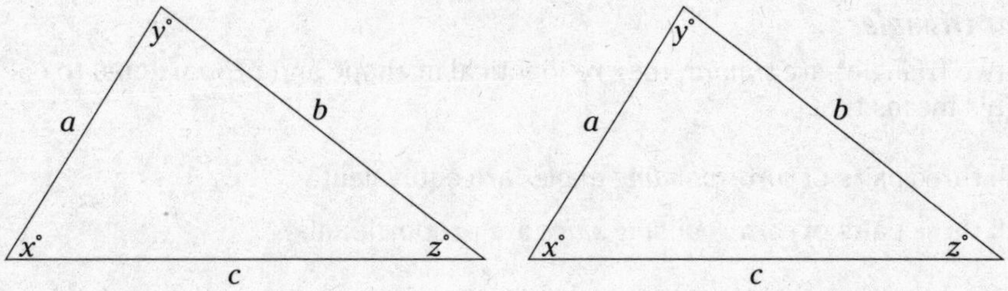

Figure 5-10: A pair of congruent triangles.

REMEMBER

Geometry provides three minimum sufficiency tests for congruency — in other words, three ways you can show that two triangles are congruent:

- **SSS:** Three sides
- **SAS:** Two sides and the angle between them
- **ASA or AAS:** One side and two angles

WARNING!

When a figure is labeled "Note: Figure not drawn to scale," a pair of triangles that appear different may turn out to be congruent. Don't let a picture of two triangles fool you into believing that they're either congruent or not congruent. Instead, rely on the rules for congruency.

On the SAT, showing that two triangles are congruent allows you to draw important conclusions that can help you answer the question.

EXAMPLE

Triangle A and triangle B are congruent triangles with a combined area of 16. If triangle A has a height of 2, which of the following must be the length of one side of triangle B?

(A) 1

(B) 2

(C) 4

(D) 8

(E) 16

Together, the two triangles have an area of 16. They're congruent, so each triangle has an area of 8. Triangle A has a height of 2, so plug this information into the formula for a triangle:

$$A = \frac{1}{2}bh$$
$$8 = \frac{1}{2}(b)(2)$$
$$8 = b$$

Thus, triangle A has a base of length 8. The triangles are congruent, so triangle B also has one side with a length of 8, so the right answer is **(D).**

Similar triangles

When two triangles are *similar*, they're identical in shape and proportional to each other in size. This means that

- All three pairs of *corresponding angles* are equivalent.
- All three pairs of *corresponding sides* are proportional.

For example, the two triangles in Figure 5-11 are similar. As you can see, they're the same basic shape, with corresponding pairs of angles that are equivalent. However, each side of the triangle on the left is twice as long as the corresponding side of the triangle on the right.

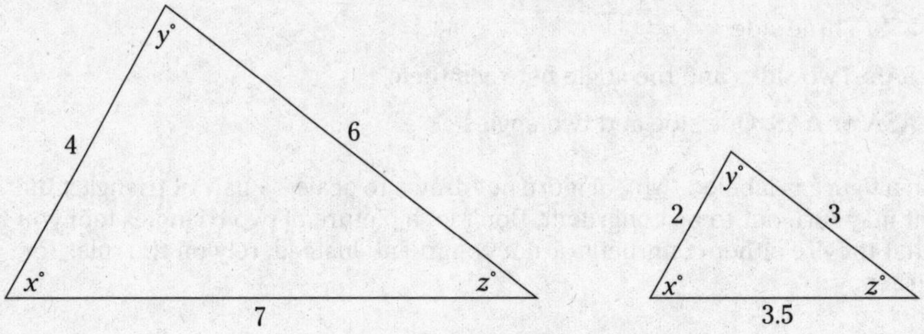

Figure 5-11: A pair of similar triangles.

REMEMBER

Two triangles are similar if all three pairs of corresponding angles are equivalent.

EXAMPLE

In the figure below, $90 - p = q$, $HI = 4$, and $IG = 9$. What is the length of $\overline{FI}$?

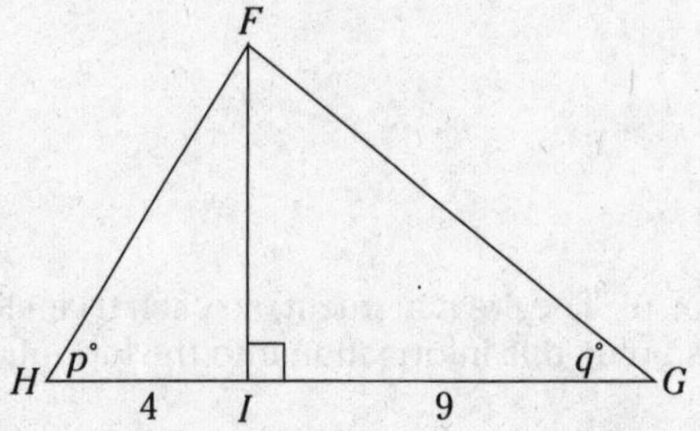

Triangle *HFI* is a right triangle, and it has one angle that measures *p* degrees, so its other angle measures $90 - p$ degrees. This equals *q* degrees because

$$90 - p = q$$

Thus, triangles *HFI* and *FGI* both have the same angles (90°, *p* degrees, and *q* degrees) so they're similar triangles. Therefore, their corresponding sides are in proportion, so *HI* : *FI* = *FI* : *IG*. Turn both ratios into fractions, and substitute 4 for *HI* and 9 for *IG*:

$$\frac{4}{FI} = \frac{FI}{9}$$

The question asks you to find *FI*. To keep things clear, let $x = FI$ and solve for x:

$$\frac{4}{x} = \frac{x}{9}$$
$$36 = x^2$$
$$6 = x$$

Thus, *FI* is **6**.

Going for Four: Quadrilaterals

A *quadrilateral* is a polygon with four sides. On the SAT, the quadrilaterals you need to work with are squares, rectangles, and parallelograms. In this section, I show you how to find the area of each and perimeter of squares and rectangles, as well as the area of parallelograms.

Squares

A *square* is a quadrilateral that has four equal sides and four right angles (see Figure 5-12). The formulas for the area and perimeter of a square both require the length of one side *(s)*. Here's the formula for the area of a square:

$$A = s^2$$

And here's the formula for the perimeter of a square:

$$P = 4s$$

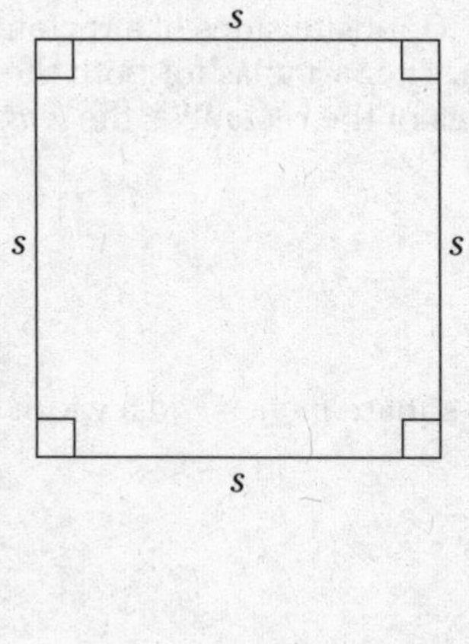

Figure 5-12: Sides of a square.

EXAMPLE

The perimeter of a square is $2x$ and its area is $5x$. What is the value of x?

(A) 2

(B) 5

(C) 10

(D) 20

(E) 50

To solve this problem, first plug the value of the perimeter into the perimeter formula and solve for s to find the length of one side:

$$P = 4s$$
$$2x = 4s$$
$$\frac{2x}{4} = \frac{4s}{4}$$
$$\frac{x}{2} = s$$

Each side of the square is $\frac{x}{2}$. Now plug this value into the formula for the area, along with the area of $5x$:

$$A = s^2$$
$$5x = \left(\frac{x}{2}\right)^2$$
$$5x = \frac{x^2}{4}$$

Simplify and solve for x:

$$20x = x^2$$
$$20 = x$$

Thus, the right answer is **(D).**

Rectangles

A *rectangle* is a quadrilateral that has four right angles. Opposite sides of a rectangle are always the same length as each other (see Figure 5-13). The formulas for both the area and perimeter of a rectangle both require two adjacent sides of the rectangle: the *length (l)* and the *width (w)*.

- $A = lw$
- $P = 2l + 2w$

EXAMPLE

What is the perimeter of a rectangle with an area of 27 square inches and a width of 3 inches?

(A) 9 inches

(B) 12 inches

(C) 24 inches

(D) 36 inches

(E) 60 inches

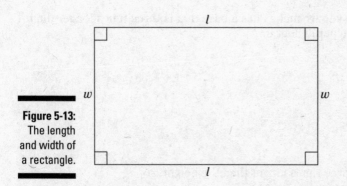

Figure 5-13: The length and width of a rectangle.

Plug the area and width into the area formula to find the length of the rectangle:

$$A = lw$$
$$27 = 3l$$
$$9 = l$$

Now plug the length and width into the formula for the perimeter:

$$P = 2l + 2w = 2(9) + 2(3) = 18 + 6 = 24$$

So the right answer is **(C).**

Parallelograms

A *parallelogram* is a quadrilateral whose opposite sides are parallel and of equal length and whose opposite angles are also equal. The formula for the area of a parallelogram requires measurements of both the base *(b)* and the height *(h)*:

$$A = bh$$

In this formula, the *base* is the length of one side and the *height* is the shortest distance from the base to the opposite base. The height is perpendicular to the bases (see Figure 5-14).

Notice why this formula works: Imagine cutting off the triangle on the left side of this parallelogram and attaching it to the right side. The result is a rectangle with a length of *b* and a width of *h*.

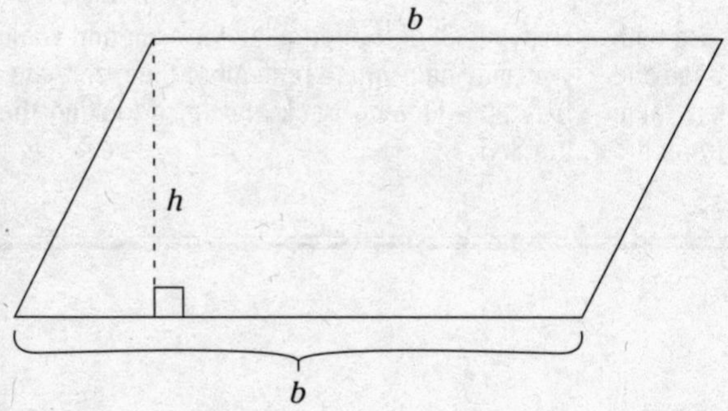

Figure 5-14: The base and height of a parallelogram.

A parallelogram with an area of 75 square inches has a base that is three times longer than its height. What is the height of the parallelogram?

(A) 3 inches

(B) 5 inches

(C) 6.25 inches

(D) 7.5 inches

(E) 15 inches

The base of the parallelogram is three times longer than the height, so

$$b = 3h$$

Substitute $3h$ for b into the parallelogram area formula, along with the area of 75. Then simplify and solve for h:

$$A = bh$$

$$75 = (3h)(h)$$

$$75 = 3h^2$$

$$25 = h^2$$

$$5 = h$$

Thus, the height is 5 inches, so the right answer is **(B).**

Taking a basic idea to new heights

There are so many formulas for area that the SAT folks give you a bunch of them as part of the *Reference Information* at the beginning of each section. One of the main reasons for all these formulas is the number of terms — *side, length, width, base,* and *height.* Are they really all necessary? I don't think so. With the proper perspective, you only need two area formulas — one for quadrilaterals and another for triangles — both using only the concepts of *base* and *height:*

- **Quadrilaterals:** $A = bh$
- **Triangles:** $A = \frac{1}{2}bh$

Think about it: In a square, the base and height are both sides, which are equal. And in a rectangle, the base and height are the length and width. But if you think of them as the base and height, you can dispense with all the extra formulas.

Even better, when you get to solid geometry, the same idea allows you to collapse formulas for the volume of a solid into two formulas — one for prisms and cylinders (solids that are flat on top) and another for pyramids and cones (solids that come to a point on top). In these formulas, the base is the *area* of the shape (square, rectangle, circle, or whatever) at the bottom of the solid, and the height is the vertical distance between the base and the top:

- **Cubes, boxes, prisms, and cylinders:** $V = bh$
- **Pyramids and cones:** $V = \frac{1}{3}bh$

Unifying all of the formulas for area and volume in this way may help you to remember them so that you spend less time flipping back and forth looking them up on the SAT.

Rolling Along with Circles

A *circle* is the set of all of the points on a plane that are all the same distance from a single center point. In this section, you discover the basic formulas and concepts related to circles that you need to succeed on the SAT.

From center stage: Radius and diameter

The *radius (r)* of a circle is the distance from the center to any point on the circle. The *diameter (d)* is the distance from any point on the circle through the center to the opposite point on the circle.

REMEMBER

The diameter of any circle is twice the radius, as you see in Figure 5-15. This is expressed in the following formula:

$$d = 2r$$

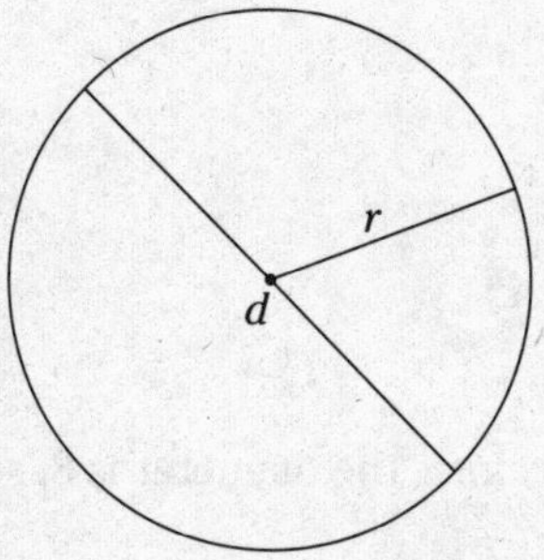

Figure 5-15: The diameter of a circle is twice the radius.

EXAMPLE

The radius of a circle is $2x$ and the diameter is $3y$. What is the value of $\frac{x}{y}$?

Begin by plugging the values of the diameter and radius into the formula:

$$d = 2r$$
$$3y = 2(2x)$$
$$3y = 4x$$

Now solve for $\frac{x}{y}$:

$$\frac{3y}{4} = \frac{4x}{4}$$
$$\frac{3y}{4} = x$$
$$\frac{3}{4} = \frac{x}{y}$$

Thus, the right answer is **3/4** or **.75**.

Finding the area of a circle

The formula for the *area (A)* of a circle depends upon the measurement of the radius. It also uses the value π, an irrational number that has an approximate value of 3.14. (***Tip:*** In your calculations on the SAT, just keep your answers in terms of π unless otherwise instructed — no need to multiply by 3.14.) Here's the formula for the area of a circle:

$$A = \pi r^2$$

Which of the following is the diameter of a circle whose area is 16π?

(A) 2π

(B) 4

(C) 4π

(D) 8

(E) 8π

Plug the area of the circle into the area formula:

$$16\pi = \pi r^2$$

Divide both sides by π and solve for r:

$$16 = r^2$$

$$4 = r$$

The radius is 4, so the diameter is twice this value. Therefore, the diameter is 8, so the right answer is **(D).**

Getting around to the circumference

The *circumference (C)* of a circle is the distance around the circle. The formula for the circumference depends on the measurement of the radius. It also uses the value π, a constant. Here's the formula for the circumference of a circle:

$$C = 2\pi r$$

What is the circumference of a circle whose area is 100π?

(A) 10

(B) 20

(C) 25

(D) 10π

(E) 20π

To find the circumference, you need the radius. You're given the area, so first use the area formula for a circle to get the radius:

$$A = \pi r^2$$
$$100\pi = \pi r^2$$
$$100 = r^2$$
$$10 = r$$

Thus, the radius of the circle is 10. Plug this value into the formula for the circumference:

$$C = 2\pi(10) = 20\pi$$

Thus, the circumference is 20π, so the right answer is **(E).**

Not quite full circle: Finding arc length

An *arc* is part of the distance around a circle. A useful way to think of arc length is as a fraction of the circumference.

EXAMPLE

In the figure below, a regular pentagon is embedded in a circle with a radius of 5. What is the arc length from Point *A* to Point *B?*

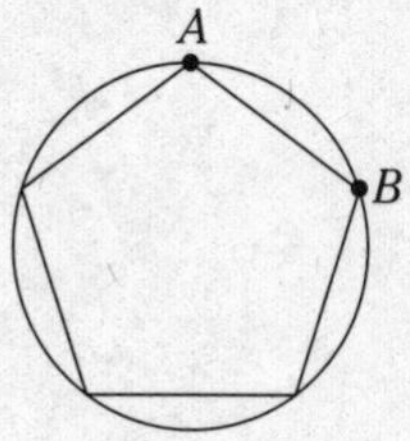

(A) π

(B) 2π

(C) 3π

(D) 4π

(E) 5π

To find the arc length, first find the circumference of this circle:

$$C = 2\pi r = 2\pi(5) = 10\pi$$

Because this pentagon is regular, the distance from *A* to *B* is one-fifth of the circumference:

$$\text{Arc length} = \frac{1}{5}(10\pi) = 2\pi$$

Therefore, the right answer is **(B).**

Often, an SAT question asks you to calculate arc length based on a number of degrees. Remember that a complete circle has 360°, so the circumference of a circle is equivalent to 360° of arc length. You can use a proportion to find a shorter arc length.

EXAMPLE

In the figure below, O is the center of the circle, angle $O = 80°$, and $OQ = 13.5$. What is the arc length from point Q to point R?

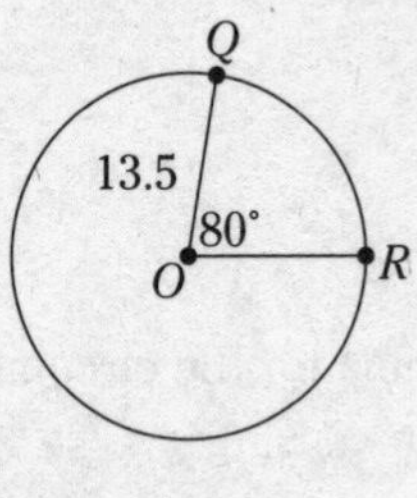

(A) 2π

(B) 3π

(C) 6π

(D) 9π

(E) 12π

The radius of the circle (OQ) is 13.5, so use this information to find the circumference:

$$C = 2\pi r = 2\pi(13.5) = 27\pi$$

This circumference is essentially 360° of arc length for this circle, so you can set up a proportion to find out the corresponding arc length for 80°:

$$\frac{80}{360} = \frac{x}{27\pi}$$

Cross-multiply and solve for x:

$$2{,}160\pi = 360x$$

$$6\pi = x$$

Therefore, the right answer is **(C)**.

Touching on tangent lines

REMEMBER

A line that's *tangent* to a circle touches that circle at exactly one point. When a tangent line and a radius intersect at a point on the circle, they always form a right angle. In Figure 5-16, $\overline{JK}$ is tangent at L to the circle that is centered at O. Thus, $\overline{JK}$ is perpendicular to $\overline{OL}$.

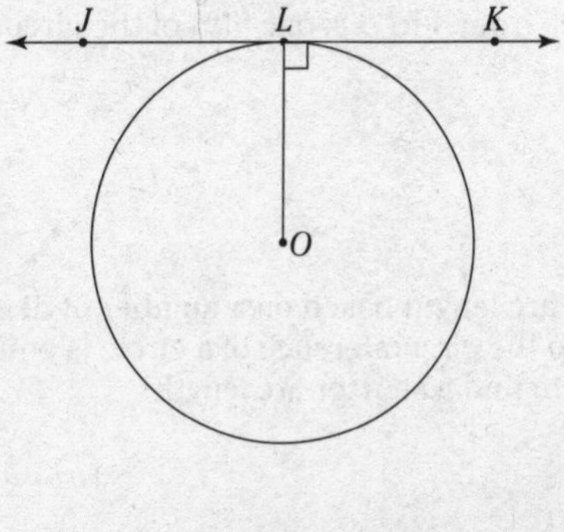

Figure 5-16: A line tangent to a circle.

SAT questions commonly use the right angle formed by a tangent line and a radius to form a right triangle. To answer this type of question, look for special right triangles — 3:4:5 triangles, 45:45:90 triangles, and 30:60:90 triangles (I introduce them earlier in this chapter in "Recognizing ratios for three common types of right triangles"). Also, remember that when a circle inscribed in a polygon (a shape with straight sides), the sides of the polygon are tangent to the circle. This information is often essential for answering some of the more difficult geometry questions.

In the figure below, line $\overline{PQ}$ is tangent at P to the circle centered at O. If $PQ = 4$ and $OQ = 5$, what is the area of the circle?

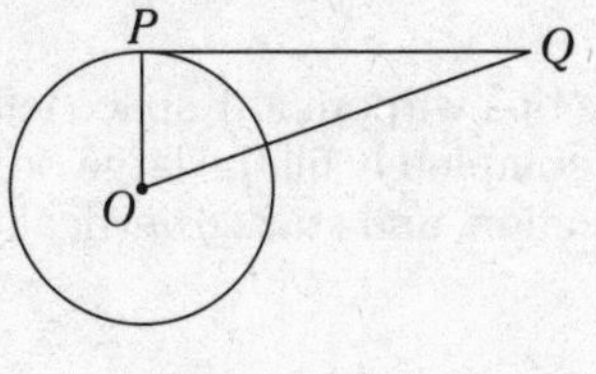

Note: Figure not drawn to scale.

(A) π

(B) 3

(C) 3π

(D) 9

(E) 9π

The tangent and the radius meet at P, so they form a right angle. Thus, $\triangle OPQ$ is a right triangle. Its hypotenuse, $\overline{OQ}$, has a length of 5. One of its legs, $\overline{PQ}$, has a length of 4. Therefore, $\triangle OPQ$ is a 3-4-5 right triangle, so $OP = 3$. (If you don't spot this, you can find OP using the Pythagorean theorem, where $4^2 + OP^2 = 5^2$.) Thus, the radius of the circle is 3, so plug this value into the formula for the area of a circle:

$$A = \pi r^2 = \pi(3^2) = 9\pi$$

Therefore, the right answer is **(E)**.

Solidifying Your Understanding of Solid Geometry

Solid geometry is geometry that occurs in three dimensions. Some SAT questions focus on a short list of topics in this area, particularly volume. In this section, I provide you with a solid grounding in solid geometry.

Volume of a rectangular solid

A *rectangular solid* is a solid with six rectangular sides — that is, a box-shaped solid, as in Figure 5-17. The formula for the volume of a rectangular solid is based on the length, width, and height of its sides:

$$V = lwh$$

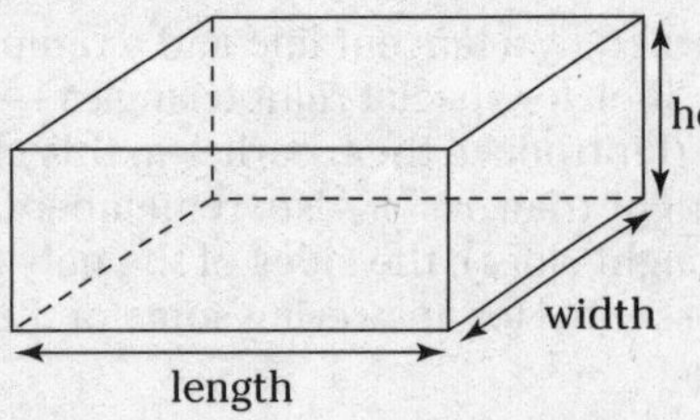

Figure 5-17: A rectangular solid.

A small rectangular box has a length of 4 inches, a width of 1 inch, and a height of 2 inches. A large box is a cube with a length, width, and height of 12 inches. What is the maximum number of small boxes that can fit inside a large box?

First make sure that the small boxes can fit into the large box without any space left over. The numbers 4, 1, and 2 all divide evenly into 12, so you can completely fill the large box (you can put 3 small boxes in one direction, put 12 in another direction, and stack 6 vertically).

Now find the volume of a small box:

$$V_{\text{small box}} = (4)(1)(2) = 8 \text{ cubic inches}$$

Next, find the volume of a large box:

$$V_{\text{large box}} = (12)(12)(12) = 1{,}728 \text{ cubic inches}$$

Now divide the volume of a large box by the volume of a small box:

$$\frac{1{,}728}{8} = 216$$

Therefore, the right answer is **216**.

Volumes of a cylinder

A *cylinder* is a projection of a circle into three dimensions — that is, a can-shaped solid, as in Figure 5-18. The formula for a cylinder is based on the area of its circular base (πr^2) and its height *(h)*:

$$V = \pi r^2 h$$

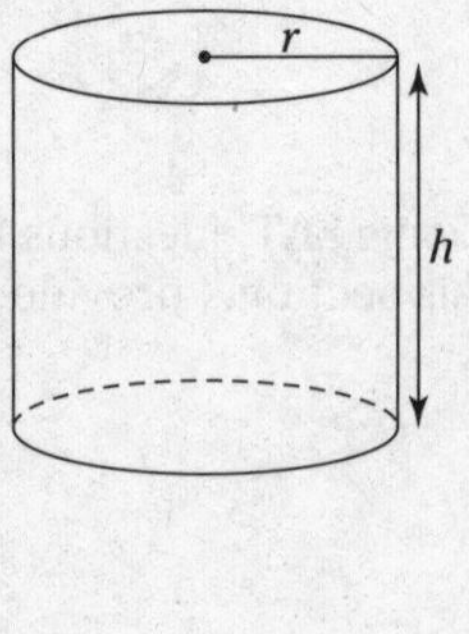

Figure 5-18: A cylinder.

In the figure below, the volume of the cylinder is 54π. What is the radius of this cylinder if its height is equal to its diameter?

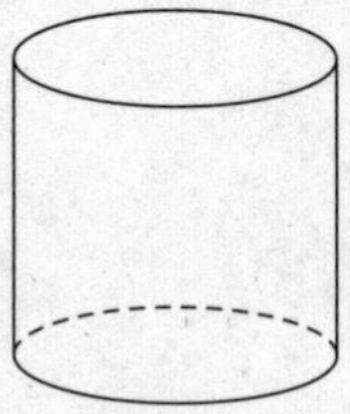

The height of the cylinder is equal to its diameter, which is twice the radius, so $h = 2r$. Plug in the given volume and substitute $2r$ for h into the formula for the volume of a cylinder:

$$V = \pi r^2 h$$

$$54\pi = \pi r^2(2r)$$

$$54\pi = 2\pi r^3$$

Divide both sides by 2π and solve for r:

$$27 = r^3$$

$$3 = r$$

Therefore, the right answer is **3**.

Pyramids and cones

Two popular solids on the SAT are pyramids and cones, as in Figure 5-19. On the SAT, you probably won't need to find the volume of a pyramid or a cone. Instead, questions often focus on surfaces or shapes within these solids. In this section, I give you a few tips on answering questions that provide you with one of these solids.

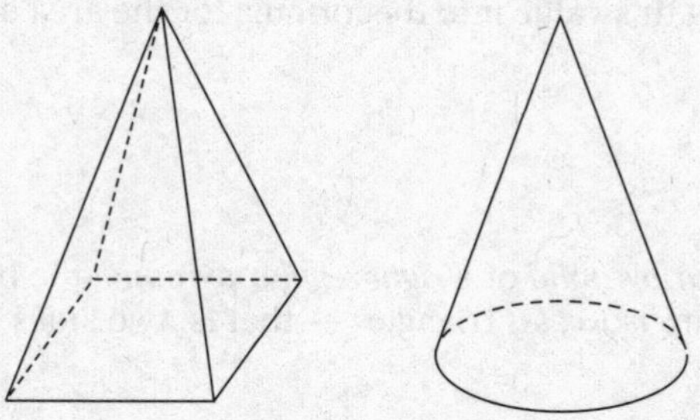

Figure 5-19: A pyramid and a cone.

When a question contains either a pyramid or a cone, it often gives you a right triangle to work with. Finding this right triangle can make the question easy to answer.

In the figure below, the height of the cone is 4 and the distance from the top to an edge of the base is 5. What is the area of the base?

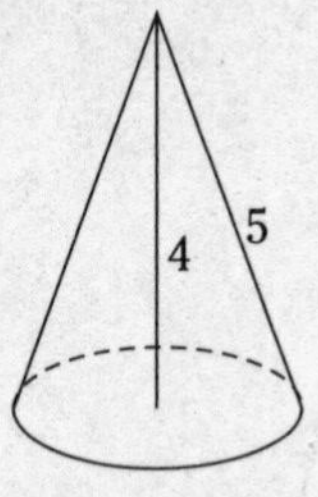

Note: Figure not drawn to scale

(A) 6π

(B) 9π

(C) 16π

(D) 25π

(E) 36π

The line from the top of the cone to the center forms a right angle with the line from the center to the edge of the base. This right angle becomes the basis of a 3-4-5 right triangle.

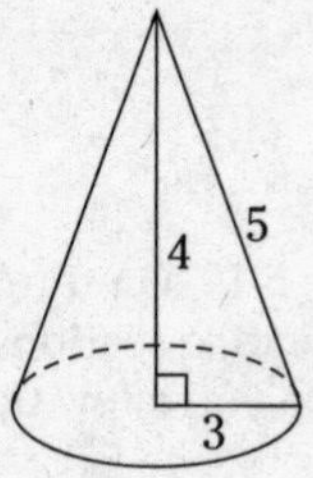

Thus, the radius of the base is 3, so plug this value into the formula for the area of a circle:

$$A = \pi r^2 = \pi(3^2) = 9\pi$$

Therefore, the right answer is **(B)**.

When a pyramid is described as a *regular pyramid* or a *right regular pyramid*, the base is a square and all four triangular surfaces are *isosceles* triangles — that is, two sides are the same length.

The figure below shows a right regular pyramid with $AB = AC$. The base of this pyramid has an area of 9 square centimeters and the distance from N to A is 7 centimeters. What is the area of the shaded side in square centimeters?

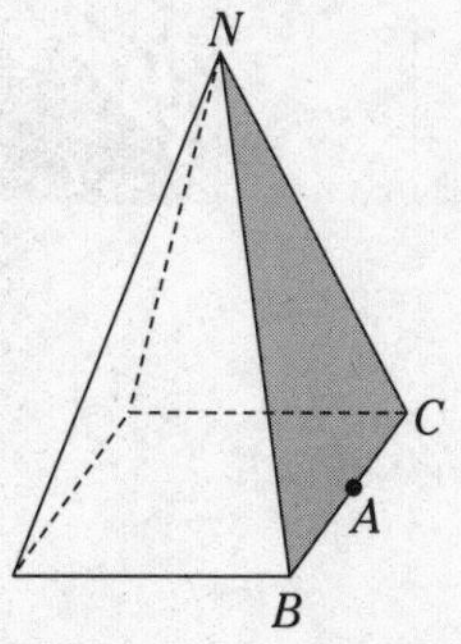

The area of the square base is 9, so use the formula for the area of a square to find the length of one side:

$$A = s^2$$
$$9 = s^2$$
$$3 = s$$

Thus, the side has a length of 3. This is the length of the base of the triangle whose height is 7, so use the formula for the area of a triangle:

$$A = \frac{1}{2}bh = \frac{1}{2}(3)(7) = \frac{21}{2}$$

Therefore, the area of the shaded triangle is **21/2**, or **10.5**, square centimeters.

Improving Your Geometric Perception

One type of SAT question tests your *geometric perception*, which is the ability to imagine a geometric object when it's turned and viewed from a different perspective. These types of questions are tricky only because you probably haven't spent much time developing the skills you need to answer them. In this section, I show you a few ways to think about geometric perception questions.

Getting your head around rotations

A *rotation* shows a picture of a figure turned in a different direction on the plane. For example, Figure 5-20 shows a single object rotated in four different directions around its center point. Each rotation is a counterclockwise turn of 90°.

A rotation never requires that you pick up an object in space and flip it over.

To test whether an answer is a rotation of an original figure, turn your test book, placing a *unique* part of the answer figure into the position shown in the original figure. Choose a feature or cluster of features that stands out from the rest of the figure. Then all other parts of the figure should fall into place. If they don't, the figure is not a rotation.

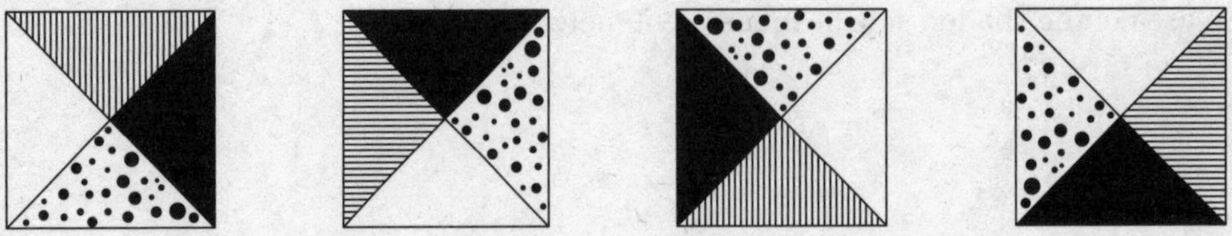

Figure 5-20: A figure and three rotations of 90°, 180°, and 270° counter-clockwise.

Which of the following is NOT a rotation of the figure shown below?

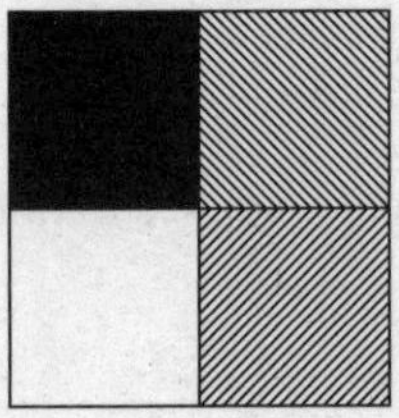

(A)

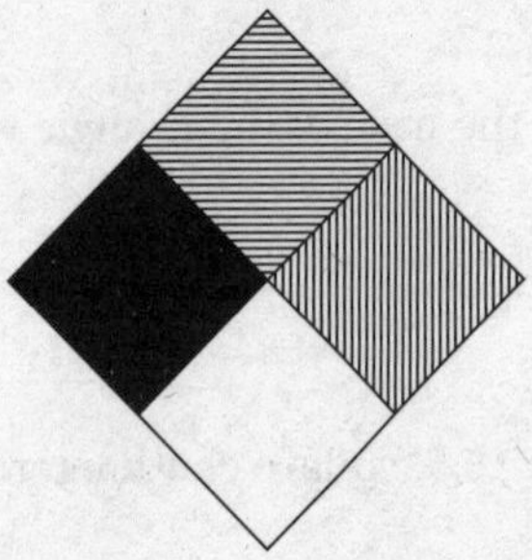

(B)

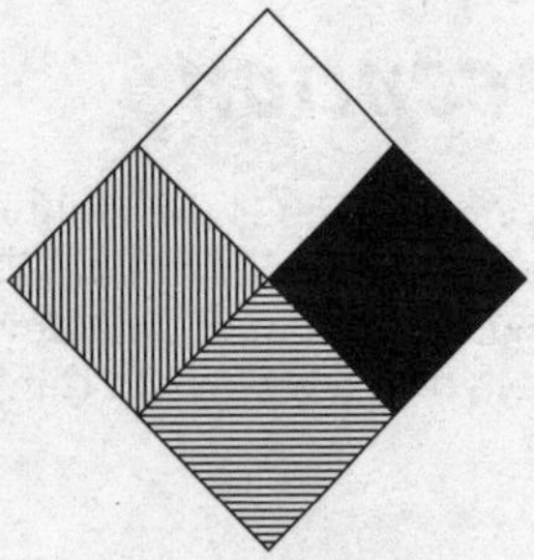

(C)

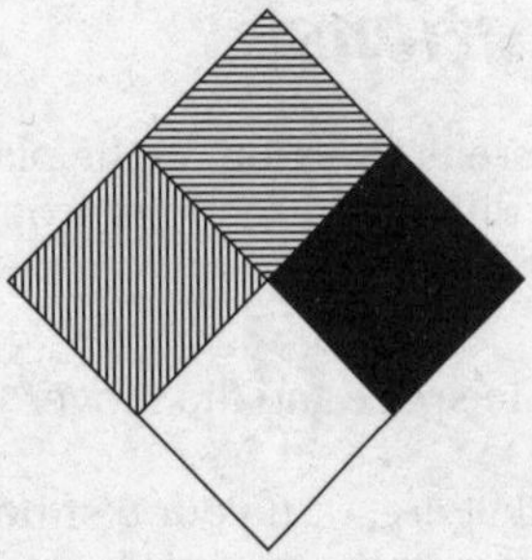

(D)

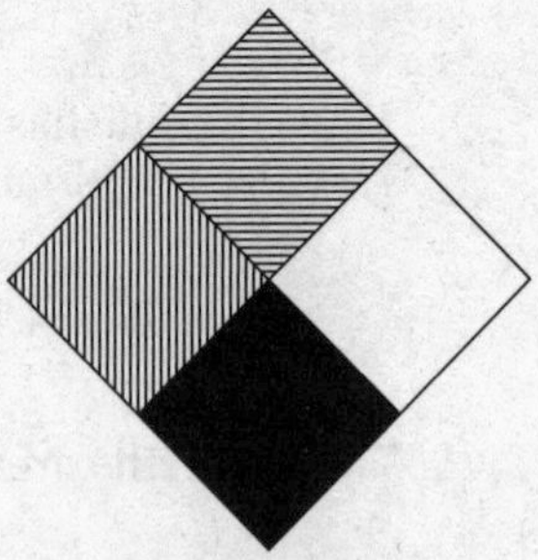

(E)

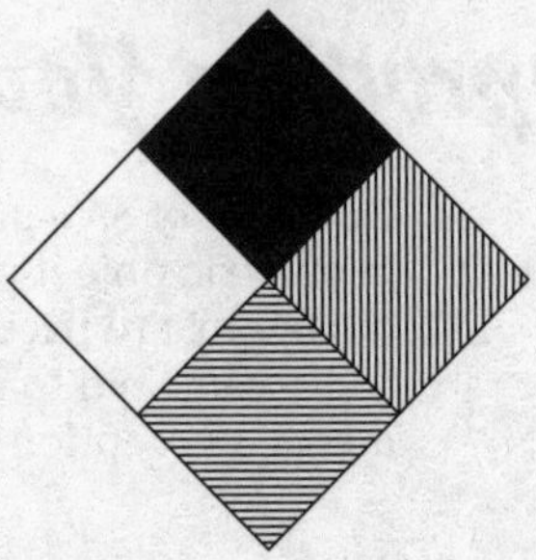

For all rotations, when you turn this book to place the black square in the upper left corner, the white square should appear in the lower left corner, as in the original figure. The only answer for which this doesn't work (try it!) is **(C)**, so this is the right answer.

Adding a dimension: Getting other views of 3-D objects

Some geometric-perception questions test your ability to imagine a 3-D object from another perspective. The most likely object you'll face for this type of question is a cube or another type of rectangular solid.

Figure 5-21 shows a regular six-sided die from four different perspectives. You can mentally rotate the cube in three dimensions to get the other perspectives:

- **Around the axis that comes straight out of the page:** When you rotate the first picture in Figure 5-21 clockwise around the dot on the 1 side, the result is the second picture: The 2 side rotates from the right side to the bottom, and the 5 side rotates from the hidden left side to the top.
- **Around the vertical axis:** Next, notice that when you rotate the second picture clockwise around the center dot on the 5 side, the result is the third picture: The 1 side rotates from the front out of sight to the left, and the 6 side rotates from the back around to the right.
- **Around the horizontal axis:** Finally, notice that when you rotate the third picture counterclockwise around the center of the 6 side, the result is the fourth picture: The 3 side rotates from the front to the bottom, and the 4 side rotates from the back to the top.

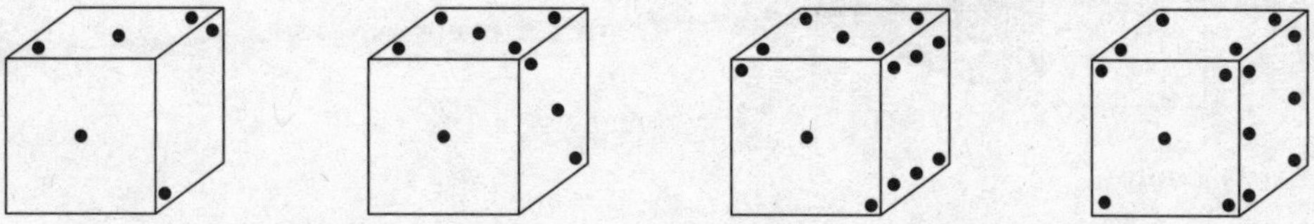

Figure 5-21: Four perspectives of a six-sided die.

TIP

With practice, you can really improve your geometric perception, so spend a few minutes practicing with Figure 5-21. For each image, see whether you can visualize the die turning 90° in the direction necessary to change it to the next image. Notice that in each case, one face rotates but stays in place, another face moves but stays in view, and the third face turns out of view.

When you can see each rotation clearly in your head, move on to another activity, but return later and see whether you can recall how the rotations happen. When you think you can see them clearly, show the figure to a friend and practice explaining how each image is a rotation of the previous image. For a greater challenge, you can even try drawing your own examples.

All six sides of the rectangular solid below are either gray or white, with opposite sides always being different colors. Which of the following could be the same rectangular solid from a different perspective?

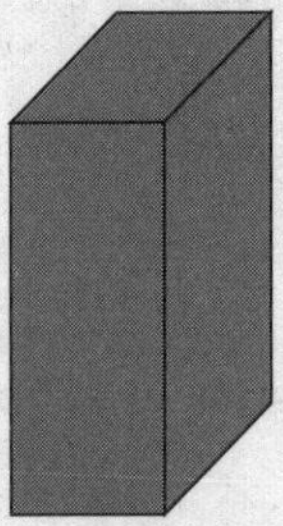

I.

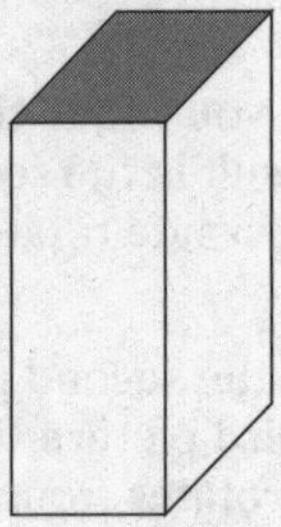

II.

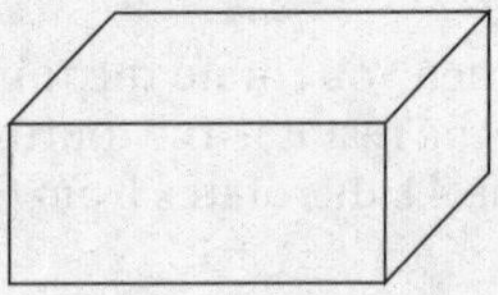

III.

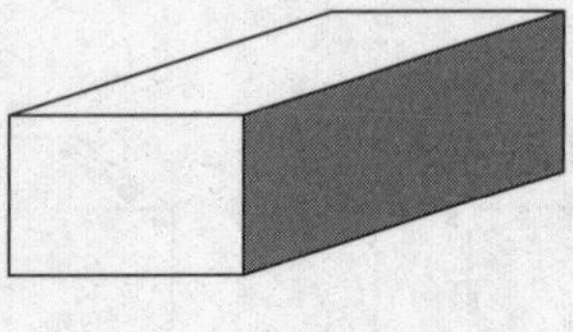

(A) I only

(B) III only

(C) I and III only

(D) II and III only

(E) I, II, and III

Option I shows a 180° rotation around the center of the top face of the original figure. Option II shows a 90° counterclockwise rotation around the center of the front face of the figure in Option I. And Option III shows a 90° clockwise rotation around the center of the top face of the figure in Option II. Thus, all three figures are different perspectives of the original figure, so the right answer is **(E)**.

Folding in information about surfaces

One type of question that tests geometric perception requires you to imagine folding a two-dimensional shape into a solid. A common transformation of this type turns a cross made from six squares into a cube, as in Figure 5-22.

To answer a folded-shape question, try to see the way in which some faces are adjacent and others are opposite each other. For example, in Figure 5-22, sides 2 and 4 are opposite, as are sides 1 and 5 and sides 3 and 6. However, side 6 folds all the way around to become adjacent with side 1.

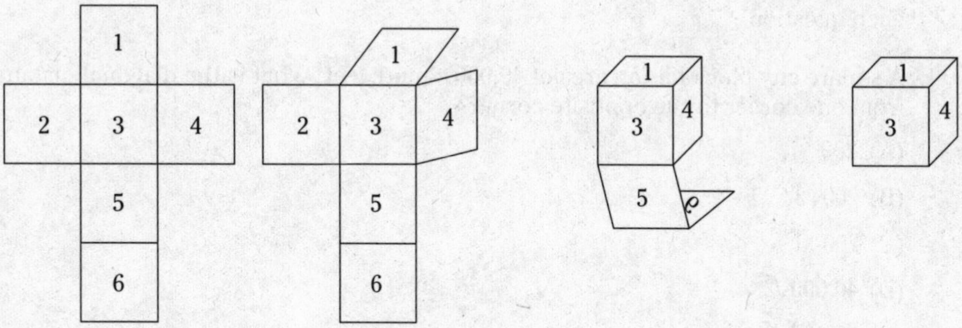

Figure 5-22: Folding a cross into a cube.

Which of the following CANNOT be the folded up version of the cube shown below?

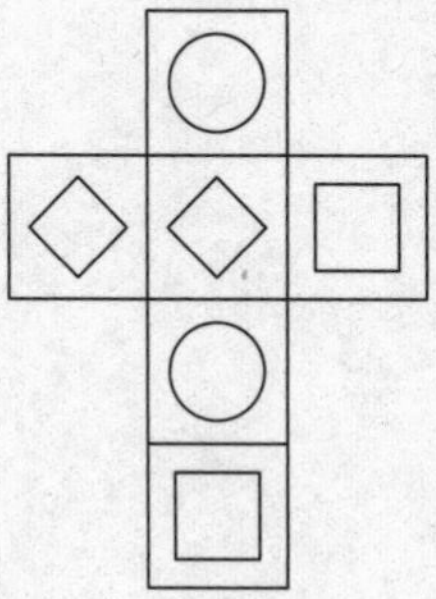

(A)

(B)

(C)

(D)

(E)

The two circles must appear on opposite sides of the cube when it's folded up. Thus, they can't be shown adjacently, so **(B)** isn't a folded up version of the cube and is, therefore, the right answer.

Practice Problems for Geometry

Ready for some practice? These 20 questions are designed to test the geometry skills covered in this chapter. If you get stuck on a question, flip back through the chapter for ideas. In the next section, I provide the answers plus a thorough explanation of how to answer each question.

1. A square city block has an area of 40,000 square feet. What is the diagonal distance in feet from one corner to the opposite corner?

(A) 200

(B) $200\sqrt{2}$

(C) $200\sqrt{3}$

(D) $40{,}000\sqrt{2}$

(E) $40{,}000\sqrt{3}$

2. In the figure below, $\triangle ABC$ is an equilateral triangle whose sides are 2 inches, and *ADEF* is a square. What is the area of *ADEF* in square inches?

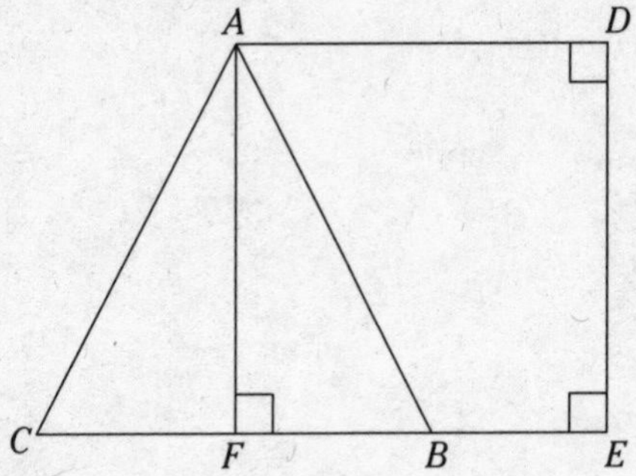

(A) 2

(B) $2\sqrt{2}$

(C) $2\sqrt{3}$

(D) 3

(E) $3\sqrt{2}$

3. In the figure below, what is the value of x?

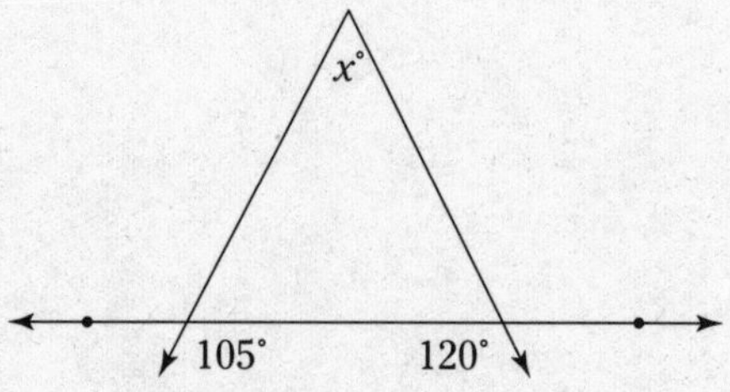

Note: Figure not drawn to scale.

(A) 30

(B) 40

(C) 45

(D) 55

(E) 60

4. In the figure below, both A and B are points on the circle centered at O, and $\triangle AOB$ is an equilateral triangle. If the area of the circle is 16π, what is the length of $\overline{AB}$?

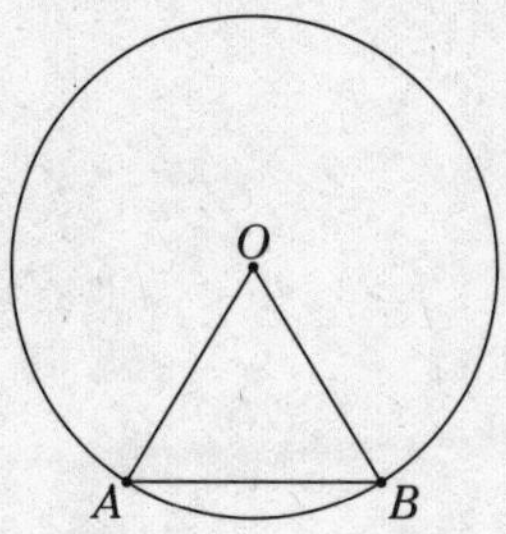

(A) π

(B) 2

(C) 2π

(D) 4

(E) 4π

5. In the figure below, $ABCD$ is a parallelogram and $\overline{AD} \perp \overline{BE}$. If $AB = 5$, $AE = 3$, and $ED = 7$, what is the area of $ABCD$?

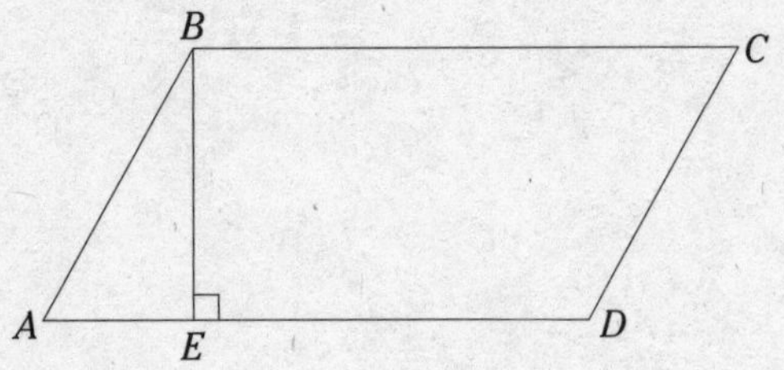

(A) 28

(B) 30

(C) 35

(D) 40

(E) 50

6. $\overline{AD}$ is a diameter of the circle centered at O, and $ABCD$ is a rectangle. If the area of the circle is 36π and the area of the rectangle is 192, what is the length of $\overline{AB}$?

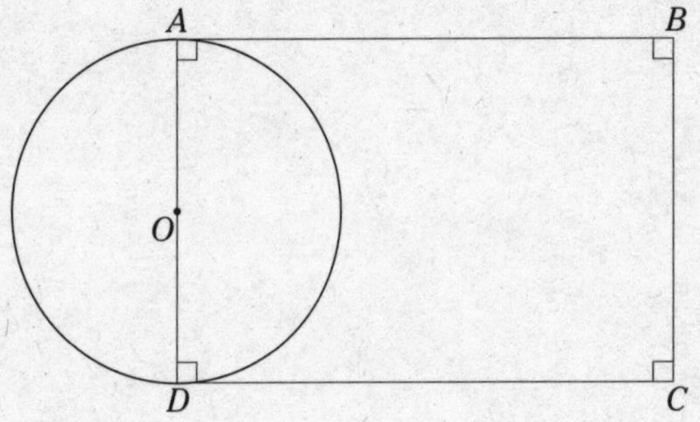

(A) 6

(B) 8

(C) 12

(D) 16

(E) 18

7. Which of the following is a rotation of the figure below around the point *P*?

(A)
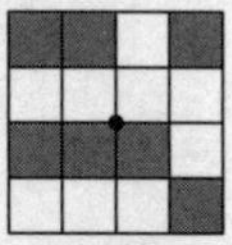

(B)
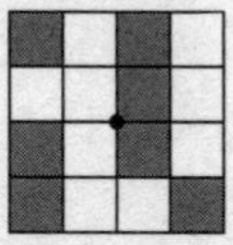

(C)
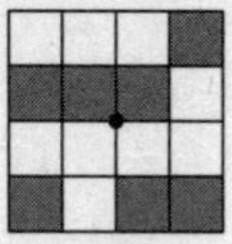

(D)
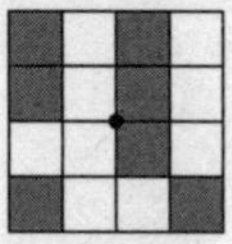

(E)
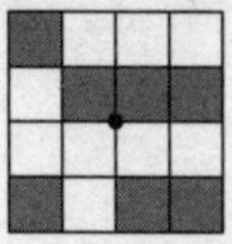

8. In the figure below, $\triangle GHI$ and $\triangle JKL$ are similar triangles. $\overline{GH}$ and $\overline{KL}$ are both 4 units in length, and $\overline{HI}$ and $\overline{JL}$ are both 6 units in length. What is the length of $\overline{GI}$?

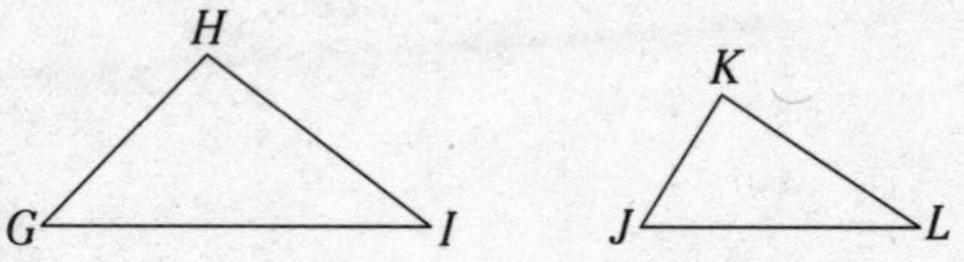

(A) 7.5

(B) 8

(C) 8.4

(D) 9

(E) 9.6

9. In the figure below, the two horizontal lines are parallel, and $m + 30 = n$. What is the value of p?

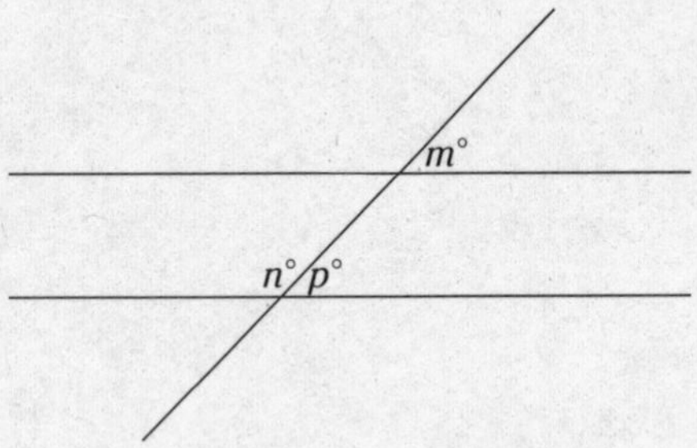

Note: Figure not drawn to scale.

(A) 55

(B) 60

(C) 75

(D) 85

(E) 105

10. A rectangular box has a volume of $10x^2$ and a length of $3x$ and a width of $2x$. What is the height of the box?

(A) $\frac{3}{5}$

(B) $\frac{5}{3}$

(C) $\frac{3x}{5}$

(D) $\frac{5x}{3}$

(E) $\frac{3x^2}{5}$

11. One side of a triangle is 3 inches. Which of the following CANNOT be the measurements of the other two sides?

(A) 1 inch and 3 inches

(B) 2 inches and 6 inches

(C) 3 inches and 3 inches

(D) 5 inches and 7 inches

(E) 10 inches and 11 inches

12. In the figure below, $\overline{SV} \perp \overline{UT}$. Two angles in $\triangle TWV$ are 120 degrees and x degrees. What is the value of n in terms of x?

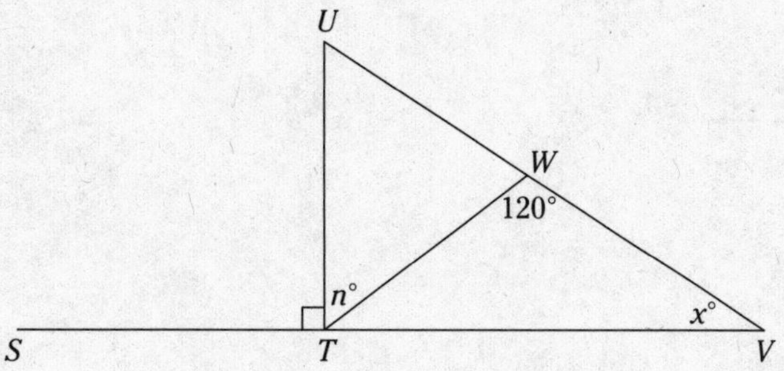

(A) x

(B) $30 + x$

(C) $30 - x$

(D) $60 + x$

(E) $90 - x$

13. In the cylinder below, the height h and the diameter d are equal. What is the volume of the cylinder in terms of d?

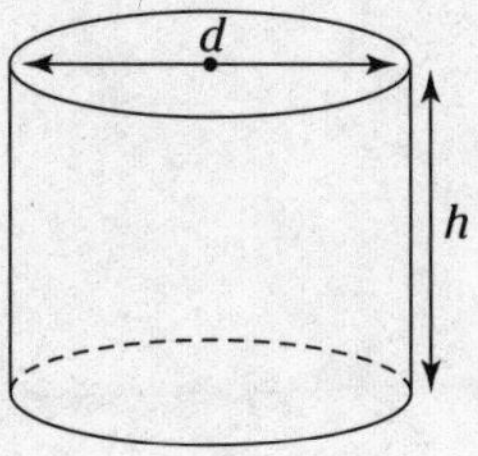

(A) $\frac{1}{2}\pi d^2$

(B) $\frac{1}{4}\pi d^2$

(C) $\frac{1}{8}\pi d^2$

(D) $\frac{1}{4}\pi d^3$

(E) $\frac{1}{8}\pi d^3$

14. In the figure below, if $x = y$, what is the value of z in terms of x?

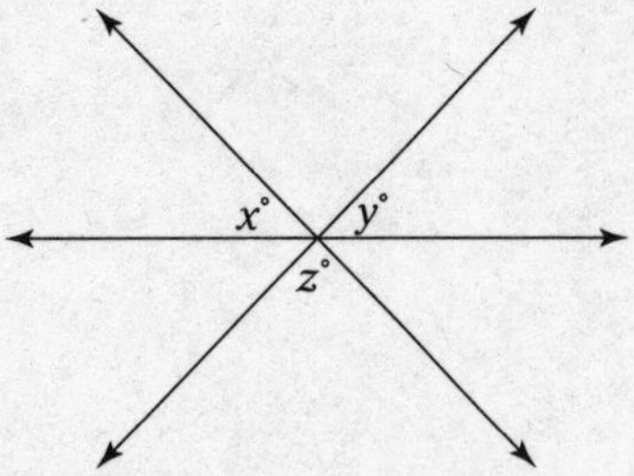

(A) $90 - x$

(B) $90 - 2x$

(C) $180 - x$

(D) $180 - 2x$

(E) It cannot be determined from the information given.

15. The figure below shows a child's building block containing the letters *A*, *B*, *C*, *D*, *E*, and *F*. Which of the following could be the same block shown from another perspective?

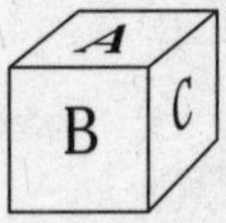

(A)
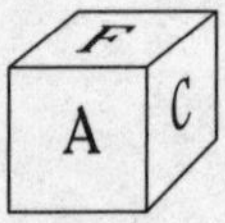

(B)
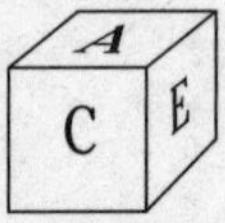

(C)
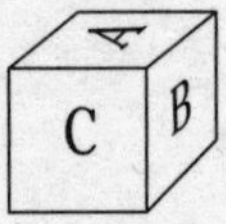

(D)
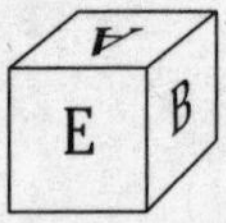

(E)
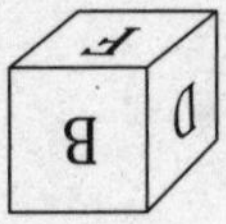

16. In the figure below, the pyramid has a height of 4. Each of the four edges that meet at N has a length of 5. What is the area of the square base?

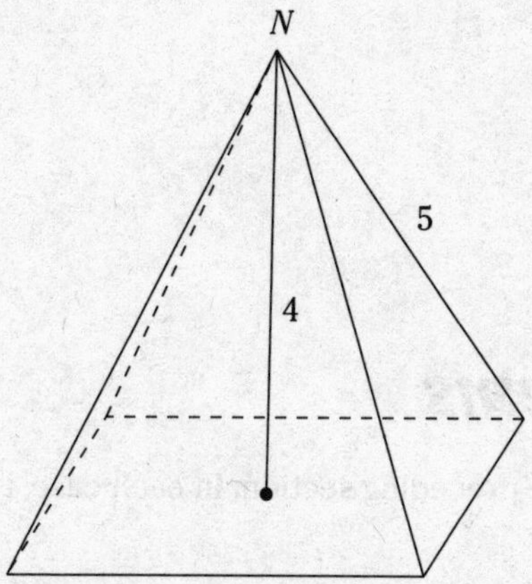

17. In the figure below, the area of $\triangle PQS$ is one-fifth of the area of $\triangle PQR$. If $PS = 4$, what is the length of $\overline{SR}$?

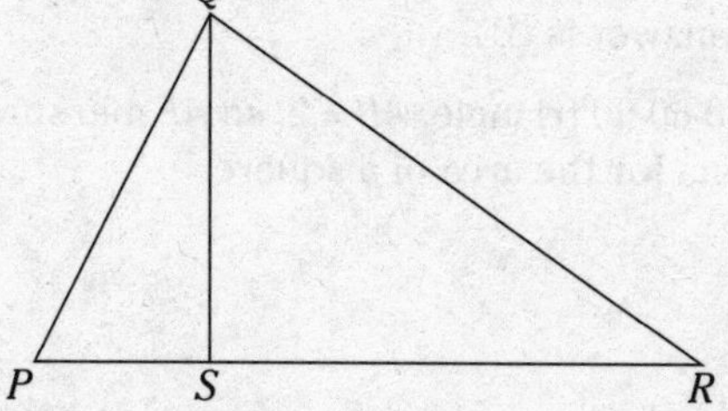

18. A rectangle has a perimeter that is six times its width. If its area is 8 square meters, what is its length in meters?

19. In the figure below, A and C are two points on the circle centered at O, and equilateral $\triangle CAO$ has a side whose length is $\sqrt{3}$. If $\overline{AB}$ is a tangent to the circle, what is the length of $\overline{AB}$?

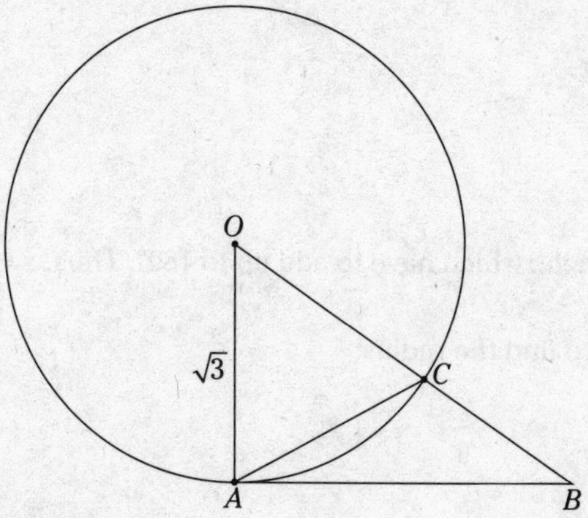

20. *PQRS* is a square with all four corners on the circle centered at *O*. If the area of the circle is 81π, what is the area of the square?

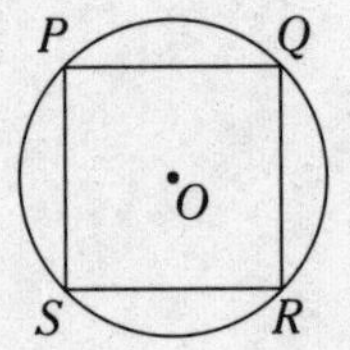

Solutions to Practice Problems

Here are the answers to the 20 questions in the preceding section. In each case, I explain how to arrive at the correct answer.

1. **B.** First use the formula for the area of a square to find the length of the side:

$$40{,}000 = s^2$$

$$200 = s$$

Thus, the diagonal of this square is the hypotenuse of a 45-45-90 triangle with a side of 200, so its length is $200\sqrt{2}$. Therefore, the right answer is (B).

2. **D.** Angle *ABF* measures 60°, so $\triangle ABF$ is a 30-60-90 triangle. $AB = 2$, so *AF* measures $\sqrt{3}$. $\overline{AF}$ is a side of the square, so use the formula for the area of a square:

$$A = s^2 = \left(\sqrt{3}\right)^2 = 3$$

Therefore, the right answer is (D).

3. **C.** To begin, fill in the supplementary angles as follows:

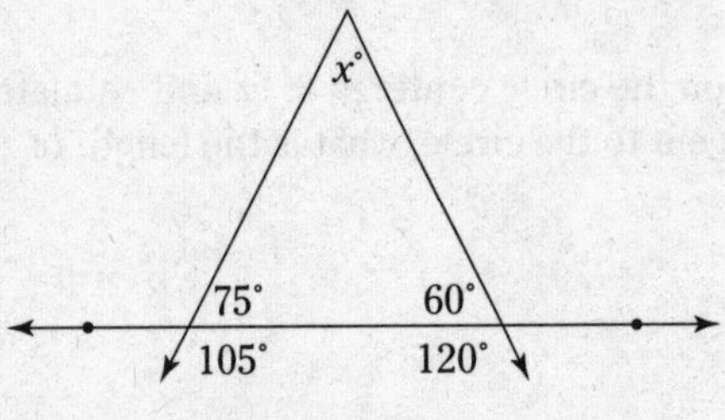

Note: Figure not drawn to scale.

Now you have three angles of a triangle, which have to add up to 180°. Thus, $x = 180 - 75 - 60 = 45$, so the right answer is (C).

4. **D.** Use the area formula for a circle to find the radius:

$$A = \pi r^2$$

$$16\pi = \pi r^2$$

$$16 = r^2$$

$$4 = r$$

The radius of the circle is 4, and this is also the side of the equilateral triangle. Thus, $AB = 4$, so the right answer is (D).

5. **D.** $AE = 3$ and $ED = 7$, so $AD = 10$; therefore, the base of the parallelogram is 10. Triangle *ABE* is a 3-4-5 right triangle, so $BE = 4$; therefore, the height of the parallelogram is 4. Use the formula for the area of a parallelogram:

$$A = bh = (4)(10) = 40$$

Thus, the right answer is (D).

6. **D.** Plug the area of the circle (36π) into the area formula for a circle to find the radius:

$$A = \pi r^2$$
$$36\pi = \pi r^2$$
$$36 = r^2$$
$$6 = r$$

Thus, the radius is 6, so the diameter of the circle is 12. This is also the width of the rectangle, so use the area formula for a rectangle to find the length:

$$A = lw$$
$$192 = l(12)$$
$$16 = l$$

AB is the length of the rectangle, so $AB = 16$ and the right answer is (D).

7. **D.** In the original figure, notice that the set of three adjacent squares and the other set of two adjacent squares look like a three-story building on the left and a two-story building on the right. When you use this feature to orient the figure, Choices (A) and (E) have the two buildings in the wrong positions. Answers (B) and (C) are lacking this feature no matter which direction you turn the page. However, rotating (D) 180° about point *P* gives you the two buildings in the correct positions, with the other two squares also aligned correctly, so this is a rotation of the original figure.

8. **D.** The triangles are similar, so corresponding sides $\overline{HI}$ and $\overline{KL}$ are in the same ratio as corresponding sides $\overline{GI}$ and $\overline{JL}$:

$$\frac{HI}{KL} = \frac{GI}{JL}$$

You know the values of three of these sides, so plug them in and let *x* equal the length of $\overline{GI}$:

$$\frac{6}{4} = \frac{x}{6}$$

You have two fractions set equal to each other, so cross-multiply and solve for *x*:

$$36 = 4x$$
$$9 = x$$

Therefore, $GI = 9$, so the right answer is (D).

9. **C.** Angle *n* and angle *p* are supplementary angles, so $p + n = 180$. Angle *m* and angle *p* are corresponding angles, so they're equal. Thus, you can substitute *m* for *p* in the preceding equation:

$$m + n = 180$$

The problem tells you that $m + 30 = n$, so substitute $m + 30$ for *n* in the equation:

$$m + (m + 30) = 180$$

Solve for m:

$$2m + 30 = 180$$

$$2m = 150$$

$$m = 75$$

Because m and p are equal, $p = 75$, so the right answer is (C).

10. **B.** Plug the volume, length, and width into the formula for the volume of a box:

$$V = lwh$$

$$10x^2 = (2x)(3x)h$$

$$10x^2 = 6x^2h$$

Divide both sides by $6x^2$:

$$\frac{10}{6} = h$$

$$\frac{5}{3} = h$$

Therefore, the right answer is (B).

11. **B.** According to the triangle inequality, the sum of the lengths of the other two sides must be greater than 3 inches. Plug in the answer choices:

Choice (A): $1 + 3 = 4$

Choice (B): $2 + 6 = 8$

Choice (C): $3 + 3 = 6$

Choice (D): $5 + 7 = 12$

Choice (E): $10 + 11 = 21$

All the answer choices check out. Similarly, the difference between the lengths of the other two sides of a triangle must be less than 3 inches.

Choice (A): $3 - 1 = 2$

Choice (B): $6 - 2 = 4$ Wrong!

Thus, the other two sides of the triangle cannot be 2 inches and 6 inches, so the right answer is (B).

12. **B.** Two angles in the lower triangle measure 120° and x°, so you can find the third angle in terms of x as follows:

$$180 - 120 - x = 60 - x$$

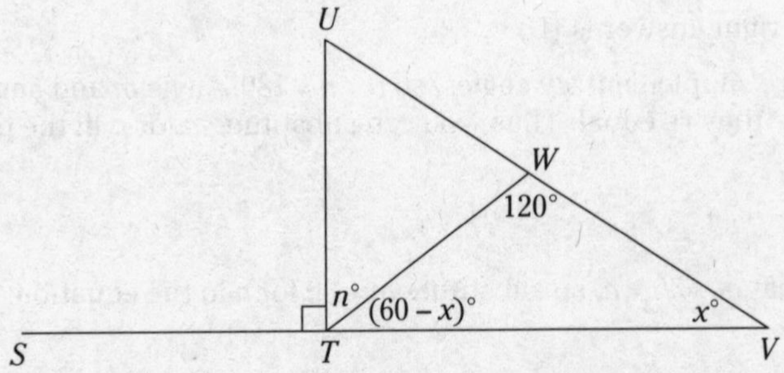

Thus, the third angle in the lower triangle measures $(60 - x)°$. This angle and angle n are complementary, so they add up to 90°:

$$n + 60 - x = 90$$

Now solve for n in terms of x:

$$n - x = 30$$
$$n = 30 + x$$

So the right answer is (B).

13. **D.** The formula for the volume of a cylinder is

$$V = \pi r^2 h$$

The problem tells you that the cylinder's height equals the diameter, and you know that the radius is half the diameter, so substitute d for h and $d/2$ for r:

$$V = \pi\left(\frac{d}{2}\right)^2 d$$
$$= \pi\frac{d^2}{2^2}d$$
$$= \pi\frac{d^3}{4}$$
$$= \frac{1}{4}\pi d^3$$

So the right answer is (D).

14. **D.** Vertical angles allow you to determine that the angle between angle y and angle z is equivalent to x. Additionally, you can substitute x for y in the figure:

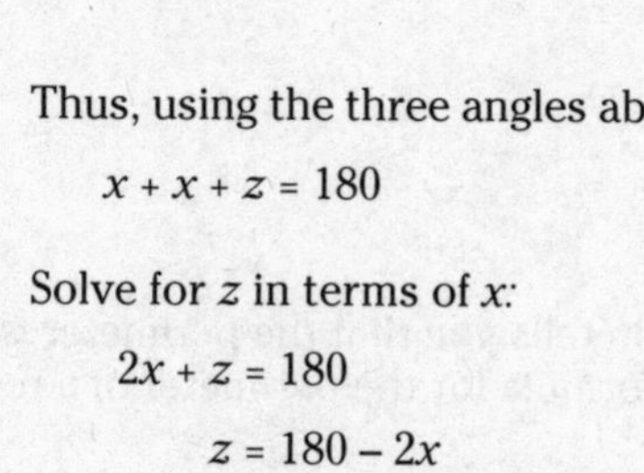

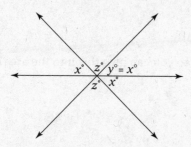

Thus, using the three angles above the horizontal line, you can set up the following equation:

$$x + x + z = 180$$

Solve for z in terms of x:

$$2x + z = 180$$
$$z = 180 - 2x$$

So the right answer is (D).

15. **E.** Answer (A) shows Side C unchanged but Side A rotated, so this is wrong. Answer (B) shows the bottom of the letter A facing the letter C, so this is wrong. Answer (C) shows the right side of the letter C facing the letter B, so this is wrong. Answer (D) shows the top of the letter B pointing toward the side rather than the bottom of the letter A, so this is wrong. Thus, the right answer is (E).

16. **18.** The height and edge of the pyramid form a 3-4-5 right triangle with $\overline{AB}$ in the following figure:

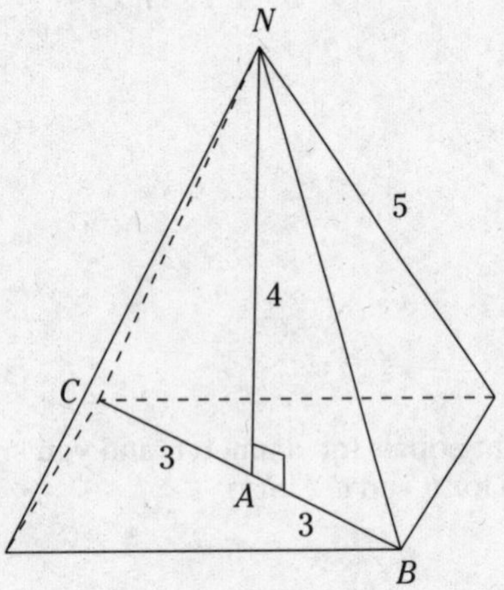

Thus, $AB = 3$, so $BC = 6$. So the side of the base is $\frac{6}{\sqrt{2}}$. Use this in the formula for the area of a square:

$$A = s^2 = \left(\frac{6}{\sqrt{2}}\right)^2 = \left(\frac{6}{\sqrt{2}}\right)\left(\frac{6}{\sqrt{2}}\right) = \frac{36}{2} = 18$$

Therefore, the area of the base is 18.

17. **16.** Let $QS = h$. Then you can calculate the area of $\triangle PQS$ in the figure in terms of h by plugging in 4 as the base:

$$\text{Area } PQS = \frac{1}{2}bh = \frac{1}{2}(4)(h) = 2h$$

The area of the $\triangle PQR$ is five times that, or $10h$, so you can plug this into the area formula to find the base of this triangle (that is, PR):

$$\text{Area } PQR = \frac{1}{2}bh$$
$$10h = \frac{1}{2}bh$$
$$10 = \frac{1}{2}b$$
$$20 = b$$

Therefore, $PR = 20$ and $PS = 4$, so $SR = 20 - 4 = 16$.

18. **4.** Let w = the width of the rectangle. The problem tells you that the perimeter is six times the width, so it's $6w$. Plug these values into the formula for the perimeter of a rectangle to find the length in terms of the width:

$$P = 2l + 2w$$
$$6w = 2l + 2w$$
$$4w = 2l$$
$$2w = l$$

The area of this rectangle is 8 square meters, so use the area formula for a rectangle and solve for w, giving you the width:

$$A = lw$$
$$8 = (2w)(w)$$
$$8 = 2w^2$$
$$4 = w^2$$
$$2 = w$$

Thus, the width is 2, but the problem asks for the length. The length equals $2w$, which is 4.

19. **3**. $\overline{AB}$ is tangent to the circle, so $\triangle BAO$ is a right triangle. Triangle CAO is equilateral, so angle AOC (which is also angle AOB) measures 60°. Therefore, $\triangle BAO$ is a 30-60-90 triangle. $AO = \sqrt{3}$, so that's the length of the short leg, x. To find the length of the long leg, multiply by $\sqrt{3}$:

$$AB = \left(\sqrt{3}\right)\left(\sqrt{3}\right) = 3$$

Thus, the right answer is 3.

20. **162**. Use the formula for the area of a circle to find the radius:

$$A = \pi r^2$$
$$81\pi = \pi r^2$$
$$81 = r^2$$
$$9 = r$$

$\overline{OP}$ is a radius and so is $\overline{OQ}$, so both are 9 units long. Triangle OPR is a 45-45-90 triangle, so $PQ = 9\sqrt{2}$.

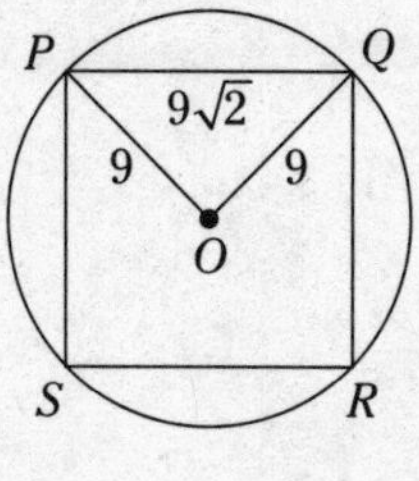

$\overline{PQ}$ is a side of the square, so use the area formula for a square:

$$A = s^2 = \left(9\sqrt{2}\right)^2 = \left(9\sqrt{2}\right)\left(9\sqrt{2}\right) = (81)(2) = 162$$

Thus, the area of the square is 162.

Chapter 6

Functions and Coordinate Geometry

In This Chapter

- Understanding mathematical functions
- Calculating the domain and the range of a function
- Plotting points and lines on the *xy*-plane
- Working with linear and quadratic functions
- Seeing how basic transformations affect a function

In this chapter, you expand your understanding of algebra to two slightly more advanced topics: functions and coordinate geometry. To start, I explain the basic concept of a mathematical *function* — essentially, a rule linking one variable to another. I show you how functions model real-world relationships between numbers. You also discover how to find the domain and range of a function — which numbers you're allowed to put in and what kinds of numbers come out.

The next topic is *coordinate geometry,* which is geometry on the *xy*-plane. I start with a discussion of plotting points and graphing lines. You use the *distance formula* to find the distance between any two points and the *midpoint formula* to find the coordinates of the midpoint between two points. From there, I discuss the *slope* of a line, which is its steepness and orientation relative to the *x*-axis. This leads naturally to a discussion of *linear functions,* which are functions that plot lines on the *xy*-plane.

Next, I discuss *quadratic functions* — functions that plot parabolas — and show you how to solve quadratic equations for *x*. I also show you how to identify the graphs of quadratic equations quickly by looking at a few basic parameters. Finally, I discuss some basic *transformations* of functions — how making slight changes to a function can affect the graph of the function in predictable ways.

The last two sections of the chapter are filled with 20 practice questions — 15 multiple-choice and 5 grid-in — and a set of solutions with detailed explanations.

Knowing How Mathematical Functions Function

A *function* is an equation that links two variables — an *input variable* (usually *x*) and an *output variable* (usually *y*) — so that any value of *x* produces no more than one value of *y*. In this section, I discuss the basics of functions.

Understanding the basic idea of a function

A function is a rule for changing one number into another. You can think of a function as a machine: You put a number (called the *input*) into the function, and the function returns a new number back to you (called the *output*):

Input → FUNCTION → Output

Functions help you build upon algebra to model real-world situations. For example, the following question shows you how to use a function to set up an algebraic equation to input a number of minutes and output a dollar amount.

Suppose your cellphone plan charges you a flat rate of 20 dollars a month plus 10 cents per minute of usage. How much do you owe in dollars if you use the phone for 690 minutes?

You can use the model of a function to find out how much the charges will be for any number of minutes. In this case, the input is the number of minutes (690). The function is the rule for turning a number of minutes into a number of dollars ($20 + $0.10 per minute). And the output is the resulting amount that you owe, in dollars. So here's what happens if you used the phone for 690 minutes last month:

Input: Number of Minutes	***Function: $20 + $0.10 per Minute***	***Output: Dollars***
690	$20 + $0.10(690)	$89

Thus, the right answer is **89**.

Solving functions with an input-output table

A useful tool for understanding functions is an *input-output table.* In this kind of table, input values for *x* are paired with output values for *y*. The table provides a way to see how *x* and *y* values change in relation to each other, and it often helps clarify patterns in these changes.

Set up an input-output table by writing in a set of *x* values that seem plausible and will be easy to work with. Then use the function to find the value of each corresponding *y* value.

The ZYX company pays its salespeople a commission of 3% of their sales. During the last pay period, Annabelle sold $8,000 in merchandise and received a commission check that was $90 greater than Bertram's. How much merchandise did Bertram sell?

This problem is a little confusing, and even with a calculator you may make a mistake. An input-output table can help sort out the information. Begin with the understanding that a commission of 3% means that for every $100 in sales, a salesperson receives $3. So for every $1,000 in sales, a salesperson receives $30. You can make a table to show the commission on every $1,000 of merchandise sold:

Input: Merchandise sold	$1,000	$2,000	$3,000	$4,000	$5,000	$6,000	$7,000	$8,000
Output: Commission	$30	$60	$90	$120	$150	$180	$210	$240

Thus, Annabelle's commission was $240 and Bertram's was $90 less, so it was $150. Therefore, Bertram sold $5,000 in merchandise, so the right answer is **5000**.

Using function notation

When you understand the basic idea of a function, the notation that mathematicians use to talk about functions makes sense:

- **Input value:** x
- **Output value:** $f(x)$ (or alternatively, $g(x)$, $h(x)$, and so forth)

A good way to think of $f(x)$ is as a separate variable such as y. So when you're given a function such as $f(x) = 3x + 4$, feel free to think of it as $y = 3x + 4$.

The notation $f(x)$ stands all on its own, so *don't* try to multiply f by x, or you'll have a big old mess on your hands.

A restaurant manager estimates that she needs seven customers to cover the cost of every employee who works the shift. Which of the following functions shows the number of customers needed as a function of employees who are hired to work a shift?

(A) $f(x) = x + 7$

(B) $f(x) = x - 7$

(C) $f(x) = 7x$

(D) $f(x) = \frac{x}{7}$

(E) $f(x) = \frac{7}{x}$

Given a number of employees hired for a shift, the manager wants to know how to calculate the number of customers she needs to break even. So in this function, the input value is the number of employees hired to work and the output value is the number of customers needed.

An input-output table can be a visual tool to answer this type of question. You can make a table easily by jotting down some simple x values such as 1 through 5. Then fill in the values for $f(x)$, adding 7 customers for each additional employee hired. Here's the result:

x = Employees hired	1	2	3	4	5
$f(x)$ = Customers needed	7	14	21	28	35

Now compare each value of x to the corresponding value of $f(x)$. In each case, x is multiplied by 7 to give you $f(x)$, so here's the function:

$$f(x) = 7x$$

Thus, the right answer is **(C).**

The big idea behind $f(x)$ notation is to create a compact system of changing input values into output values. This system works by allowing you to plug in the value of x into the notation $f(x)$ to output a new value. So in the preceding problem, you can express the five values in the table as follows:

$$f(1) = 7 \qquad f(2) = 14 \qquad f(3) = 21 \qquad f(4) = 28 \qquad f(5) = 35$$

Given the function $f(x) = 6x - 1$, what is the value of $f(2) + f(5)$?

Begin by finding the values of $f(2)$ and $f(5)$. To do this, plug the numbers 2 and 5 into the function separately and solve:

$$f(2) = 6(2) - 1 \qquad f(5) = 6(5) - 1$$
$$= 12 - 1 \qquad = 30 - 1$$
$$= 11 \qquad = 29$$

To answer the question, find the value of $f(2) + f(5)$:

$$f(2) + f(5) = 11 + 29 = 40$$

So the right answer is **40**.

Functioning within certain limits: Finding the domain and the range

Every function has both a domain and a range, which are limits placed on which values can be inputted to and outputted from functions. In this section, I discuss the domain and the range and show you how to find both for a variety of functions.

Dominating the domain

The *domain* of a function is the set of allowed input values — that is, all possible x values that don't violate any of the sacred rules of math. For the SAT, there are two such rules you need to keep in mind:

- The denominator (bottom) of a fraction cannot equal zero.
- The value inside a square root must be greater than or equal to zero.

Which of the following values is not in the domain of $f(x) = \frac{1}{2x-6}$?

(A) 0

(B) 1

(C) –1

(D) 3

(E) –3

The denominator of a fraction cannot equal zero, so $2x - 6 \neq 0$. To find the value of x that isn't part of the domain, set $2x - 6$ equal to zero and solve for x:

$$2x - 6 = 0$$

$$2x = 6$$

$$x = 3$$

Therefore, when $x = 3$, the denominator $2x - 6$ equals 0, which isn't allowed. Thus, 3 isn't in the domain of the function, so the right answer is **(D)**.

Which of the following inequalities expresses the domain of x for the function $f(x) = \sqrt{7-2x}$?

(A) $x > \frac{7}{2}$

(B) $x \geq \frac{7}{2}$

(C) $x < \frac{7}{2}$

(D) $x \leq \frac{7}{2}$

(E) None of the above

Answers on the SAT are always real numbers, so the value inside the square root $(7 - 2x)$ must always be greater than or equal to 0. Use this rule to set up an inequality:

$$7 - 2x \geq 0$$

This equation enables you to rule out two answers immediately. The ≥ sign may change to ≤, but it cannot change to > or <, so you can rule out answers (A) and (C). Now, continue by solving this inequality for x:

$$-2x \geq -7$$

Divide both sides by –2, switching the sign from ≥ to ≤, because you're dividing by a negative number (as I explain in Chapter 4):

$$x \leq \frac{7}{2}$$

Therefore, the right answer is **(D).**

Homing in on the range

The *range* of a function is the set of possible output values — that is, all possible values of $f(x)$. On SAT questions, a question about range usually focuses on functions that include absolute values and even-numbered exponents. Absolute values are never negative (as I explain in Chapter 3). Similarly, square numbers and the results of other even-numbered exponents such as x^4 and x^6 can't be negative, because multiplying any number by itself an even number of times always results in a nonnegative number. Here are some guidelines:

- Absolute values and even-numbered exponents always produce an output of zero or greater:
  - The range of $f(x) = |x|$ is $f(x) \geq 0$
  - The range of $f(x) = x^2$ is $f(x) \geq 0$
- Extra constants and coefficients *inside* absolute values and expressions raised to even-numbered exponents have no effect on the range:
  - The range of $f(x) = |2x + 1|$ is $f(x) \geq 0$
  - The range of $f(x) = (4x - 3)^2$ is $f(x) \geq 0$
- Extra constants *outside* absolute values and expressions raised to even-numbered exponents may affect the range:
  - The range of $f(x) = |x| + 1$ is $f(x) \geq 1$
  - The range of $f(x) = x^2 - 3$ is $f(x) \geq -3$

Which of the following functions have a range of $f(x) \geq 5$?

I. $f(x) = |x + 5|$

II. $f(x) = |x| + 5$

III. $f(x) = (x + 5)^2$

(A) I only

(B) II only

(C) III only

(D) I and II only

(E) I and III only

The function $f(x) = |x + 5|$ is entirely an absolute value, so its range is $f(x) \geq 0$. The function $f(x) = |x| + 5$ is an absolute value plus 5, so its minimum value is $0 + 5 = 5$; therefore, its range is $f(x) \geq 5$. The function $f(x) = (x + 5)^2$ is entirely raised to an even power, so its range is $f(x) \geq 0$. Therefore, the right answer is **(B).**

Coordinating Your Grasp of Coordinate Geometry

Coordinate geometry focuses on graphing points, lines, and other shapes on the *xy-plane*. As you can see in Figure 6-1, the *xy*-plane is basically a pair of number lines that cross at 0. The horizontal line is called the *x-axis,* and the vertical line is called the *y-axis*. The point at which they cross is called the *origin*. In this section, you get up to speed on the basics of coordinate geometry for the SAT.

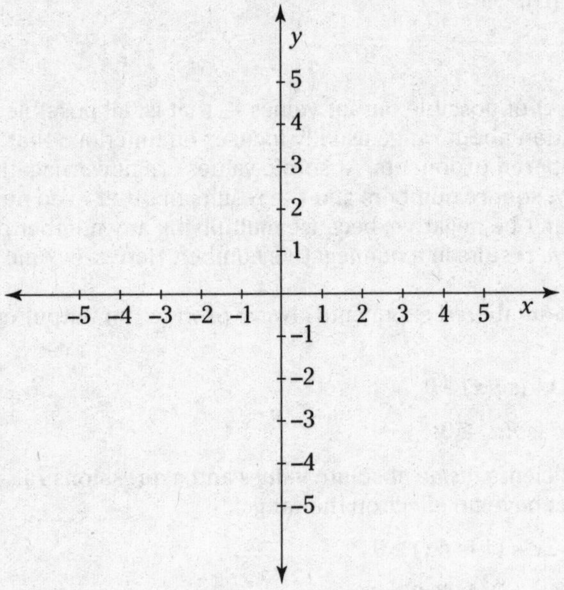

Figure 6-1: The *xy*-plane.

Getting to the point

Every point on the *xy*-plane corresponds to a different *ordered pair* of the form (*x*, *y*): a pair of numbers representing an *x* value and a *y* value. Ordered pairs are the link between points on a graph and *x* and *y* values in a function. The next example gives you practice plotting points on a graph.

EXAMPLE

JKLM is a rectangle, with *J* = (2, 2), *K* = (2, 4), and *L* = (6, 4). What are the coordinates of point *M?*

(A) (2, 6)

(B) (4, 2)

(C) (4, 6)

(D) (6, 2)

(E) (6, 6)

The information that *JKLM* is a rectangle allows you to draw conclusions about the remaining point. Drawing a graph and plotting the points is a useful step to answering the question:

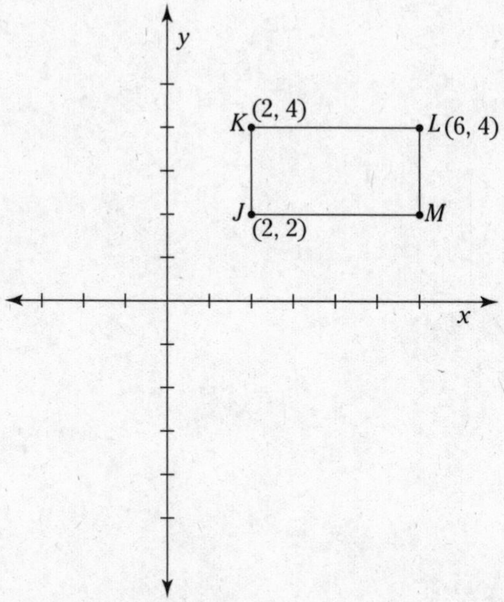

Points *J* and *K* have the same *x*-coordinate (2), so points *L* and *M* should also have the same *x*-coordinate, which is 6. Similarly, points *K* and *L* have the same *y*-coordinate (4), so points *J* and *M* should have the same *y*-coordinate, which is 2. Thus, $M = (6, 2)$, so the right answer is **(D)**.

Lining things up

In coordinate geometry, two points determine a line, and a length of a line between any two points is called a *line segment,* just as in plane geometry. In this section, I show you how to use two important formulas that apply to line segments.

The distance formula

The *distance formula* gives you the distance between any two points on a graph — in other words, it tells you the length of the line segment between any two points.

REMEMBER

The distance between any two points (x_1, y_1) and (x_2, y_2) is given by the following formula:

$$\text{Distance} = \sqrt{(x_2 - x_1)^2 + (y_2 - y_1)^2}$$

Distances are always positive.

TIP

If you have trouble remembering the distance formula, you can use the Pythagorean theorem ($a^2 + b^2 = c^2$). The distance formula is really just an adaptation of the Pythagorean theorem solved for *c*. The distance between two points is the hypotenuse of a right triangle whose legs are parallel to the *x*- and *y*-axes. One leg of the triangle is the difference between the two points' *x* values ($x_2 - x_1$), and the other leg is the difference between the *y* values ($y_2 - y_1$).

To see the connection between the distance formula and the Pythagorean theorem, look at the following figure:

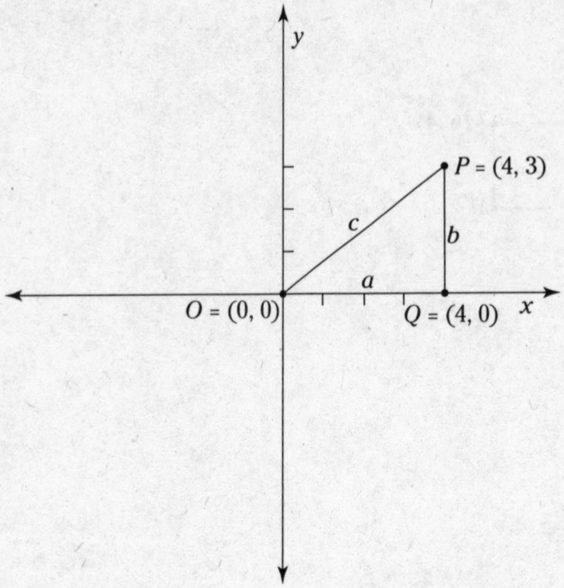

You can find the distance from O to P using the distance formula by plugging in the values (0, 0) and (4, 3):

$$\text{Distance} = \sqrt{(4-0)^2 + (3-0)^2}$$

Now simplify to find the answer:

$$= \sqrt{4^2 + 3^2} = \sqrt{16+9} = \sqrt{25} = 5$$

So the distance from O to P is 5. You can find the same result using the Pythagorean theorem, with $\overline{OP}$ as the hypotenuse (c) of the right triangle OPQ. Notice that the two legs of this triangle are of lengths $a = 4$ and $b = 3$, so

$$a^2 + b^2 = c^2$$

$$4^2 + 3^2 = c^2$$

$$16 + 9 = c^2$$

$$25 = c^2$$

$$5 = c$$

As you can see, both distance formula and the Pythagorean theorem give you the same answer.

What is the distance from (–3, 2) to (5, –4) on an *xy*-plane?

To solve this problem, use the distance formula:

$$\text{Distance} = \sqrt{(5-(-3))^2 + (-4-2)^2}$$

Now simplify:

$$= \sqrt{(8)^2 + (-6)^2}$$
$$= \sqrt{(8)(8) + (-6)(-6)}$$
$$= \sqrt{64 + 36}$$
$$= \sqrt{100}$$
$$= 10$$

So the distance between these two points is **10**.

The midpoint formula

The *midpoint formula* tells you the coordinates of the midpoint between any two points on a graph — that is, the midpoint of the line segment between those two points.

REMEMBER

The coordinates of the point directly between any two points (x_1, y_1) and (x_2, y_2) is given by the following formula:

$$\text{Midpoint} = \left(\frac{x_1 + x_2}{2}, \frac{y_1 + y_2}{2} \right)$$

TIP

The midpoint formula is an application of the formula for a mean average, which I discuss in Chapter 7. You're just finding the mean average of the x values and the mean average of the y values.

EXAMPLE

On the graph below, which of the following is the midpoint between point S and point T?

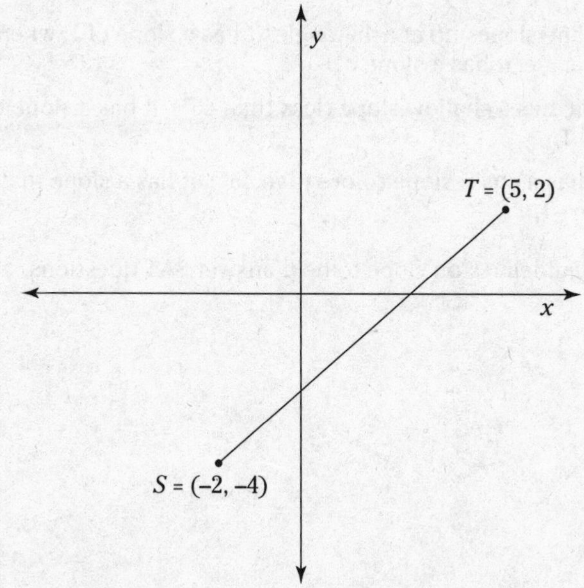

(A) $\left(\frac{1}{2}, -2\right)$

(B) $(2, -1)$

(C) $\left(\frac{3}{2}, -1\right)$

(D) $(1, -2)$

(E) $\left(\frac{3}{2}, -\frac{3}{2}\right)$

Plug the four values into the midpoint formula:

$$\text{Midpoint} = \left(\frac{-2+5}{2}, \frac{-4+2}{2}\right)$$

Then simplify:

$$= \left(\frac{3}{2}, \frac{-2}{2}\right) = \left(\frac{3}{2}, -1\right)$$

So the right answer is **(C)**.

Feeling inclined to measure slope

In coordinate geometry, every line has a *slope:* its orientation with respect to the *x*-axis. You can think of the slope of a line as its steepness as you progress from left to right — that is, forward along the *x*-axis. Here are some guidelines on the direction of slope:

- **Positive slope:** When a line goes up as you follow it from left to right, it has a positive slope.
- **Negative slope:** When a line goes down as you follow it from left to right, it has a negative slope.
- **Zero slope:** When a line is parallel to the *x*-axis, it has a slope of 0.
- **Undefined slope:** When a line is vertical, its slope is undefined.

And here are some guidelines on the steepness of slope:

- **Slope of 1 or –1:** When a line slopes up at a 45° angle, it has a slope of 1; when a line slopes down at a 45° angle, it has a slope of –1.
- **Shallow slope:** When a line has a shallow slope (less than 45°), it has a slope that's a fraction between –1 and 1.
- **Steep slope:** When a line has a steep slope (more than 45°), it has a slope that's either greater than 1 or less than –1.

You can often use these basic guidelines on slope to help answer SAT questions.

EXAMPLE

On the graph below, which of the following could be slope of the line?

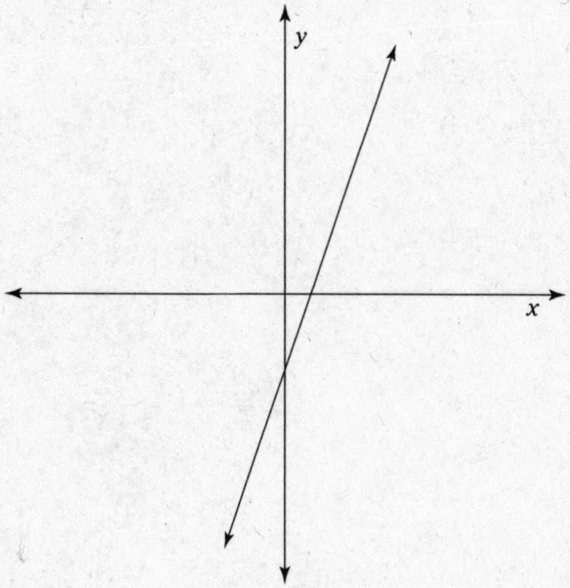

(A) 1

(B) 4

(C) –4

(D) $\frac{1}{4}$

(E) $-\frac{1}{4}$

The slope is positive, so you can rule out answers (C) and (E). The slope is steep — that is, greater than 45° — so you can rule out answers (A) and (D). Therefore, the right answer is **(B).**

Finding slope by counting off points on a graph

An SAT question may give you two points on a graph — with or without an actual picture of the graph — and require you to find the slope of the line that connects them. The slope of a line may be the result you're looking for or may be a necessary first step to finding other information.

TIP

An easy way to calculate the slope of a line is by thinking of it as *up and over* or *down and over.* For the *over* part, always move from left to right, just as you would when reading.

On the graph below, what is the slope of the line connecting point *A* and point *B*?

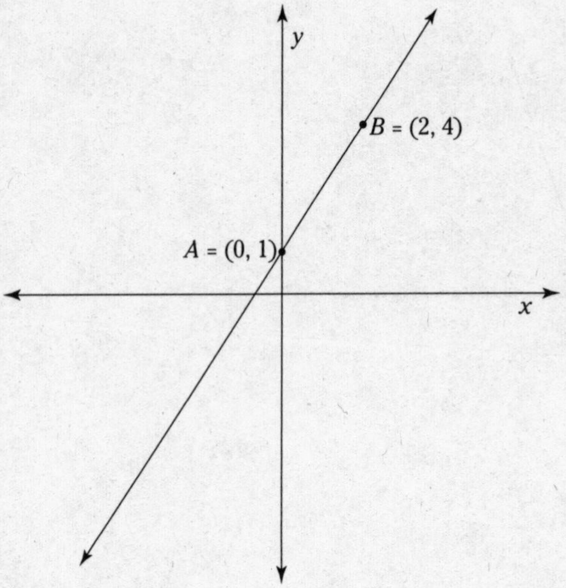

Starting at point *A*, you need to go *up 3* and *over 2* to get to point *B*. To find the slope, translate each of these words as follows:

Up	***3***	***Over***	***2***
+	3	/	2

Therefore, the slope is $+\frac{3}{2}$, which you write as **3/2** or **1.5** on the answer grid.

If the slope of the line on the graph below is *m*, which of the following is correct?

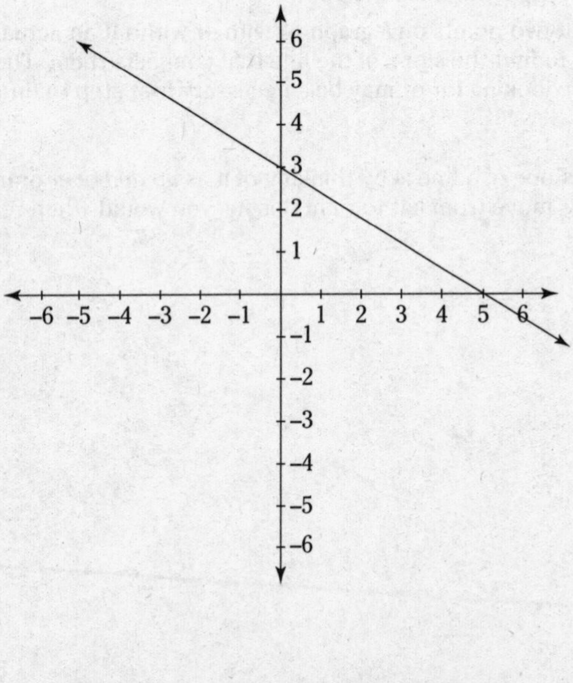

(A) $m = -0.3$

(B) $m = -0.4$

(C) $m = -0.5$

(D) $m = -0.6$

(E) $m = -0.7$

In this question, you're given only a line without the coordinates of two points. So find two convenient points on the graph where you can easily see the coordinates, such as (0, 3) and (5, 0).

From the first point, you need to go *down 3* and *over 5* to reach the second point. Translate each of these words as follows:

Down	***3***	***Over***	***5***
–	3	/	5

Thus, the slope of this line is

$$-\frac{3}{5} = -0.6$$

So the right answer is **(D)**.

Using the two-point formula for slope

Even when you don't have a graph of a line, you can still calculate the slope of a line if you know the coordinates of two points on that line — (x_1, y_1) and (x_2, y_2) — by using the following formula:

$$\text{Slope} = \frac{\text{rise}}{\text{run}} = \frac{y_2 - y_1}{x_2 - x_1}$$

What is the slope of a line passing through the points (–2, –3) and (5, –1)?

Use the formula for the slope:

$$\text{Slope} = \frac{-1-(-3)}{5-(-2)} = \frac{-1+3}{5+2} = \frac{2}{7}$$

Therefore, the right answer is **2/7**, which you can also write as **.285** (a cut-off decimal) or **.286** (rounded) on the answer grid.

Graphing Linear Functions

A linear function — the equation for a line — is any function of the following form:

$$f(x) = mx + b$$

For graphing, the $f(x)$ is usually replaced by y, so the equation becomes $y = mx + b$. In this section, I show you a variety of tools for answering SAT questions about linear functions.

The slope-intercept form

The slope-intercept form of a linear function (line) is as follows:

$$y = mx + b$$

Note that when an equation is in the slope-intercept form, the left side of the equation equals y with no coefficient. The form gets its name because from the two variables m and b:

- The variable m (the coefficient of the x term) is the slope of the line.
- The variable b (the constant term) is the *y-intercept* — the value of y where the line crosses the y-axis.

And x and y just stand for the x- and y-coordinates of various points along the line.

What are the slope and y-intercept of the equation $4x - 3y = 6$?

(A) slope = 4, y-intercept = –3

(B) slope = –3, y-intercept = 4

(C) slope = –4, y-intercept = 6

(D) slope = $\frac{4}{3}$, y-intercept = –2

(E) slope = $-\frac{4}{3}$, y-intercept = –2

To find the slope and y-intercept, use algebra to put the equation into the slope-intercept form — that is, get y alone on one side of the equation. First isolate the y term on the left side of the equation:

$$-3y = -4x + 6$$

Then divide both sides of the equation by –3:

$$y = \frac{4}{3}x - 2$$

Therefore, the slope is $\frac{4}{3}$ and the y-intercept is –2, so the right answer is **(D)**.

The point-slope form

The point-slope form of a linear function allows you to write the equation of any line given the slope m and one point (x_1, y_1) on the line. Here is the point-slope form:

$$y - y_1 = m(x - x_1)$$

A typical question using this form may give you the slope and a point and then ask you to write the equation for the line in slope-intercept form. Here's an example:

Which of the following is the equation for a line that has a slope of –2 and that includes the point (–1, 3)?

(A) $y = -2x - 3$

(B) $y = -2x - 1$

(C) $y = -2x$

(D) $y = -2x + 1$

(E) $y = -2x + 3$

In this question, (x_1, y_1) is (–1, 3). To begin, plug in the values of the slope *m* and the values of x_1 and y_1:

$$y - 3 = -2(x - (-1))$$

Next, put this equation into slope-intercept form by isolating *y* and simplifying:

$$y = -2(x - (-1)) + 3$$
$$y = -2(x + 1) + 3$$
$$y = -2x - 2 + 3$$
$$y = -2x + 1$$

So the right answer is **(D).**

REMEMBER

Parallel lines

When two lines on a graph are *parallel,* they have the same slope. You can use this fact to answer SAT questions.

EXAMPLE

What is the equation of a line that passes through the point (2, –4) and is parallel to the line whose equation is $y = -4x + 5$?

(A) $y = 4x + 4$

(B) $y = 4x - 4$

(C) $y = -4x + 4$

(D) $y = -4x - 4$

(E) $y = -\frac{1}{4}x - 4$

The line you're looking for is parallel to the line whose equation is $y = -4x + 5$, so the two lines have the same slope. Thus, the slope of the line you're looking for is –4, so you can rule out answers (A), (B), and (E).

Because you have the slope and a point on the line, you can use the point-slope form (as I show you in the preceding section):

$$y - (-4) = -4(x - 2)$$
$$y + 4 = -4x + 8$$
$$y = -4x + 4$$

Therefore, the right answer is **(C).**

REMEMBER

Perpendicular lines

Two lines are *perpendicular* when they meet at a right angle. In coordinate geometry, when two lines are perpendicular, their slopes are negative reciprocals of one another. To find the *negative reciprocal* of a number, express it as a fraction and flip it over, and then change its sign. For example,

The negative reciprocal of $\frac{2}{3}$ is $-\frac{3}{2}$.

The negative reciprocal of $-\frac{1}{4}$ is $\frac{4}{1}$, which equals 4.

The negative reciprocal of 5 (which equals $\frac{5}{1}$) is $-\frac{1}{5}$.

Here's a problem that deals with perpendicular lines on the *xy*-plane:

What is the equation of a line that passes through (0, –3) and is perpendicular to the line whose equation is $y = \frac{4}{5}x - 1$?

(A) $y = \frac{4}{5}x + 1$

(B) $y = \frac{4}{5}x - 3$

(C) $y = -\frac{4}{5}x - 3$

(D) $y = -\frac{5}{4}x - 1$

(E) $y = -\frac{5}{4}x - 3$

The line you're looking for is perpendicular to the line whose equation is $y = \frac{4}{5}x - 1$, so their slopes are negative reciprocals of each other. Thus, the slope of the line you're looking for is $-\frac{5}{4}$, so you can rule out answers (A), (B), and (C).

You could use the point-slope formula to find the equation, but there's an easier way: The point you're given is (0, –3), which is the *y*-intercept of the line. Thus, the equation is $y = -\frac{5}{4}x - 3$, so the right answer is **(E).**

Quadratic Functions

A *quadratic function* takes the following form:

$$f(x) = ax^2 + bx + c$$

The presence of the x^2 term makes this quadratic.

Quadratic functions are one of the Algebra II topics that the SAT covers. Fortunately, in their infinite mercy, the SAT folks don't test you on everything about quadratic functions that a typical Algebra II course covers. For example, the much-dreaded quadratic formula is *not* on the SAT. But you do need to know how to solve a *quadratic equation*, which is a quadratic function that's set to 0:

$$ax^2 + bx + c = 0$$

You also need to know how to graph quadratic functions, which are parabolas, on the *xy*-plane. For graphing purposes, the quadratic function takes the following form:

$$y = ax^2 + bx + c$$

In this section, I show you the basic skills you need to answer SAT questions about quadratic functions.

Solving quadratic equations

A *quadratic equation* has the following basic form:

$$ax^2 + bx + c = 0$$

Your main task when you see an equation that looks like this is almost always solving it for x. In this section, I show you how to solve every type of quadratic equation that you encounter on the SAT.

Solving easy two-term forms of quadratics

Every quadratic equation has an x^2 term. When a quadratic has an x^2 term with only one of the other terms (either bx or c), it's relatively easy to solve. The easiest is of the form

$$ax^2 + c = 0$$

It has only one variable term, so you simply isolate that term and solve for x. Check out an example:

If $4x^2 - 9 = 0$ and $x > 0$, what is the value of x^3?

Your first step in answering this question is solving the quadratic equation. To do this, just isolate the variable term:

$$4x^2 = 9$$

Next, divide both sides by 4:

$$x^2 = \frac{9}{4}$$

Now take the square root of both sides:

$$x = \sqrt{\frac{9}{4}} = \frac{\sqrt{9}}{\sqrt{4}} = \pm\frac{3}{2}$$

Notice that the answer could be positive or negative, because when you square either $\frac{3}{2}$ or $-\frac{3}{2}$, the result is $\frac{9}{4}$. However, the question specifies that x is positive. Plug this value of x into x^3:

$$\left(\frac{3}{2}\right)^3 = \left(\frac{3}{2}\right)\left(\frac{3}{2}\right)\left(\frac{3}{2}\right) = \frac{27}{8}$$

So the right answer is **27/8,** which you can also write as **3.37** (cut off) or **3.38** (rounded) on the test.

Another relatively simple form of the quadratic equation is

$$ax^2 + bx = 0$$

Here, factoring out an x is the key to solving this problem. Try an example:

Which two values of x satisfy the equation $3x^2 + 5x = 0$?

(A) 0 and $\frac{3}{5}$

(B) 0 and $-\frac{3}{5}$

(C) 0 and 1

(D) 1 and $\frac{5}{3}$

(E) 0 and $-\frac{5}{3}$

For starters, you can easily see that 0 must be one of the current values, so you can rule out Choice (D).

Because x is the greatest common factor, you can factor out an x on the left side:

$$x(3x + 5) = 0$$

Now notice that the equation is correct if either factor — x or $3x + 5$ — equals zero. So you can split this equation into two equations:

$$x = 0 \quad \text{or} \quad 3x + 5 = 0$$

The first equation verifies that $x = 0$. The second solves easily:

$$3x = -5$$

$$x = \frac{-5}{3}$$

Thus, $x = 0$ or $x = -\frac{5}{3}$, so the right answer is **(E)**.

Factoring to solve standard three-term quadratic equations

With quadratics, the main event is the bona fide three-term equation of the following form:

$$ax^2 + bx + c = 0$$

In an Algebra II class, you sometimes need the hairy quadratic formula to solve some of these equations. Fortunately, every quadratic of this type that you encounter on the SAT can be solved by factoring — that is, changing the equation into something of the following form:

$$(px + q)(rx + t) = 0$$

Then set the values inside each set of parentheses equal to zero and solve as two separate equations to get the two values for x. Check out an example:

If a and b are the two values of x that satisfies the equation $x^2 + 5x - 6 = 0$, what is the value of $a^2 + b^2$?

(A) 5

(B) –5

(C) 35

(D) 37

(E) –37

To solve this equation, you need to factor $x^2 + 5x - 6$. This is often a matter of trial and error, but on the SAT, factoring a quadratic usually isn't super-difficult. Here's how it works:

1. **Begin by setting up a pair of parentheses equal to 0.**

   $$(\quad)(\quad) = 0$$

2. **Put an x in each set of parentheses (include coefficients on the x's if your x^2 term has a coefficient other than 1 on it).**

   Because x^2 has a coefficient of 1, both x terms inside the parentheses also have coefficients of 1:

   $$(x\quad)(x\quad) = 0$$

3. **List all possible pairs of numbers that multiply to give you the *c* term, the constant.**

   Here are the factors of –6:

   1×-6 $\quad -1 \times 6$ $\quad 2 \times -3$ $\quad -2 \times 3$

4. **Look for the factors of the *c* term (from Step 3) that add to give you *b;* place these numbers in parentheses.**

   Because $x^2 + 5x - 6$, you're looking for the pair that adds up to 5:

   $-1 + 6 = 5$

   Note: If you have coefficients on your *x*'s, these factors should add to give you the *b* term *after* you multiply them by those coefficients in some combination.

   Place these numbers into the parentheses:

   $(x - 1)(x + 6) = 0$

5. **Set the contents of each set of parentheses equal to zero and solve to find two values for *x*.**

   If either factor — $(x - 1)$ or $(x + 6)$ — equals zero, the whole equation is correct. So you can split this into two equations and solve each individually:

   $x - 1 = 0$ or $x + 6 = 0$

   $x = 1$ $\quad x = -6$

Now to finish the example problem, plug these values into $a^2 + b^2$:

$$a^2 + b^2 = 1^2 + (-6)^2 = 1 + 36 = 37$$

Therefore, the right answer is 37, so the right answer is **(D).**

Graphing quadratic functions

When you graph a quadratic function, the result is a *parabola* — an open-ended bullet-nosed shape that goes on infinitely. For example, Figure 6-2 is the graph of the most basic quadratic function, $y = x^2$.

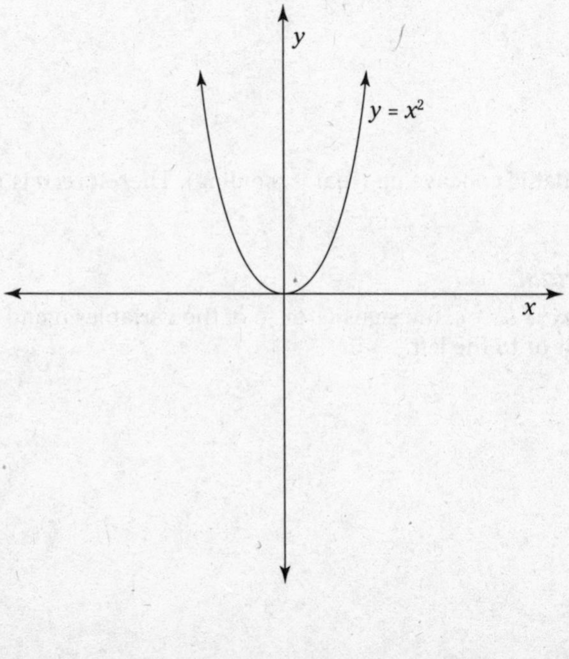

Figure 6-2: A graph of the function $y = x^2$.

Feeling happy or sad? Finding whether the parabola faces up or down

In a quadratic function $f(x) = ax^2 + bx + c$, the sign (+ or –) of the variable a governs the most important quality of the parabola:

- A positive a gives a parabola that is concave up.
- A negative a gives a parabola that is concave down.

TIP

As a memory device, remember that a positive a gives a smiling parabola, and a negative a gives a frowning parabola.

EXAMPLE

The figure below is the graph of the function $f(x) = ax^2 + bx + c$. Which of the following must be true?

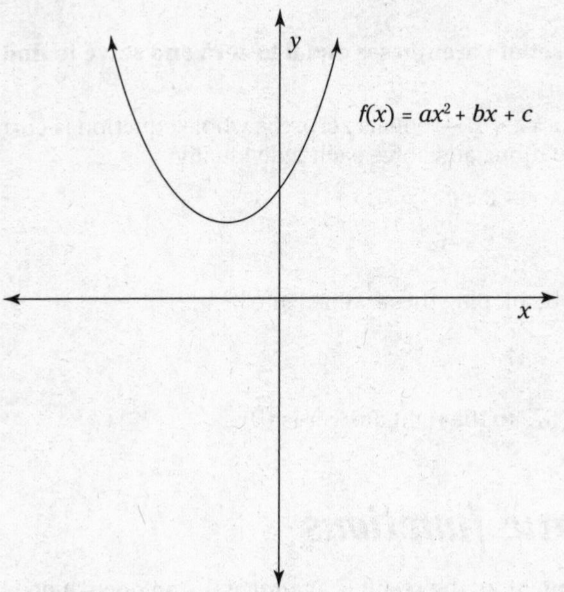

(A) $a > 0$

(B) $b < 0$

(C) $c < 0$

(D) $a < b$

(E) $a = c$

The figure shows a parabola that is concave up (that is, smiling). Therefore, a is positive, so the right answer is **(A).**

REMEMBER

Moving over: Shifts left or right

In a quadratic function $f(x) = ax^2 + bx + c$, the signs (+ or –) of the variables a and b displace the parabola either to the right or to the left:

- When a and b have the same sign, the parabola moves to the *left* (that is, in the negative direction).
- When a and b have different signs, the parabola moves to the *right* (that is, in the positive direction).

The words *same* and *left* both have four letters, reminding you that these two words are linked.

The figure below shows the graph of a function $f(x) = ax^2 + bx + c$. Which of the following could be true?

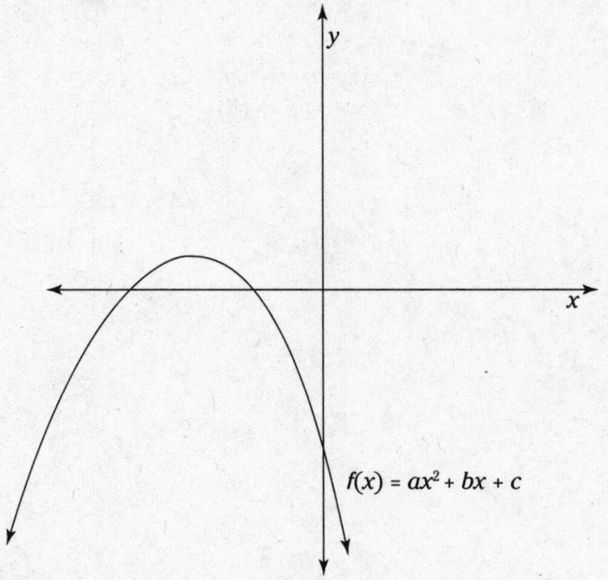

(A) $0 < a < b$

(B) $0 < b < a$

(C) $a < 0 < b$

(D) $b < 0 < a$

(E) $a < b < 0$

The parabola is concave down (that is, frowning), so a is negative. And the parabola is displaced to the left, so a and b have the same sign; therefore, b is also negative. The right answer is **(E)**.

Crossing the line: The y-intercept

In a quadratic function $f(x) = ax^2 + bx + c$, the variable c is the y-intercept, the place where the parabola crosses the y-axis.

Don't get confused between quadratic functions (where the y-intercept is c) and linear functions (where the y-intercept is b). Remember that the *constant* term is the y-intercept.

If the function f is defined by $f(x) = x^2 + bx + c$, where $b < c < 0$, which of the following could be a graph of f?

(A)

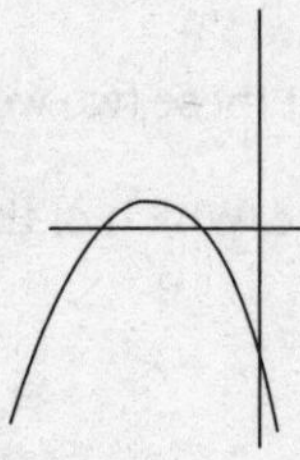

(D)

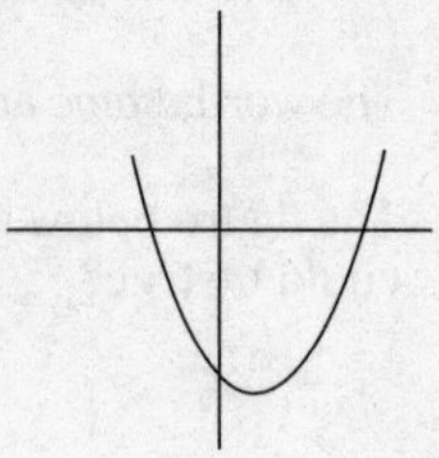

(B)

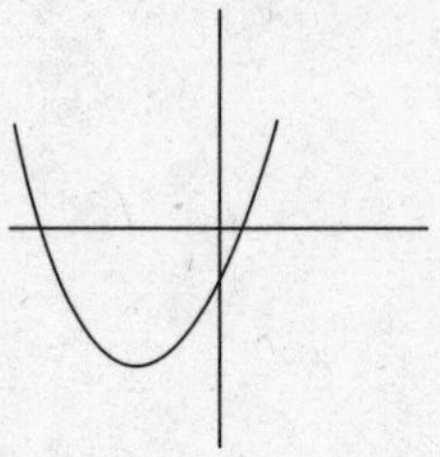

(E)

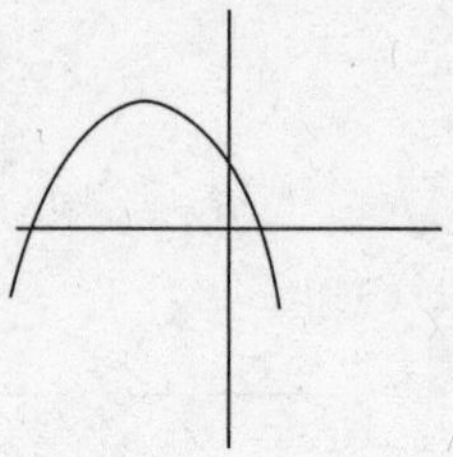

(C)

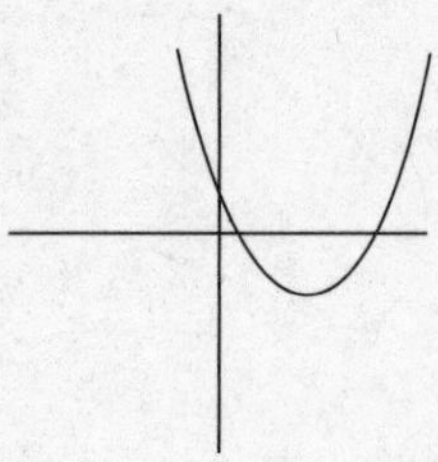

In this equation, $a = 1$, so a is positive. Thus, the graph is concave up, so you can rule out (A) and (E). The variable b is negative, so a and b have different signs. Thus, the graph is displaced to the right, so you can rule out (B). The variable c is negative, so the y-intercept is negative, so you can rule out (C). Thus, the right answer is **(D).**

Transformations: Moving and Flipping Graphs

One common SAT question asks you to identify a simple *transformation* of a function — an adjustment to the equation that causes the whole graph to move. This type of movement is usually one of two kinds:

- **Reflection:** Transformation of a function to its mirror image along either the x-axis or y-axis
- **Shift:** Displacement of a function up, down, left, or right

For each of these questions, the basic form of the function is $y = f(x)$. In this section, I show you how to handle both types of transformations.

Reflecting on reflections

The simplest type of transformation is a *reflection,* which changes a function to its mirror image. This kind of transformation can happen in one of two ways:

- **Vertical flip:** Changing $y = f(x)$ to $y = -f(x)$ reflects the function *vertically* with respect to the *x*-axis. (This happens because you're reversing signs on the *y* values, so everything at the top moves to the bottom and vice versa.)
- **Horizontal flip:** Changing $y = f(x)$ to $y = f(-x)$ reflects the function *horizontally* with respect to the *y*-axis. (This happens because you're reversing signs on the *x* values, so what was on the left goes to the right and vice versa.)

If the function $y = f(x)$ is shown below, which of the following is a graph of the function $y = f(-x)$?

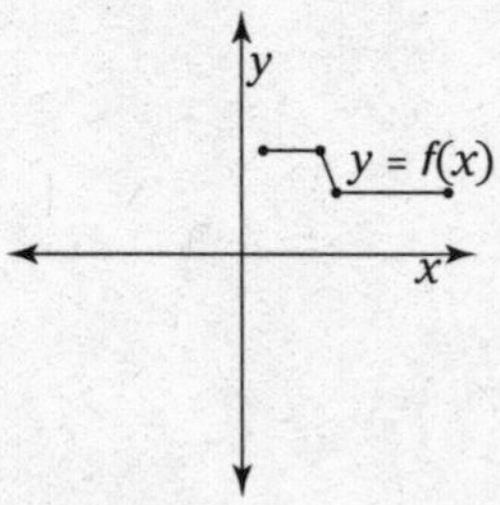

(A)

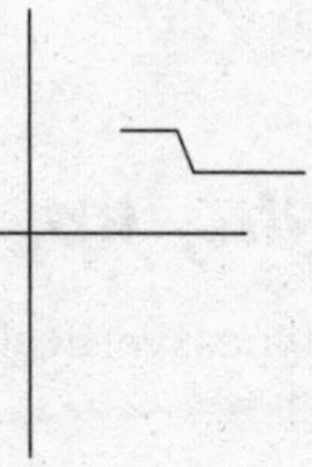

(B)

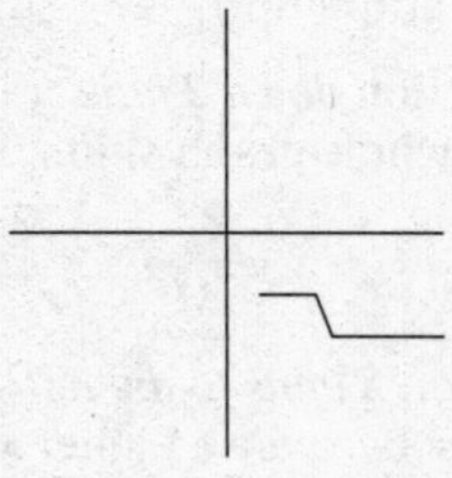

(C)

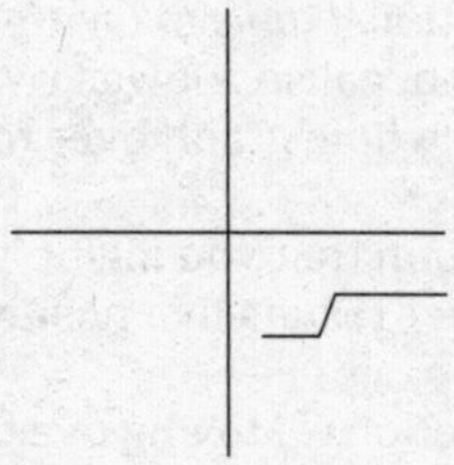

(D)

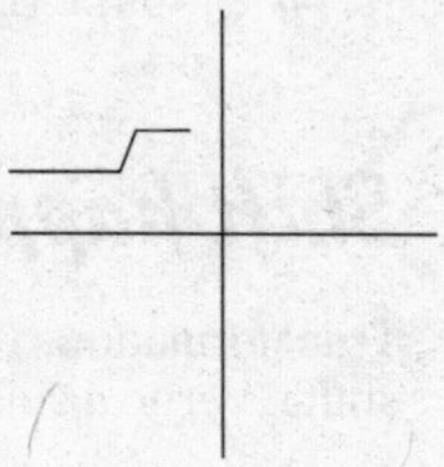

(E)

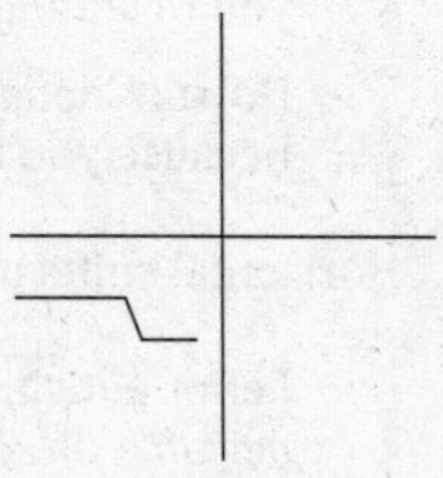

The graph of $y = f(-x)$ is a reflection of the original function horizontally across the y-axis, so the right answer is **(D).**

EXAMPLE

The graph below shows two functions, $f(x)$ and $g(x)$. Which of the following is true?

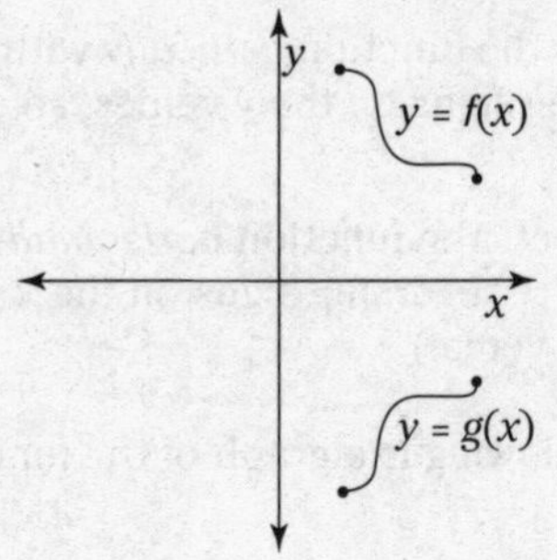

(A) $f(x) = g(x - 1)$

(B) $f(x) = g(x) + 1$

(C) $f(x) = -g(x)$

(D) $f(x) = g(-x)$

(E) $f(x) = -g(-x)$

The graphs of $f(x)$ and $g(x)$ are reflections vertically across the x-axis. So if $y = f(x)$, then $y = -g(x)$, so the right answer is **(C).**

Shift happens: Moving left, right, up, or down

REMEMBER

Transformations that shift a function are of two basic types: vertical shifts and horizontal shifts. Vertical shifts move the graph either up or down:

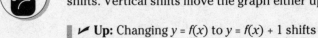

- **Up:** Changing $y = f(x)$ to $y = f(x) + 1$ shifts the function *up 1 unit.* (This happens because you're adding to the y value, which shifts the whole graph up.)
- **Down:** Changing $y = f(x)$ to $y = f(x) - 2$ shifts the function *down 2 units.* (This happens because you're subtracting from the y value, so the whole graph shifts down.)

REMEMBER

Horizontal shifts move the graph either left or right:

- **Left:** Changing $y = f(x)$ to $y = f(x + 3)$ shifts the function *3 units to the left* — that is, in the *negative* direction. (This seems weird, but it happens because a higher x value — in this case, 3 — replaces 0 on the graph, shifting the whole graph over to the left.)
- **Right:** Changing $y = f(x)$ to $y = f(x - 4)$ shifts the function *4 units to the right* — that is, in the *positive* direction. (Also weird, but this happens because a lower x value — in this case, –4 — replaces 0 on the graph, which shifts the whole graph over to the right.)

WARNING!

Note that a horizontal shift happens in the *opposite* direction that you might imagine: Adding a number causes a negative shift, and subtracting a number results in a positive shift.

For info on shifts specific to parabolas, see the earlier sections "Moving over: Shifts left or right" and "Crossing the line: The y-intercept."

Which of the following transformations shifts the function $y = f(x)$ three units down and two units to the right?

(A) $y = f(x + 2) - 3$

(B) $y = f(x - 3) + 2$

(C) $y = f(x - 2) + 3$

(D) $y = f(x + 3) - 2$

(E) $y = f(x - 2) - 3$

The transformation that shifts the function three units down is $y = f(x) - 3$. The transformation that shifts the function two units to the right (that is, in the positive direction) is $y = f(x - 2)$. Putting these two transformations together gives you $y = f(x - 2) - 3$, so the right answer is **(E)**.

Practice Problems on Functions and Coordinate Geometry

Ready for some practice on functions and coordinate geometry? Here are 20 questions — 15 multiple-choice and 5 grid-in — based on the work in this chapter. If you get stuck on a question, feel free to flip back to the section where I cover this information. You can find a complete explanation of how to find every answer in the next section.

1. What is the value of $f(6) - f(5)$ for the function $f(x) = x^2 - 1$?

(A) 1

(B) 9

(C) 10

(D) 11

(E) −11

2. Which of the following transformations of $y = f(x)$ will displace the function two units to the right and reflect it across the x-axis?

(A) $y = f(-x + 2)$

(B) $y = f(-x - 2)$

(C) $y = -f(x - 2)$

(D) $y = f(-x) + 2$

(E) $y = -f(x) + 2$

3. If $J = (1, -1)$ and $K = (-3, 2)$ are two points on an xy-plane, what is the value of the distance JK?

(A) 1

(B) 2

(C) 3

(D) 4

(E) 5

4. What is the domain of the function $f(x)=\sqrt{3-4x}$?

(A) $x>\frac{3}{4}$

(B) $x\geq\frac{3}{4}$

(C) $x\neq\frac{3}{4}$

(D) $x<\frac{3}{4}$

(E) $x\leq\frac{3}{4}$

5. If a, b, and c are all positive integers, which of the following could be the equation of the graph shown in the figure below?

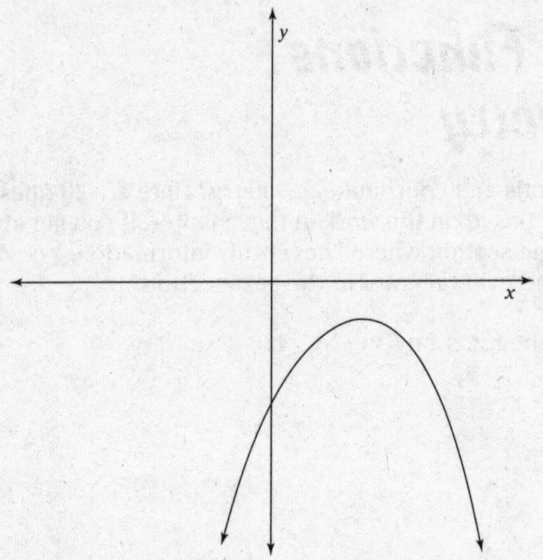

(A) $f(x) = ax^2 + bx + c$

(B) $f(x) = ax^2 - bx - c$

(C) $f(x) = -ax^2 + bx - c$

(D) $f(x) = -ax^2 - bx + c$

(E) $f(x) = -ax^2 - bx - c$

6. Which of the following functions is parallel to $f(x)=\frac{3}{4}x+2$?

I. $f(x)=\frac{3}{4}x-1$

II. $f(x)=\frac{4}{3}x+2$

III. $f(x)=-\frac{4}{3}x+2$

(A) I only

(B) II only

(C) III only

(D) I and II only

(E) II and III only

7. In the figure below, what is the midpoint of point U and point V?

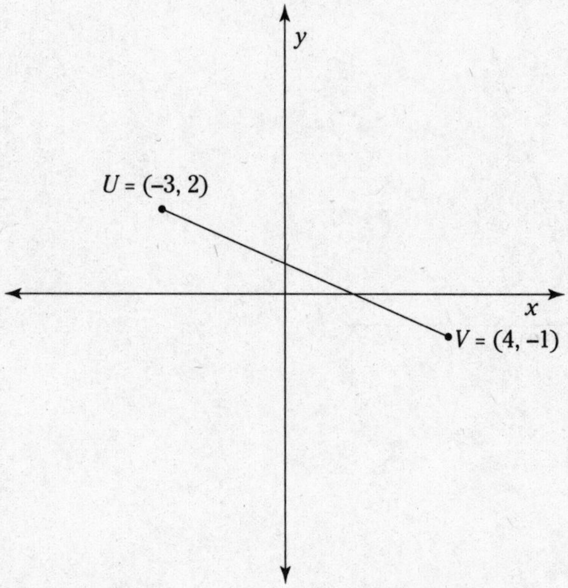

(A) $\left(1, \frac{1}{4}\right)$

(B) $\left(\frac{3}{2}, 0\right)$

(C) (0, 0)

(D) $\left(\frac{1}{2}, \frac{1}{2}\right)$

(E) $\left(\frac{1}{3}, \frac{1}{2}\right)$

8. What is the equation of a line with a slope of $-\frac{1}{3}$ that passes through the point (3, –6)?

(A) $y = -\frac{1}{3}x$

(B) $y = -\frac{1}{3}x + 1$

(C) $y = -\frac{1}{3}x - 5$

(D) $y = -\frac{1}{3}x + 6$

(E) $y = -\frac{1}{3}x + 7$

9. Which of the following could be the equation of a line that is perpendicular to the line shown in the figure below?

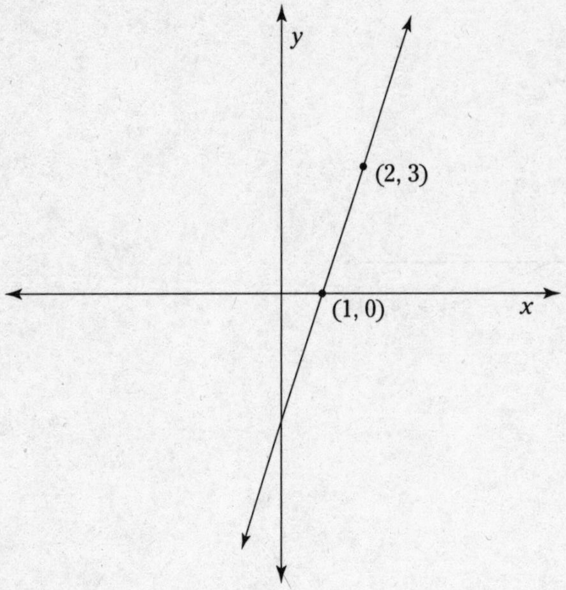

(A) $y = -3x$

(B) $y = 3x - 4$

(C) $y = \frac{1}{3}x$

(D) $y = \frac{1}{3}x + 1$

(E) $y = -\frac{1}{3}x - 1$

10. A hotel charges $100 for the first night and $80 for each additional night. Which of the following is a function that allows you to input a number of nights and output the cost in dollars?

(A) $f(x) = 80x + 100$

(B) $f(x) = 100x + 80$

(C) $f(x) = 80x + 20$

(D) $f(x) = 80(x + 1) + 100$

(E) $f(x) = 80(x - 1) + 20$

11. Which of the following functions has a range of $f(x) \geq 2$?

(A) $f(x) = |x + 2|$

(B) $f(x) = |x - 2|$

(C) $f(x) = |x| - 2$

(D) $f(x) = (x + 2)^2$

(E) $f(x) = x^2 + 2$

12. The figure below shows the graphs of $f(x)$ and $f(x + a)$. What is the value of a?

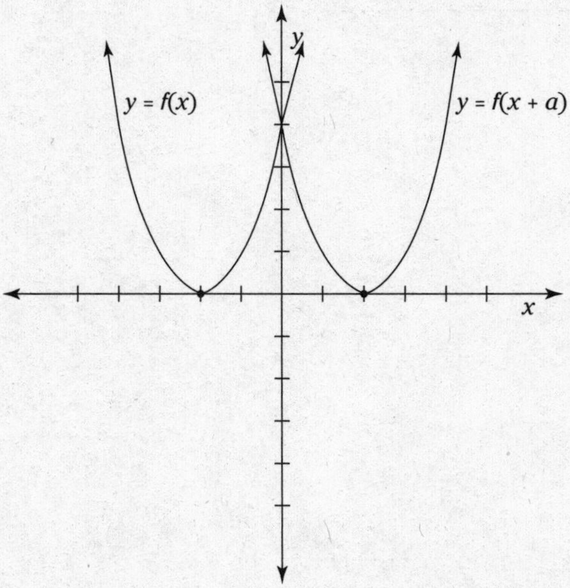

(A) 0

(B) 2

(C) –2

(D) 4

(E) –4

13. The graph below shows the function $f(x) = ax^2 + bx + c$. Which of the following CANNOT be true?

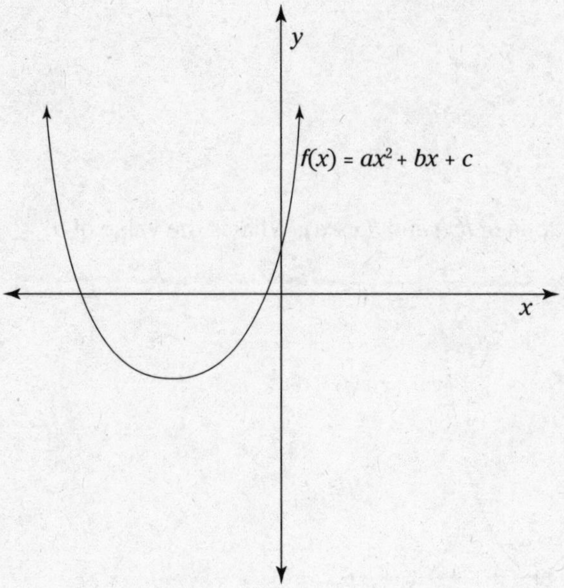

(A) $a = 1$

(B) $b = -2$

(C) $c = 3$

(D) $a < b$

(E) $a > b$

14. What is the midpoint of a line on an *xy*-plane between (–4, –3) and (2, 0)?

(A) $\left(1, -\frac{3}{2}\right)$

(B) $\left(-1, \frac{3}{2}\right)$

(C) $\left(-1, -\frac{3}{2}\right)$

(D) $\left(\frac{7}{2}, 1\right)$

(E) $\left(-\frac{7}{2}, 1\right)$

15. The figure below shows a graph of the function $y = f(x)$. If $g(x) = f(x - 1)$, which of the following could be a graph of $g(x)$?

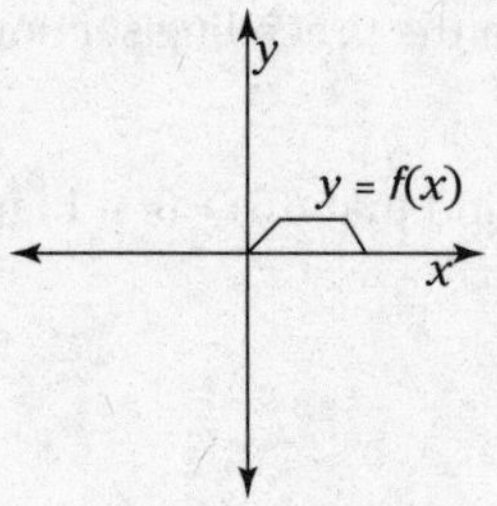

(A)

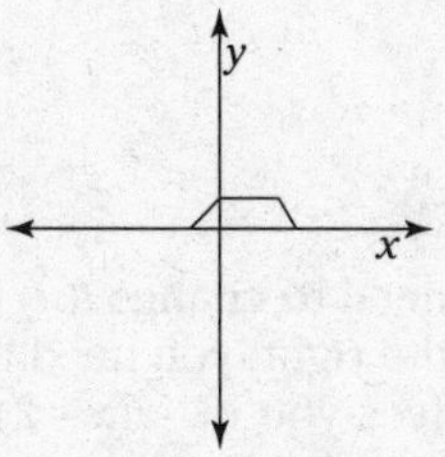

(B)

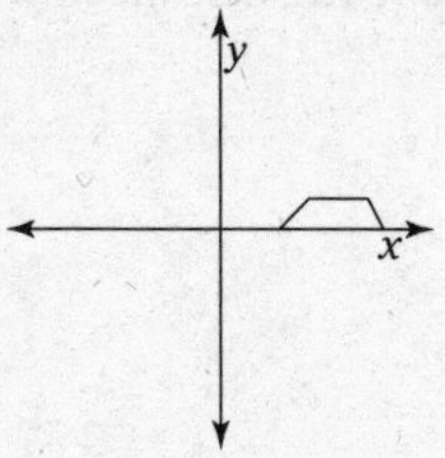

(C)

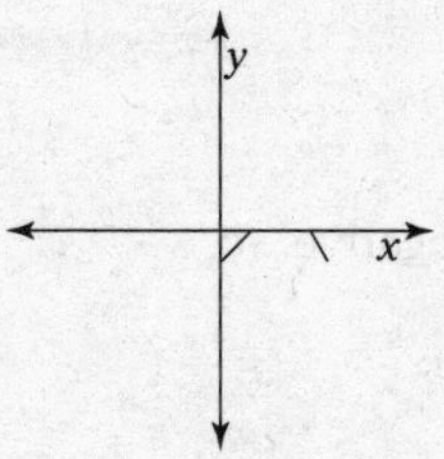

(D)

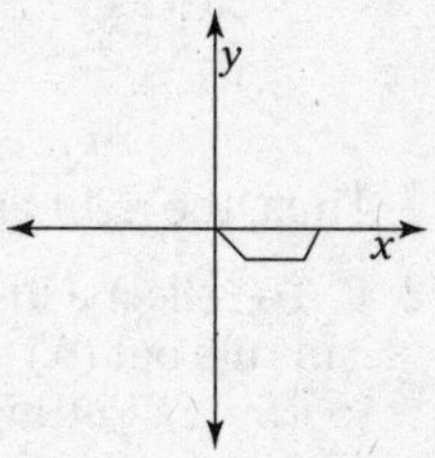

(E)

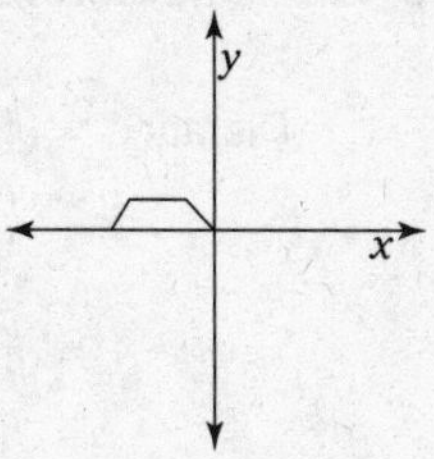

16. On the xy-plane, what is the distance from (–4, 5) to (1, –7)?

17. What value of x is excluded from the domain of $f(x) = \frac{1}{x^2 - 6x + 9}$?

18. What is the value of $f(-5)$ for the function $f(x) = 3x^2 + 5x - 10$?

19. What is the y-intercept of a line that passes through the point (2, 4) and is parallel to $y = \frac{2}{3}x + 5$?

20. What is the sum of all possible values of x for the equation $x^2 - 4x - 12 = 0$?

Solutions to Practice Problems

Here are the answers to each of the practice problems from the preceding section, complete with a detailed explanation of each.

1. **D.** For the function $f(x) = x^2 - 1$, plug in 6 and 5 for x. You find that $f(6) = 6^2 - 1$ and $f(5) = 5^2 - 1$. So calculate as follows:

   $f(6) - f(5)$

   $= (6^2 - 1) - (5^2 - 1)$

   $= (36 - 1) - (25 - 1)$

   $= 35 - 24$

   $= 11$

   Thus, the right answer is (D).

2. **C.** To reflect a function vertically across the x-axis, you need to change $f(x)$ to $-f(x)$, so you can rule out (A), (B), and (D). To displace a function to the right, you need to change $f(x)$ to $f(x - 2)$. Putting these two transformations together gives you $y = -f(x - 2)$, so the right answer is (C).

3. **E.** The question tells you that $J = (1, -1)$ and $K = (-3, 2)$. Use the distance formula:

   $$\begin{aligned}\text{Distance} &= \sqrt{(x_2 - x_1)^2 + (y_2 - y_1)^2}\\ &= \sqrt{(1-(-3))^2 + (-1-2)^2}\\ &= \sqrt{(4)^2 + (-3)^2}\\ &= \sqrt{16+9}\\ &= \sqrt{25}\\ &= 5\end{aligned}$$

   Thus, the right answer is (E).

4. **E.** The value inside the square root $(3 - 4x)$ cannot be negative, so

   $3 - 4x \geq 0$

   Subtract 3 from both sides of the equation:

   $-4x \geq -3$

   Divide both sides by -4, flipping the $\geq$ sign to $\leq$ (see Chapter 4 for details on working with inequalities):

   $$x \leq \frac{-3}{-4}$$

   $$x \leq \frac{3}{4}$$

   Thus, the right answer is (E).

5. **C.** The parabola is concave down (frowning), so a is negative. It is displaced to the right, so a and b have different signs, which makes b positive. And the y-intercept is below the x-axis, so c is negative. Thus, the right answer is (C).

6. **A.** One linear function is parallel to another only if their slopes are the same. The slope of $f(x)=\frac{3}{4}x+2$ is $\frac{3}{4}$, so only $f(x)=\frac{3}{4}x-1$ is parallel to it. Thus, the right answer is (A).

7. **D.** Use the midpoint formula for the points $U = (-3, 2)$ and $V = (4, -1)$:

$$\text{Midpoint}=\left(\frac{x_1+x_2}{2},\ \frac{y_1+y_2}{2}\right)$$
$$=\left(\frac{-3+4}{2},\ \frac{2+(-1)}{2}\right)$$
$$=\left(\frac{1}{2},\ \frac{1}{2}\right)$$

Therefore, the right answer is (D).

8. **C.** The problem asks you to find the equation of a line with a slope of $-\frac{1}{3}$ that passes through the point (3, –6). Use the point-slope form for the equation of a line:

$$y-y_1=m(x-x_1)$$
$$y-(-6)=-\frac{1}{3}(x-3)$$
$$y+6=-\frac{1}{3}x+1$$
$$y=-\frac{1}{3}x-5$$

Thus, the right answer is (C).

9. **E.** First find the line's slope. The line in the figure passes through (1, 0) and (2, 3). To move from the first point to the second, you need to go *up 3 and over 1*, so translate this as follows:

Up	***3***	***Over***	***1***
+	3	/	1

So the slope of this line is 3. Thus, the slope of any perpendicular line is the negative reciprocal of 3, which is $-\frac{1}{3}$. Therefore, the right answer is (E).

10. **C.** To help you see the pattern so you can write the function, begin by making an input-output table showing the relationship between number of nights and cost in dollars:

x = number of nights	1	2	3	4	5
$f(x)$ = cost in dollars	100	180	260	340	420

Notice that for each extra night, the dollar amount increases by $80. The only function that gives the correct output is $f(x) = 80x + 20$, so the right answer is (C).

11. **E.** When an entire function is either an absolute value or raised to an even power, its range is $f(x) \geq 0$, so you can rule out (A), (B), and (D). The function $f(x) = |x| - 2$ has a minimum value of $0 - 2 = -2$, so (C) is incorrect. Therefore, the answer is (E).

12. **E.** The graph of $f(x + a)$ is displaced four units to the right from $f(x)$. Thus, $f(x + a) = f(x - 4)$, so $a = -4$. Therefore, the right answer is (E).

13. **B.** The parabola is concave up, so $a > 0$. And the parabola is displaced to the left, so a and b have the same signs. Thus, $b > 0$, so $b \neq -2$. The right answer is (B).

14. **C.** Use the midpoint formula for the points (–4, –3) and (2, 0):

$$\begin{aligned}\text{Midpoint} &= \left(\frac{x_1+x_2}{2}, \frac{y_1+y_2}{2}\right)\\ &= \left(\frac{-4+2}{2}, \frac{-3+0}{2}\right)\\ &= \left(\frac{-2}{2}, \frac{-3}{2}\right)\\ &= \left(-1, -\frac{3}{2}\right)\end{aligned}$$

Thus, the right answer is (C).

15. **B.** The function $f(x-1)$ displaces the function $f(x)$ one unit to the right, so the right answer is (B).

16. **13.** Use the distance formula for the points (–4, 5) and (1, –7):

$$\begin{aligned}\text{Distance} &= \sqrt{(x_2-x_1)^2+(y_2-y_1)^2}\\ &= \sqrt{(-4-1)^2+(5-(-7))^2}\\ &= \sqrt{(-5)^2+12^2}\\ &= \sqrt{25+144}\\ &= \sqrt{169}\\ &= 13\end{aligned}$$

So the right answer is 13.

17. **3.** The domain of the function $f(x)=\frac{1}{x^2-6x+9}$ cannot include a value of x that results in a denominator of 0. So to find the value of x that's excluded from the domain, set the denominator equal to 0 and solve for x:

$x^2 - 6x + 9 = 0$

Solve by factoring. First put your x's in parentheses:

$(x\quad)(x\quad) = 0$

List all pairs of integers that multiply to 9:

$1 \times 9 \qquad 3 \times 3$

$-1 \times -9 \qquad -3 \times -3$

Find the pair whose sum is –6:

$-3 + -3 = 6$

Substitute this pair into the parentheses:

$(x - 3)(x - 3) = 0$

Split the equation to solve. Both parentheses include the same values, so you only have to do the math once:

$$x - 3 = 0$$
$$x = 3$$

So the right answer is 3.

18. **40.** Substitute –5 for x into the function $f(x) = 3x^2 + 5x - 10$ as follows:

$$\begin{aligned} f(-5) &= 3(-5)^2 + 5(-5) - 10 \\ &= 3(25) - 25 - 10 \\ &= 75 - 25 - 10 \\ &= 50 - 10 \\ &= 40 \end{aligned}$$

Thus, the right answer is 40.

19. **8/3** or **2.66** or **2.67**. The line you're looking for is parallel to $y = \frac{2}{3}x + 5$, so its slope is also $\frac{2}{3}$. Use the point-slope form for the equation of a line:

$$\begin{aligned} y - y_1 &= m(x - x_1) \\ y - 4 &= \frac{2}{3}(x - 2) \\ y - 4 &= \frac{2}{3}x - \frac{4}{3} \\ y &= \frac{2}{3}x - \frac{4}{3} + 4 \\ y &= \frac{2}{3}x + \frac{8}{3} \end{aligned}$$

So you can write the right answer as 8/3 or give its decimal equivalent.

20. **4**. Solve $x^2 - 4x - 12 = 0$ for x by factoring. To begin, set up the equation as follows, with your x's inside the parentheses:

$$(x \quad)(x \quad) = 0$$

Now find all pairs of numbers that multiply to the c value of –12:

$$1 \times -12 \qquad 2 \times -6 \qquad 3 \times -4$$
$$-1 \times 12 \qquad -2 \times 6 \qquad -3 \times 4$$

Add each of these pairs to find the one whose sum is the b value, 4:

$$2 + (-6) = -4$$

Thus, 2 and –6 are the two values that go into the parentheses:

$$(x + 2)(x - 6) = 0$$

Split the equation into two separate equations and solve each:

$$x + 2 = 0 \quad \text{or} \quad x - 6 = 0$$
$$x = -2 \qquad\qquad x = 6$$

So the only two values of x are –2 and 6. The sum of these values is $-2 + 6 = 4$, so this is the right answer.

Chapter 7

From the Grab Bag: A Variety of Other SAT Math Skills

In This Chapter

- Working with number sequences
- Making sense of set theory, Venn diagrams, and logic questions
- Sorting out statistical information with the arithmetic mean, median, and mode
- Predicting the future with probability
- Analyzing statistical data with tables and graphs

This chapter fills in the remaining math skills that you need to succeed on the SAT. I call this bunch of skills the "grab bag" because, quite honestly, I couldn't think of a more clever way to group them. This is math that's not really arithmetic, algebra, geometry, or coordinate geometry — that is, it's the stuff that your teachers have been slipping in for years, disguising problems as puzzles and games to take the edge off between tests. My conservative estimate is that about 15 percent of the SAT — say, eight or nine questions — focuses on this information. The good news is that these topics are relatively simple and, dare I say, fun?

I start you off with *number sequences,* which are number patterns generated by a simple mathematical rule. Next, you tackle some simple problems in set theory. I introduce some important mathematical sets that help you with questions of this type. You also discover how to work with Venn diagrams — overlapping circles that represent sets visually. I also show you how to handle logic questions, which require you to draw new conclusions from a bunch of disorganized facts.

After that, you move on to questions involving statistics and probability. I discuss the three most common types of averages: the arithmetic mean, the median, and the mode. I also show you how to solve algebra problems involving the arithmetic mean, folding in the skills from Chapter 4.

Next, I discuss problems in counting and probability. First, I show you how to answer questions about counting, which gives you a foundation for answering probability questions. You also see how to apply this type of thinking to answer certain types of geometry questions. Finally, you focus on questions involving graphs, including scatterplots and pictograms.

Lining Things Up with Sequences

A *sequence* is a list of numbers that follows a pattern. For example,

2, 4, 6, 8, 10, ...

A sequence usually has a rule for generating the next number in the sequence. After you know the rule, you can figure out what any number in the sequences will be. Often, the rule that governs a sequence of numbers is based on simple math such as addition or multiplication.

Usually, the rule is applied to one number to get the next number in the sequence. For example, the rule for the preceding sequence is *add 2* — that is, add 2 to the first number to get the second, add 2 to the second number to get the third, and so forth.

What is the tenth number in the sequence that begins 2, 5, 8, 11, 14?

In this sequence, each new number is generated by adding three to the previous number, so the rule is *add 3*. Apply this rule to continue the sequence as follows: 17, 20, 23, 26, 29. Thus, the tenth number in the sequence is **29**.

You can also use a rule to work backward and find earlier numbers in a sequence.

A sequence continues infinitely in both directions. If three numbers in this sequence, consecutively and in order, are 48, 96, and 192, which of the integers below is lowest in the sequence?

(A) 0

(B) 1

(C) 2

(D) 3

(E) 6

Examine the three numbers in this sequence and you find that each is, in turn, twice that of the previous number. So the rule is *multiply by two*. You can use this rule to generate more numbers, but to answer the question, you need to work backward from 48. To find the number just before, divide by two. So just before 48 was 24, and before that were the numbers 12, 6, and 3. But if you try to divide 3 by 2, you get 1.5, which isn't an integer. Thus, the lowest integer in the sequence is 3, so the right answer is **(D)**.

You can also use algebra to help you answer questions about sequences. To do this, assign the variable x to the first number in the sequence, and then represent the remaining numbers using x.

In a number sequence, each number is three times the previous number. The sum of five of these five numbers is 605. What is the greatest of these five numbers?

To solve this problem, let x equal the first of the five numbers. The rule tells you that the second number is three times the first, so it's $3x$. By the same rule, the third, fourth, and fifth numbers are $9x$, $27x$, and $81x$. The sum of these five numbers is 605, so

$$x + 3x + 9x + 27x + 81x = 605$$

Simplify and solve for x:

$$121x = 605$$

$$x = 5$$

The question asks for the greatest of the five numbers, which is $81x$:

$$81x = 81(5) = 405$$

Therefore, the answer is **405**.

In some cases, a more-difficult sequence may depend on a pair of alternating rules, as in this next example:

What is the next number in the sequence that begins 0, 1, 3, 4, 12, 13, 39, 40?

A quick look at this sequence shows you that pairs of numbers are sequential, so one part of the rule is *add 1*. The rule between these pairs is *multiply by 3*. Taken together, the alternating rule for generating this series is *add 1, multiply by 3*. The last two numbers given are 39 and 40, so to find the next number, multiply 40 by 3:

$40 \times 3 = 120$

Thus, the next number in the sequence is **120**.

Setting up for Success: Set Theory

A *set* is simply a collection of things. For example,

{cup, plate, spoon, fork}

Each of the four items in this set is called an *element* (or *member*) of that set. On the SAT, questions about sets usually focus on sets of numbers.

A set can be defined in words, provided the definition is clear and unambiguous, so you may have to list the elements of a set yourself. For example, if set V is "the set of all two-digit integers," then you know that

Set $V = \{10, 11, 12, \ldots, 97, 98, 99\}$

This set is too large to list all the elements, so the ellipsis (...) stands for all the integers between 12 and 96. Similarly, given that set W is "the set of integers greater than 7," then

Set $W = \{8, 9, 10, 11, 12, \ldots\}$

This set is not just large but infinite. In this case, the ellipsis stands for an infinite number of integers greater than 12.

In this section, I introduce some key information to help you answer SAT questions about sets.

Understanding union and intersection

Two important operations on sets are *union* and *intersection:*

- **Union:** The union of two sets is the set of every element in at least one of the two sets.
- **Intersection:** The intersection of two sets is the set of every element in both sets.

For example, suppose you have the following sets:

Set $A = \{1, 2, 3, 4, 5\}$
Set $B = \{2, 4, 6, 8, 10\}$

The union of sets A and B is $\{1, 2, 3, 4, 5, 6, 8, 10\}$, and the intersection of sets A and B is $\{2, 4\}$. Now check out some example problems.

If set $M = \{4, 5, 6, 7, 8, 9, 10\}$ and set $N = \{1, 4, 9, 16, 25\}$, how many elements are contained in the union of sets *M* and *N?*

(A) 2

(B) 5

(C) 7

(D) 10

(E) 12

The union of sets *M* and *N* is {1, 4, 5, 6, 7, 8, 9, 10, 16, 25}. This set contains 10 elements, so the right answer is **(D)**.

Set *Y* is the set of all positive integers less than 5, and set *Z* is the set of all integers that are both greater than 3 and less than 8. What is the intersection of sets *Y* and *Z?*

(A) {0, 1, 2, 3, 4, 5, 6, 7}

(B) {0, 1, 2, 3, 4, 5, 6, 7, 8}

(C) {1, 2, 3, 4, 5, 6, 7}

(D) {3, 4, 5}

(E) {4}

First, find out which elements are in sets *Y* and *Z:*

Set $Y = \{1, 2, 3, 4\}$

Set $Z = \{4, 5, 6, 7\}$

The intersection of sets *Y* and *Z* includes every number found in both of these sets, so the right answer is **(E)**.

Knowing a few important sets of numbers

Sometimes, questions about sets also test your understanding about numbers. Here are a few important sets of numbers that may be useful on the SAT:

- **Set of integers:** {..., –2, –1, 0, 1, 2, ...}
- **Set of positive integers:** {1, 2, 3, 4, 5, ...}
- **Set of even integers:** {..., –4, –2, 0, 2, 4, ...}
- **Set of odd integers:** {..., –5, –3, –1, 1, 3, 5, ...}
- **Set of square numbers:** {0, 1, 4, 9, 16, 25, ...}
- **Set of prime numbers:** {2, 3, 5, 7, 11, 13, ...}

Set *P* is the set of all positive odd integers, and set *Q* is the set of all one-digit numbers. If set *R* is the intersection of set *P* and set *Q*, what is the sum of all the elements in set *R?*

(A) 5

(B) 9

(C) 10

(D) 25

(E) 45

Set R is the intersection of set P and set Q, so every number in set R has all the properties of numbers in both of these sets. Thus, set R contains positive, odd, one-digit numbers, so set $R = \{1, 3, 5, 7, 9\}$. The sum of these five numbers is 25, so the right answer is **(D)**.

Intersections: Showing overlap with Venn diagrams

REMEMBER

A *Venn diagram* is a group of interlocking circles that visually represent how two or more sets are related. The following figure shows an example of a Venn diagram. Each circle represents the number of elements in a set. The area where two or more circles overlap represents the number of elements that are in both or all of these sets.

EXAMPLE

In the Venn diagram below, the number in each region indicates the number of elements in that region. How many elements are in the intersection of sets F and H?

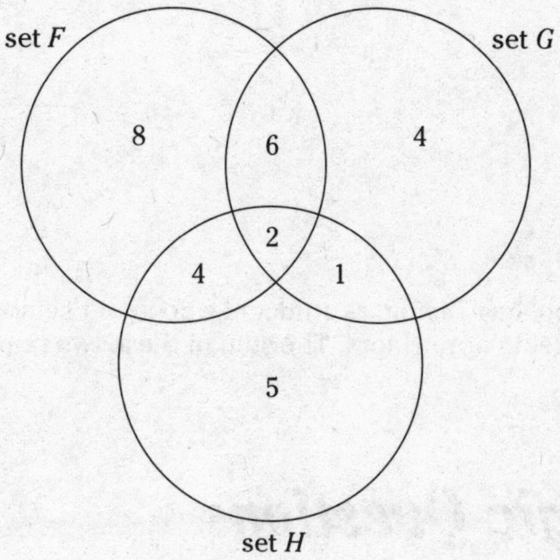

(A) 2

(B) 4

(C) 6

(D) 13

(E) 26

The intersection of sets F and H is the area shared by both of these sets. This area includes two regions, one with four elements and the other with two elements. Thus, the intersection of these two sets has six elements, so the right answer is **(C)**.

In some cases, a Venn diagram is bounded by a rectangle. A number appearing inside the rectangle but outside all the circles is the number of elements that are outside of all the sets.

EXAMPLE EXAM

The Venn diagram below provides data on all the students currently enrolled at Westphalia High School. What is the total number of students who are not seniors?

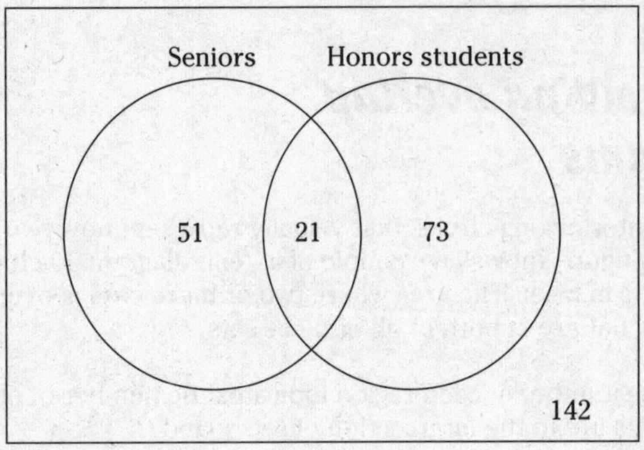

(A) 21

(B) 73

(C) 142

(D) 193

(E) 215

The diagram shows you that the school has 73 honors students who aren't seniors and 142 students who are neither honors students nor seniors. The sum of these two numbers is 215, so the right answer is **(E)**.

Thinking Logically: Logic Questions

A *logic question* provides you with a set of information and requires you to analyze it in order to make logical deductions to answer the question. Sometimes, a logic question requires you to put a set of people or items in order from first to last. In other cases, you're asked to draw a conclusion from several logical statements using words like *all* and *some*.

EXAMPLE EXAM

Four people named Irina, Jake, Kaylia, and Logan are standing in line, with no two occupying the same position. Kaylia is immediately ahead of Irina. Jake is someplace ahead of Irina and someplace behind Logan. Who is second in line?

(A) Irina

(B) Jake

(C) Kaylia

(D) Logan

(E) It cannot be determined from the information given.

To solve this type of problem, make a visual chart using the initials of the four people. Kaylia is standing directly in front of Irina, so place them together as a unit:

Front KI *Back*

Jake is standing someplace ahead of Irina, so he is also standing someplace ahead of Kaylia, because Irina and Kaylia are standing together:

Front J KI *Back*

Jake is someplace behind Logan:

Front L J KI *Back*

You can now see where all four people are standing in line. Jake is second in line, so the right answer is **(B).**

REMEMBER

Another type of logic question presents a set of logical statements. Usually, these statements focus on a set such as a group of people, giving you information about members of the group. Certain key words are important to notice:

- **All:** Refers to *every* member of the group.
- **Most:** Refers to *more than half* the members of the group, which can also mean all of the group.
- **Some:** Refers to *at least one* member of the group, which can also mean most or all of the group.
- **None:** Refers to *no members* of the group.

EXAMPLE

Some of Ms. Kessler's students have completed their essays. Most of her students have completed their math homework. All of her students have completed their astronomy labs. Which of the following statements must be true?

(A) Most of Ms. Kessler's students have completed their essays.

(B) None of Ms. Kessler's students have not completed their math homework.

(C) None of Ms. Kessler's students have completed both their essays and math homework.

(D) Some of Ms. Kessler's students have completed both their essays and math homework.

(E) Most of Ms. Kessler's students have completed both their math homework and astronomy labs.

In this question, the group is Ms. Kessler's students. You're given three statements about this group:

- Some of the group (or possibly most or all of them) have completed their essays.
- Most of the group (or possibly all of them) have completed their math homework.
- All of them have completed their astronomy labs.

The question asks you which of the five answers *must* be true. Answer (A) could be true — it's possible that most of the group completed their essays — but it also could be false, so (A) is wrong. Answer (B) could be true — it's possible that all of the group completed their math homework, so none of them failed to complete it — but it also could be false, so (B) is wrong. Answers (C) and (D) could be true — it's possible that there's no overlap between the groups that completed their essays and math homework, but it's also possible that there is overlap — (C) and (D) could also be false, so they're both wrong. The right answer is **(E)** — most of the students have completed their math homework and all of them have completed their astronomy labs, so most have completed both of these assignments.

Statistically Speaking: Understanding Averages

Statistics allow you to make mathematical sense of *data sets* — lists of numbers compiled through measuring real-world phenomena. In this section, I provide you what you need to handle SAT statistics questions.

Most of the statistics questions you face on the SAT require you to work with relatively short lists of numbers to find out key facts about them, such as the mean, the median, and the mode. You discover how to calculate a weighted mean — the mean of one or more numbers that are themselves mean averages. You also discover how to apply your algebra skills (from Chapter 4) to questions involving the mean average.

Knowing the three M's: Mean, median, and mode

The three most common types of averages all begin with the letter *m:* the mean, the median, and the mode. Each of these provides statistical information about a data set — that is, a set of numbers. In this section, I discuss these three types of averages.

Mean

The *mean* (also called the *arithmetic mean*) is the most commonly used type of average of a list of values. Compute the mean using the following formula:

$$\text{Mean} = \frac{\text{Sum of values}}{\text{Number of values}}$$

If five students score 78, 83, 89, 91, and 94 on a test, what is the average (arithmetic mean) of their scores?

(A) 87

(B) 88

(C) 89

(D) 90

(E) 91

To find the mean, add these five scores (435) and divide the sum by the number of scores (5):

$$\text{Mean} = \frac{435}{5} = 87$$

So the right answer is **(A).**

You can also use this formula in reverse to find a missing score:

Keisha and two of her friends sold magazine subscriptions. Her friends sold 14 and 19 subscriptions, and the average (arithmetic mean) of the three girls' sales was 18 subscriptions. How many subscriptions did Keisha sell?

(A) 16

(B) 17

(C) 18

(D) 19

(E) 21

In this problem, you know that the mean of the three values is 18. But you're not sure how many subscriptions Keisha sold, so call this number *k*. Plug everything you know into the formula for the mean:

$$18 = \frac{14 + 19 + k}{3}$$

Multiply both sides by 3 to simplify the equation, and then solve for *k*:

$$18(3) = 14 + 19 + k$$

$$54 = 33 + k$$

$$k = 21$$

So the right answer is **(E)**.

Median

The *median* of a list of numbers is the middle number when all the numbers are placed in order. When a list includes an even number of values, you find the median by taking the mean average of the two middle values.

If a group of salespeople sold 18, 12, 39, 16, and 11 items, what is the median number of items sold?

To answer this question, first put the five numbers in order:

11, 12, 16, 18, 39

The middle number is **16**, so this is answer.

Six students answered 21, 14, 22, 23, 25, and 19 questions right on an exam. What is the median number of questions answered correctly?

Start by putting the values in order:

14, 19, 21, 22, 23, 25

You have six values in the list, so you need to find the mean average of the third and fourth values. The two middle values are 21 and 22, so find the median by taking the mean average of these two numbers:

$$\frac{21 + 22}{2} = 21.5$$

Thus, the right answer is **21.5**, which you can also grid in as **43/2** on the test.

Mode

The *mode* of a list of values is the most frequent value in that list. A list of values may have more than one mode.

Over a series of games, nine baseball players batted in 1, 2, 5, 4, 5, 2, 3, 2, and 4 runs. What is the mode for runs batted in among these nine players?

(A) 1

(B) 2

(C) 3

(D) 4

(E) 5

The most frequent value in the list is 2, so the right answer is **(B)**.

In a recent bowling tournament, one player bowled 155, 168, and 173. A second bowled 179, 173, and 192. A third bowled 186, 145 and 181. And a fourth bowled 162, 186, and 205. Which of the following is a mode for this tournament?

I. 173

II. 176

III. 186

(A) I only

(B) II only

(C) I and II only

(D) I and III only

(E) I, II, and III

The scores 173 and 186 both appear most frequently on the list (twice each), so they're the only modes. Thus, the right answer is **(D)**.

Weighs and means: Finding weighted averages

The formula for the mean average allows you to find the mean of one data set — that is, one list of numbers. But in some cases, you may be working with more than one data set. A *weighted average* allows you to find the mean of all the values in more than one data set, using the mean value of each set.

To find a weighted average using a set of mean values, multiply each mean value by the number of items in its data set. Then add up all these totals and divide by the number of items in all the data sets. A table can help you keep track of the process.

Sondra had a mean average score of 90 after taking eight tests. She scored 100 on her next two tests. What is her mean average score for the ten tests?

(A) 92

(B) 94

(C) 95

(D) 96

(E) 97

Don't simply find the mean of 90 and 100. This answer would be 95, which is the wrong answer. These numbers aren't individual test scores but *mean* scores. You need to weight each of these scores based on the number of tests it represents. To find the answer, make a table to organize this information:

	Mean Score	×	***Number of Tests***	=	***Total***
	90		8		720
	100		2		200
Total					

Fill in the table by adding down the second and third columns:

	Mean Score	×	***Number of Tests***	=	***Total***
	90		8		720
	100		2		200
Total			**10**		**920**

To find the weighted mean average score, work backward in the bottom row by dividing the total (920) by the number of tests (10):

	Mean Score	×	***Number of Tests***	=	***Total***
	90		8		720
	100		2		200
Total	**92**		10		920

Thus, the weighted mean average is 92, so the right answer is **(A).**

Finding the mean of algebraic expressions

To answer some questions, you may need to use the formula for the mean to set up an algebraic equation. One sure sign of this type of question is that you're given the average of a set of numbers that includes a variable such as x.

If the average (arithmetic mean) of 8, $4x$, and $7x$ is 21, what is the value of x?

(A) 3

(B) 5

(C) 10.5

(D) 11

(E) 21

This question uses the arithmetic mean of three numbers, so you probably need the formula

$$\text{Mean} = \frac{\text{Sum of values}}{\text{Number of values}}$$

Plug the values you have into this formula:

$$21 = \frac{8 + 4x + 7x}{3}$$

From here, just solve the equation. Multiply both sides of the equation by 3 to remove the fraction, and then solve for x:

$$21(3) = 8 + 4x + 7x$$
$$63 = 8 + 11x$$
$$55 = 11x$$
$$x = 5$$

Therefore, **(B)** is the right answer.

Another common problem type involves the arithmetic mean of a sequence of numbers.

The average (arithmetic mean) of five numbers is 26. One of these numbers is 34, and the other four are a sequence of four consecutive odd numbers. What is the value of the greatest odd number in this sequence?

(A) 15

(B) 17

(C) 21

(D) 25

(E) 27

This question gives you mean of the five numbers (26) and the value of one of the numbers (34). Represent the other four numbers as x, $x + 2$, $x + 4$, and $x + 6$. Then plug all these values into the formula for the arithmetic mean:

$$26 = \frac{34 + x + x + 2 + x + 4 + x + 6}{5}$$

Multiply both sides by 5, and then simplify and solve for x:

$$26(5) = 34 + x + x + 2 + x + 4 + x + 6$$
$$130 = 46 + 4x$$
$$84 = 4x$$
$$x = 21$$

Therefore, 21 is the first odd number in this sequence, so the other three numbers are 23, 25, and 27. The question asks for the greatest odd number in this sequence, so the right answer is **(E)**.

Figuring the Odds: Problems in Probability

Probability is the mathematical likelihood that a given outcome will occur. Probability questions on the SAT often involve flipping a coin, rolling dice, or selecting items at random. In this section, I first show you how to solve problems in which you're required to count the number of possible outcomes of both *independent events* (events that don't affect each other) and *dependent events* (events that may affect each other). With this understanding in place, I provide the formula for probability and show you how to answer a variety of SAT questions.

Possible outcomes: Using your counting skills

A *counting problem* requires you to find the number of different *outcomes,* which are simply the ways in which two or more events can happen. An *event* in this case is simply a choice. Some SAT questions present you explicitly with a counting problem. Other questions require you to calculate probability by first counting the number of outcomes and then plugging this information into the formula for probability.

Counting outcomes of independent events

Some counting problems require you to figure out how many outcomes are possible given a group of events that are *independent* — that is, events whose results don't affect each other. To count the possible outcomes for a set of independent events, simply multiply the number of possible outcomes for each event. Consider the following example problem:

The director of a high school play wants to cast the two main characters for a production of *Romeo and Juliet.* Five boys try out for the part of Romeo and seven girls read for the part of Juliet. How many pairings of Romeo and Juliet are possible?

In this problem, an outcome is a single pairing of actors to play Romeo and Juliet. To count the number of outcomes, you need to track two different events: the casting of Romeo and the casting of Juliet. These two events are *independent* because the choice of Romeo doesn't in any way affect the choice of Juliet (mathematically, at least).

Romeo	***Juliet***	***Outcomes***
5	7	35

$$5 \times 7 = 35$$

Thus, there are **35** possible outcomes — that is, 35 different ways that the director could cast the parts of Romeo and Juliet.

Every night, Abby chooses one stuffed animal, one doll, and one pillow to sleep with. She has ten stuffed animals, eight dolls, and six pillows to choose from. How many different combinations are possible?

In this problem, an outcome is a grouping of one stuffed animal, one doll, and one pillow. To count the number of outcomes, track three independent events — choice of stuffed animal, choice of doll, and choice of pillow — and then multiply the results.

Stuffed Animals	***Dolls***	***Pillows***	***Outcomes***
10	8	6	480

$$10 \times 8 \times 6 = 480$$

Thus, there are **480** different outcomes.

Counting outcomes of dependent events

In some cases, an outcome is based on a set of dependent events — that is, events in which one choice affects the others. Calculating outcomes of dependent events can be tricky. Just as when you're working with independent events, you need to multiply the number of possible outcomes for each event. But you need to be careful that you're counting these numbers correctly. The examples that follow show you how to proceed.

James has brought four different suits to wear on the four days of a business trip, Monday through Thursday. If he wears a different suit each day, in how many different orders can he wear the four suits?

In this problem, an outcome hinges upon four events: wearing a suit on each of the four days. However, each event is *dependent* on the other events: For example, if he wears his blue suit on Monday, then he can't wear it on Tuesday.

To set up this problem, notice that he has four choices on Monday. Then on Tuesday, he has three choices left. On Wednesday, he's down to two choices. And on Thursday, he has only one option.

As in problems with independent events, after you know how many choices are available for each event, calculate the number of outcomes by multiplying:

Monday	*Tuesday*	*Wednesday*	*Thursday*	*Outcomes*
4	3	2	1	24

$$4 \times 3 \times 2 \times 1 = 24$$

Thus, there are **24** different outcomes — that is, orders in which James can wear his four suits.

For access to a security system, you need to choose a four-digit passcode. Each digit must be different, and the first digit must not be 0 or 1. How many different passcodes do you have to choose from?

In this problem, an outcome is a single passcode. To find this, you're tracking four events: the four individual digits of the code. These events are dependent, because after you choose a number, you can't choose it again. Additionally, there's a restriction on your choice of the first digit.

Set up a chart and begin by noting that you can only choose eight of the ten digits. Then, for the second digit, you have nine choices left. For the third digit, eight choices remain. Finally, for the fourth digit, you can choose among the remaining seven digits. Multiply these four numbers together to obtain the number of possible passcodes:

First Digit	*Second Digit*	*Third Digit*	*Fourth Digit*	*Possible Outcomes*
8	9	8	7	4,032

$$8 \times 9 \times 8 \times 7 = 4{,}032$$

Therefore, there are **4032** possible outcomes — that is, passcodes.

What are the odds? Calculating probability

Probability is a number representing the likelihood that an outcome will happen. When an outcome is certain, its probability is 1 (for example, the probability that 2 + 2 = 4 is 1). When an outcome is impossible, its probability is 0 (for example, the probability that 2 + 2 = 5 is 0).

Most of the time, probability falls somewhere between 0 and 1. For this reason, probability is usually expressed as a fraction, but you can also express it as a decimal or percent. Here's the formula for the probability of a given event:

$$\text{Probability} = \frac{\text{Target outcomes}}{\text{Total outcomes}}$$

In this formula, the number of *target outcomes* (or *successes*) simply means the number of ways in which the event actually happens. The number of *total events* (or *sample space*) is the total number of ways the events can happen.

If you can win a game by rolling either a 1 or a 6 on a standard six-sided die, what is the probability that you will win?

(A) $\frac{1}{6}$

(B) $\frac{1}{3}$

(C) $\frac{1}{2}$

(D) $\frac{2}{3}$

(E) $\frac{3}{4}$

In this case, there are two target outcomes — rolling a 1 and rolling a 6. And you can roll six different numbers, so the total number of outcomes is 6. Plug these numbers into the formula for probability:

$$\text{Probability} = \frac{2}{6} = \frac{1}{3}$$

Therefore, the probability that you'll win the game is $\frac{1}{3}$, so the right answer is **(B)**.

To answer some probability questions, you need to rely on some of the counting skills that I introduce earlier in "Possible outcomes: Counting on your counting skills."

Geoffrey writes the letters A, B, C, D, and E on separate slips of paper and drops them into a bag. He picks two letters at random. What is the probability that he picks two consonants?

(A) 0.1

(B) 0.2

(C) 0.3

(D) 0.4

(E) 0.5

To calculate the probability, start by calculating the total number of ways that Geoffrey can pick two letters from the bag. These are dependent events, because after he chooses a letter, he can't choose the same letter again. So for his first pick, he has five choices, and for his second pick, he has four choices:

First Pick	***Second Pick***	***Total Outcomes***
5	4	20

$5 \times 4 = 20$

So the total number of outcomes is 20.

Now calculate the number of ways in which he can pick two consonants. For his first pick, he has three choices — B, C, or D. For his second pick, one of these three letters has been removed from the bag, so he only has two choices:

First Pick	***Second Pick***	***Target Outcomes***
3	2	6

$3 \times 2 = 6$

There are six different target outcomes. Now plug these numbers into the formula:

$$\text{Probability} = \frac{6}{20} = \frac{3}{10} = 0.3$$

Thus, the right answer is **(C)**.

On target: Visualizing geometric probability

Geometric probability problems test your skill at solving both probability problems and area-measurement problems. Here's the formula for finding geometric probability:

$$\text{Geometric probability} = \frac{\text{Target area}}{\text{Total area}}$$

The figure below contains a circle inscribed in a square whose side has a length of 6. If a point in this figure is chosen at random, what is the probability that this point will lie in the shaded region?

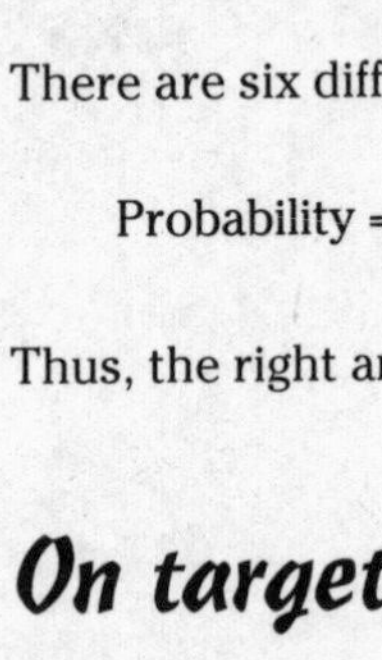

(A) 1

(B) $\frac{\pi}{4}$

(C) $\frac{4}{\pi}$

(D) $1-\frac{\pi}{4}$

(E) $\frac{4}{\pi}-1$

To set up the problem, first decide what the target area and total area mean in this problem:

- Target area = Area of square – Area of circle
- Total area = Area of square

So you can calculate the geometric probability for this problem as follows:

$$\text{Geometric probability} = \frac{\text{Area of square} - \text{Area of circle}}{\text{Area of square}}$$

Now calculate these two values (I introduce area formulas in Chapter 5). The area of the square is easier:

$$A_{\text{square}} = s^2 = 6^2 = 36$$

To calculate the area of the circle, you need to find out its radius. Note that the diameter of the circle is equal to the side of the square, so this circle has a diameter of 6. The diameter is twice the radius, so the circle has a radius of 3. Plug this value into the area formula for a circle:

$$A_{\text{circle}} = \pi r^2 = \pi(3^2) = 9\pi$$

Now plug these two values into the geometric-probability formula:

$$\text{Geometric probability} = \frac{36 - 9\pi}{36}$$

Solve using algebra:

$$= \frac{36}{36} - \frac{9\pi}{36} = 1 - \frac{9\pi}{36} = 1 - \frac{\pi}{4}$$

So the right answer is **(D)**.

Seeing Is Believing: Interpreting Data from Graphs

Tables and graphs provide visual representations of complex data that would otherwise be awkward to present. In this section, I show you how to answer SAT questions that require you to interpret data from graphs. I also show you how to merge information from more than one table or graph.

A variety of graphs exist for organizing data. Each type of graph has a slightly different function and is more or less useful for different types of data. In this section, I introduce you to five types of graphs that commonly appear on the SAT. For each type, I show you how to answer one or more typical questions.

Raising the bar with a bar graph

A *bar graph* shows comparative data, providing a visual representation of how separate values compare to one another. Both of the following questions refer to this bar graph:

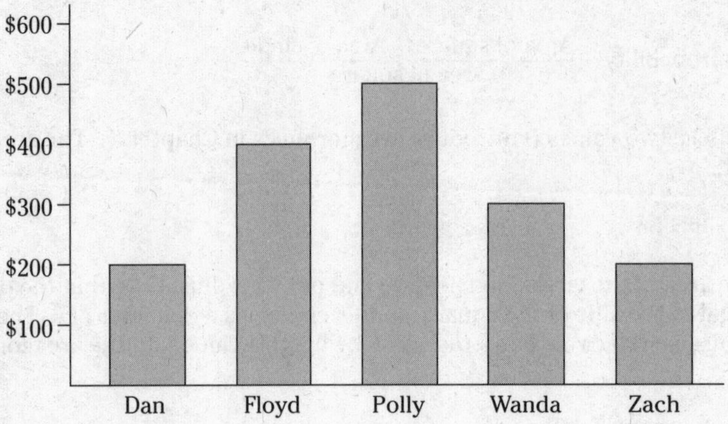

The bar graph shows the amounts of money that five fund-raisers collected in a single day. What is the total amount of money brought in by the five fund-raisers?

(A) $500

(B) $1,100

(C) $1,400

(D) $1,600

(E) $2,000

To find the answer, read the graph and add up the amount of money that each person brought in:

$200 + $400 + $500 + $300 + $200 = $1,600

So the right answer is **(D)**.

According to the bar graph, how much more money did Polly collect than Wanda?

(A) $100

(B) $200

(C) $300

(D) $400

(E) $500

Polly collected $500 and Wanda collected $300, so Polly collected $200 more than Wanda; therefore, the right answer is **(B)**.

Picturing data with a pictogram

A pictogram is very similar to a bar graph. The main difference is that data is presented as a sequence of icons, each of which has a discrete meaning.

The graph below shows the number of new houses built in Chester County during the first six months of the year. In which month were exactly seven new houses built?

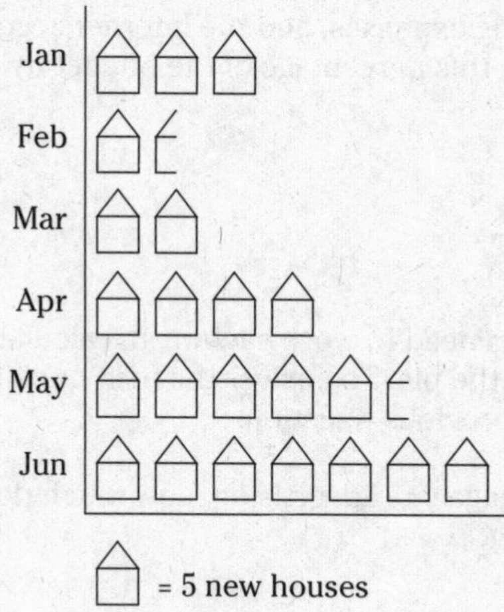

(A) February

(B) March

(C) April

(D) May

(E) June

In this graph, each icon stands for five houses, so seven houses is represented by one icon plus part of another. Therefore, seven houses were built in February, so the right answer is **(A)**.

Getting a slice of the pie chart

A *pie chart* shows a distribution of resources as a percentage of the total. To answer most questions that include a pie chart, you need to know how to work with percents (as I show you in Chapter 3). The next two example questions refer to the following pie chart:

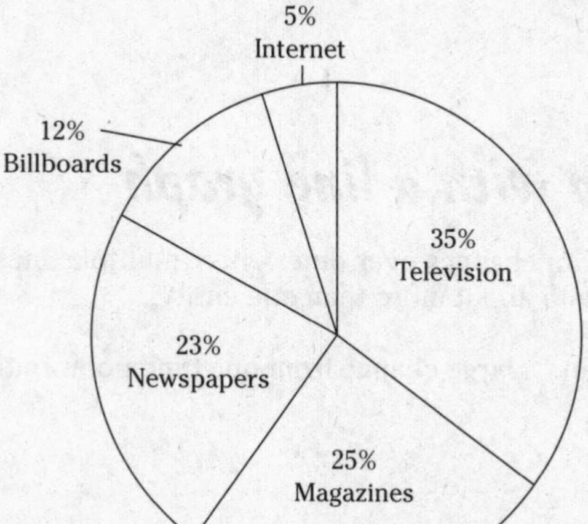

Advertising Expenses for East Coast Home Siding

The pie chart shows how the East Coast Home Siding Company allocates its advertising budget. If the company has a \$20,000 advertising budget, how much money, in dollars, does it spend in total on television and Internet advertising?

Television accounts for 35% of the advertising expenses, and the Internet accounts for 5%, so together these account for 40%. Calculate this percentage of the budget by changing the percent to a decimal and multiplying:

$$40\% \text{ of } 20{,}000 = 0.4(20{,}000) = 8{,}000$$

Therefore, the right answer is **8000**.

To answer a pie-chart question, you may also need to work backward, calculating the total expenses based the value of a single slice of the pie. To answer the next question, use the same graph but ignore the results from the previous question.

If the company spends a total of \$6,000 on magazine advertising, how much does it spend in total on billboard and newspaper advertising?

(A) \$5,250

(B) \$6,000

(C) \$8,000

(D) \$8,400

(E) \$10,500

According to the graph, the company spends 25% of its budget on magazine ads. This amount is \$6,000, so figure out the total advertising budget:

$$25\% \text{ of } ? = \$6{,}000$$

Convert this to an algebraic equation and solve:

$$0.25x = 6{,}000$$
$$x = \$24{,}000$$

So the total advertising budget is \$24,000. Now use this information to calculate how much is spent on billboards (12%) and newspaper advertising (23%) altogether:

$$35\% \text{ of } \$24{,}000 = 0.35(24{,}000) = 8{,}400$$

So the right answer is **(D)**.

Lining up information with a line graph

A *line graph* shows how information data changes over time. Often, multiple lines placed on a single graph allow you to compare data about more than one entity.

On a line graph, a steep slope represents a large change from one time point to the next.

Use the following line graph for the next two example questions:

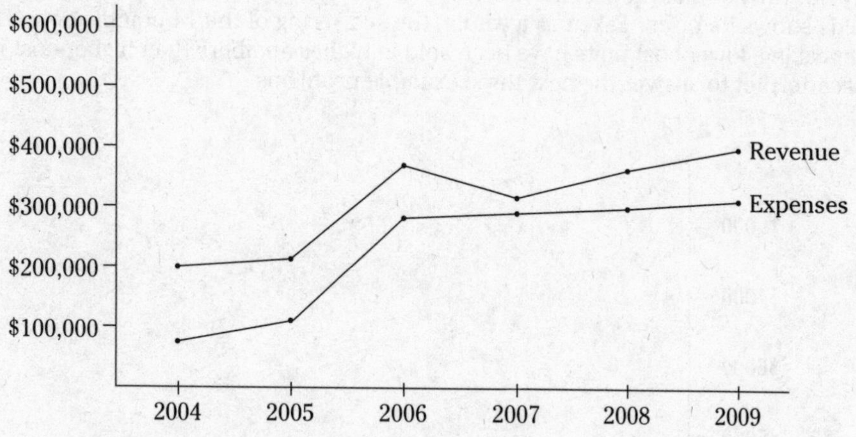

The line graph shows the revenue and expenses for Filterfresh Coffee Exporters from 2004 to 2009. Between which two years did revenue show the greatest increase?

(A) 2004 and 2005

(B) 2005 and 2006

(C) 2006 and 2007

(D) 2007 and 2008

(E) 2008 and 2009

Increase is measured on a line graph by slope; a large slope indicates a large increase. Therefore, the greatest increase in revenue occurred from 2005 to 2006, so the right answer is **(B)**.

According to the line graph, if profit margin is measured by subtracting expenses from revenue, which year showed the smallest profit margin?

(A) 2005

(B) 2006

(C) 2007

(D) 2008

(E) 2009

A small profit margin means a small difference between revenue and expenses. The smallest such difference occurred in 2007 — where the lines are closest together — so the right answer is **(C)**.

Unscattering data with a scatterplot

A *scatterplot* gives a visual representation of how data falls along two axes — for example, the price of an item and number of unit sales for that item. Scatterplots are useful for making comparisons between two different sets of data.

For example, the following graph provides information on 14 different models of hot tubs. Each dot represents a different model. A dot's position along the horizontal axis shows how many hot tubs of that model have been sold so far this year. A dot's position along the vertical axis shows its price. Taken as a whole, the scattering of the 14 points shows that, generally speaking, lower-cost units have been sold in higher numbers than higher-cost units. Use this scatterplot to answer the next three example problems.

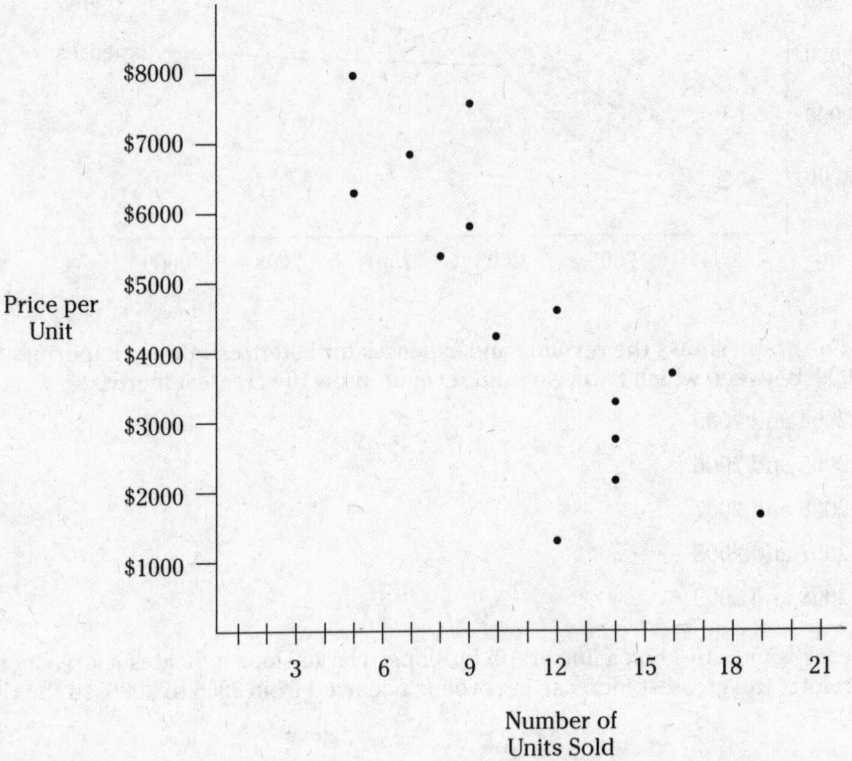

The scatterplot provides year-to-date data from the Hot Spas Company, comparing the price and sales on 14 different models of hot tubs. What is the approximate cost for the model of hot tub that has sold the most units so far this year?

(A) $1,800

(B) $4,000

(C) $5,000

(D) $7,500

(E) $8,000

According to the scatterplot, the best-selling hot tub has sold 19 units so far this year. It sells for about $1,800, so the right answer is **(A)**.

In the scatterplot, what is the approximate difference in cost between the highest- and lowest-priced models of hot tubs?

(A) $6,000

(B) $6,800

(C) $7,300

(D) $8,000

(E) $9,200

The graph shows that the cost of the highest-priced hot tub is about $8,000 and the lowest priced hot tub sells for about $1,200: $8,000 – $1,200 = $6,800. Therefore, the right answer is **(B)**.

Among the 14 different models of hot tubs shown in the scatterplot, what is the approximate median price of a hot tub?

(A) $3,500

(B) $4,400

(C) $4,900

(D) $5,300

(E) $6,000

The median price falls in the middle of the range of prices. The two models in the middle of the range, represented by the two dots halfway down the graph, sell for approximately $4,200 and $4,600. The median falls directly between these two numbers, so it's $4,400; therefore, the right answer is **(B)**.

Practice Problems for Grab-Bag Skills

Ready for some practice? Here are 20 problems designed to test your understanding of the topics covered in this chapter. The first 15 are multiple-choice questions, and the last five are grid-in questions. If you get stuck on a problem, flip back to the info earlier in the chapter. You can turn to the next section for a complete explanation of how you can answer each question.

1. If the average of x, $9x$, $10x$, and $12x$ is 64, what is the value of x?

   (A) 4

   (B) 6

   (C) 8

   (D) 9

   (E) 16

2. Set F is the set of all positive integers less than 100, and set G is the set of all square numbers. If set H is the intersection of sets F and G, what is the number of elements in set H?

   (A) 9

   (B) 10

   (C) 11

   (D) 19

   (E) 99

3. In the Venn diagram below, the number in each region indicates the number of elements in that region. How many elements are in the union of sets K and L?

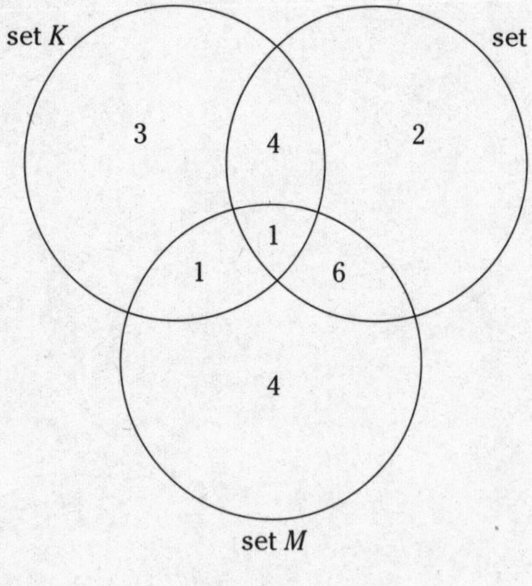

   (A) 4

   (B) 5

   (C) 9

   (D) 17

   (E) 21

4. What is the difference between the median and the mode in the following list of values: 4, 9, 12, 12, 12, 18, 23, 23, 31, and 40?

(A) 0

(B) 3

(C) 6

(D) 8

(E) 15

5. Five people are standing in line, from first to fifth, with no two people standing together. Max is standing immediately ahead of Oliver. Oliver is standing someplace ahead of Petra. Petra is standing immediately behind Quentin. Norma is standing someplace between Oliver and Quentin. Who is third in line?

(A) Max

(B) Norma

(C) Oliver

(D) Petra

(E) Quentin

6. If you flip five coins, what is the probability that exactly two of them will come up heads?

(A) $\frac{1}{2}$

(B) $\frac{1}{4}$

(C) $\frac{2}{5}$

(D) $\frac{5}{8}$

(E) $\frac{5}{16}$

7. The graph below shows average daily high and low temperature in a Midwestern city for each of the 12 months of the year. Between which pair of consecutive months is there the greatest rise in the average low temperature?

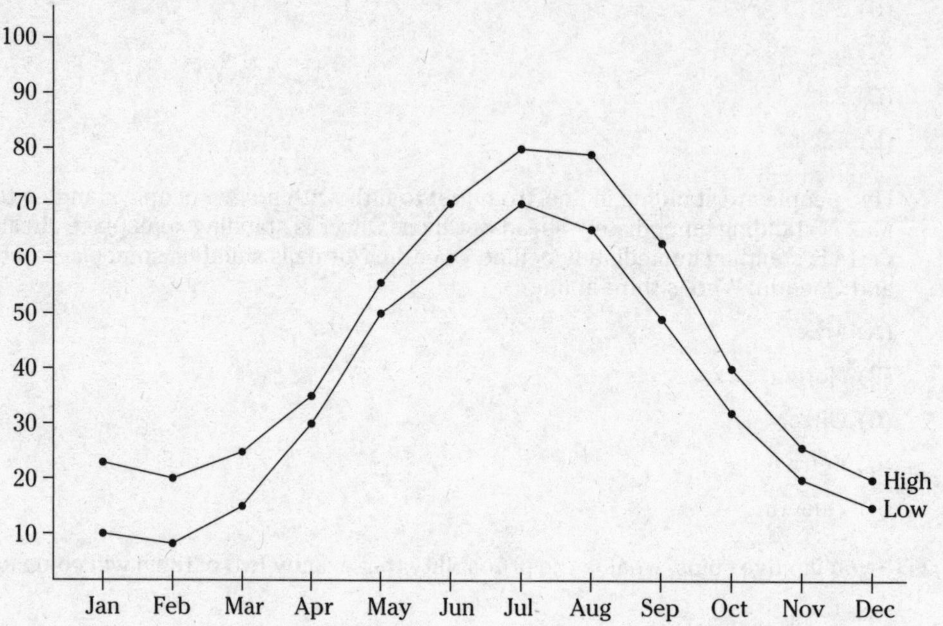

(A) January to February

(B) February to March

(C) April to May

(D) June to July

(E) September to October

8. The first number in a sequence is –4, and every subsequent number is obtained by multiplying the previous number by –3. What are the fourth and fifth numbers in the sequence?

(A) –108 and 324

(B) 108 and –324

(C) 324 and –972

(D) –324 and 972

(E) –324 and –972

9. The average (arithmetic mean) of five integers is 11. One of these five integers is 13, and the others are four consecutive integers. What is the lowest of the five integers?

(A) 8

(B) 9

(C) 10

(D) 12

(E) 13

10. Carol always puts six things on her hamburger: ketchup, lettuce, mustard, onion, relish, and tomato. She always puts either the ketchup or the mustard on first. In how many different orders can Carol place these six items on her hamburger?

(A) 30

(B) 120

(C) 240

(D) 720

(E) 1,440

11. The graph below shows the results of a survey taken outside a movie theater. Each participant was asked his or her age and the number of movies that he or she had attended in the last month. According to the data, the oldest person in the survey who attends six or more movies per month is approximately how many years old?

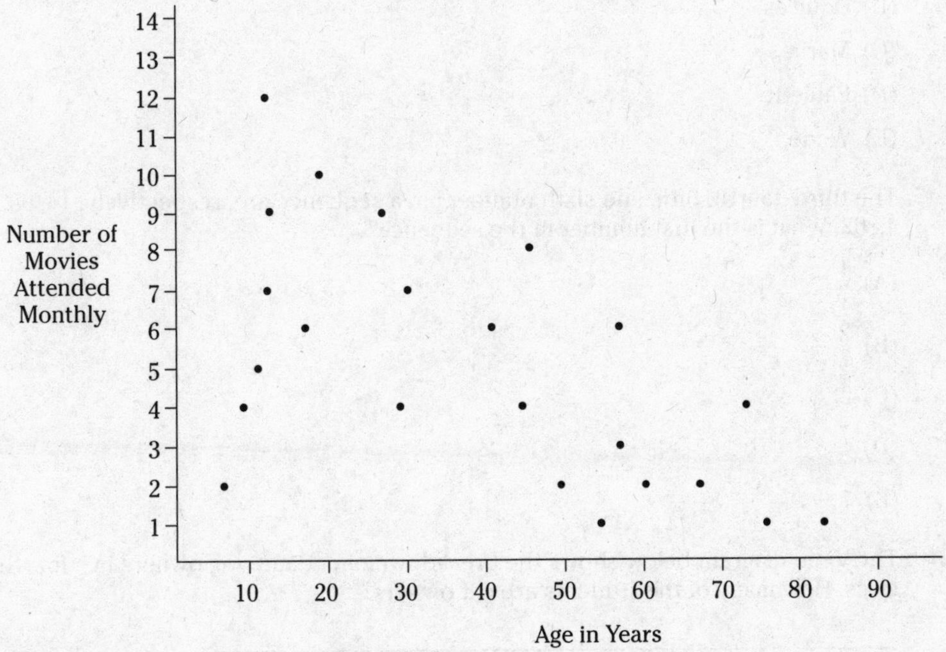

(A) 13

(B) 22

(C) 40

(D) 58

(E) 65

12. From Monday through Thursday, Eleanor sold a total of $1,550 in merchandise. How much does she need to sell on Friday so that her average sales on each of the five days is $450?

(A) $450

(B) $600

(C) $625

(D) $700

(E) $740

13. If you roll three dice, what is the probability that all three of them will show the same value?

(A) $\frac{1}{6}$

(B) $\frac{1}{18}$

(C) $\frac{1}{36}$

(D) $\frac{1}{108}$

(E) $\frac{1}{216}$

14. Wade arrives sometime before Clarese and sometime after Douglas. Maria arrives sometime before Douglas. Paulette arrives immediately before Wade. Who arrives first?

(A) Clarese

(B) Douglas

(C) Maria

(D) Paulette

(E) Wade

15. The third, fourth, fifth, and sixth numbers in a sequence are, respectively, 14, 98, 686, and 4,802. What is the first number in the sequence?

(A) $\frac{1}{7}$

(B) $\frac{2}{7}$

(C) 2

(D) $\frac{7}{2}$

(E) 7

16. The Venn diagram below shows the breakdown of cat and dog owners in a fourth-grade class. How many of the students are cat owners?

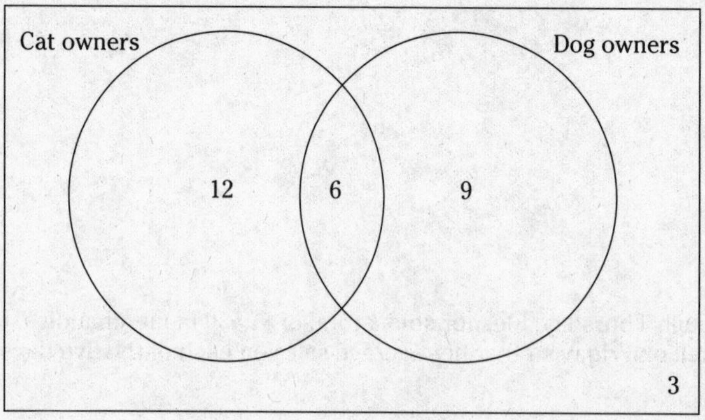

17. Ms. Rosen's first-period class has 25 students. On a recent exam, the 15 juniors scored an average (arithmetic mean) of 90 points and the 10 seniors scored an average of 85. What was the average score for the entire class?

18. In the diagram below, the diameter of the smaller circle is equal to the radius of the larger circle. If a point inside the larger circle is selected at random, what is the probability that it will fall inside the shaded region?

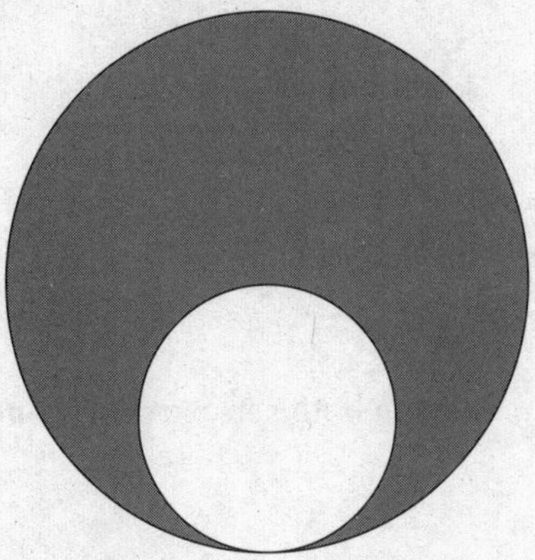

19. The pie chart below shows the results of a recent study of how many households, by percentage, have various numbers of televisions in their homes. If 530 households have televisions in three or fewer rooms, how many have televisions in more than three rooms?

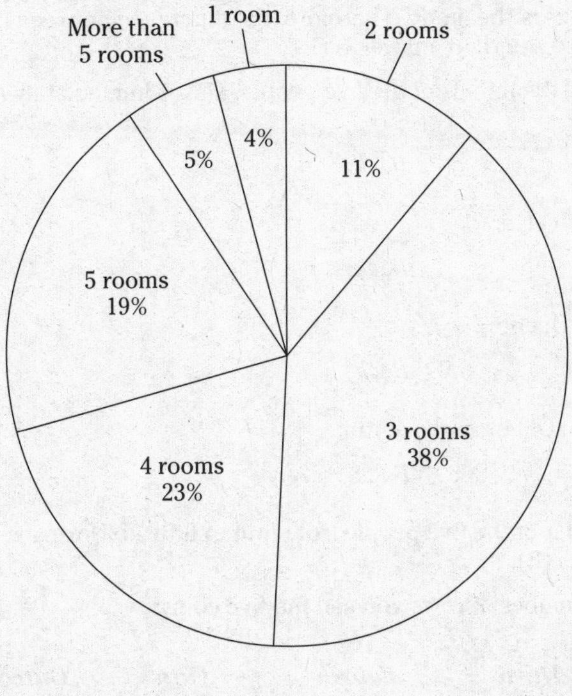

20. The first five numbers in a sequence are 17, 34, 35, 70, and 71. What is the eighth number in the sequence?

Solutions to Practice Problems

Here are the answers to the questions from the preceding section.

1. **C.** Use the formula for the mean to set up the equation and solve for *x*:

$$\text{Mean} = \frac{\text{Sum of values}}{\text{Number of values}}$$
$$64 = \frac{x + 9x + 10x + 12x}{4}$$
$$64(4) = x + 9x + 10x + 12x$$
$$256 = 32x$$
$$x = 8$$

Therefore, the right answer is (C).

2. **A.** The intersection of *F* and *G* contains only numbers in both sets, so set *H* contains positive square numbers less than 100:

Set *H* = {1, 4, 9, 16, 25, 36, 49, 64, 81}

Therefore, set *H* has nine elements, so the right answer is (A).

3. **D.** The union of sets *K* and *L* is everything in either one or both of these sets, so add up the six numbers inside these regions in the Venn diagram: 3 + 4 + 2 + 1 + 1 + 6 = 17. Therefore, the right answer is (D).

4. **B.** The list has two middle numbers, 12 and 18, so the median is 15. The most repeated number in the list is 12, so this is the mode. Therefore, the difference between the median and the mode is 15 – 12 = 3, so the right answer is (B).

5. **B.** Set up a visual chart using the initials of the five people. Max is immediately ahead of Oliver:

Front	MO			*Back*

Oliver is someplace ahead of Petra:

Front	MO	P		*Back*

Petra is immediately behind Quentin:

Front	MO	QP		*Back*

Norma is someplace between Oliver and Quentin:

Front	MO	N	QP	*Back*

The chart shows you the order of the five people from first to fifth, so Norma is third. Therefore, the right answer is (B).

6. **E.** Begin by calculating the number of ways you can flip five coins:

First	***Second***	***Third***	***Fourth***	***Fifth***	***Outcomes***
2	2	2	2	2	32

$2 \times 2 \times 2 \times 2 \times 2 = 2^5 = 32$

So there are a total of 32 possible events. Next, list and count all the possible ways in which exactly two heads could land. A quick way to do this is list all the possible combinations, starting with first and second coins (1-2), then first and third coins (1-3), and so forth:

1-2			
1-3	2-3		
1-4	2-4	3-4	
1-5	2-5	3-5	4-5

As you can see, there are 10 possible ways that exactly two heads can come up. Plug these numbers into the formula for probability and reduce the fraction:

$$\text{Probability} = \frac{10}{32} = \frac{5}{16}$$

Therefore, the probability is $\frac{5}{16}$, so the right answer is (E).

7. **C.** The bottom line on the graph shows the average low temperature. This line has the steepest positive slope from April to May, so the right answer is (C).

8. **B.** According to the rule, here are the first five numbers of the sequence:

   –4, 12, –36, 108, –324

   Therefore, the right answer is (B).

9. **B.** Represent the sequence of four consecutive integers as x, $x + 1$, $x + 2$, and $x + 3$. Use the formula for the arithmetic mean, plugging in these values and others from the problem:

   $$11 = \frac{13 + x + x + 1 + x + 2 + x + 3}{5}$$

   Multiply both sides by 5 and solve for x:

   $$55 = 13 + x + x + 1 + x + 2 + x + 3$$

   $$55 = 19 + 4x$$

   $$36 = 4x$$

   $$x = 9$$

   Thus, the numbers are 9, 10, 11, 12, and 13. The lowest of these is 9; therefore, the right answer is (B).

10. **C.** Carol must place either ketchup or mustard on her burger first. After that, she can choose any of the remaining items in each case. So she has five options for her second choice, four options for her third choice, and so forth. Multiply these six numbers together to get the number of outcomes:

First	*Second*	*Third*	*Fourth*	*Fifth*	*Sixth*	*Outcomes*
2	5	4	3	2	1	240

$$2 \times 5 \times 4 \times 3 \times 2 \times 1 = 240$$

Thus, Carol can place these six items on her burger in 240 different ways, so the right answer is (C).

11. **D.** Starting on the vertical axis, the number 6 indicates people who attended six movies in the last month. Moving horizontally to the right, the graph shows that the oldest person who gave this response is about 58 years old. Therefore, the right answer is (D).

12. **D.** Use the formula for the mean average:

$$\text{Mean} = \frac{\text{Sum of values}}{\text{Number of values}}$$

$$450 = \frac{1{,}550 + x}{5}$$

Now solve for *x*:

$$450(5) = 1{,}550 + x$$

$$2{,}250 = 1{,}550 + x$$

$$x = 700$$

Thus, Eleanor needs to sell $700 in merchandise on Friday. Therefore, the right answer is (D).

13. **C.** First, calculate the total number of events:

First Die	***Second Die***	***Third Die***	***Outcomes***
6	6	6	216

$$6 \times 6 \times 6 = 6^3 = 216$$

There are only six ways for all three numbers to come up the same: 111, 222, 333, 444, 555, and 666. Use the probability formula:

$$\text{Probability} = \frac{6}{216} = \frac{1}{36}$$

Thus, the right answer is (C).

14. **C.** To answer this question, set up a visual chart. Wade arrives sometime before Clarese and sometime after Douglas:

First D W C *Last*

Maria arrives sometime before Douglas:

First M D W C *Last*

Paulette arrives immediately before Wade:

First M D PW C *Last*

Therefore, Maria arrives first, so the right answer is (C).

15. **B.** The numbers are all increasing, so the jump from one number to the next could be based on addition, multiplication, or some combination of the two. Because the numbers are increasing so quickly, try multiplication first. Start with the two lowest numbers you have to work with: What number multiplied by 14 gives you 98?

$98 \div 14 = 7$, so $14 \times 7 = 98$

Check to see whether you can generate the rest of the sequence by multiplying each number by 7 to get the next number:

$$14 \times 7 = 98$$

$$98 \times 7 = 686$$

$$696 \times 7 = 4{,}802$$

This checks out, so the rule for generating each next number in the sequence is *multiply by 7*. Now work backward to the first number by dividing 14 by 7 and then by 7 again:

$$14 \div 7 = 2$$
$$2 \div 7 = \frac{2}{7}$$

So here's the sequence, from the first number to the sixth:

$$\frac{2}{7},\ 2,\ 14,\ 98,\ 686,\ 4{,}802$$

Thus, the first number in the sequence is $\frac{2}{7}$, so the right answer is (B).

16. **18**. The chart shows that 12 children own a cat but not a dog and that six own both a cat and a dog. Therefore, the total number of cat owners is 18.

17. **88**. Set up a chart organizing the information from the problem as follows:

	Score	×	*Number*	=	*Weighted Score*
Juniors	90		15		1,350
Seniors	85		10		850
Total	88		25		2,200

In the last row, you divide the total weighted score by the total number of tests to get the weighted average score. Thus, the weighted average score is 88.

18. **3/4** or **.75**. Use the formula for geometric probability:

$$\text{Geometric probability} = \frac{\text{Area of large circle} - \text{Area of small circle}}{\text{Area of large circle}}$$

To find the area of the two circles, you need the radius. You don't know the exact radius of either circle, but you do know that the radius of the large circle equals the diameter of the small circle and that the diameter is twice the radius.

Radius of small circle = r

Radius of large circle = $2r$

Use this information to find the areas of the two circles in terms of r:

$$A_{\text{small circle}} = \pi r^2$$
$$A_{\text{large circle}} = \pi(2r)^2 = 4\pi r^2$$

Plug these two values into the geometric-probability formula:

$$\text{Geometric probability} = \frac{4\pi r^2 - \pi r^2}{4\pi r^2}$$

Simplify:

$$= \frac{3\pi r^2}{4\pi r^2} = \frac{3}{4}$$

Thus the right answer is $\frac{3}{4} = 0.75$, which you can grid in as 3/4 or .75.

19. **470**. First, read the graph and find out the percentage of households that have televisions in three or fewer rooms:

    $4\% + 11\% + 38\% = 53\%$

    Now figure out the total number of households in the study:

    $53\% \text{ of } ? = 530$

    Make an equation out of this:

    $$0.53x = 530$$
    $$x = 1{,}000$$

    So the study included 1,000 households, 530 of whom have three or fewer TVs. The remaining households have more than three TVs, so subtract:

    $1{,}000 - 530 = 470$

    So the right answer is 470.

20. **286**. The sequence is produced by alternating two rules: *multiply by two* and *add one*. So the next three numbers in the sequence are 142, 143, and 286, making 286 the right answer.

Part III

Your Problems Are Solved! SAT Problem-Solving Techniques

"I'm studying all areas of math – algebra, geometry, blackjack, roulette..."

In this part . . .

In Part III, I provide a variety of ways to improve some of the more-advanced SAT skills you need to succeed on the test: handling word problems, working with multiple formulas, and identifying the best approach for each specific question.

Chapter 8

What's in a Word? SAT Word Problems

In This Chapter

- Turning words into numbers, symbols, and equations
- Choosing variables to make the math easier
- Using charts to organize complex information
- Visualizing a problem by drawing a picture

Question: What's the only thing that makes word problems different from other math problems?

Answer: Words.

This answer may sound too simple, but it's true. I'm aware that many students are intimidated by word problems. Unfortunately, the folks who write the SAT are also aware of this fact. That's one of the reasons that word problems appear on the test.

Word problems don't require any more math than you already know. The only additional skill that word problems test is reading comprehension. To solve them, you need only to understand the words in the problem, keep a clear head, and practice turning the words into some kind of tool that allows your math skills to take over. This *something* may be an equation, a chart, a picture, or just a scribble — whatever works best.

That's what this chapter is all about. I start out by showing you how to turn basic math words and phrases into expressions and equations. Then I show you how making a chart or sketch can help you unravel certain types of word problems. As always, I finish up the chapter with plenty of practice problems, complete with worked-out solutions.

Solving Word Problems Using Equations

When faced with a word problem on the SAT, you can let a variable such as x (or any letter you choose) represent a number whose value you're trying to find. This allows you to translate words into expressions and equations — strings of symbols that contain variables, numbers, and other math symbols.

After you've set up an equation, most of the hard work of solving a word problem is done, and you can use algebra to solve for the variable. In this section, I show you how to set up equations to solve word problems. I give you hints on handling some of the trickier translations, and I give you tips on choosing variables that make the math as easy as possible.

Getting the groupings right: Translations with parentheses

As the complexity of statements in a problem increases, so does the potential for ambiguity. For example, suppose you want to translate the expression $2(x + 7)$ into words. You may consider using the words "two times a number plus seven." This phrase is ambiguous, because two translations are possible: either $2(x + 7)$ or $2x + 7$.

To avoid ambiguity, the SAT writers sometimes include the word *quantity,* which indicates that the words that follow are to be grouped. For example,

"Two times the quantity of a number plus seven" becomes $2(x + 7)$

As you can see, the use of the word *quantity* tells you that the words "a number plus seven" are to be grouped with parentheses, which eliminates the ambiguity. Here's another example:

"One-third the quantity of six minus a number" becomes $\frac{6-x}{3}$

In this case, the words "six minus a number" are grouped as the numerator of a fraction.

The expression "ten times the quantity of five minus a number" is equivalent to which of the following?

(A) $5 - 10x$

(B) $10 - 50x$

(C) $50 - x$

(D) $50 - 10x$

(E) $10x - 50$

The word *quantity* indicates that "five minus a number" is to be grouped as $(5 - x)$ and then multiplied by 10:

$10(5 - x)$

This doesn't match any of the answer choices, so do a little math:

$= 50 - 10x$

Thus, the right answer is **(D).**

The words *sum*, *difference*, *product*, and *quotient* are also used to group the words that follow them. For example,

"Twice the sum of seven and a number" becomes $2(x + 7)$

"Half the difference of a number and ten" becomes $\frac{x-10}{2}$

"Three minus the product of a number and six" becomes $3 - 6x$

"Seven more than the quotient of two and a number" becomes $7 + \frac{2}{x}$

The expression "five less than the quotient of three and a number" is equivalent to

(A) $\frac{2}{x}$

(B) $-\frac{2}{x}$

(C) $5-\frac{3}{x}$

(D) $\frac{3}{x}-5$

(E) $\frac{3}{x-5}$

Translate the words "the quotient of three and a number" first; then subtract 5:

$$\frac{3}{x}-5$$

Therefore, the right answer is **(D)**.

Translating equations that involve fractions

The word *of* in a statement with a fraction (or percentage) stands for *multiplication*. For example,

"Kathy's age is $\frac{3}{4}$ of Wanda's age" becomes $k=\frac{3}{4}w$

The words *as much* and *as many* also stand for multiplication. For example,

"Henry has $\frac{5}{8}$ as much money as Jennifer" becomes $h=\frac{5}{8}j$

This week, Norm worked $\frac{5}{6}$ as many hours as Patricia, and together they put in 77 hours. How many hours did Patricia work?

To get started, let n equal Norm's hours and p equal Patricia's hours. Norm worked $\frac{5}{6}$ as many hours as Patricia:

$$n=\frac{5}{6}p$$

Together, Norm and Patricia worked for 77 hours:

$$n+p=77$$

Now you can substitute $\frac{5}{6}p$ for n into the second equation:

$$\frac{5}{6}p+p=77$$

Multiply every term by 6 to get rid of the denominator:

$$5p+6p=462$$

Now solve for p:

$$11p=462$$

$$p=42$$

Thus, Patricia worked for **42** hours.

TIP

You can use either the fraction $\frac{1}{100}$ or the decimal 0.01 to translate the word *percent.*

"p percent" becomes $\frac{p}{100}$ or $p(0.01)$

Generally speaking, the decimal 0.01 is easier to use on your calculator, so I recommend it.

Choosing a variable to avoid fractions

Although you need to be able to handle fractions in word problems (as I show you in the preceding section), you sometimes have an opportunity to make your work easier by avoiding fractions entirely.

TIP

Generally speaking, when choosing which value to represent directly with a variable, choose the *lesser* value. The following example shows you why.

EXAMPLE

Sherilyn has four times as much money as Maybil, and together they have $45. How many dollars does Sherilyn have?

To answer this question, you need to represent the amount that one girl has as a variable. Then you need to represent the amount that the other girl has in terms of that variable. If you use s to represent the amount of money Sherilyn has, here's what you get:

$$\text{Sherilyn} = s$$

$$\text{Maybil} = \frac{s}{4}$$

The result here is the following equation:

$$s + \frac{s}{4} = 45$$

To solve this equation for s, you need to work with fractions, which is nobody's idea of a good time. However, you can avoid this difficulty with a little planning. Instead of starting with Sherilyn's amount, start by representing Maybil's amount as the variable m:

$$\text{Maybil} = m$$

$$\text{Sherilyn} = 4m$$

Here's the equation that results:

$$m + 4m = 45$$

This equation practically solves itself:

$$5m = 45$$

$$m = 9$$

Thus, Maybil has $9, so Sherilyn has $36 and the answer is **36**.

Before moving on from this example, notice why using m is easier: The question states that Sherilyn has four times as much money as Maybil, so Maybil has the *lesser* amount. Using m to represent Maybil's amount is easier because it allows you to avoid fractions.

EXAMPLE

Darryl has one dollar less than twice as many dollars as Alex and exactly half as much money as Thom. Together, they have $60. How many dollars does Thom have?

Before jumping into this problem, step back and take a look at it. Darryl has about twice as many dollars as Alex but half as many dollars as Thom. So Alex probably has less money than the other two; therefore, use the variable a to represent his amount.

Alex = a

Next, represent Darryl's dollar amount in terms of Alex's (that is, in terms of a):

Darryl = $2a - 1$

Finally, represent Thom's dollar amount in terms of Darryl's. Darryl has half as many dollars as Thom, so Thom has twice as many dollars as Darryl:

Thom = $2(2a - 1) = 4a - 2$

Altogether, the three boys have $60:

$$a + 2a - 1 + 4a - 2 = 60$$

Solve for a:

$$7a - 3 = 60$$
$$7a = 63$$
$$a = 9$$

Thus, Alex has $9. Plug this information into $4a - 2$ to find Thom's amount:

$$4(9) - 2 = 36 - 2 = 34$$

Thus, the right answer is **34**.

Writing systems of equations: Using more than one variable

Some word problems are relatively simple to solve using one variable. In other cases, however, you may find setting up a problem using two or more variables — and two or more equations — an easier way to start out. Then you can solve the problem just as you'd solve any other system of equations — by using substitution or by combining equations (see Chapter 4 for more on working with multiple variables).

EXAMPLE

If Caroline had five dollars more than she does, she would have twice as much money as Jacob. And if Jacob had five dollars less than he does, he would have one-third as much money as Caroline. How much money do Caroline and Jacob have together?

(A) $10

(B) $15

(C) $20

(D) $24

(E) $25

The question is stated in a complicated way that may be easier to approach using two variables:

Caroline = c Jacob = j

Now take the problem sentence by sentence. First, translate the first sentence into an equation:

$$c + 5 = 2j$$

Next, translate the second sentence; then simplify it, multiplying both sides by 3:

$$j - 5 = \frac{c}{3}$$
$$3(j - 5) = c$$
$$3j - 15 = c$$

Now substitute $3j - 15$ for c into the first equation:

$$3j - 15 + 5 = 2j$$
$$3j - 10 = 2j$$

This equation solves easily:

$$-10 = -j$$
$$10 = j$$

Thus, Jacob has $10, so substitute 10 for j into the first equation:

$$c + 5 = 2(10)$$
$$c + 5 = 20$$
$$c = 15$$

Thus, Caroline has $15, so together Caroline and Jacob have $25, making the right answer **(E).**

Don't stress too much wondering whether to use one variable or two to solve a problem. Many problems can be solved using either one variable or several. To illustrate this point, here's another look at a question from the earlier section "Choosing a variable to avoid fractions":

EXAMPLE

Darryl has one dollar less than twice as many dollars as Alex and exactly half as much money as Thom. Together, they have $60. How many dollars does Thom have?

In the previous section, I answer this question using one variable. This time, I set up the problem using three variables — a, d, and t — to represent the amounts that the three boys have. The first sentence tells you that Darryl has one dollar less than twice as many dollars as Alex:

$$d = 2a - 1$$

The second sentence tells you that Darryl has exactly half as much money as Thom, so Thom has twice as much money as Darryl:

$$t = 2d$$

The third sentence tells you that altogether, the boys have $60:

$$a + d + t = 60$$

With three equations and three variables, you can solve the problem. In this case, use a few substitutions to rewrite the final equation using one variable. First, substitute $2d$ for t into the final equation:

$$a + d + 2d = 60$$
$$a + 3d = 60$$

Next, substitute $2a - 1$ for d:

$$a + 3(2a - 1) = 60$$
$$a + 6a - 3 = 60$$
$$7a - 3 = 60$$

Note that this equation is the same as the one you arrive at when you answer this question in the previous section, and it solves easily:

$$7a = 63$$
$$a = 9$$

Thus, Alex has $9 dollars, so you can find Darryl's amount and then Thom's:

$$d = 2a - 1 = 2(9) - 1 = 18 - 1 = 17$$
$$t = 2d = 2(17) = 34$$

Thus, Thom has $34, so the right answer is (still!) **34**.

Charting a Course: Drawing Charts to Solve Word Problems

Some of the more difficult SAT questions may contain too much information to turn directly into equations. For these questions, making a chart can be useful way to organize information so that you can see how to turn it into an equation.

You probably have at least some experience making charts to solve algebra problems. And here's some good news: Even difficult SAT questions are often easier than a lot of the questions you've faced on homework assignments. So don't worry that making a chart necessarily means a question is going to take a huge amount of time to solve. Furthermore, you don't have to spend a lot of time on making a chart. Sometimes, scribbling a few words and numbers may provide enough information to give you an idea how to proceed. Check out an example problem:

Anna and Bryan are both celebrating their birthday today. Bryan is now twice as old as Anna. Six years from today, Anna's age will be $\frac{2}{3}$ of Bryan's. How old is Anna today?

You can use the following chart to organize the information:

	Today	*Six Years from Today*
Anna		
Bryan		

The chart provides four boxes for both people's ages today and in six years. To begin filling it in, let a equal Anna's current age. Bryan is twice as old as Anna, so his age today is $2a$:

	Today	***Six Years from Today***
Anna	a	
Bryan	$2a$	

In six years, each person's age will be (surprise!) six years greater, so you can fill in these numbers as well.

	Today	***Six Years from Today***
Anna	a	$a + 6$
Bryan	$2a$	$2a + 6$

Now use the information from the last column to create an equation. Anna's age in six years will be $\frac{2}{3}$ of Bryan's age then:

$$a+6=\frac{2}{3}(2a+6)$$

Multiply both sides by 3 and solve:

$$3(a + 6) = 2(2a + 6)$$
$$3a + 18 = 4a + 12$$
$$6 = a$$

Thus, Anna's age today is **6**.

Each of the 27 children in Ms. Witherspoon's class has either two or three siblings. If the total number of siblings is 68, how many children have exactly two siblings?

To solve this problem, make a chart with three rows and three columns:

Siblings per Child	***Children***	***Total Siblings***
2		
3		
Total	**27**	**68**

The first two rows of the chart account for children with two or three siblings. The last row gives the total for each column. I've already filled in the information that there are a total of 27 children with a total of 68 siblings.

Now let x equal the number of children who have two siblings. Because there are 27 children altogether, the number of children with three siblings is $27 - x$:

Siblings per Child	***Children***	***Total Siblings***
2	x	
3	$27 - x$	
Total	**27**	**68**

Next, multiply the number of siblings per child by the number of children in each row:

Siblings per Child	***Children***	***Total Siblings***
2	x	$2x$
3	$27 - x$	$3(27 - x)$
Total	**27**	**68**

Now make an equation by adding up everything in the *Total Siblings* column to equal the number in the bottom right corner:

$$2x + 3(27 - x) = 68$$

Solve this equation for x:

$$2x + 81 - 3x = 68$$
$$81 - x = 68$$
$$-x = -13$$
$$x = 13$$

Thus, 13 children have exactly two siblings, so the answer is **13**.

EXAMPLE

Alison ran at a constant rate of seven miles per hour. Then she walked for the same amount of time at three miles per hour. If the total distance she covered was five miles, how much time did she spend running?

(A) 10 minutes

(B) 15 minutes

(C) 20 minutes

(D) 30 minutes

(E) 60 minutes

This is a classic *rate-time-distance* problem, which uses the following formula:

$$\text{Rate} \times \text{Time} = \text{Distance}$$

To solve this type of problem, make a chart:

	Rate	***Time***	***Distance***
Run	7	x	
Walk	3	x	

As you can see, I've filled in Alison's running and walking rates. I've also chosen x to represent the amount of time *in hours* that she spent running and then walking. Using the formula for rate, time, and distance, you can multiply across the chart to find the distance she ran and walked:

	Rate	*Time*	*Distance*
Run	7	x	$7x$
Walk	3	x	$3x$

Alison covered a total distance of 5 miles, so you can make an equation by adding up the *Distance* column:

$$7x + 3x = 5$$

Solve for x:

$$10x = 5$$
$$x = \frac{1}{2}$$

She spent a total of half an hour running; therefore, the answer is **(D).**

Picturing Success: Sketching to Solve Word Problems

Sometimes, a picture's worth a thousand words. This applies on the SAT as well. Drawing a little sketch can often jog your brain in just the right way so you can see the answer. In this section, I give you a few tips for sketching your way to success.

Distance drawings: Moving with a purpose

Students find some rate-time-distance problems confusing because they're not sure how to find the distance between two vehicles, such as cars, trains, or planes. Often, a quick sketch can clarify how to proceed.

EXAMPLE

Two trains leave a station at the same time, with the train that's heading east traveling at half the speed of the one that's heading west. After two hours, the trains are 192 miles apart. What is the speed of the westbound train?

(A) 16 miles per hour

(B) 32 miles per hour

(C) 48 miles per hour

(D) 64 miles per hour

(E) 96 miles per hour

To start this problem, sketch a picture to see where you stand:

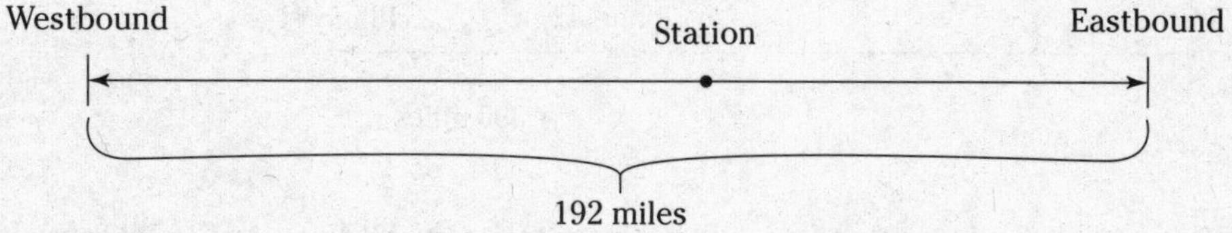

Now make a chart and plug in the information:

	Rate	***Time***	***Distance***
West	$2x$	2	$4x$
East	x	2	$2x$

If you like, you can place the two distances in the sketch.

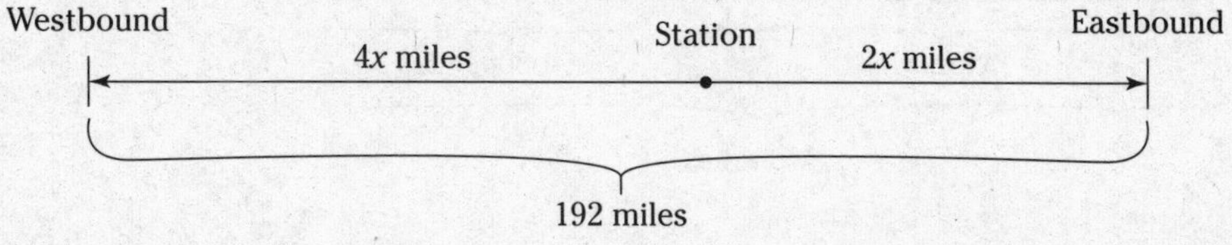

The sketch shows you that the distance between the two trains is the distance that the westbound train travels *plus* the distance that the eastbound train travels. This distance equals 192 miles, so you now have an equation to work with:

$$4x + 2x = 192$$

Solve for x:

$$6x = 192$$

$$x = 32$$

Thus, the eastbound train is traveling at 32 miles per hour, so the speed of the westbound train is 64 miles per hour. Therefore, the right answer is **(D).**

A plane leaves New York for Paris at 12:00 p.m. traveling at 500 miles per hour. A second plane leaves New York for Paris at 2:00 p.m. At 5:00 p.m., the second plane is 1,300 miles behind the first plane. What is the speed of the second plane?

(A) 200 miles per hour

(B) 300 miles per hour

(C) 400 miles per hour

(D) 450 miles per hour

(E) 650 miles per hour

In this problem, the two planes are traveling in the same direction. Here's a sketch:

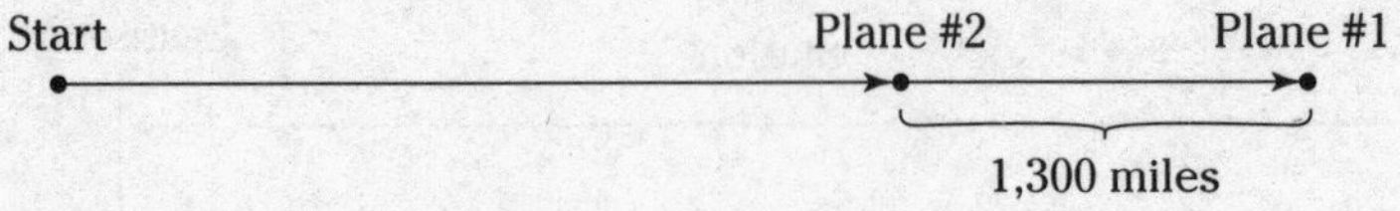

You can enter information from the problem into a chart. Note that at 5:00 p.m., the first plane has been traveling for 5 hours and the second plane, for 3 hours:

	Rate	***Time***	***Distance***
Plane #1	500	5	2,500
Plane #2	x	3	$3x$

When you know the distances, you can place them in the sketch:

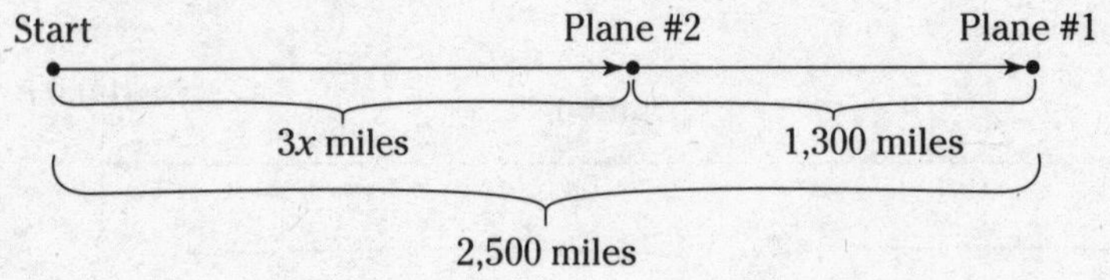

The sketch clarifies how to build an equation:

$$3x + 1{,}300 = 2{,}500$$

Solve for x:

$$3x = 1{,}200$$

$$x = 400$$

The second plane is traveling at 400 miles per hour, so the right answer is **(C)**.

Timelines: Avoiding algebra with a number line

Often, drawing a picture can help you figure out a problem that doesn't appear to be visual at all. In fact, sometimes you can avoid algebra entirely with a good sketch. For example, if you're doing a problem that concerns how much of a task is complete, a number line can be a big help. Check it out:

Shawn is working a night shift at his job. An hour ago, he had completed one-third of his shift. Two hours from now, he will have completed two-thirds of his shift. How long is the whole shift?

(A) 6 hours

(B) 7 hours

(C) 7.5 hours

(D) 8.5 hours

(E) 9 hours

You could solve this with algebra, but there's an easier way. Instead, sketch a picture showing the shift from start to finish as a line segment:

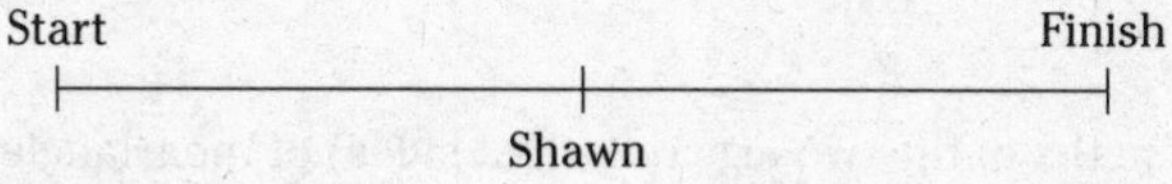

The sketch shows the beginning and the end of the shift, plus where Shawn is in the shift right now. Next, fill in the remaining information from the question:

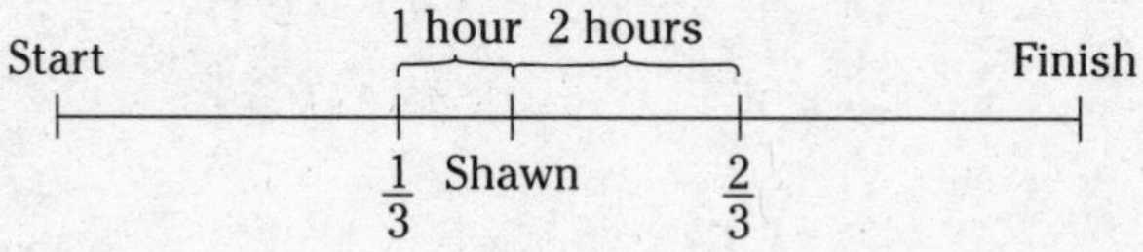

The chart shows you that an hour ago, Shawn was $\frac{1}{3}$ of the way through the shift, and two hours from now, he will be $\frac{2}{3}$ of the way through it. So you can see that the middle $\frac{1}{3}$ of the shift is exactly three hours. Therefore, the entire shift is 9 hours, so the right answer is **(E)**.

Spacing out: Uncovering hidden geometry

Not every geometry question has an accompanying figure. In some cases, however, when you sketch out information from the question, a geometry problem emerges. This is especially common with map problems, like the one that follows:

Jessica lives 15 miles west of Kaitlin and 20 miles south of Martine. How many miles apart do Kaitlin and Martine live?

At first glance, this may seem like an arithmetic or algebra problem. But when you sketch it out, you find that the three girls' houses form the three corners of a right triangle.

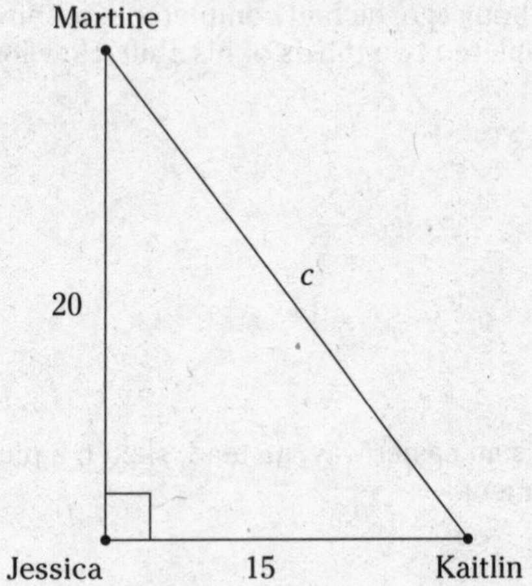

The problem gives you the lengths of the two legs (shortest sides) of the triangle, so you can find the hypotenuse (longest side) using the Pythagorean theorem, $a^2 + b^2 = c^2$. Substitute in the lengths of the legs:

$$15^2 + 20^2 = c^2$$

Solve for c:

$$225 + 400 = c^2$$
$$625 = c^2$$
$$25 = c$$

Thus, Kaitlin and Martine live **25** miles apart.

Practice Word Problems

All set to practice some word problems? Here are 20 questions — 15 multiple-choice and 5 grid-in — testing the skills covered in this chapter. Along the way, if you hit a rough spot, flip through this chapter for ways to break through. For each question, I provide a step-by-step solution in the next section.

1. If you multiply a number by ten and then subtract one, the result is divisible by three. But if you add twelve to the number, the result is divisible by eleven. Which of the following could be the number?

   (A) 6

   (B) 10

   (C) 13

   (D) 16

   (E) 21

2. As part of their finale, each of the 18 members of a juggling troupe is juggling either six or seven balls. Altogether, the troupe is juggling 120 balls. How many members are juggling exactly seven balls?

   (A) 7

   (B) 9

   (C) 10

   (D) 12

   (E) 14

3. The sum of two numbers is 44, and their difference is 4. What is the product of these two numbers?

   (A) 420

   (B) 440

   (C) 480

   (D) 520

   (E) 600

4. Bob lives 24 miles north of his office and 10 miles east of the university he attends. How far apart are the office and the university?

   (A) 26 miles

   (B) 28 miles

   (C) 30 miles

   (D) 32 miles

   (E) 34 miles

5. The expression "seven times the difference of four and a number" is equivalent to which of the following?

(A) $7x - 4$

(B) $4 - 7x$

(C) $28 - x$

(D) $28 - 4x$

(E) $28 - 7x$

6. If Sheila had one more dollar, Eileen would have three times as much money as Sheila does. And if Eileen had six dollars more, she would have four times as much money as Sheila. How much money do they have altogether?

(A) \$18

(B) \$21

(C) \$25

(D) \$32

(E) \$39

7. David sells *d* boxes of cookies, Tyrone sells three times as many boxes as David, and Kendall sells half as many boxes as Tyrone. How many boxes did they sell altogether?

(A) $4.5d$

(B) $5.5d$

(C) $d + 4.5$

(D) $d + 5.5$

(E) $4d + 0.5$

8. Two cars leave from the same starting point at the same time on a straight road heading west. The faster car is traveling at 60 miles per hour, and after two and a half hours, it's 40 miles ahead of the slower car. What is the speed of the slower car?

(A) 40 mph

(B) 42 mph

(C) 44 mph

(D) 48 mph

(E) 50 mph

9. Xavier left his office and drove 75 miles south for his first appointment of the day. After that, he drove east for 40 miles for a second appointment. To finish up, he took a direct route back to his office. How much distance did he cover altogether?

(A) 85 miles

(B) 115 miles

(C) 170 miles

(D) 200 miles

(E) 230 miles

10. Six added to the product of a number *n* and two is equal to five less than the product of *n* and three. Which of the following is true of *n*?

(A) $n \leq 0$

(B) $1 \leq n \leq 6$

(C) $7 \leq n \leq 12$

(D) $13 \leq n \leq 18$

(E) $n > 18$

11. Marion is reading a book for a report. So far, she has read half the book plus 10 pages. When she reads another 35 pages, she'll be finished with $\frac{3}{4}$ of the book. What is the total length of the book?

(A) 120 pages

(B) 140 pages

(C) 160 pages

(D) 180 pages

(E) 200 pages

12. The sum of two numbers *x* and *y* is 30, and the quotient of *x* and *y* is 4. What is the difference of *x* and *y*?

(A) 6

(B) 8

(C) 12

(D) 16

(E) 18

13. Tracy's age in whole years is three times greater than the age of his sister, Maxine. In three years, Maxine's age will be $\frac{3}{7}$ of Tracy's age. How much older is Tracy than Maxine?

(A) 3 years

(B) 7 years

(C) 10 years

(D) 12 years

(E) 14 years

14. Stephanie set a goal of running a certain number of laps on a track in four days. She completed $\frac{1}{3}$ of her goal on Monday and completed another $\frac{1}{4}$ of her goal on Tuesday. Then she completed her goal by running an equal number of laps on both Wednesday and Thursday. If her goal was to run 24 laps, how many laps did she run on Thursday?

(A) 2

(B) 3

(C) 4

(D) 5

(E) 6

15. Coltonville is located due north of Bellemeade and exactly 80 miles east of Ramsay. If Ramsay is 100 miles from Bellemeade, what is the distance from Coltonville to Bellemeade?

(A) 20 miles

(B) 60 miles

(C) 70 miles

(D) 90 miles

(E) 180 miles

16. Angel has half as much money as his older sister and three times as much money as his younger brother. Altogether, the three children have $230. How many dollars does Angel have?

17. Eight minus the product of seven and a positive number is equal to the same number multiplied by itself. What is the number?

18. At 10:00 a.m., two boats leave a port headed in opposite directions, one traveling 5 miles per hour faster than the other. At noon, the boats are 44 miles apart. What is the speed of the faster boat in miles per hour?

19. The product of two positive numbers is 27 more than their sum. If the greater number minus the smaller number equals 3, what is the smaller number?

20. Roger had three times more money than Stephen at the beginning of the day. They each earned $200, and now Roger has twice as much money as Stephen. How many dollars do they both have together now?

Solutions to Practice Problems

In this section, I provide the correct answers to all 20 questions in the previous section. I also give you a detailed explanation that shows you how you can arrive at each answer.

1. **B.** Let x equal the number. Then the following two statements are true:

   $10x - 1$ is divisible by 3 $\quad\quad$ $x + 12$ is divisible by 11

   The second statement is easier to test, so try it on all five answer choices:

   $6 + 12 = 18$ no

   $10 + 12 = 22$ yes

   $13 + 12 = 25$ no

   $16 + 12 = 28$ no

   $21 + 12 = 33$ yes

   Only 10 or 21 could be the number. Test both of these numbers against the first statement:

   $10(10) - 1 = 99$ yes

   $21(10) - 1 = 209$ no

   Thus, 10 could be the number, so the right answer is (B).

2. **D.** Let x equal the number of jugglers who are juggling exactly seven balls. Then, $18 - x$ jugglers are juggling exactly six. Make a chart to organize this information:

Balls	***Jugglers***	***Total***
6	$18 - x$	$108 - 6x$
7	x	$7x$
Total	**18**	**120**

Now make an equation by adding in the *Total* column:

$$108 - 6x + 7x = 120$$

Solve for x:

$$108 + x = 120$$

$$x = 12$$

Thus, 12 jugglers are juggling exactly seven balls, so the answer is (D).

3. **C.** Let x equal the greater number and y equal the smaller number. You can make two equations:

$$x + y = 44$$

$$x - y = 4$$

Add the two equations together:

$$\begin{array}{l} x + y = 44 \\ \underline{x - y = \ \ 4} \\ 2x \qquad = 48 \end{array}$$

Solve for x:

$$x = 24$$

Thus, the greater number is 24, so the smaller number is 20. The problem asks for the product, so multiply these two numbers:

$$24 \times 20 = 480$$

The product of these two numbers is 480, so the right answer is (C).

4. **A.** Sketch a picture of Bob's home, the office, and the university:

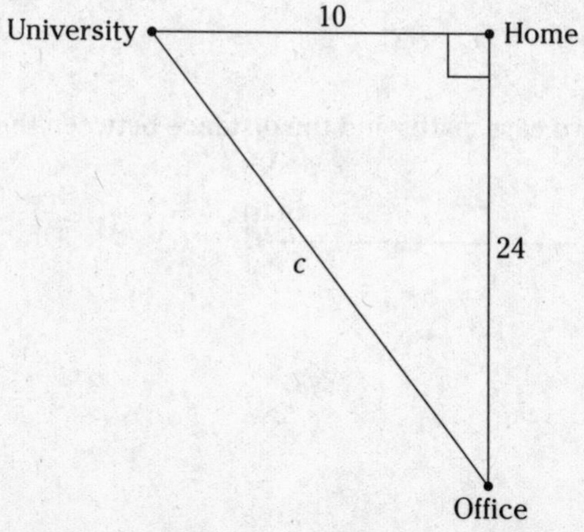

These three locations form the points of a right triangle, so use the Pythagorean theorem, $a^2 + b^2 = c^2$. The distance between the office and the university is the hypotenuse of the triangle, so you want to solve for c. Substitute in the other distances and solve:

$$24^2 + 10^2 = c^2$$
$$576 + 100 = c^2$$
$$676 = c^2$$
$$26 = c$$

Thus, the right answer is (A).

5. **E.** The word *difference* indicates that the expression that follows is to be grouped as $(4 - x)$ and then multiplied by seven:

$$7(4 - x) = 28 - 7x$$

Thus, the right answer is (E).

6. **E.** Let s represent Sheila's money and e represent Eileen's money. You can make two equations as follows:

$$3(s + 1) = e$$
$$4s = e + 6$$

Substitute $3(s + 1)$ for e into the second equation and solve for s:

$$4s = 3(s + 1) + 6$$
$$4s = 3s + 3 + 6$$
$$4s = 3s + 9$$
$$s = 9$$

That's how much money Sheila has. Now find how much Eileen has by substituting 9 for s into the second equation and solving for e:

$$4(9) = e + 6$$
$$36 = e + 6$$
$$30 = e$$

Thus, Sheila has \$9 and Eileen has \$30. They have \$39 together, so the right answer is (E).

7. **B.** David sold d boxes, so Tyrone sold $3d$ and Kendall sold $\frac{3}{2}d$. Thus, altogether the boys sold the following:

$$d + 3d + \frac{3}{2}d = 4d + \frac{3}{2}d = \frac{11}{2}d = 5.5d$$

Therefore, the right answer is (B).

8. **C.** Start by drawing a sketch of the two cars' paths and the distance between the cars.

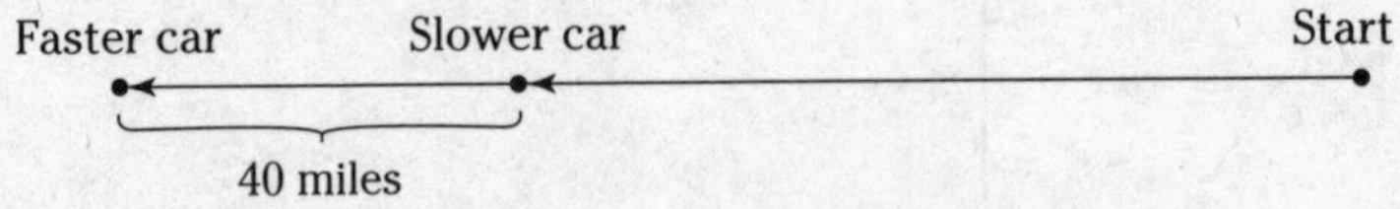

Now make a chart and enter the information:

	Rate	***Time***	***Distance***
Faster car	60	2.5	150
Slower car	x	2.5	$2.5x$

Place the distances into the sketch:

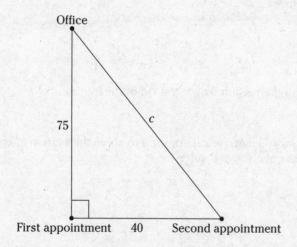

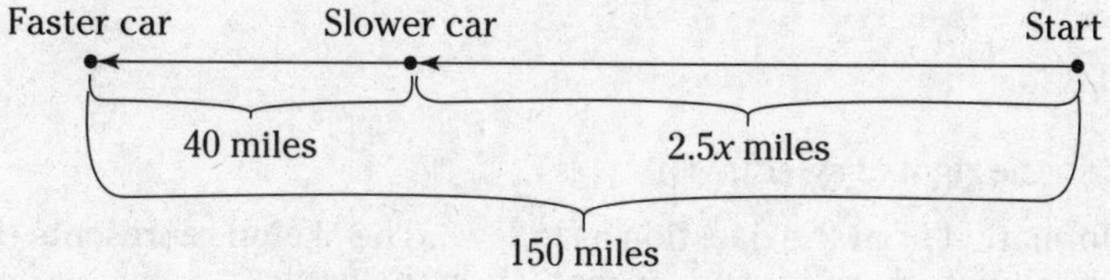

Use the sketch to set up the following equation:

$$40 + 2.5x = 150$$

Solve for x to find the speed of the lower car:

$$2.5x = 110$$

$$x = \frac{110}{2.5}$$

$$x = 44$$

Thus, the speed of the slower car is 44 miles per hour, so the right answer is (C).

9. **D.** Begin by sketching three parts of Xavier's drive:

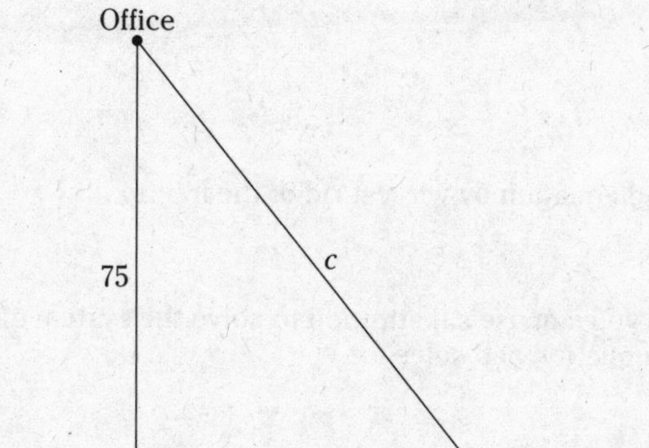

These three parts are in the shape of a right triangle, so you can find the distance Xavier traveled on the third part of his trip using the Pythagorean theorem, $a^2 + b^2 = c^2$. The trip from the second appointment to the office is the hypotenuse of the triangle, so you need to find c. Substitute in the given distances and solve for c:

$$75^2 + 40^2 = c^2$$

$$5{,}625 + 1{,}600 = c^2$$

$$7{,}225 = c^2$$

$$85 = c$$

The problem asks for the total distance Xavier traveled, so add up the three parts of his trip:

$75 + 40 + 85 = 200$

Thus, Xavier drove 200 miles, so the right answer is (D).

10. **C.** Translate the statement as follows:

$6 + 2n = 3n - 5$

Solve for n:

$6 = n - 5$

$11 = n$

Thus, $7 \leq n \leq 12$, so the right answer is (C).

11. **D.** Sketch the information from the question as follows. The sketch represents the book as a line segment and shows where Marion currently is in the book:

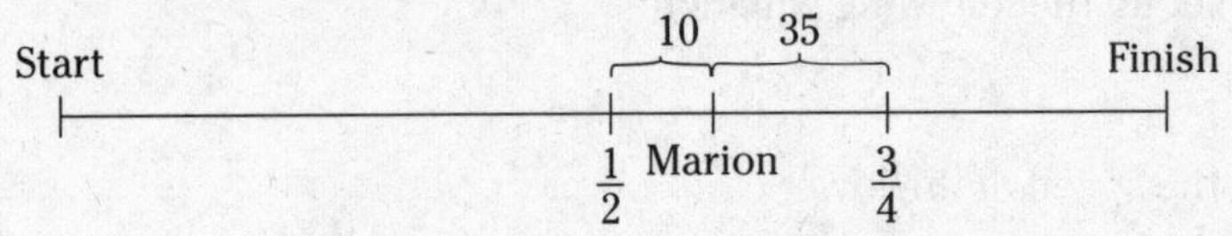

Ten pages ago, she was halfway through the book; in 35 pages, she'll be done with $\frac{3}{4}$ of it. Thus, $\frac{1}{4}$ of the book is 45 pages, so the whole book is four times this length:

$45 \times 4 = 180$

Thus, the book is 180 pages long, so the right answer is (D).

12. **E.** Begin by making two equations:

$x + y = 30$

$\frac{x}{y} = 4$

Multiply both sides of the second equation by y to get rid of the fraction:

$x = 4y$

This equation is solved for x, so you can use substitution to solve the system of equations. Substitute $4y$ for x into the first equation and solve for y:

$4y + y = 30$

$5y = 30$

$y = 6$

Now substitute 6 for y into the first equation so you can find x:

$x + 6 = 30$

$x = 24$

Next, find the difference between x and y so you can answer the given question:

$x - y = 24 - 6 = 18$

Thus, the right answer is (E).

13. **D.** Let Maxine's current age be m. Tracy is three times older, so his age is $3m$. Use the following chart:

	Current Age	***Age in 3 Years***
Maxine	m	$m + 3$
Tracy	$3m$	$3m + 3$

In 3 years, Maxine's age will be $\frac{3}{7}$ of Tracy's, so set up the following equation:

$$m+3=\frac{3}{7}(3m+3)$$

Distribute (multiply) the right side to remove the parentheses:

$$m+3=\frac{9}{7}m+\frac{9}{7}$$

Multiply every term in the equation by 7 to get rid of the fractions:

$$7m + 21 = 9m + 9$$

Solve for m:

$$21 = 2m + 9$$

$$12 = 2m$$

$$6 = m$$

Thus, Maxine's current age is 6, so Tracy is 18. Therefore, Tracy is 12 years older than Maxine, so the right answer is (D).

14. **D.** Sketch a picture of the week from Monday to Thursday as follows:

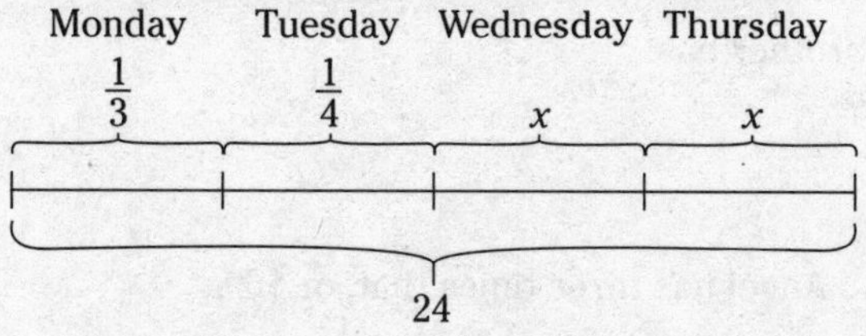

You can replace $\frac{1}{3}$ and $\frac{1}{4}$ with the number of laps:

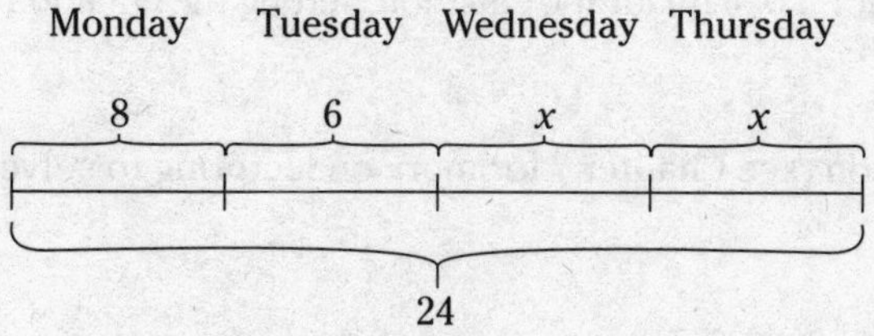

Now notice that she ran 14 laps on the first two days, so she ran a total of 10 laps on the last two days. Thus, she ran 5 laps on each of these days, so the right answer is (D).

15. **B.** Sketch the locations of the three towns:

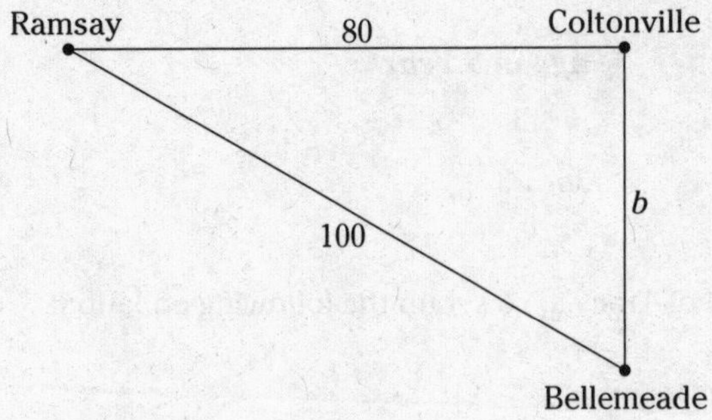

Thus, the three towns form the corners of a right triangle, so you can use the Pythagorean theorem, $a^2 + b^2 = c^2$. The hypotenuse of this triangle is 100 miles and one leg is 80 miles, so substitute as follows:

$$80^2 + b^2 = 100^2$$

Solve for b, the distance between Coltonville and Bellemeade:

$$6{,}400 + b^2 = 10{,}000$$
$$b^2 = 3{,}600$$
$$b = 60$$

Thus, the distance between the two towns is 60 miles, so the right answer is (B).

16. **69**. Angel's brother has the least money, so to avoid fractions, let b equal the number of dollars that the brother has. Thus, Angel has $3b$ dollars and his sister has $2(3b)$, or $6b$ dollars. Altogether, they have \$230, so

$$b + 3b + 6b = 230$$

Solve for b, the amount Angel's brother has:

$$10b = 230$$
$$b = 23$$

Thus, Angel's brother has \$23, so Angel has three times that, or \$69.

17. **1**. Translate this equation as follows:

$$8 - 7x = x^2$$

Rearrange to the more common form of a quadratic equation, setting the equation equal to 0:

$$x^2 + 7x - 8 = 0$$

Factor the left side of the equation (see Chapter 7 for more on factoring to solve a quadratic equation):

$$(x - 1)(x + 8) = 0$$

Now split the equation into two separate equations:

$$x - 1 = 0 \quad \text{or} \quad x + 8 = 0$$
$$x = 1 \quad\quad\quad x = -8$$

The number has to be positive, so it's 1.

18. **13.5** or **27/2**. First, sketch the problem:

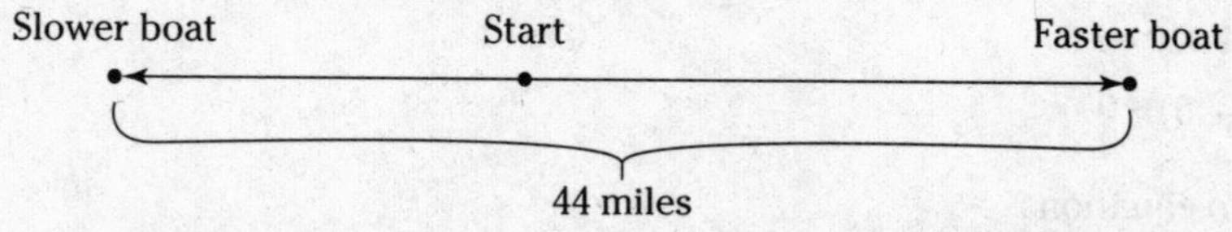

Now set up a chart. Note that the boats travel for two hours:

	Rate	***Time***	***Distance***
Faster boat	$x + 5$	2	$2x + 10$
Slower boat	x	2	$2x$

Enter the distances from the chart into the sketch:

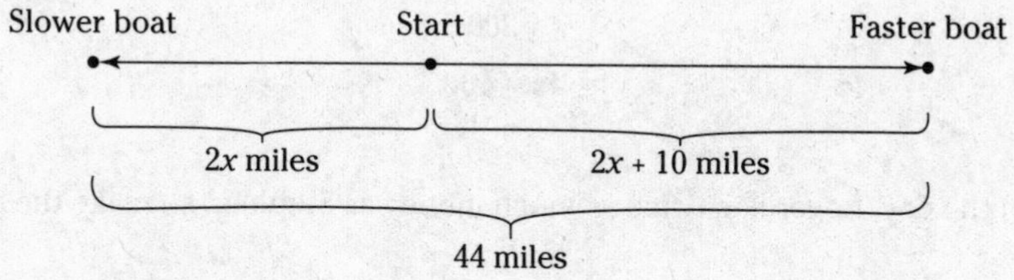

Use the sketch to set up an equation:

$$2x + 10 + 2x = 44$$

Solve for x:

$$4x + 10 = 44$$

$$4x = 34$$

$$x = 8.5$$

Thus, the slower boat traveling at 8.5 miles per hour, so the speed of the faster boat is 13.5 miles per hour, which you can also write in as 27/2.

19. **5**. Let g equal the greater number and s equal the smaller number. Thus, you can make two equations:

$$gs = g + s + 27$$

$$g - s = 3$$

Solve the second equation for g:

$$g = 3 + s$$

Now you can use substitution to solve the system of equations. Substitute $3 + s$ for g into the first equation and simplify:

$$(3 + s)s = 3 + s + s + 27$$

$$3s + s^2 = 30 + 2s$$

This equation contains a quadratic term (s^2), so put the equation in quadratic form and solve by factoring (see Chapter 7 for more on solving quadratic equations):

$$s^2 + s - 30 = 0$$

$$(s + 6)(s - 5) = 0$$

Split into two equations:

$s + 6 = 0$ or $s - 5 = 0$

$s = -6$ $s = 5$

The answer is a positive number, so the smaller number, s, is 5.

20. **1200**. Let s equal the number of dollars that Stephen had at the beginning of the day. Then Roger had $3s$ dollars at the beginning of the day. Each man earned $200 during the day, so place this information into a chart:

	Beginning	***End***
Roger	$3s$	$3s + 200$
Stephen	s	$s + 200$
Total	**4s**	**4s + 400**

At the end of the day, Roger has twice as much money as Stephen, so make the following equation:

$$3s + 200 = 2(s + 200)$$

Solve for s:

$$3s + 200 = 2s + 400$$

$$s + 200 = 400$$

$$s = 200$$

According to the chart, the two men together have $4s + 400$ dollars at the end of the day, so substitute 200 for s:

$$4(200) + 400 = 800 + 400 = 1{,}200$$

Therefore, together they have $1,200, which you write as 1200.

Chapter 9

SAT Math Strategy

In This Chapter

- Identifying the easy, medium, and hard questions
- Using more than one formula to answer a question
- Approaching tough problems
- Using all your resources

If you play basketball, your practice time probably includes skills training for running, jumping, shooting, passing, and so forth. This training is important because when you get to the game, you need to know *how* to move. But a winning player needs more: He or she needs to know not just how to move but how to *respond*. No matter how good you are at shooting, there are times when the winning move is to pass the ball to a teammate who's wide open down the court. And no amount of skills training in shooting or passing is going to give you the ability to know when to use each of your skills. The only way to develop this ability is to play the game.

The analogy carries over to the SAT. When you're studying math — either in school or on your own time — you tend to focus on building one skill at a time: reading a number line, solving an equation, using the formula for the area of a square, and so on. Of course, skills-building practice is important. But when you get to the SAT, you face 54 separate questions that all require different responses.

How do you figure out which skills you'll need to answer a specific SAT question? That's what this chapter is all about. It takes a wide view of SAT strategy, giving you a few perspectives on how to approach the questions. I discuss the fact that the early questions are generally easier than the later ones. I show you how to match the skills in your math toolbox to each question as you face it. You leave this chapter feeling confident that the stuff you've been studying is actually the stuff that you need to answer most of the SAT questions they can throw at you.

Performing SA-Triage: How Difficult Is This Problem?

In a medical emergency, *triage* means prioritizing patients based on their needs so that limited resources can be allocated wisely. On the SAT, your most limited resource is time. And because every question is scored the same regardless of difficulty, your best bet is to focus on the easy questions before proceeding to the hard ones.

Fortunately, each of the three SAT math sections order their questions, roughly speaking, from easiest to hardest. So early questions — the first six or so questions in a section — tend to be easier than later ones. This fact doesn't mean that you'll always find each question progressively harder than the last. But it does give you a clue about how much of your math arsenal you'll need to use to solve a particular problem.

TIP

Even when an early question appears tough, it may be easier than it looks. Here are a few points to consider with early questions on the SAT:

- Early questions usually have a relatively simple way to find the answer. Look for it!
- Don't skip over an early question until you're sure you're not making any headway.
- Consider circling back to any early questions you skipped over *before* you finish the test. On second glance, you may find them easier than what awaits you at the end of the section.

The questions you find in the middle third of a section are of average difficulty. This usually means that they're focusing on one thing, without too much else to distract you. In many cases, middling questions require you to remember and apply a formula. (In the next section, I provide a few pointers on using formulas.)

Sometimes a question of middling difficulty appears confusing because of unusual terminology or symbols. Don't let math jargon throw you: A relatively easy question may look harder because of how it's stated. When a question feels a little impenetrable, it's tempting to skip over it. But if it isn't in the difficult third of the test, you can probably figure it out, so read it again.

The last five to seven problems on each section on the SAT are, generally speaking, harder than the ones that precede them. Usually, the difficulty stems from the fact that they require multiple steps and, in some cases, more than one formula to remember and apply. The later sections of this chapter focus on a few ideas for approaching difficult problems.

Formulas for Success: Working with Math Formulas

In this section, the special focus is on using the formulas from Part II of this book. I give a short review of the formulas you need, including which ones are provided on the test and those you need to commit to memory. I show you how to read a question and anticipate the formulas that may be most helpful to answer it. You also discover how to use more than one formula to answer a question. Finally, I show you how to work through a problem that uses formulas from several different areas of math.

Knowing the right formulas

In this section, I list some formulas that you should know when you take the SAT. I can't say for sure that you'll need absolutely all of them for *your* SAT, but you'll need a bunch of them, so familiarize yourself with them as much as possible.

Using the formulas provided

The nice folks who write the SAT give you seven important geometric formulas for reference. These formulas appear at the beginning of each math section, so you don't have to memorize any of this information. However, you should know when and how to use it (see Chapter 5 for more info on these and other important geometry formulas):

- **Area of a circle:** $A = \pi r^2$
- **Circumference of a circle:** $C = 2\pi r$

- **Area of a rectangle:** $A = lw$
- **Area of a triangle:** $A = \frac{1}{2}bh$
- **Volume of a box (rectangular solid):** $V = lwh$
- **Volume of a cylinder:** $V = \pi r^2 h$
- **Pythagorean theorem:** $c^2 = a^2 + b^2$

The test-makers also provide the relationships of the sides in 30-60-90 and 45-45-90 right triangles:

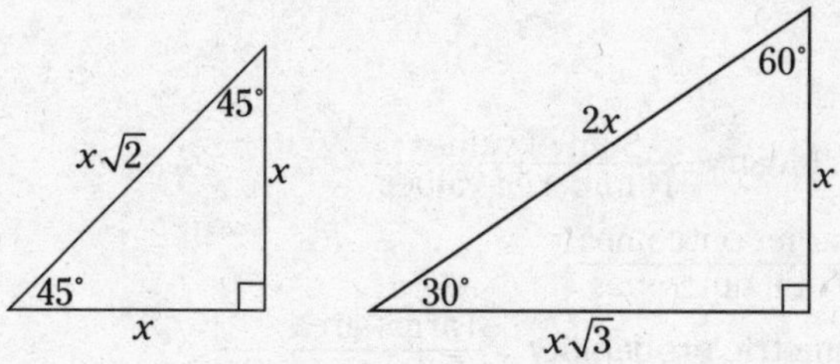

Two additional facts are included:

- The number of degrees of arc in a circle is 360.
- The sum of the measures of degrees of a triangle is 180.

I address these important formulas and facts in Chapter 5. The most important thing to remember is that you don't have to *remember* them for the test — you just have to know how and when to use them.

Remembering the formulas you need

Here I provide you with 17 formulas that you may need for your SAT but that aren't provided on the SAT list of formulas. Make sure you get to know these formulas well and how to use them.

Arithmetic and algebra formulas (Chapters 3 and 4):

- **Calculating percent:** Percent × Number = Result
- **Percent increase and decrease:**

  $$\text{Percent increase or decrease} = \frac{\text{Amount of increase or decrease}}{\text{Old number}}$$
- **Difference of two squares:** $x^2 - y^2 = (x + y)(x - y)$

Geometry formulas (Chapter 5):

- **Supplementary angles:** $\angle 1 + \angle 2 = 180°$
- **Complementary angles:** $\angle 1 + \angle 2 = 90°$
- **Triangle inequality:** $a - b < c < a + b$ (that is, the length of a side of a triangle is greater than the difference of the lengths of the two other sides, and it's less than the sum of the lengths of the two other sides)
- **Perimeter of a rectangle:** $P = 2l + 2w$
- **Area of a parallelogram:** $A = bh$

Coordinate geometry formulas (Chapter 6):

- **Distance formula:** Distance $= \sqrt{(x_2 - x_1)^2 + (y_2 - y_1)^2}$
- **Midpoint formula:** Midpoint $= \left(\frac{x_1 + x_2}{2}, \frac{y_1 + y_2}{2}\right)$
- **Two-point slope formula:** Slope $= \frac{y_2 - y_1}{x_2 - x_1}$
- **Slope-intercept form:** $y = mx + b$
- **Point-slope form:** $y - y_1 = m(x - x_1)$
- **Quadratic function (standard form):** $y = ax^2 + bx + c$

Additional formulas (Chapter 7):

- **Average (arithmetic mean):** Mean $= \frac{\text{Sum of values}}{\text{Number of values}}$
- **Probability:** Probability $= \frac{\text{Target outcomes}}{\text{Total outcomes}}$
- **Geometric probability:** Geometric probability $= \frac{\text{Target area}}{\text{Total area}}$

Memorize these formulas and be able to work with them. Part II of this book (Chapters 3 through 7) gives a detailed look at all of them. Throughout the next section, I provide some tips for working with formulas.

Answering formula questions

Knowing the formulas I've listed in the preceding section is essential for a good SAT score, but it isn't quite enough. You need to feel comfortable using these formulas so that you can move through a problem and come up with the right answer quickly. Fortunately, all formulas have certain things in common. Every formula is simply an equation with more than one variable, so a lot of what you know about working with equations applies to formulas.

Some tougher questions may require you to remember and use two formulas to get the right answer. Generally speaking, the two formulas you need can be distinguished in this way:

- **Formula #2:** The formula that you need answer the specific question
- **Formula #1:** The formula that makes sense of the information you're given

I list these two formulas apparently out of order for a good reason: Formula #2 is easy to spot, but you can't really use it until you use Formula #1. A couple of examples should help make sense of this oddity.

What is the area of the triangle shown in the figure below, given that the average (arithmetic mean) of 5, $3x$, and $8x$ is 20?

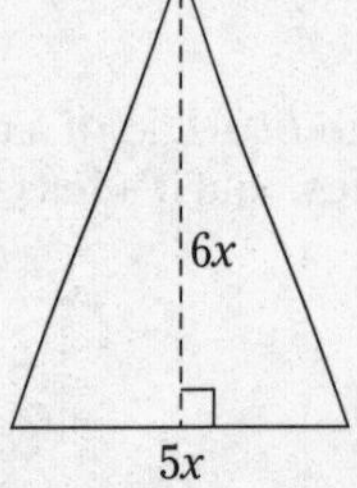

Note: Figure not drawn to scale.

This question specifically asks for the area of a triangle, so here's Formula #2:

$$A = \frac{1}{2}bh$$

However, if you try to use this formula immediately, here's what you get:

$$A = \frac{1}{2}(5x)(6x) = 15x^2$$

At this point, you're stuck: You can't find the area of the triangle because you don't know the value of *x*. To get this value, you need to find an arithmetic mean. So here's Formula #1:

$$\text{Mean} = \frac{\text{Sum of values}}{\text{Number of values}}$$

This formula should be easier to work with, given the information provided in the question. Start by plugging this information into the formula:

$$20 = \frac{5 + 3x + 8x}{3}$$

From here, just solve the equation. Multiply both sides by 3 to remove the fraction, and then solve for *x:*

$$20(3) = \frac{5 + 3x + 8x}{3}$$

$$60 = 5 + 11x$$

$$55 = 11x$$

$$x = 5$$

The base of the triangle is $5x = 5(5) = 25$, and the height is $6x = 6(5) = 30$, so plug these numbers into the formula for the area of a triangle:

$$A = \frac{1}{2}bh = \frac{1}{2}(25)(30) = 375$$

So the area of the triangle is **375**.

EXAMPLE

In the figure below, the area of the rectangular cross-section of the cylinder is 36. What is the volume of the cylinder?

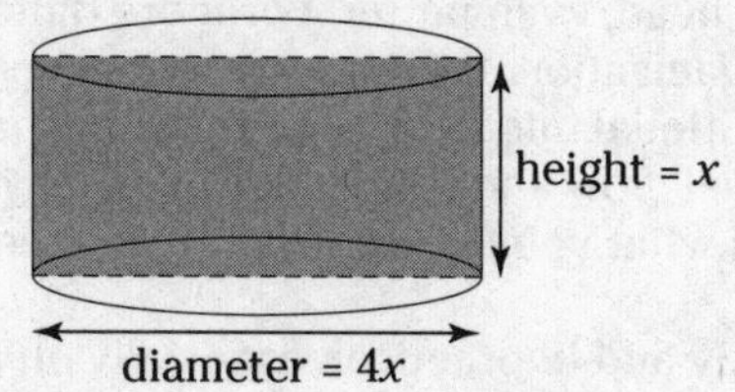

(A) 14π

(B) 18π

(C) 28π

(D) 56π

(E) 108π

The question asks for the volume of the cylinder, so here's Formula #2:

$$V = \pi r^2 h$$

However, you can't use this information yet, because the radius and the height of the cylinder are expressed in terms of x. And to find x, you need to work with the area of the rectangle, so here's Formula #1:

$$A = lw$$

Now plug in the values for the area, length, and width of the rectangle:

$$36 = 4x(x)$$

Solve for x:

$$36 = 4x^2$$

$$9 = x^2$$

$$3 = x$$

Thus, the height of the cylinder is $x = 3$, and the diameter is $x = 12$, so the radius is $x = 6$. Now plug the values for the height and radius into the formula for the volume of a cylinder:

$$V = \pi r^2 h = \pi(6^2)(3) = \pi(36)(3) = 108\pi$$

Therefore, the right answer is **(E)**.

Plotting a Course to Answer Tough Questions

TIP

If an SAT question is difficult, try breaking it down into manageable steps. You need to be clear what an SAT question is asking and what you're given to answer it, so here are the first two questions to ask if you're not immediately clear on how to proceed with an SAT math question:

- What *specifically* is this question asking?
- What information do I have to start with?

TIP

For some questions, outlining the start and end of the problem may be all the planning you need to do. If you can do the outlining in your head, even better. For more difficult questions, however, you may need a little more organization. If the way from the beginning to the end isn't totally clear, write down any additional info from the problem. That way, you can begin to get a sense of how this problem will flow and which skills you may need along the way. Then you can build a bridge between what you have and what you need.

At first glance, this practice may seem unwieldy and impractical, especially on a timed test. Admittedly, what I describe in the following example may seem a bit formal. Nevertheless, taking a few seconds to read a question and plot out a strategy before you leap in can save you a lot of time in the long run.

EXAMPLE

Referring to the number line below, what is the volume of a rectangular solid with a width of *PQ*, a length of *PR*, and a height of *QS*?

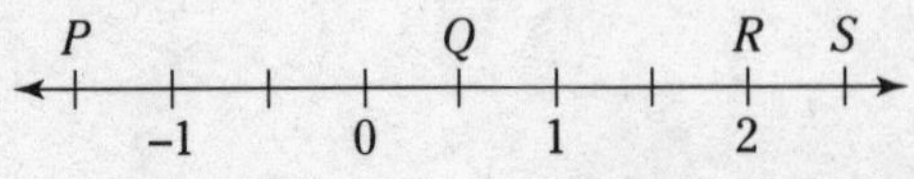

To start, figure out what the question is specifically asking and what information you have to start with. This problem asks for the volume of the box, and it gives you a number line. So you can outline this problem in this way:

Start:	***End:***
Number line	Volume of box

To build a bridge from the number line problem to the area problem, add additional information from the problem as seems appropriate:

Start:		***End:***
Number line	Width = *PQ*	Volume of box = *lwh*
Length of interval?	Length = *PR*	
	Height = *QS*	

Now you get a sense of how this problem will go. Begin by working on the number-line portion of the problem, getting the length of the interval:

Interval = 0.5

Next, find the lengths *PQ*, *PR*, and *QS*. Then plug these values into the formula for the area of a rectangle, and the problem is solved.

$PQ = 4 \text{ intervals} = 2$

$PR = 7 \text{ intervals} = 3.5$

$QS = 4 \text{ intervals} = 2$

Plug these numbers into the formula for the area of a box:

$V = (2)(3.5)(2) = 14$

Therefore, the right answer is **14**.

Tips and Tricks: Looking for Fast, Easy Approaches

The SAT demands not only a thorough knowledge of math but also the ability to think through problems. Here are a few more ways to approach problems.

Using the five resources at your service

REMEMBER

When taking the SAT, you have five resources — aside from your brain — available to help you answer the questions:

- The question itself
- The five possible answers (for multiple-choice questions)

- The *Reference Information* at the beginning of each SAT math section
- Your pencil and the test-book margins
- Your calculator

Using them all can help you push through questions that may otherwise back you up. In this section, I discuss them all.

Reading the question carefully: The truth is in there

REMEMBER

Every question contains all the information you need to answer it — really! So take an extra second or two with each question to make sure you're clear on the information it contains and what it's asking. And if you get stuck, don't just stare at your notes — reread the question to scan for any information that you haven't used yet or may have misunderstood on your first reading.

Scanning your choices: The right answer is staring you in the face

All but ten of the questions on the SAT are multiple-choice questions. A multiple-choice question gives you an advantage that you don't have in your math classes: The right answer is right in front of you — along, of course, with four wrong answers.

TIP

Some problems — especially algebra problems — may be easier to solve if you plug in potential answers to see which one fits best. Even glancing at the answers and ruling out wrong ones can cut down on the calculations you have to do, especially if you're plugging in test numbers or drawing figures.

You can also rule out answers to help you complete a half-finished problem. For example, suppose you're stuck on a problem, but you've figured out that the answer must be negative. To save time, consider ruling out the positive answers and guessing one of the negative answers; then move on. The SAT penalizes you ¼ point for wrong multiple-choice answers, but a good strategy is to guess if you can rule out at least one wrong answer.

Utilizing the Reference Information

The first page of each SAT math section includes a wealth of *Reference Information* that contains formulas and other useful math stuff that you receive free of charge. So don't strain your brain to remember the formula for the volume of a cylinder — look it up!

Also, if you get stuck on a problem — especially a geometry problem — flip back to this information and glance over it. You may notice a formula that comes in handy for answering the question you're working on.

Using work space to take short, effective notes

You can use the margins of your SAT test book as work space for jotting down notes and solving equations. Use this space to your advantage, but don't overwrite. Usually, there's a perfect balance between trying to figure out too much in your head (which can lead to errors) and writing down everything (which can be time-consuming and still not help you get the right answer).

For example, suppose you need to know how many numbers between 10 and 40 are divisible by 3. You may want to jot down these numbers as you think of them (12, 15, 18, and so on) so you don't miscount. But if you find yourself listing every possible number and then crossing out the wrong ones, you're probably taking more time than you need to.

Often, the best way to use work space is to draw a small visual aid, such as a picture, a table, or a graph. In some cases, drawing the right picture will practically cause the answer to jump off the page.

Calculating the smart way

Your calculator can be indispensible if you use it correctly. If you're reasonably adept with a calculator, you can save yourself from lots of number-crunching. And if you get really good at using your calculator, you can solve equations and graph functions to gain a real advantage over the other test-takers.

At the same time, don't rely on your calculator to do every little thing for you. Keying in numbers and symbols takes time, and if you make a mistake punching in numbers, you won't get the right answer.

TIP

Don't enter long strings of symbols into your calculator — longer calculations are far more likely to contain errors that you won't catch. Instead, break problems down into small calculations that you can reality-check: If you enter 133 – 56 and get the answer 8,432,789, you probably should enter it again!

Putting your brain to work

On the SAT, your brain is your most important resource. In fact, it's the resource that manages all your other problem-solving tools. Unlike computers, brains can solve problems not only by plodding away at them but by scanning a set of options and intuitively drawing on the one that feels most useful.

TIP

If you get stuck on a problem by using one approach, think creatively and try another. Here are some problem-solving options:

- **Think about the problem logically.** Sometimes if you understand the math concepts, you can rule out wrong answers or find a shortcut that allows you to do fewer calculations. For instance, instead of calculating how much of a pie someone ate and subtracting that from the whole, you may want to start with a fraction that represents how much pie is left over. You may then be able to do the problem without having to subtract fractions.
- **Fill in some made-up numbers.** Test numbers can sometimes help you get a handle on what's going on with a problem, allowing you to think through the problem more clearly than if you were to use the variables you've been given. Plugging in a 0 or a 1 (whichever seems easiest to work with) can be especially helpful. Or if the given numbers are large, you may be able to substitute some smaller numbers and pick up on a pattern.
- **Use your calculator in a different way.** Solving an equation for *y* and graphing it or setting up a table of values is sometimes useful. Graphing an equation and then zooming in on the *zeros* (where the graph crosses the *x*-axis) may help you pick out the right answer.
- **Draw a picture that illustrates the problem you're working on.** Even problems that aren't strictly visual can sometimes be made easier with the right picture. You may even want to redraw some given geometry figures to better understand what's going on.
- **Scan the five answer choices to see whether one of them makes sense given the work you're already done.** Or try plugging answers one by one to see which one's correct.

The next sections show how two of these strategies — using logic and plugging in test numbers — can help you solve SAT problems.

Thinking through problems logically before doing the math

In many cases, there's more than one way to solve a problem. Sometimes thinking logically about the situation can help you cut down on the actual math you have to slog through. If you see an easy way in, go ahead and follow it. For instance, here's a question I show you how to solve in Chapter 8:

Each of the 27 children in Ms. Witherspoon's class has either two or three siblings. If the total number of siblings is 68, how many children have exactly two siblings?

This is a grid-in question, which means it isn't among the first eight questions in a section. Still, if it's among the first couple of grid-in questions, it may not be all that difficult.

You could solve this problem by coming up with the equation $2x + 3(27 - x) = 68$, where x is the number of students with two siblings (as I show you in Chapter 8). But there's a simple way to look at it: Consider that every child has *at least* two siblings, so this accounts for $2 \times 27 = 54$ siblings. This leaves 14 siblings unaccounted for, so 14 of the 27 children have three siblings. Therefore, the remaining 13 children have only two siblings, so the right answer is **13**.

Plug and play: Tackling property questions by plugging in test numbers

Problems that deal with properties of a number can seem very tricky, but there's often an easy way to solve them: Choose a simple number that has the stated property and then use it to rule out wrong answers. A few examples should help make this procedure clear.

If n is the product of any three consecutive positive integers, which of the following must be a property of n?

(A) n is divisible by 4.

(B) n is divisible by 5.

(C) n is divisible by 6.

(D) n is divisible by 7.

(E) n is divisible by 8.

This question tells you that the property is true of *every* possible n, provided that n is the product of three consecutive positive integers. So find an easy value n to work with and test it. Try using 1, 2, and 3:

Let $n = 1 \times 2 \times 3 = 6$

The goal now is to *rule out* all answers that don't fit. The number 6 isn't divisible by 4, 5, 7, or 8, so you can rule out (A), (B), (D), and (E). Therefore, the right answer is **(C).**

This procedure of plugging in numbers works only for ruling out wrong answers, not for choosing the right answer. In one variation on this type of question, you're asked to identify a property that a number *cannot* have. This time, you can rule out an answer by finding at least one example of when the property holds true.

If x is an integer and $n = 4x + 3$, which of the following CANNOT be a property of n?

(A) n is an odd number.

(B) n is an even number.

(C) n is divisible by 3.

(D) n is divisible by 5.

(E) n is divisible by 7.

To start out, pick an easy integer for x: Let $x = 0$.

$$n = 4(0) + 3 = 0 + 3 = 3$$

In this case, n is both odd and divisible by 3, so you can rule out answers (A) and (C). Next, let $x = 1$.

$$n = 4(1) + 3 = 4 + 3 = 7$$

This time, n is divisible by 7, so you can rule out answer (E). Now let $x = 2$:

$$n = 4(2) + 3 = 8 + 3 = 11$$

You can't rule out any answers, so let $x = 3$:

$$n = 4(3) + 3 = 12 + 3 = 15$$

In this case, n is divisible by 5, so you can rule out answer (D). By elimination, the right answer is **(B).**

Part IV
Practice Makes Perfect: SAT Math Practice Tests

The 5th Wave
By Rich Tennant
Jimmy spent all day concentrating on his upcoming SAT. This proved an excellent study habit up until he tried milking his father's prize bull.
©RICHTENNANT

In this part . . .

Part IV provides you with an opportunity to put your training to the test — literally. Try your skills on three practice tests, each with three parts, just like the real SAT math sections. I also give you not just the answer but a detailed solution to each question.

Chapter 10

Practice Test 1

Ready to put your preparation to the test? This practice test includes three math sections, just like the ones you'll face on your actual SAT. Work through each section in the time stated at the top of that section.

As on the SAT, you may use a calculator. I also recommend that you tear out and use the answer sheet provided at the beginning of this chapter.

Good luck!

Answer Sheet for Practice Test 1

Use the ovals and grid-ins provided with this practice exam to record your answers.

Section 1

1. Ⓐ Ⓑ Ⓒ Ⓓ Ⓔ
2. Ⓐ Ⓑ Ⓒ Ⓓ Ⓔ
3. Ⓐ Ⓑ Ⓒ Ⓓ Ⓔ
4. Ⓐ Ⓑ Ⓒ Ⓓ Ⓔ
5. Ⓐ Ⓑ Ⓒ Ⓓ Ⓔ
6. Ⓐ Ⓑ Ⓒ Ⓓ Ⓔ
7. Ⓐ Ⓑ Ⓒ Ⓓ Ⓔ
8. Ⓐ Ⓑ Ⓒ Ⓓ Ⓔ
9. Ⓐ Ⓑ Ⓒ Ⓓ Ⓔ
10. Ⓐ Ⓑ Ⓒ Ⓓ Ⓔ
11. Ⓐ Ⓑ Ⓒ Ⓓ Ⓔ
12. Ⓐ Ⓑ Ⓒ Ⓓ Ⓔ
13. Ⓐ Ⓑ Ⓒ Ⓓ Ⓔ
14. Ⓐ Ⓑ Ⓒ Ⓓ Ⓔ
15. Ⓐ Ⓑ Ⓒ Ⓓ Ⓔ
16. Ⓐ Ⓑ Ⓒ Ⓓ Ⓔ
17. Ⓐ Ⓑ Ⓒ Ⓓ Ⓔ
18. Ⓐ Ⓑ Ⓒ Ⓓ Ⓔ
19. Ⓐ Ⓑ Ⓒ Ⓓ Ⓔ
20. Ⓐ Ⓑ Ⓒ Ⓓ Ⓔ

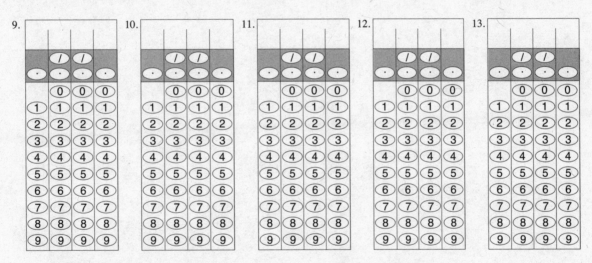

Section 2

1. Ⓐ Ⓑ Ⓒ Ⓓ Ⓔ
2. Ⓐ Ⓑ Ⓒ Ⓓ Ⓔ
3. Ⓐ Ⓑ Ⓒ Ⓓ Ⓔ
4. Ⓐ Ⓑ Ⓒ Ⓓ Ⓔ
5. Ⓐ Ⓑ Ⓒ Ⓓ Ⓔ
6. Ⓐ Ⓑ Ⓒ Ⓓ Ⓔ
7. Ⓐ Ⓑ Ⓒ Ⓓ Ⓔ
8. Ⓐ Ⓑ Ⓒ Ⓓ Ⓔ

Grid-ins 9–18 (each grid identical):

	/	/	
.	.	.	.
	0	0	0
1	1	1	1
2	2	2	2
3	3	3	3
4	4	4	4
5	5	5	5
6	6	6	6
7	7	7	7
8	8	8	8
9	9	9	9

9. 10. 11. 12. 13. 14. 15. 16. 17. 18.

Section 3

1. (A) (B) (C) (D) (E)	5. (A) (B) (C) (D) (E)	9. (A) (B) (C) (D) (E)	13. (A) (B) (C) (D) (E)
2. (A) (B) (C) (D) (E)	6. (A) (B) (C) (D) (E)	10. (A) (B) (C) (D) (E)	14. (A) (B) (C) (D) (E)
3. (A) (B) (C) (D) (E)	7. (A) (B) (C) (D) (E)	11. (A) (B) (C) (D) (E)	15. (A) (B) (C) (D) (E)
4. (A) (B) (C) (D) (E)	8. (A) (B) (C) (D) (E)	12. (A) (B) (C) (D) (E)	16. (A) (B) (C) (D) (E)

Section 1

Time: 25 minutes for 20 questions

Directions: Choose the *best* answer to each question. Mark the corresponding oval on the answer sheet.

Notes:

- You may use a calculator.
- All numbers used in this exam are real numbers.
- All figures lie in a plane.
- All figures may be assumed to be to scale unless the problem specifically indicates otherwise.

Reference Information:

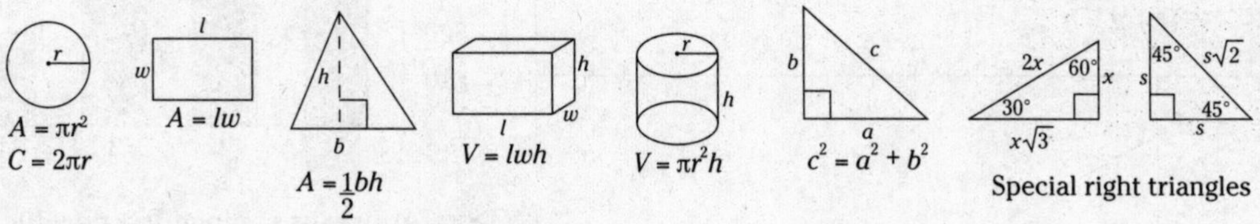

Special right triangles

There are 360 degrees of arc in a circle.

There are 180 degrees in the sum of the interior angles of a triangle.

1. The mean average of $2x$, $3x$, and 17 is 24. What is the value of x?

   (A) 8
   (B) 9
   (C) 11
   (D) 13
   (E) 14

2. If $4n - 5 > 15$, which of the following could be the value of n?

   (A) –6
   (B) –5
   (C) 0
   (D) 5
   (E) 6

3. If $f(x) = \frac{-6 + x^2}{3x}$ for all nonzero values of x, then $f(3)$ =

   (A) 1
   (B) –1
   (C) $\frac{1}{3}$
   (D) $\frac{2}{3}$
   (E) $-\frac{2}{3}$

Go on to next page

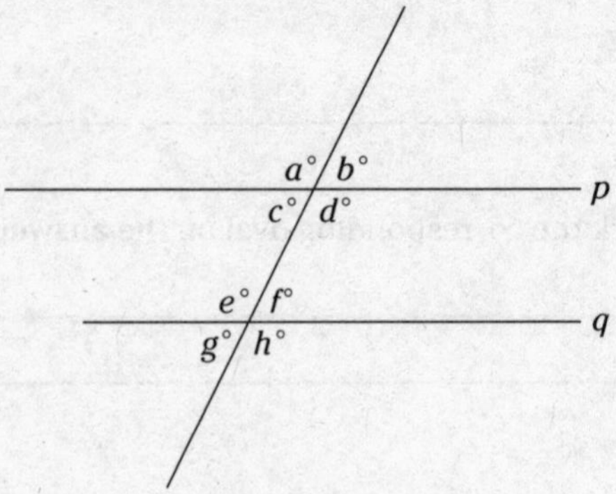

4. In the figure above, if $p \parallel q$, which of the following must be true?

(A) $a + d = 180$

(B) $a + e = 180$

(C) $a + h = 180$

(D) $b = g$

(E) $g = h$

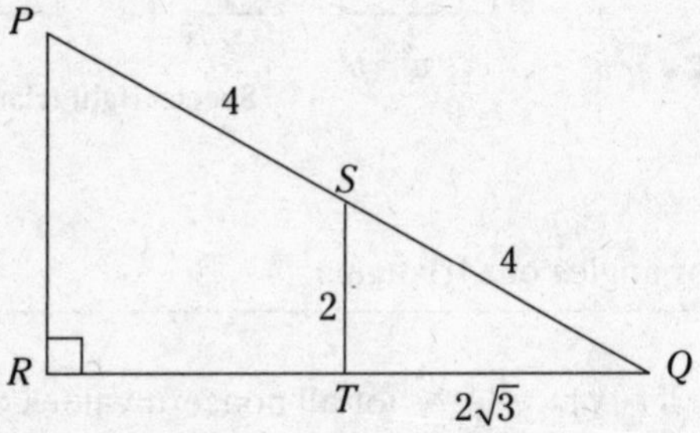

5. In the figure above, $\triangle QRP$ is similar to $\triangle QTS$. What is the length of $\overline{RT}$?

(A) $\sqrt{2}$

(B) $\sqrt{3}$

(C) $2\sqrt{3}$

(D) $3\sqrt{2}$

(E) $4\sqrt{3}$

6. Set P is the set of all positive integers less than 50, and set Q is the set of all integers that are divisible by 7. How many elements are in the intersection of set P and set Q?

(A) Fewer than 5

(B) 5

(C) 6

(D) 7

(E) More than 7

7. If m is a positive number and $m^2 - 11 = 39$, then $m =$

(A) $2\sqrt{2}$

(B) $5\sqrt{2}$

(C) $7\sqrt{2}$

(D) $2\sqrt{5}$

(E) $2\sqrt{7}$

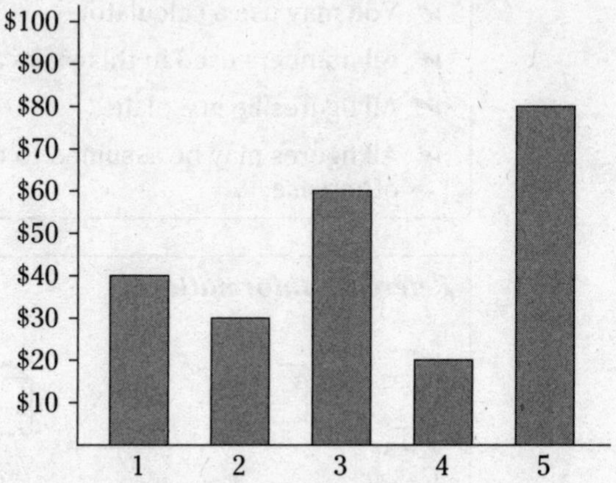

8. Andrea is saving for a new bicycle, and she's been putting away money from her weekly paycheck in \$10 increments for the last five weeks. According to the graph above, in which two weeks did she save a total of exactly \$100?

(A) Weeks 1 and 5

(B) Weeks 2 and 3

(C) Weeks 2 and 5

(D) Weeks 3 and 5

(E) Weeks 4 and 5

Go on to next page

9. Eve's house number is a three-digit number that satisfies the conditions below:

The first digit is an even number greater than 2.

The second digit is an odd number less than 8.

The third digit is the product of the first two digits.

How many three-digit numbers satisfy all of these conditions?

(A) One

(B) Two

(C) Three

(D) Four

(E) More than four

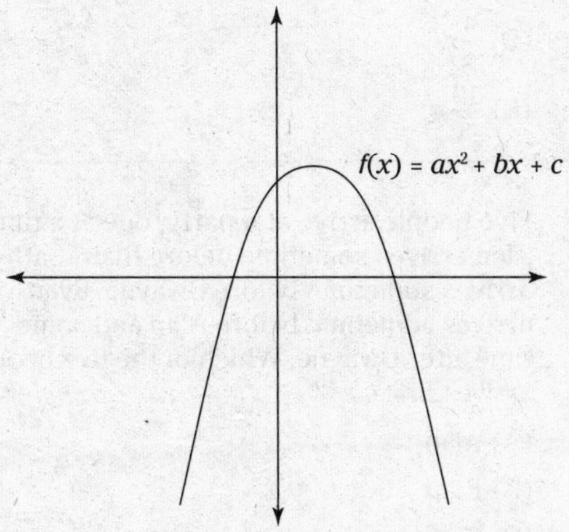

10. The graph above shows the function $f(x) = ax^2 + bx + c$. Which of the following CANNOT be true?

(A) $a < 0$

(B) $b > 0$

(C) $c > 0$

(D) $a < b$

(E) $a > c$

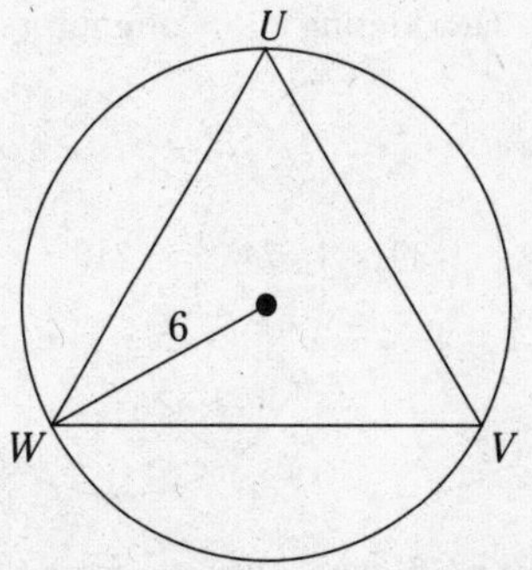

11. In the figure above, the circle has a radius of 6 and $\triangle UVW$ is equilateral. What is the arc length along the circle clockwise from point U to point V?

(A) π

(B) 2π

(C) 3π

(D) 4π

(E) 6π

12. A circle has a radius of 3, and another circle has a diameter of 3. What is the combined area of the two circles?

(A) 9π

(B) 18π

(C) $\frac{9}{2}\pi$

(D) $\frac{9}{4}\pi$

(E) $\frac{45}{4}\pi$

13. What is the equation of a line that passes through the point (0, –7) and is perpendicular to $y = 4x + 3$?

(A) $y = -4x + 3$

(B) $y = 4x - 7$

(C) $y = -\frac{1}{4}x + 3$

(D) $y = \frac{1}{4}x - 7$

(E) $y = -\frac{1}{4}x - 7$

Go on to next page

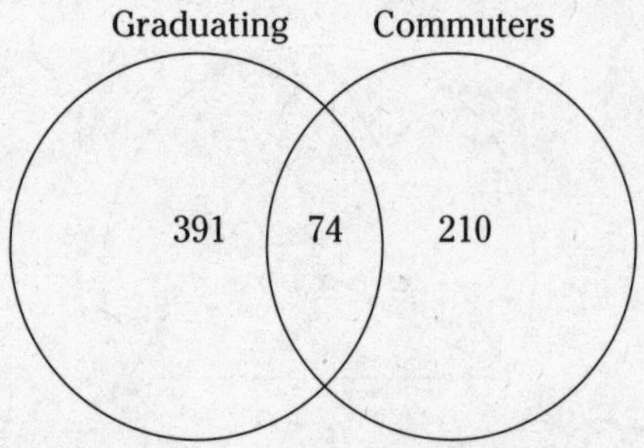

14. The Venn diagram above gives the breakdown of students at Averill College who are graduating this year and those who are commuters. If 10% of all students at the college are commuters who are graduating this year, how many students are noncommuters who are not graduating this year?

(A) 65

(B) 284

(C) 465

(D) 601

(E) 675

15. What is the difference between the mode and the median of the following list of values: 8, 10, 10, 15, 16, 18, 18, 18, 27, 36?

(A) 1

(B) 2

(C) 3

(D) 4

(E) 5

16. In the figure above, all circles are tangent as shown. What is the area of the shaded region if each of the small circles has a diameter of 2?

(A) π

(B) 2π

(C) 7π

(D) $\frac{9}{4}\pi$

(E) $\frac{19}{4}\pi$

17. Five people arrive at a party, one at a time. Alan arrives sometime before Blair. Cathy arrives sometime before Dwayne. Evan arrives sometime before Alan and sometime after Dwayne. Which of the five people arrives first?

(A) Alan

(B) Blair

(C) Cathy

(D) Dwayne

(E) Evan

Go on to next page

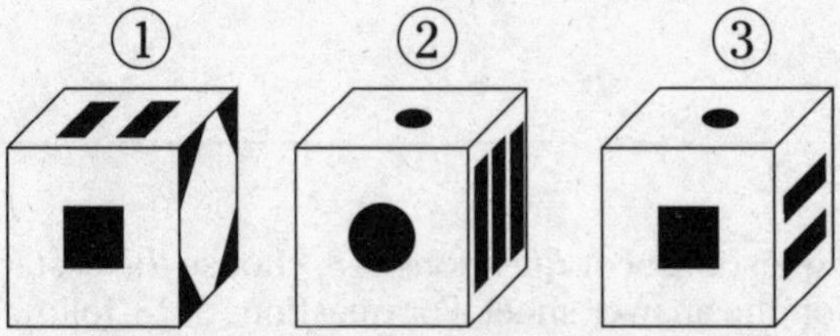

18. The figure above shows three perspectives of the same cube. Which of the following shapes can be folded up to form the same cube?

(A)

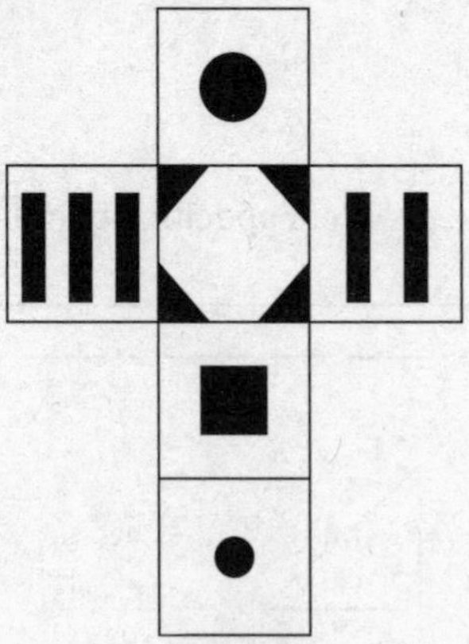

(B)

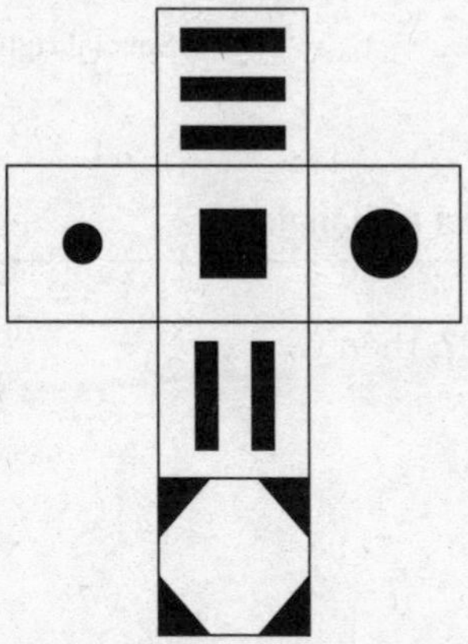

(C)

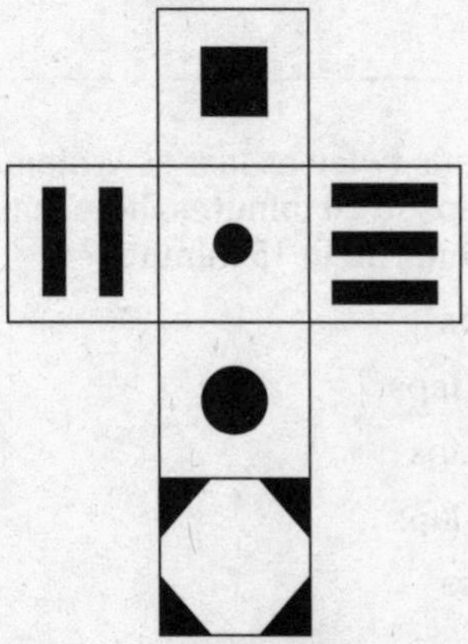

(D)

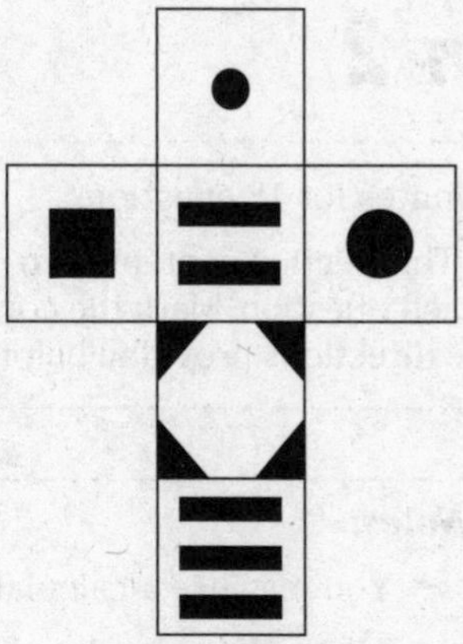

(E)

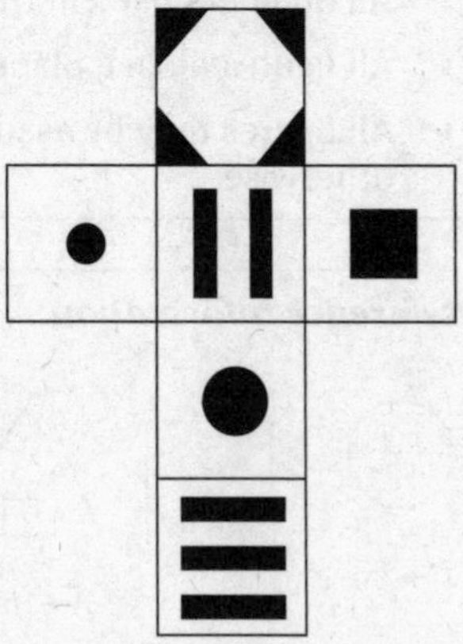

19. If $x^2 - 4y^2 = 2x + 4y$, with $x > 0$ and $y > 0$, what is the value of y in terms of x?

(A) $x - 1$

(B) $x + 2$

(C) $x - 2$

(D) $\frac{x}{2} + 1$

(E) $\frac{x}{2} - 1$

20. How many positive two-digit numbers n are divisible by 1, n, and exactly one other number?

(A) One

(B) Two

(C) Three

(D) Four

(E) More than four

STOP DO NOT TURN THE PAGE UNTIL TOLD TO DO SO.
DO NOT RETURN TO A PREVIOUS TEST.

Section 2

Time: 25 minutes for 18 questions

Directions: This section contains two different types of questions. For questions 1–8, choose the *best* answer to each question. Mark the corresponding oval on the answer sheet. For questions 9–18, follow the separate directions provided before those questions.

Notes:

- You may use a calculator.
- All numbers used in this exam are real numbers.
- All figures lie in a plane.
- All figures may be assumed to be to scale unless the problem specifically indicates otherwise.

Reference Information:

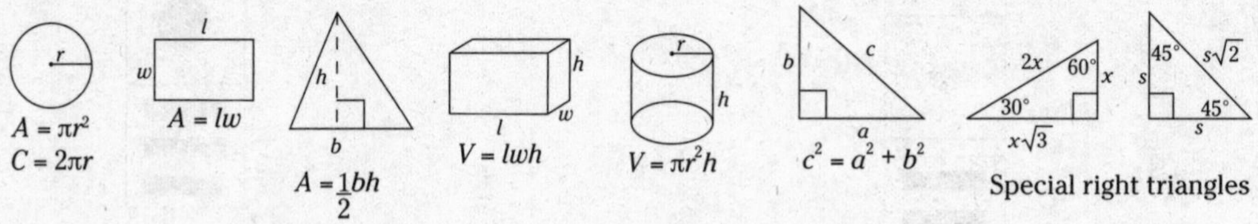

Special right triangles

There are 360 degrees of arc in a circle.

There are 180 degrees in the sum of the interior angles of a triangle.

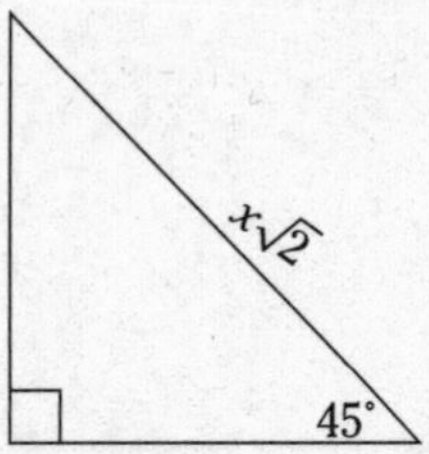

1. In the figure above, the area of the triangle is 8 square inches. How many inches is *x?*
   (A) 1
   (B) 2
   (C) 4
   (D) 8
   (E) 16

2. If $3^{y-1} = 27$, then y =
   (A) 2
   (B) 3
   (C) 4
   (D) 5
   (E) 9

3. Tasha runs twice as fast as Willem. If Tasha runs 8 laps in 20 minutes, how many laps can Willem run in 15 minutes?
   (A) 3 laps
   (B) 3.25 laps
   (C) 3.5 laps
   (D) 3.75 laps
   (E) 4 laps

Go on to next page

4. If $v > 8$ and $vw = 120$, which of the following must be true?

(A) $v < 120$

(B) $v > 120$

(C) $w < 15$

(D) $w = 15$

(E) $w > 15$

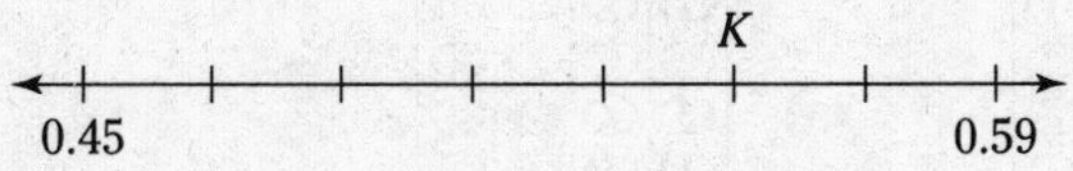

5. On the number line above, what is the value of *K?*

(A) 0.50

(B) 0.54

(C) 0.55

(D) 0.57

(E) 0.58

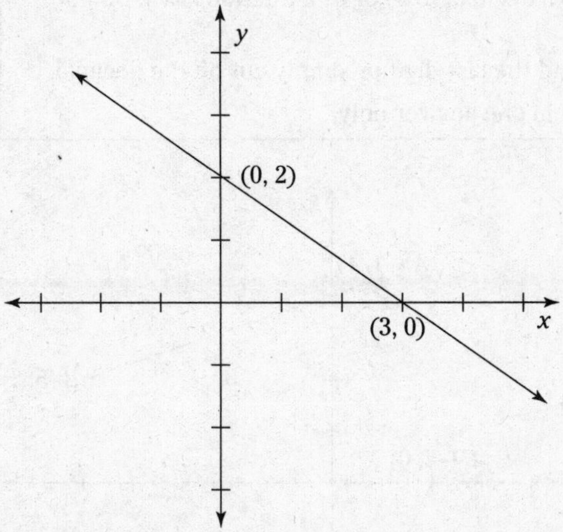

6. What is the equation of a line that is parallel to the line shown in the figure above and that passes through the point (0, –4)?

(A) $y = \frac{2}{3}x$

(B) $y = -\frac{3}{2}x + 4$

(C) $y = \frac{2}{3}x + 4$

(D) $y = -\frac{2}{3}x - 4$

(E) $y = -\frac{3}{2}x - 4$

7. Beth can wash a car by herself in 10 minutes, and Liza can wash one in 15 minutes. If they work together, how many minutes will they take to wash one car?

(A) 3 minutes

(B) 4 minutes

(C) 4.5 minutes

(D) 5 minutes

(E) 6 minutes

8. After the first number, each number in a sequence is one less than twice the previous number. The sixth number in the sequence is 33. What is the sum of the first three numbers?

(A) 5.5

(B) 8

(C) 10

(D) 10.5

(E) 17

Go on to next page

Directions for student-produced response questions 9–18: Solve the problem and then write your answer in the boxes on the answer sheet. Then mark the ovals corresponding to your answer, as shown in the following examples. Note the fraction line and the decimal points.

Answer: 7/2 Answer: 3.25 Answer: 853

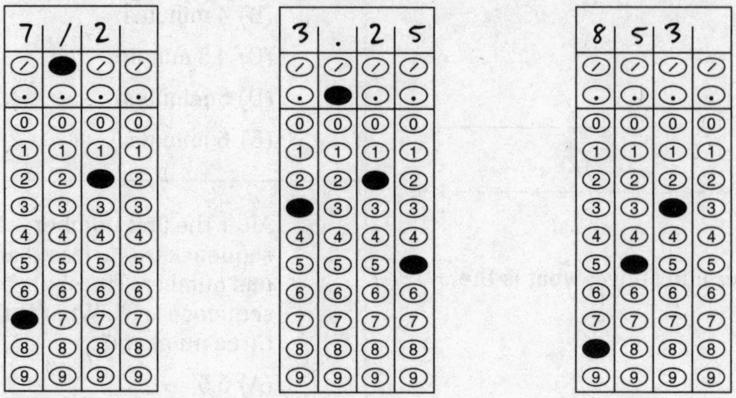

- Although you do not have to write the solutions in the boxes, you do have to blacken the corresponding ovals. You should fill in the boxes to avoid confusion. Only the blackened ovals will be scored. The numbers in the boxes will not be read.
- There are no negative answers.
- Mixed numbers, such as 3½, may be gridded in as a decimal (3.5) or as a fraction (7/2). Do not grid in 31/2; it will be read as 31/2.
- Grid in a decimal as far as possible. You may round the last digit or simply cut off the decimal.
- A question may have more than one answer. Grid in one answer only.

9. A small rectangular box has a length of 6 inches, a width of 4 inches, and a height of 2 inches. How many of these boxes can fit inside a larger box that is a cube whose side is 12 inches?

10. Let $x|y|z$ be defined as $x^y + y^z$. What is the value of $9|2|8$?

11. If p percent of 1,300 is 156, then 36 is p percent of what number?

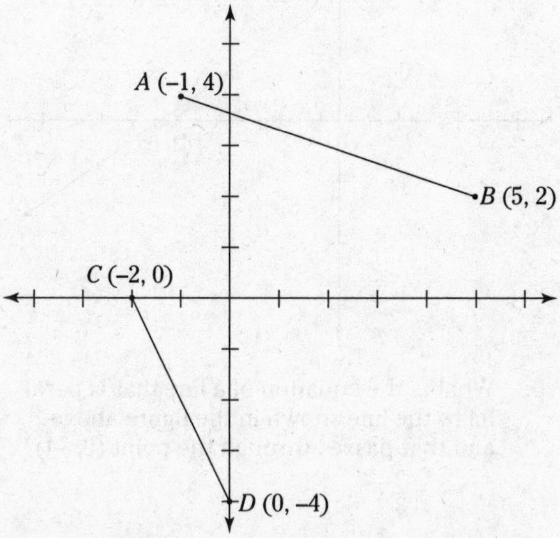

12. In the figure above, what is the slope of the line connecting the midpoint of $\overline{AB}$ with the midpoint of $\overline{CD}$?

Go on to next page

13. Jeffrey has a cell phone plan that gives him 800 minutes per month for $45, charges $0.10 per minute for the next 800 minutes, and charges $0.25 for each additional minute after that. How many minutes did he use last month if his bill was $168?

14. Together, Darren and Errol did 53 pushups. If Darren had done seven more pushups, he would have done twice as many pushups as Errol. How many pushups did Errol do?

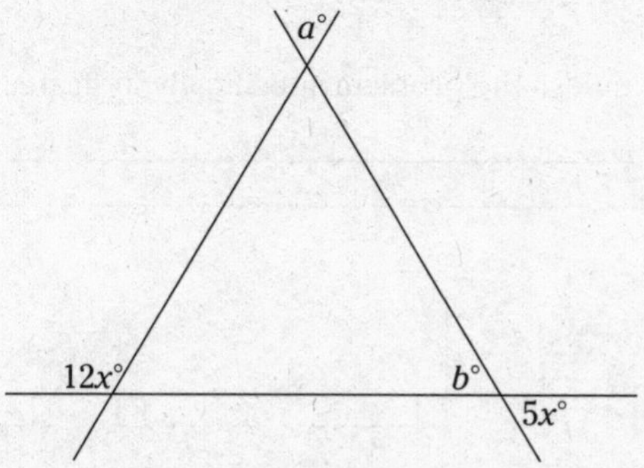

15. In the figure above, what is the ratio of b to a?

16. If $2x - 5y = 0$, what number does $\frac{x}{y} - \frac{y}{x}$ equal?

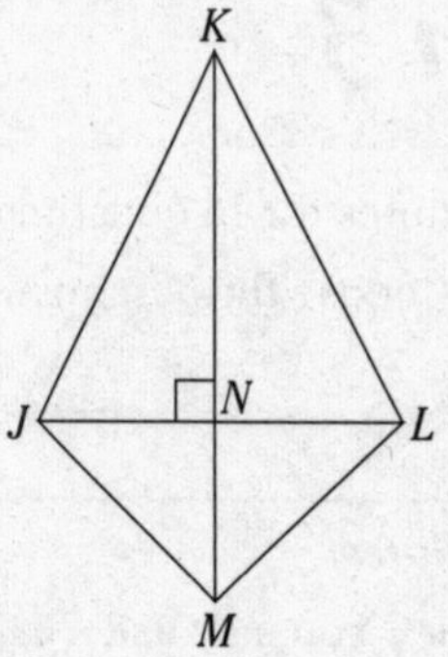

Note: Figure not drawn to scale.

17. In the figure above, $NM = 3$, $ML = 5$, the area of $\triangle JKM$ is 10, and the area of $\triangle JLM$ is 9. What is the area of $JKLM$?

18. How many different ways can you roll five dice such that you roll five different numbers, including either 1 or 6 but not both?

STOP DO NOT TURN THE PAGE UNTIL TOLD TO DO SO. DO NOT RETURN TO A PREVIOUS TEST.

Section 3

Time: 20 minutes for 16 questions

Directions: Choose the *best* answer to each question. Mark the corresponding oval on the answer sheet.

Notes:

- You may use a calculator.
- All numbers used in this exam are real numbers.
- All figures lie in a plane.
- All figures may be assumed to be to scale unless the problem specifically indicates otherwise.

Reference Information:

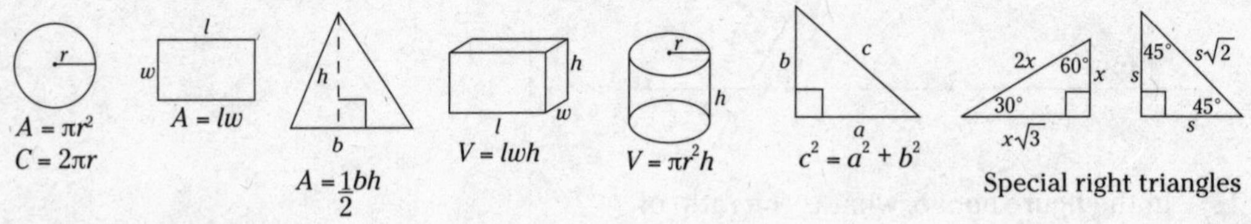

There are 360 degrees of arc in a circle.

There are 180 degrees in the sum of the interior angles of a triangle.

1. If $x = -2$ and $y = 6$, what is the value of $4x^3 - xy^2$?

(A) 40

(B) –40

(C) 104

(D) –104

(E) –176

2. If $a - b = 1$, then $a + 2b =$

(A) $1 + b$

(B) $1 - b$

(C) $1 + 2b$

(D) $1 + 3b$

(E) $1 - 3b$

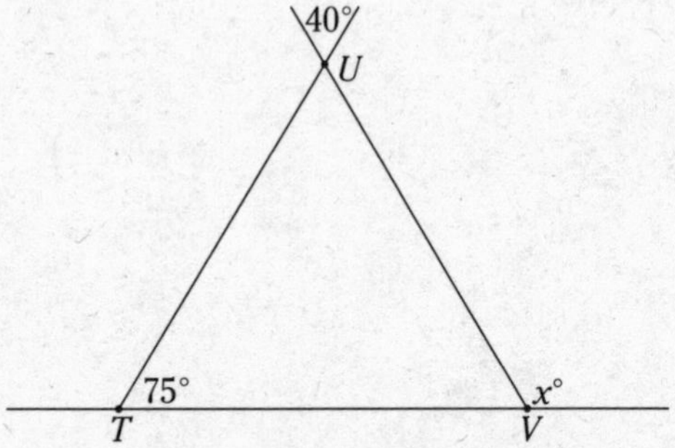

Note: Figure not drawn to scale.

3. In the figure above, what is the value of x?

(A) 115

(B) 120

(C) 125

(D) 130

(E) 135

Go on to next page

4. Which of the following values of x is NOT in the domain of $f(x)=\dfrac{1}{2x^2-18}$?

(A) –3

(B) –1

(C) 0

(D) 2

(E) 9

5. Let $x \&\& y$ be defined as $1-\dfrac{x}{y}$. What is the value of $\dfrac{2\&\&3}{4\&\&5}$?

(A) $\frac{2}{5}$

(B) $\frac{3}{5}$

(C) $\frac{5}{3}$

(D) $\frac{1}{15}$

(E) $\frac{8}{15}$

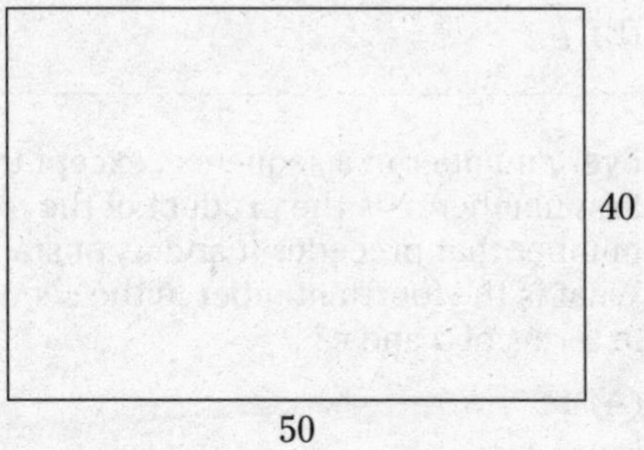

6. If the length and width of the rectangle in the figure above are each increased by 30%, what will the perimeter of the rectangle be?

(A) 117

(B) 180

(C) 234

(D) 2,000

(E) 3,505

7. Set P contains only prime numbers, and set S contains only square numbers. Which of the following sets could be the union of set P and set S?

(A) {1, 3, 5, 7, 9, 11, 13}

(B) {2, 4, 6}

(C) {15, 16, 17}

(D) {35, 36, 37}

(E) {97, 99, 101, 103}

8. If $\sqrt{x^2+3}=n$ and x is a positive number, what is the value of x in terms of n?

(A) $(n^2+3)^2$

(B) $(n^2-3)^2$

(C) $\left(\sqrt{n}-3\right)^2$

(D) $\sqrt{n^2+3}$

(E) $\sqrt{n^2-3}$

9. Elaine can run three miles in the time it takes her to walk one mile. If she can run five miles in 40 minutes, how long will it take her to walk four miles?

(A) 60 minutes

(B) 72 minutes

(C) 84 minutes

(D) 96 minutes

(E) 108 minutes

Go on to next page

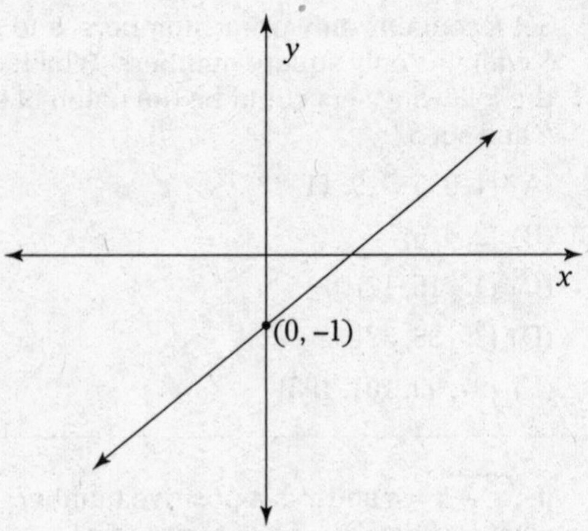

10. In the figure above, the line has a slope of $\frac{2}{3}$. What is the value of x when $y = 4$?

(A) $\frac{5}{3}$

(B) $\frac{11}{3}$

(C) $\frac{9}{2}$

(D) $\frac{11}{2}$

(E) $\frac{15}{2}$

11. Which of the following numbers are divisible by exactly two different prime numbers?

I. 60

II. 80

III. 100

(A) I only

(B) II only

(C) III only

(D) I and II only

(E) II and III only

12. A math class has 12 boys and 15 girls. The first three students to arrive today were all boys. What is the probability that the fourth student to arrive was also a boy?

(A) $\frac{1}{2}$

(B) $\frac{1}{3}$

(C) $\frac{3}{4}$

(D) $\frac{3}{8}$

(E) $\frac{4}{9}$

13. The sum of four different positive integers is 27. If one of the integers is 20, which of the following must be one of the numbers?

(A) 3

(B) 4

(C) 5

(D) 6

(E) 7

14. Every number in a sequence, except the first number *a*, is the product of the number that precedes it and a constant *c*. What is the fourth number in the sequence in terms of *a* and *c*?

(A) ac

(B) ac^2

(C) $(ac)^2$

(D) ac^3

(E) $(ac)^3$

Go on to next page

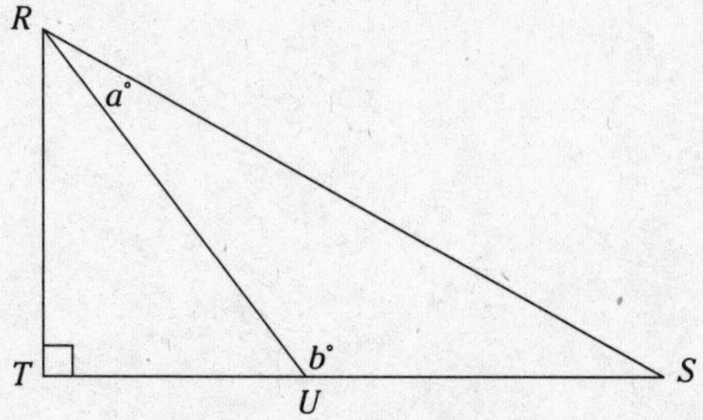

Note: Figure not drawn to scale.

15. In the figure above, $\triangle RST$ is a right triangle, $a = 15$, $b = 135$, and $TU = 4$. What is the area of $\triangle RSU$?

(A) $8\sqrt{2}$

(B) $8\sqrt{3}$

(C) $8\sqrt{3} - 8$

(D) $16\sqrt{2}$

(E) $16\sqrt{3} - 16$

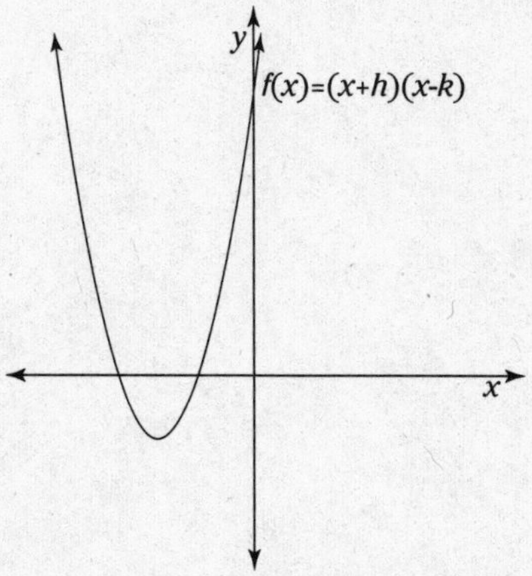

16. In the figure above, $f(x) = (x + h)(x - k)$. Which of the following could be values of h and k?

(A) $h = 2, k = 1$

(B) $h = -2, k = 4$

(C) $h = -1, k = -3$

(D) $h = -3, k = \frac{1}{2}$

(E) $h = 5, k = -2$

DO NOT TURN THE PAGE UNTIL TOLD TO DO SO.
DO NOT RETURN TO A PREVIOUS TEST.

Chapter 11

Answers and Explanations for Practice Test 1

Here are the answers to the 54 questions from Practice Test 1 in Chapter 10. For each question, I provide a detailed explanation showing a possible way to find the correct answer. I recommend reading these explanations to further hone your SAT math skills. If you just want to check your answers quickly, you can skip to the end of the chapter, where I've provided a basic Answer Key.

Solutions to Section 1 Questions

1. **C.** Use the formula for a mean average: Mean $= \frac{\text{Sum of values}}{\text{Number of values}}$. Substitute in the three values from the problem, as well as the mean:

   $$24 = \frac{2x+3x+17}{3}$$

   Multiply both sides by 3 and solve for *x:*

   $$72 = 2x + 3x + 17$$

   $$72 = 5x + 17$$

   $$55 = 5x$$

   $$11 = x$$

   Thus, the right answer is (C).

2. **E.** Solve the inequality for *n:*

   $$4n - 5 > 15$$

   $$4n > 20$$

   $$n > 5$$

   Thus, *n* could be 6, so the right answer is (E). (An alternative approach to this problem is to notice that the goal is to maximize the value of $4n - 5$, so the right answer must be the greatest value of *n*.)

3. **C.** Plug in 3 for *x* into the function:

   $$f(3) = \frac{-6+3^2}{3(3)} = \frac{3}{9} = \frac{1}{3}$$

   Therefore, the right answer is (C).

4. **D.** Angle b and angle c are vertical angles, so $b = c$. And angle c and angle g are corresponding angles, so $c = g$. Therefore, $b = g$, so the right answer is (D).

5. **C.** The two triangles are similar, and $\triangle QRP$ is a right triangle, so $\triangle QTS$ is a right triangle with a side of length 2 and a hypotenuse of length 4. Therefore, $\triangle QTS$ is a 30-60-90 triangle, because its hypotenuse is twice as long as its shortest leg. Thus, $TQ = 2\sqrt{3}$. (Or you can find this length using the Pythagorean theorem: $TQ^2 + 2^2 = 4^2$.)

   The two triangles are similar, and $\overline{PQ}$ is twice as long as $\overline{SQ}$, so $\overline{RT}$ is twice as long as $\overline{TQ}$. Therefore, $RQ = 4\sqrt{3}$, so $RT = 2\sqrt{3}$. Thus, the right answer is (C).

6. **D.** The intersection of these two sets includes only the numbers that appear in both sets, so list the positive integers less than 50 that are divisible by 7:

   {7, 14, 21, 28, 35, 42, 49}

   Thus, this set has seven elements, so the right answer is (D).

7. **B.** Solve the equation for m:

$$m^2 - 11 = 39$$
$$m^2 = 50$$
$$\sqrt{m^2} = \sqrt{50}$$
$$m = \sqrt{25}\sqrt{2}$$
$$m = 5\sqrt{2}$$

   Therefore, the right answer is (B).

8. **E.** Andrea saved \$20 in Week 4 and \$80 in Week 5, which totals \$100, so the right answer is (E).

9. **C.** The first digit could be 4, 6, or 8. The second digit could be 1, 3, 5, or 7. The third digit is the product of the first two digits, so only three combinations of these numbers are possible:

$$4 \times 1 = 4$$
$$6 \times 1 = 6$$
$$8 \times 1 = 8$$

   Therefore, the only possible house numbers are 414, 616, or 818, so the right answer is (C).

10. **E.** The graph is concave down, so a is negative. The graph is displaced to the right (toward the positive direction), so a and b have different signs — that is, one is positive and the other is negative. Therefore, b is positive. The y-intercept is positive, so c is positive. Thus, the right answer is (E).

11. **D.** Plug in 6 as the radius into the formula for the circumference of a circle: $C = 2\pi r = 2\pi(6) = 12\pi$. The triangle is equilateral, so the distance from U to V is $\frac{1}{3}$ of the circumference of the circle: $\frac{1}{3}(12\pi) = 4\pi$. Therefore, the distance is 4π, so the right answer is (D).

12. **E.** The problem asks for the combined area of two circles. The first circle has a radius of 3, so plug this value into the area formula for a circle:

$$A = \pi r^2 = \pi(3^2) = 9\pi$$

The second circle has a diameter of 3, so it has a radius of $\frac{3}{2}$. Plug this value into the area formula for a circle:

$$A = \pi r^2 = \pi\left(\frac{3}{2}\right)^2 = \frac{9}{4}\pi$$

Now add the two areas together:

$$9\pi + \frac{9}{4}\pi = \frac{36}{4}\pi + \frac{9}{4}\pi = \frac{45}{4}\pi$$

Therefore, the right answer is (E).

13. **E.** The slope of a line perpendicular to $y = 4x + 3$ is the negative reciprocal of 4, which is $-\frac{1}{4}$ (see Chapter 6 for details). The point (0, –7) is the *y*-intercept of the line. Thus, the equation is $y = -\frac{1}{4}x - 7$, so the right answer is (E).

14. **A.** Seventy-four students are both graduating and commuters. That's 10 percent of all students in the college, so the college has a total of 740 students. Calculate the number of students who are either graduating or commuters, or both, by adding all the numbers shown in the Venn diagram: 391 + 74 + 210 = 675. The remaining students are neither graduating nor commuters, so calculate this number by subtracting: 740 – 675 = 65. Therefore, the right answer is (A).

15. **A.** The *mode* is the most common number in the list, which is 18. You have an even number of items in the list, and the numbers are already in order from smallest to largest, so to calculate the median, just find the mean average of the middle two numbers, 16 and 18:

$$\text{Mean} = \frac{16+18}{2} = \frac{34}{2} = 17$$

Thus, the difference between the mode and the median is 18 – 17 = 1. Therefore, the right answer is (A).

16. **B.** To find the area of the shaded region, subtract the area of the small circles from the area of the large circle. Each small circle has a diameter of 2, so each has a radius of 1. Plug this value into the formula for the area of a circle:

$$A_{\text{small circle}} = \pi r^2 = \pi(1^2) = \pi$$

The small circles are tangent to each other, and exactly three circles fit across the large circle. So the diameter of the large circle is 6. Thus, its radius is 3, so plug this value into the formula for the area of a circle:

$$A_{\text{large circle}} = \pi r^2 = \pi(3^2) = 9\pi$$

To find the shaded area, take the area of the large circle minus the area of seven small circles: $9\pi - 7\pi = 2\pi$. Thus, the right answer is (B).

17. **C.** Use the letters A through E to represent the five guests, and make a chart to organize the order from first to last. Alan arrives sometime before Blair:

First A B *Last*

Evan arrives sometime before Alan:

First E A B *Last*

Evan arrives sometime after Dwayne:

First D E A B *Last*

Cathy arrives sometime before Dwayne:

First C D E A B *Last*

Therefore, Cathy arrives first, so the right answer is (C).

18. **C.** The first and third perspectives both show the sides with the square and the two lines. If you were to tip the cube in the first perspective over to the right, you'd get perspective three. Thus, the side with the dot and the side with the four triangles are opposite each other, so you can rule out Choices (B) and (E).

    The second and third perspectives both show the side with the dot on top. Thus, these two perspectives show the cube spun 180° around an axis through this dot. So the side with two lines and the side with three lines are opposite each other, and the lines on each of these sides are perpendicular to each other. Therefore, you can rule out answers (A) and (D), so the right answer is (C).

19. **E.** Although you may be tempted to separate out the x and y terms as the first step, there is a better way. The key to this problem is to recognize that the left side can be factored as the difference of squares, and the right side has a greatest common factor of 2:

$$x^2 - 4y^2 = 2x + 4y$$

$$(x + 2y)(x - 2y) = 2(x + 2y)$$

Divide both sides by $x + 2y$:

$$x - 2y = 2$$

Solve for y:

$$-2y = -x + 2$$

$$\frac{-2y}{-2} = \frac{-x}{-2} + \frac{2}{-2}$$

$$y = \frac{x}{2} - 1$$

Thus, the right answer is (E).

20. **B.** A number n is divisible by exactly three numbers — 1, n, and another number — if and only if n is the square of a prime number. For example,

    Factors of 2^2 = 4: 1, 2, and 4

    Factors of 3^2 = 9: 1, 3, and 9

    Factors of 5^2 = 25: 1, 5, and 25

    Factors of 7^2 = 49: 1, 7, and 49

    Factors of 11^2 = 121: 1, 11, and 121

    Only two such numbers — 25 and 49 — have exactly two digits, so the right answer is (B).

Solutions to Section 2 Questions

1. **C.** The triangle is a 45-45-90 triangle. It has a hypotenuse of $x\sqrt{2}$, so the length of each leg is x. The two legs of a right triangle are also the base and height, so you can use the area formula for a triangle:

   $$A = \frac{1}{2}bh$$
   $$8 = \frac{1}{2}(x)(x)$$
   $$8 = \frac{x^2}{2}$$

   Multiply both sides by 2 and then solve for x: $16 = x^2$; $4 = x$. Thus, the right answer is (C).

2. **C.** If you can get the bases on both sides of the equation equal to each other, then you can set the exponents equal to each other. The easiest way to get the bases equal is to express 27 as a power of 3:

   $$3^{y-1} = 27$$
   $$3^{y-1} = 3^3$$

   Because the bases are equal, the exponents are also equal, so $y - 1 = 3$; $y = 4$. Therefore, the right answer is (C).

3. **A.** This problem may look a little confusing, but it's early in the set, so try to just reason it out. Tasha runs 8 laps in 20 minutes, and she's twice as fast as Willem. So Willem covers half her distance in the same amount of time; therefore, he runs 4 laps in 20 minutes. Thus, he runs 1 lap in 5 minutes, so he runs 3 laps in 15 minutes. Therefore, the right answer is (A).

4. **C.** Begin with the inequality that's given:

   $$v > 8$$

   Multiply both sides by w:

   $$vw > 8w$$

   Now, because $vw = 120$, you can substitute 120 for vw into this inequality and solve for w: $120 > 8w$; $15 > w$. Because 15 is greater than w, $w < 15$, so the right answer is (C).

5. **C.** Subtract to find the distance between the two labeled points: $0.59 - 0.45 = 0.14$. This distance is divided into seven intervals, so divide by 7 to find the value of one interval:

   $$\frac{0.14}{7} = 0.02$$

   Each interval represents an increase of 0.02, so you can label the number line as follows:

   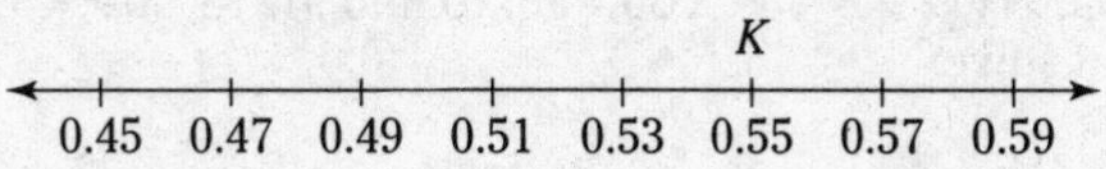

   Thus, K equals 0.55, so the right answer is (C).

6. **D.** The equation for a line on a graph is $y = mx + b$. You need to know the slope, m, and b (the y-intercept, where $x = 0$) to fill in this equation. The graph shows a line that passes through (0, 2) and (3, 0), so plug these numbers into the formula for slope m:

$$m = \frac{y_2 - y_1}{x_2 - x_1} = \frac{2-0}{0-3} = \frac{2}{-3} = -\frac{2}{3}$$

Thus, a parallel line also has a slope of $-\frac{2}{3}$. The point (0, –4) is the y-intercept for this line, so $b = -4$. Plugging these values for m and b gives you the following equation:

$$y = -\frac{2}{3}x - 4$$

Therefore, the right answer is (D).

7. **E.** Beth takes 10 minutes to wash a car, so she can wash $\frac{1}{10}$ of a car in one minute. Liza takes 15 minutes, so she can wash $\frac{1}{15}$ of a car in one minute. Add these two fractions to find out what part of a car they can wash in one minute when working together:

$$\frac{1}{10} + \frac{1}{15} = \frac{3}{30} + \frac{2}{30} = \frac{5}{30} = \frac{1}{6}$$

Working together, they can wash $\frac{1}{6}$ of a car in a minute, so they can wash a whole car in 6 minutes. Therefore, the right answer is (E).

8. **C.** The sixth number in the sequence, which is 33, was produced by taking the fifth number, doubling it, and subtracting 1. So to find the fifth number, add 1 to 33 and take half of it:

$$\textit{Fifth number} = \frac{33+1}{2} = \frac{34}{2} = 17$$

Repeat this procedure to find each earlier number in the sequence:

$$\textit{Fourth number} = \frac{17+1}{2} = \frac{18}{2} = 9$$

$$\textit{Third number} = \frac{9+1}{2} = \frac{10}{2} = 5$$

$$\textit{Second number} = \frac{5+1}{2} = \frac{6}{2} = 3$$

$$\textit{First number} = \frac{3+1}{2} = \frac{4}{2} = 2$$

Thus, the first three numbers are 2, 3, and 5. Add them to find your answer: 2 + 3 + 5 = 10. Therefore, the sum of the first three numbers in the sequence is 10, so the right answer is (C).

9. **36.** First find the volume of the small box: $V_{small} = lwh = (6)(4)(2) = 48$. Now find the volume of the larger box: $V_{large} = s^3 = 12^3 = (12)(12)(12) = 1{,}728$. To find how many small boxes fit inside the larger box, divide: $\frac{1{,}728}{48} = 36$. Therefore, the right answer is 36.

10. **337.** According to the definition, $x|y|z = x^y + y^z$. You want to find $9|2|8$, so $x = 9$, $y = 2$, and $z = 8$. Plug in your numbers and solve:

$$9|2|8 = 9^2 + 2^8 = 81 + 256 = 337$$

So the right answer is 337.

11. **300**. The problem says *p* percent of 1,300 is 156, which you can translate as

$$1{,}300p = 156$$

Divide to find *p:*

$$p = \frac{156}{1{,}300} = 0.12 = 12\%$$

Thus, 36 is 12 percent of some number *x*, so the equation is $36 = 0.12x$. Divide both sides by 0.12 to solve for *x*: $x = 300$.

12. **5/3** or **1.66** or **1.67**. Use the midpoint formula to find the midpoint of $\overline{AB}$:

$$\text{Midpoint} = \left(\frac{x_1 + x_2}{2}, \frac{y_1 + y_2}{2}\right) = \left(\frac{5 + (-1)}{2}, \frac{4 + 2}{2}\right) = (2, 3)$$

Next, use the midpoint formula to find the midpoint of $\overline{CD}$:

$$\text{Midpoint} = \left(\frac{x_1 + x_2}{2}, \frac{y_1 + y_2}{2}\right) = \left(\frac{-2 + 0}{2}, \frac{0 + (-4)}{2}\right) = (-1, -2)$$

Then use the slope formula to find the slope of the line that connects these two points:

$$\text{Slope} = \frac{y_2 - y_1}{x_2 - x_1} = \frac{3 - (-2)}{2 - (-1)} = \frac{5}{3}$$

Therefore, the answer is 5/3 (which you can also write as 1.66 or 1.67 in the grid).

13. **1772**. The flat rate for the first 800 minutes accounts for $45 of the bill. The $0.10 per minute charge for the second 800 minutes accounts for $80. Thus, Jeffrey paid $125 for the first 1,600 minutes. This leaves the last $43 of his bill unaccounted for. He paid $0.25 per minute, so divide to find how many minutes he used at this rate:

$$\frac{43}{0.25} = 172$$

This adds an additional 172 minutes, so find the total number of minutes: 1,600 + 172 = 1,772. Therefore, Jeffrey used the phone for 1,772 minutes, which you write as 1772.

14. **20**. Let *d* equal Darren's pushups and *e* equal Errol's pushups. Then you can make two equations:

$$d + e = 53$$

$$d + 7 = 2e$$

You have a system of equations. If you take the first equation minus the second equation, the *d*'s drop out:

$$e - 7 = 53 - 2e$$

Solve for *e*: $e = 60 - 2e$; $3e = 60$; $e = 20$. Therefore, Errol did 20 pushups.

15. **5/7** or **.714**. The measure of angle *b* is 5*x* (vertical angles). The lower-left angle in the triangle and the angle labeled 12*x* degrees are supplementary, so the measure of the lower left angle is $180 - 12x$. Angle *a* and the remaining angle in the triangle are vertical angles.

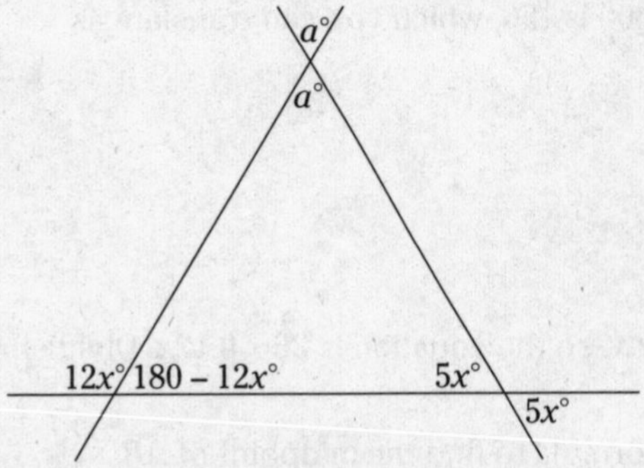

The sum of the three angles inside the triangle equals 180, so

$$a + 5x + 180 - 12x = 180$$
$$a - 7x + 180 = 180$$
$$a + 180 = 180 + 7x$$
$$a = 7x$$

So here's the ratio of b to a:

$$\frac{b}{a} = \frac{5x}{7x} = \frac{5}{7}$$

Therefore, the right answer is 5/7, which you can also write as .714 in the grid.

16. **2.1**. Start by solving the equation for $\frac{x}{y}$:

$$2x = 5y$$
$$\frac{2x}{y} = 5$$
$$\frac{x}{y} = \frac{5}{2}$$

Therefore,

$$\frac{y}{x} = \frac{2}{5}$$

Substitute these two values into the expression $\frac{x}{y} - \frac{y}{x}$:

$$\frac{x}{y} - \frac{y}{x} = \frac{5}{2} - \frac{2}{5} = \frac{25}{10} - \frac{4}{10} = \frac{21}{10} = 2.1$$

Thus, the right answer is 2.1. (You can't write this answer as a fraction because you don't have enough space in the answer grid.)

17. **30**. The basic solving strategy is to use the area formula repeatedly to find bases, heights, and areas of the various triangles that make up *JKLM*. $NM = 3$ and $ML = 5$, so $\triangle MNL$ is a 3-4-5 triangle. Therefore, $NL = 4$ (you can also get this answer using the Pythagorean theorem, where $3^2 + NL^2 = 5^2$). Calculate the area of this triangle using the area formula: $A = \frac{1}{2}bh = \frac{1}{2}(3)(4) = 6$.

The area of $\triangle JLM$ is 9, so the area of $\triangle JNM$ is 3. You can plug in its height and area to find the base *JN*:

$$A = \frac{1}{2}bh$$
$$3 = \frac{1}{2}(b)(3)$$
$$1 = \frac{b}{2}$$
$$2 = b$$

Therefore, $JN = 2$. The area of $\triangle JKM$ is 10, so the area of $\triangle JKN$ is 7. You can plug its base and area into the triangle-area formula to find its height *KN*:

$$A = \frac{1}{2}bh$$
$$7 = \frac{1}{2}(2)(h)$$
$$7 = h$$

Thus, $KN = 7$. Now use the area formula to find the area of $\triangle KLN$:

$$A = \frac{1}{2}bh = \frac{1}{2}(4)(7) = 14$$

So the area of $\triangle KLN$ is 14.

The area of quadrilateral *JKLM* equals the area of four small triangles: $A_{JKLM} = A_{\triangle MNL} + A_{\triangle JNM} + A_{\triangle JKN} + A_{\triangle KLN}$. Substitute and solve: $6 + 3 + 7 + 14 = 30$. The following figure summarizes these conclusions:

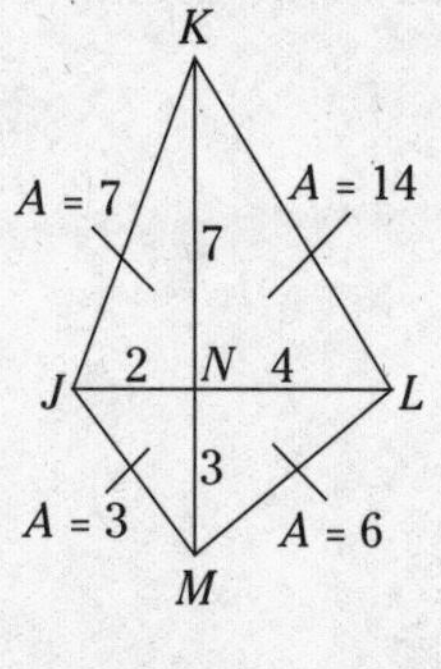

18. **240**. There are two possible numbers *not* rolled: 1 and 6. That is, you roll either a 1 or a 6 but not both. After you establish this number, there are five possible numbers you can roll on the first die, four on the second die, three on the third die, two on the fourth die, and one on the fifth die:

    $2 \times 5 \times 4 \times 3 \times 2 \times 1 = 240$

    Thus, there are 240 ways to roll five dice within the conditions stated.

Solutions to Section 3 Questions

1. **A.** Plug in –2 for x and 6 for y:

   $$4x^3 - xy^2 = 4(-2)^3 - (-2)(6)^2$$

   Now evaluate this expression:

   $$= 4(-8) - (-2)(36) = -32 + 72 = 40$$

   Therefore, the right answer is (A).

2. **D.** Begin with the given equation: $a - b = 1$. You want to change the left side of the equation to $a + 2b$, so add $3b$ to both sides of the equation: $a - b + 3b = 1 + 3b$. Then simplify: $a + 2b = 1 + 3b$. Therefore, the right answer is (D).

3. **A.** Angle $TUV = 40°$ (vertical angles), so first two angles of $\triangle TUV$ add up to 115°. Thus, angle $UVT = 65°$, because the sum of angles in a triangle is 180°. This angle and angle x are supplementary, so they add up to 180°; therefore, $x = 115°$. The right answer is (A).

4. **A.** The domain is the set of allowable values for x. Any value for x that results in a denominator of 0 is excluded from the domain, so set the denominator equal to 0 and solve for x:

   $$2x^2 - 18 = 0$$

   $$2x^2 = 18$$

   $$x^2 = 9$$

   $$x = 3, -3$$

   Thus, both 3 and –3 aren't in the domain of the function, so the right answer is (A).

5. **C.** Begin by translating the new notation. In the top of the fraction, $x = 2$ and $y = 3$. On the bottom, $x = 4$ and $y = 5$:

   $$\frac{2\,\&\,\&3}{4\,\&\,\&5} = \frac{1-\frac{2}{3}}{1-\frac{4}{5}}$$

   Now evaluate:

   $$= \frac{\frac{1}{3}}{\frac{1}{5}} = \frac{1}{3} \div \frac{1}{5} = \frac{1}{3} \times \frac{5}{1} = \frac{5}{3}$$

   Therefore, the right answer is (C).

6. **C.** First, calculate 30% of 50: (0.3)(50) = 15. So a 30% increase on a length of 50 results in a new length of 50 + 15 = 65.

   Next, calculate 30% of 40: (0.3)(40) = 12. So a 30% increase on a width of 40 results in a new width of 40 + 12 = 52.

   Plug the new length and width into the formula for the perimeter of a rectangle: $P = 2l + 2w = 2(65) + 2(52) = 130 + 104 = 234$. Therefore, the right answer is (C).

7. **A.** The union of set P and set S contains every number from both sets and only those numbers, so every number in the set must be either a prime number or a square number, or both. The numbers 6, 15, 35, and 99 are all neither prime nor square, which rules out answers (B), (C), (D), and (E). However, 1 and 9 are both square numbers, and 3, 5, 7, 11, and 13 are all prime. Thus, the right answer is (A).

8. **E.** To get the answer, you have to isolate x on one side of the equation. Start with the given equation: $\sqrt{x^2+3} = n$. Square both sides of the equation and then subtract 3: $x^2 + 3 = n^2$; $x^2 = n^2 - 3$. Then take the square root of both sides, remembering that x is a positive number: $x = \sqrt{n^2 - 3}$. So the right answer is (E).

9. **D.** Elaine can run 5 miles in 40 minutes, so it would take her three times longer to walk 5 miles: 40 minutes × 3 = 120 minutes. So she can walk 5 miles 120 minutes.

   She'd take one-fifth of this time to walk 1 mile: 120 minutes ÷ 5 = 24 minutes. Elaine can walk 1 mile in 24 minutes, so she would take four times longer to walk four miles. Multiply by 4 to get your answer: 24 minutes × 4 = 96 minutes. Therefore, the right answer is (D).

10. **E.** The line has a slope of $\frac{2}{3}$ and its y-intercept is –1, so its equation is $y = \frac{2}{3}x - 1$. Plug in 4 for y and solve for x:

$$4 = \frac{2}{3}x - 1$$
$$5 = \frac{2}{3}x$$

   Multiply both sides by 3 and divide by 2:

$$15 = 2x$$
$$\frac{15}{2} = x$$

   Therefore, the right answer is (E).

11. **E.** Begin by finding the prime factors of 60:

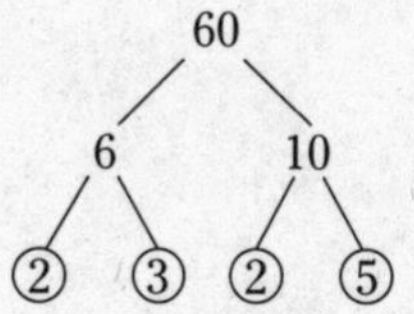

   Do the same for 80 and 100.

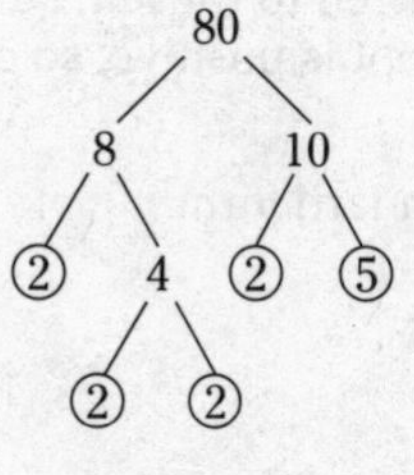

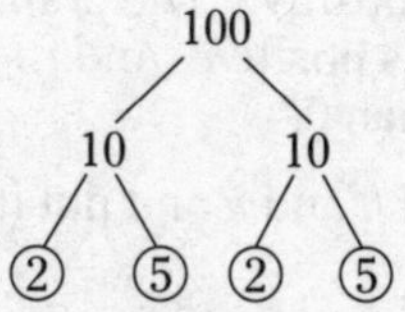

   So 60 has three distinct prime factors (2, 3, and 5), 80 has two (2 and 5), and 100 has two (2 and 5). Therefore, the right answer is (E).

12. **D.** The first three students to arrive are boys, so this leaves 24 students who haven't yet arrived. Of these, 9 are boys. So use the formula for probability: $\text{Probability} = \frac{\text{Target outcomes}}{\text{Total outcomes}} = \frac{9}{24} = \frac{3}{8}$. Therefore, the right answer is (D).

13. **B.** One of the four numbers is 20, and altogether the four numbers add up to 27. Thus, the three smallest numbers are different positive integers that add up to 7. The only possible combination is 1 + 2 + 4 = 7. Therefore, one number must be 4, so the right answer is (B).

14. **D.** The first number in the sequence is a. The second number is the first multiplied by c, so the second number is ac. The third number is the second multiplied by c, so the third is ac^2. And the fourth is the third multiplied by c, so it's ac^3. Thus, the right answer is (D).

15. **C.** Two angles in $\triangle RSU$ are 15° and 135°, so angle RSU = 30°. Thus, angle TRS = 60°, so angle TRU = 45°. Therefore, $\triangle TRU$ is a 45-45-90 triangle and $\triangle TRS$ is a 30-60-90 triangle. Now you can find the sides of these triangles. (During the test, if you don't remember how the lengths of the sides of these special right triangles relate, you can check the *Reference Information* that appears at the beginning of each math section on the SAT.) $RT = 4$, so $TS = 4\sqrt{3}$. Therefore, $US = 4\sqrt{3} - 4$.

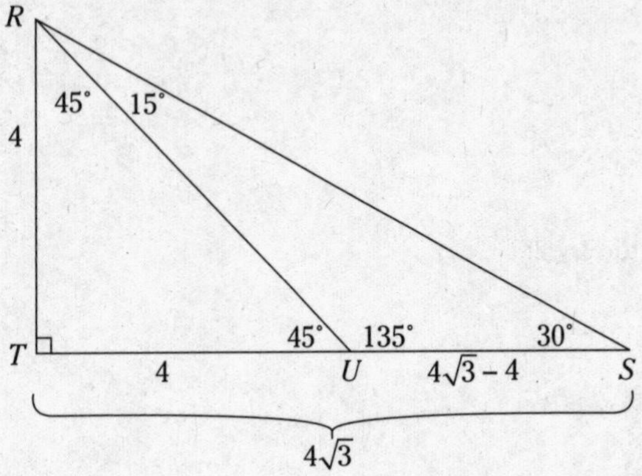

The base of $\triangle RSU$ is $4\sqrt{3} - 4$, and the height is 4. Plug these numbers into the formula for the area of a triangle:

$$A = \frac{1}{2}bh = \frac{1}{2}\left(4\sqrt{3}-4\right)(4) = 2\left(4\sqrt{3}-4\right) = 8\sqrt{3}-8$$

Therefore, the right answer is (C).

16. **E.** The key to this question is to examine the graph as a basic quadratic, $f(x) = ax^2 + bx + c$, and then use this information to find possible values of h and k.

The graph is concave up, so a is positive. The graph is displaced to the left, so a and b have the same sign; therefore, b is positive. And the y-intercept is positive, so c is positive. Thus, a, b, and c are all greater than 0.

Now take the function in terms of h and k and put it into standard form:

$$\begin{aligned} f(x) &= (x + h)(x - k) \\ &= x^2 + hx - kx - hk \\ &= x^2 + (h - k)x - hk \end{aligned}$$

Therefore, in this function, $a = 1$, $b = h - k$, and $c = -hk$. You know that b is positive, so $b > 0$ and $h - k > 0$; $h > k$. Therefore, $h > k$, so you can rule out answers (B) and (D).

You also know that c is positive, so $-hk$ is positive, which means h and k have opposite signs. So you can rule out answers (A) and (C). Therefore, the right answer is (E).

Answer Key

Section 1

1. **C**	6. **D**	11. **D**	16. **B**
2. **E**	7. **B**	12. **E**	17. **C**
3. **C**	8. **E**	13. **E**	18. **C**
4. **D**	9. **C**	14. **A**	19. **E**
5. **C**	10. **E**	15. **A**	20. **B**

Section 2

1. **C**	6. **D**	11. **300**	16. **2.1**
2. **C**	7. **E**	12. **5/3** or **1.66** or **1.67**	17. **30**
3. **A**	8. **C**	13. **1772**	18. **240**
4. **C**	9. **36**	14. **20**	
5. **C**	10. **337**	15. **5/7** or **.714**	

Section 3

1. **A**	5. **C**	9. **D**	13. **B**
2. **D**	6. **C**	10. **E**	14. **D**
3. **A**	7. **A**	11. **E**	15. **C**
4. **A**	8. **E**	12. **D**	16. **E**

Chapter 12

Practice Test 2

Well, you survived the first practice test (unless you didn't like the looks of it and decided to start with this one instead). Here's another chance to perfect your SAT math skills.

Tear out the answer sheet provided at the beginning of this chapter and do each of the three sections in this chapter in the indicated time. A calculator is permitted, as on the SAT.

Don't forget to check your answers in Chapter 13 when you're done. Good luck!

Answer Sheet for Practice Test 2

Use the ovals and grid-ins provided to record your answers for each section of this practice test.

Section 1

1. Ⓐ Ⓑ Ⓒ Ⓓ Ⓔ
2. Ⓐ Ⓑ Ⓒ Ⓓ Ⓔ
3. Ⓐ Ⓑ Ⓒ Ⓓ Ⓔ
4. Ⓐ Ⓑ Ⓒ Ⓓ Ⓔ
5. Ⓐ Ⓑ Ⓒ Ⓓ Ⓔ
6. Ⓐ Ⓑ Ⓒ Ⓓ Ⓔ
7. Ⓐ Ⓑ Ⓒ Ⓓ Ⓔ
8. Ⓐ Ⓑ Ⓒ Ⓓ Ⓔ
9. Ⓐ Ⓑ Ⓒ Ⓓ Ⓔ
10. Ⓐ Ⓑ Ⓒ Ⓓ Ⓔ
11. Ⓐ Ⓑ Ⓒ Ⓓ Ⓔ
12. Ⓐ Ⓑ Ⓒ Ⓓ Ⓔ
13. Ⓐ Ⓑ Ⓒ Ⓓ Ⓔ
14. Ⓐ Ⓑ Ⓒ Ⓓ Ⓔ
15. Ⓐ Ⓑ Ⓒ Ⓓ Ⓔ
16. Ⓐ Ⓑ Ⓒ Ⓓ Ⓔ
17. Ⓐ Ⓑ Ⓒ Ⓓ Ⓔ
18. Ⓐ Ⓑ Ⓒ Ⓓ Ⓔ
19. Ⓐ Ⓑ Ⓒ Ⓓ Ⓔ
20. Ⓐ Ⓑ Ⓒ Ⓓ Ⓔ

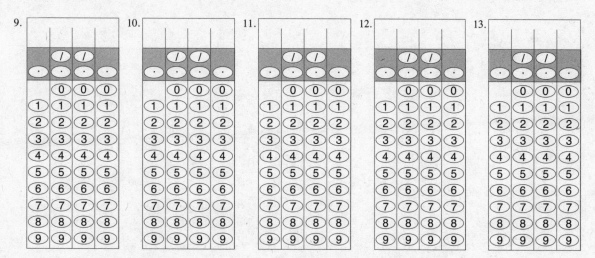

Section 2

1. Ⓐ Ⓑ Ⓒ Ⓓ Ⓔ
2. Ⓐ Ⓑ Ⓒ Ⓓ Ⓔ
3. Ⓐ Ⓑ Ⓒ Ⓓ Ⓔ
4. Ⓐ Ⓑ Ⓒ Ⓓ Ⓔ
5. Ⓐ Ⓑ Ⓒ Ⓓ Ⓔ
6. Ⓐ Ⓑ Ⓒ Ⓓ Ⓔ
7. Ⓐ Ⓑ Ⓒ Ⓓ Ⓔ
8. Ⓐ Ⓑ Ⓒ Ⓓ Ⓔ

Grid-ins 9. 10. 11. 12. 13. 14. 15. 16. 17. 18. — each grid:

	/	/	
.	.	.	.
	0	0	0
1	1	1	1
2	2	2	2
3	3	3	3
4	4	4	4
5	5	5	5
6	6	6	6
7	7	7	7
8	8	8	8
9	9	9	9

Section 3

1. (A) (B) (C) (D) (E)	5. (A) (B) (C) (D) (E)	9. (A) (B) (C) (D) (E)	13. (A) (B) (C) (D) (E)
2. (A) (B) (C) (D) (E)	6. (A) (B) (C) (D) (E)	10. (A) (B) (C) (D) (E)	14. (A) (B) (C) (D) (E)
3. (A) (B) (C) (D) (E)	7. (A) (B) (C) (D) (E)	11. (A) (B) (C) (D) (E)	15. (A) (B) (C) (D) (E)
4. (A) (B) (C) (D) (E)	8. (A) (B) (C) (D) (E)	12. (A) (B) (C) (D) (E)	16. (A) (B) (C) (D) (E)

Section 1

Time: 25 minutes for 20 questions

Directions: Choose the *best* answer and darken the corresponding oval on the answer sheet.

Notes:

- You may use a calculator.
- All numbers used in this exam are real numbers.
- All figures lie in a plane.
- All figures may be assumed to be to scale unless the problem specifically indicates otherwise.

Reference Information:

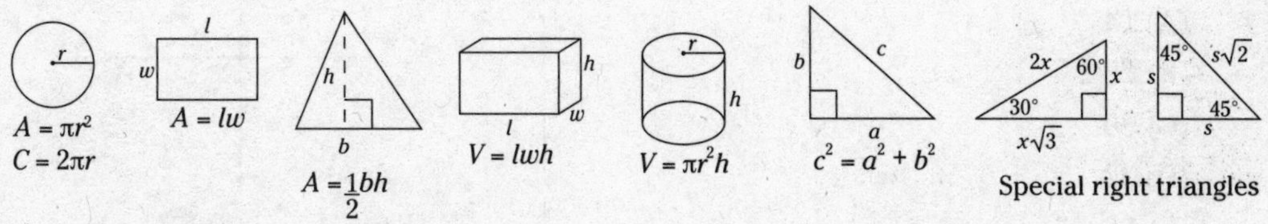

Special right triangles

There are 360 degrees of arc in a circle.

There are 180 degrees in the sum of the interior angles of a triangle.

1. Josh is stocking shelves at the grocery store. He stocked 4 boxes containing packages of cookies. One box contained 9 packages, and the rest contained 16 packages each. How many packages of cookies did he put on the shelves?

(A) 25

(B) 36

(C) 48

(D) 57

(E) 73

2. If the average (arithmetic mean) of 4, 11, $3x$, $7x$, and $8x$ is 39, what is the value of x?

(A) 5

(B) 6

(C) 8

(D) 10

(E) 11

Go on to next page

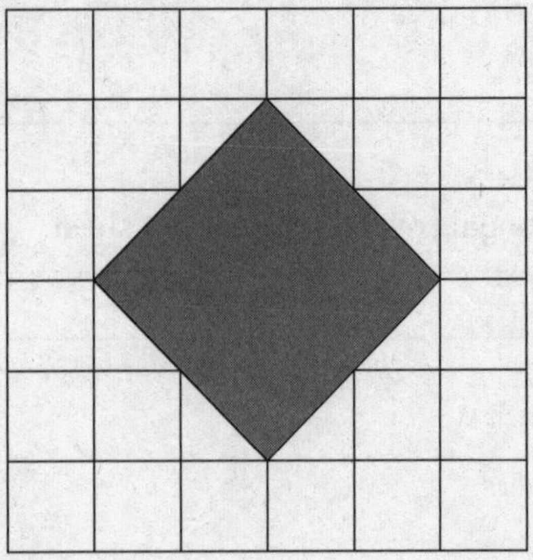

3. In the figure above, each individual square has an area of 1, and each triangle is half the area of a square. What the total area of the large square, excluding the shaded region?

(A) 24

(B) 28

(C) 30

(D) 32

(E) 36

4. Anthony washed 40% of his laundry on Monday morning and 60% of what was left over on Monday afternoon. What percentage of his laundry does he have left to finish up on Monday night?

(A) 0%

(B) 20%

(C) 24%

(D) 46%

(E) 64%

5. The first five numbers in a sequence are 1, 3, 7, 15, 31. What is the next number in the sequence?

(A) 47

(B) 59

(C) 61

(D) 63

(E) 77

Questions 6 and 7 refer to the following table.

Sales	Commission
$2,000	$350
$4,000	$450
$6,000	$550
$8,000	$650

6. The table above shows the commission as a linear function of gross sales for every $2,000 of merchandise sold each week. Which of the following graphs describes the given data?

(A)
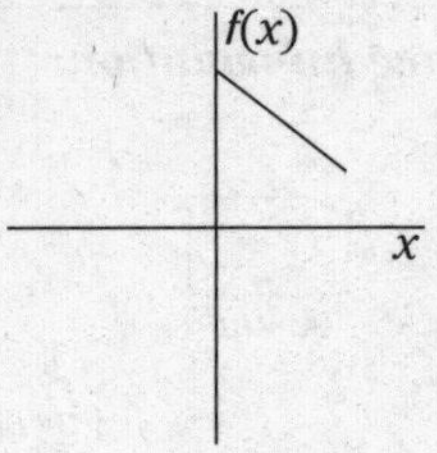

(B)
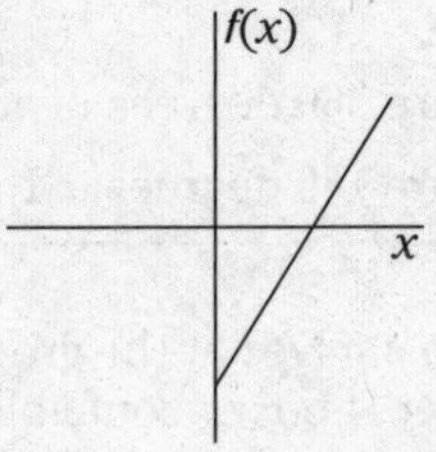

(C)
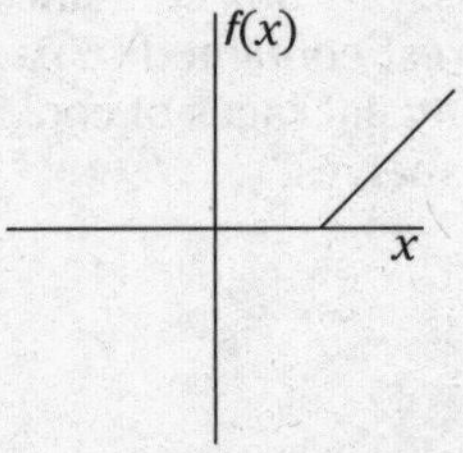

(D)
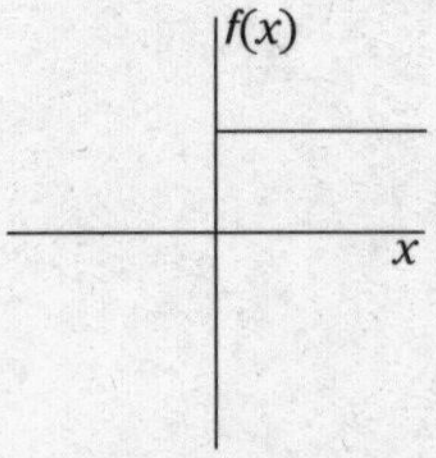

(E)
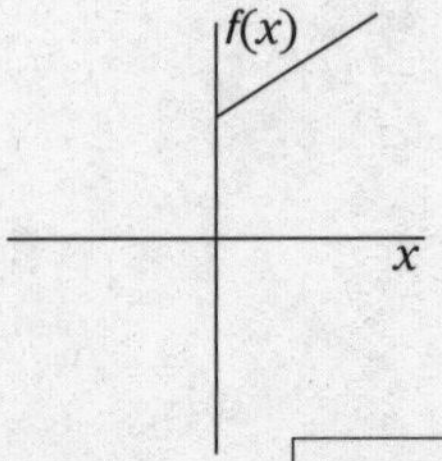

Go on to next page

7. The equation for the function producing the numbers in this chart is $f(x) = 0.05x + b$, where x is the dollar amount of sales and $f(x)$ is the dollar amount of the commission. What is the value of b in this function?

(A) \$150

(B) \$250

(C) \$350

(D) \$400

(E) \$500

8. Sister Theresa received a generous donation of a apples from a local orchard. She divided them evenly among t teachers in her school, each of whom distributed her share evenly among the s students in her class. In terms of a, s, and t, how many apples did each child receive?

(A) ast

(B) $\frac{as}{t}$

(C) $\frac{st}{a}$

(D) $\frac{at}{s}$

(E) $\frac{a}{st}$

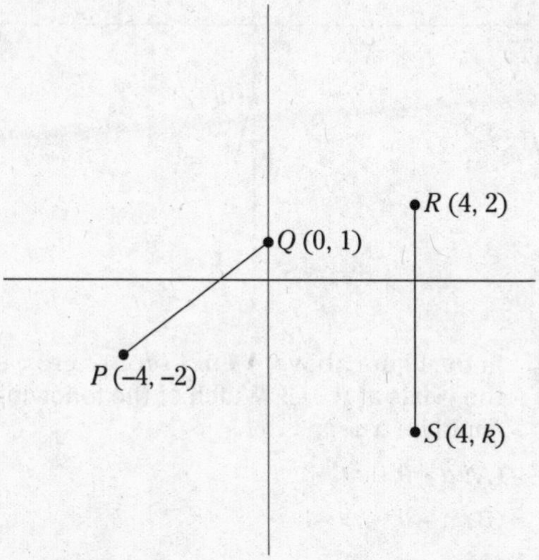

9. In the figure above, $PQ = RS$. What is the value of k?

(A) –1

(B) –2

(C) –3

(D) –4

(E) –5

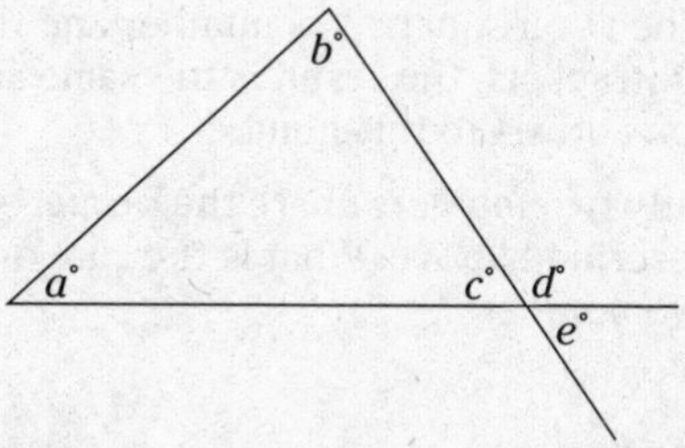

10. In the figure above, which of the following must be true?

(A) $a = e$

(B) $a + b + d = 180$

(C) $a + c + e = 180$

(D) $a + b = d + e$

(E) $a + b + c + d + e = 360$

11. Set F is the set of all integers greater than 25 and less than 45, and set G is the set of all prime numbers. How many elements are in the intersection of set F and set G?

(A) Three

(B) Four

(C) Five

(D) Six

(E) More than six

12. For a certain fraction, if you add one to the numerator and subtract two from the denominator, the resulting fraction is the same as subtracting four from the denominator. Which of the following could be this fraction?

(A) $\frac{1}{5}$

(B) $\frac{1}{6}$

(C) $\frac{1}{7}$

(D) $\frac{1}{8}$

(E) $\frac{1}{9}$

Go on to next page

13. When you square this number and then subtract six, the result is the same as when you add six to this number.

Only two integers share the property described above. What is the sum of these two numbers?

(A) 2

(B) 1

(C) 0

(D) –1

(E) –2

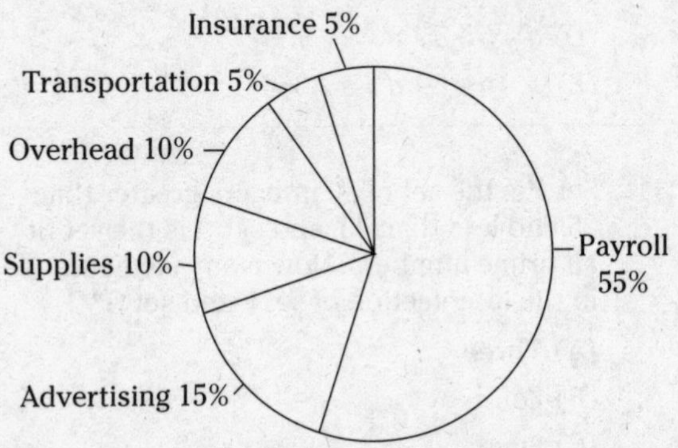

14. The pie chart above shows the monthly breakdown of expenses for Dome Housecleaning Services. If advertising costs $825 a month, then the monthly payroll expense is

(A) Less than $2,000

(B) Between $2,000 and $2,500

(C) Between $2,500 and $3,000

(D) Between $3,000 and $3,500

(E) More than $3,500

Points	Number of Quizzes
10	3
9	6
8	4
7	2

15. Keishaun has taken 15 quizzes in his math class this semester. Each test is graded on a 10-point scale, and the table above shows how many of each grade he has received. If he receives 10 points on each of the next five quizzes, what will his semester average be?

(A) 9.6

(B) 9.2

(C) 9.0

(D) 8.8

(E) 8.4

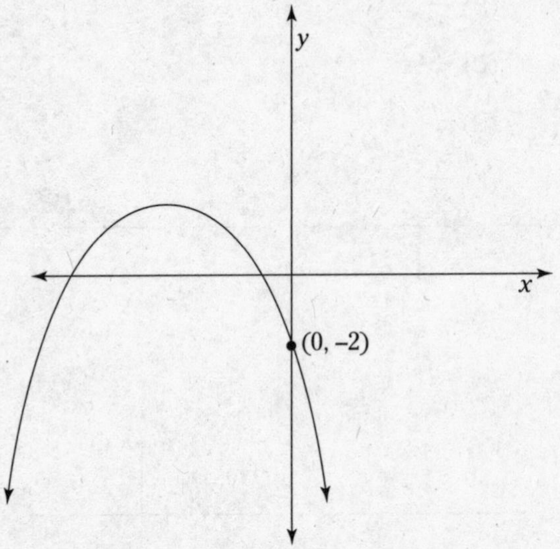

16. In the figure above, $y = ax^2 + bx + c$ crosses the y-axis at $y = -2$. Which of the following could be true?

(A) $a + b + c = -3$

(B) $a + b + c = -1$

(C) $a + b + c = 0$

(D) $a + b + c = 2$

(E) $a + b + c = 4$

Go on to next page

17. If $25^{x-3} = \sqrt{5}^{2x}$, then $x =$

(A) 2

(B) 3

(C) 4

(D) 6

(E) 10

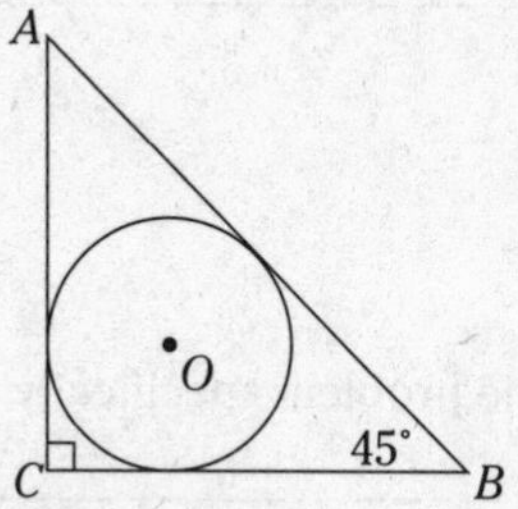

18. In the figure above, each side of the right triangle *ABC* is tangent to the circle centered at *O*. If the radius of the circle is 1, what is the area of the triangle?

(A) $\sqrt{2}$

(B) $2\sqrt{2}$

(C) $1+\sqrt{2}$

(D) $2+2\sqrt{2}$

(E) $3+2\sqrt{2}$

19. Ms. D'Agostino has only seniors and juniors in her college prep class. She has five more seniors than juniors. If she has *s* seniors, what percent of her class are juniors?

(A) $\frac{s}{s-5}\%$

(B) $\frac{s-5}{2s-5}\%$

(C) $\frac{100s}{s-5}\%$

(D) $\frac{s-5}{100(2s-5)}\%$

(E) $\frac{100(s-5)}{2s-5}\%$

20. How many ounces of a 70% alcohol solution should be mixed with an unspecified amount of a 95% alcohol solution to yield 32 ounces of an 80% alcohol solution?

(A) 19.2

(B) 19.6

(C) 20.4

(D) 22.0

(E) 23.8

STOP

DO NOT TURN THE PAGE UNTIL TOLD TO DO SO.
DO NOT RETURN TO A PREVIOUS TEST.

Section 2

Time: 25 minutes for 18 questions

Directions: This section contains two different types of questions. For questions 1–8, choose the *best* answer to each question. Mark the corresponding oval on the answer sheet. For questions 9–18, follow the separate directions provided before those questions.

Notes:

- You may use a calculator.
- All numbers used in this exam are real numbers.
- All figures lie in a plane.
- All figures may be assumed to be to scale unless the problem specifically indicates otherwise.

Reference Information:

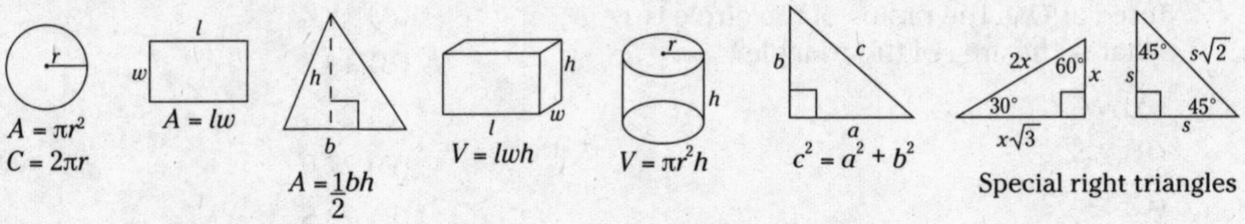

There are 360 degrees of arc in a circle.

There are 180 degrees in the sum of the interior angles of a triangle.

1. Two sides of a triangle have lengths of 7 and 4. Which of the following could be the length of the third side?

   (A) 2

   (B) 3

   (C) 10

   (D) 11

   (E) 12

2. Eleanor likes just five types of fruit: apples, bananas, mangos, oranges, and pears. She likes to bring three different types of fruit to work each day. For how many days can she bring a different combination of fruit to work without repeating the same combination twice?

   (A) 6

   (B) 8

   (C) 9

   (D) 10

   (E) 15

Go on to next page

3. The sum of four consecutive odd integers is 80. What is the product of the two lowest numbers?

(A) 195

(B) 255

(C) 323

(D) 399

(E) 483

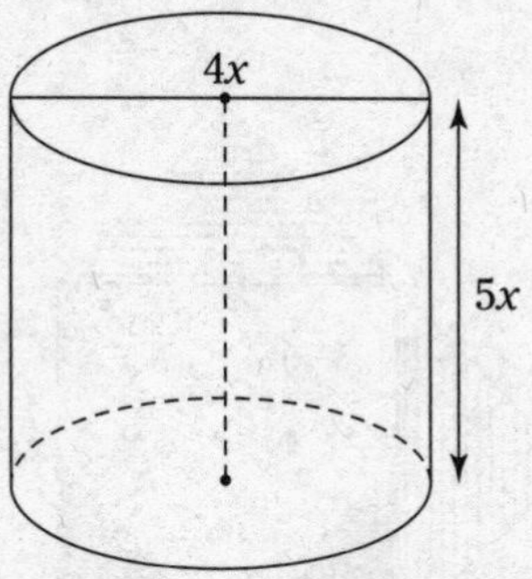

4. The cylinder above has a diameter of $4x$ and a height of $5x$. What is its volume?

(A) $10\pi x^2$

(B) $20\pi x^2$

(C) $20\pi x^3$

(D) $25\pi x^3$

(E) $40\pi x^3$

5. Let $x\$y\$z$ be defined as $5^x - 3^y - 2^z$. What is the value of 2\$0\$4?

(A) 8

(B) 9

(C) 10

(D) 11

(E) 12

Go on to next page

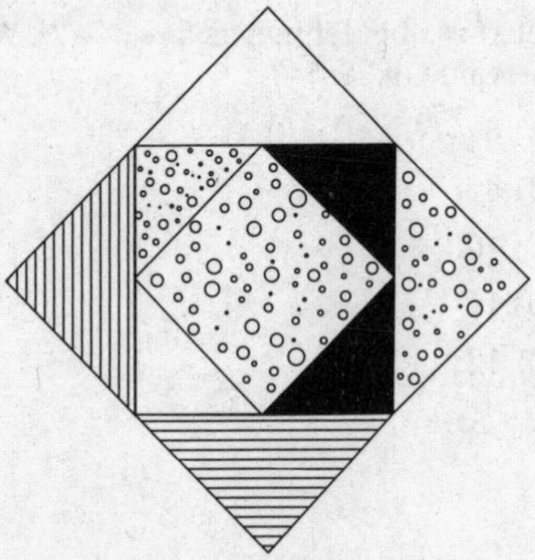

6. Which of the following is a rotation of the figure shown above?

(A)

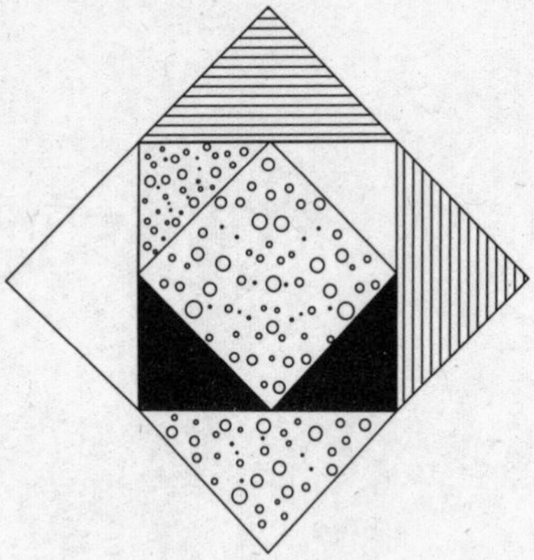

(B)

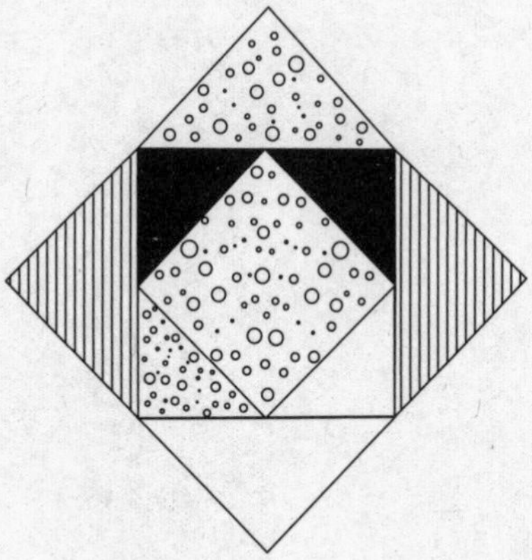

(C)

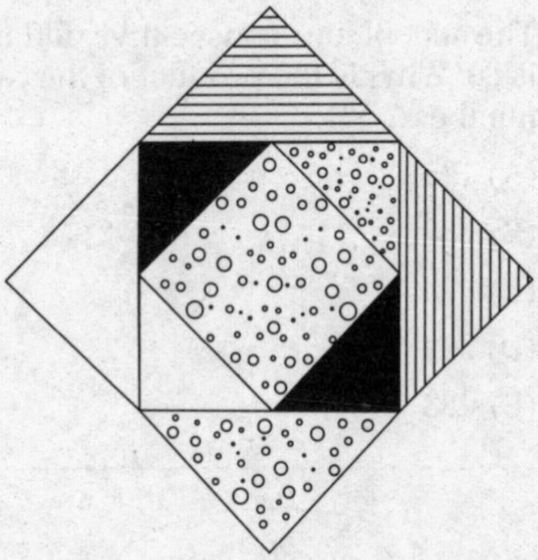

(D)

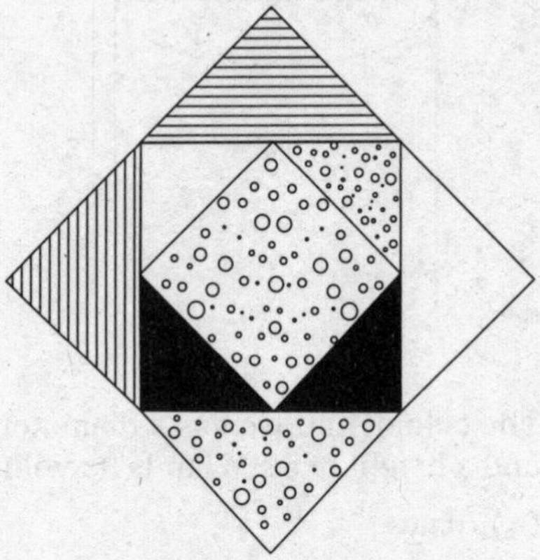

(E)

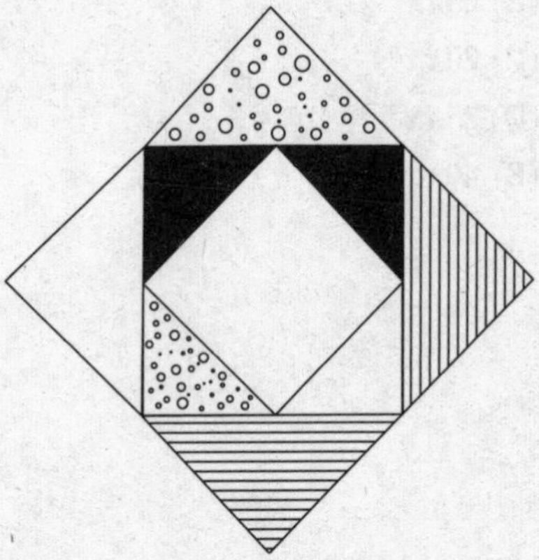

Go on to next page

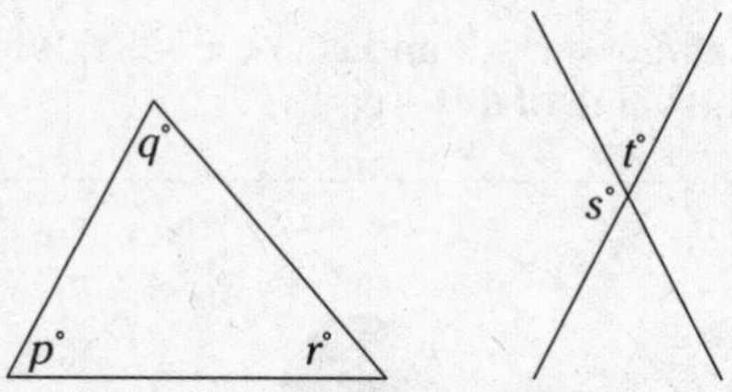

7. In the figure above, what is the average (arithmetic mean) of *p*, *q*, *r*, *s*, and *t*?

(A) 36

(B) 45

(C) 54

(D) 60

(E) 72

8. Bill and Nikki each received a whole number of dollars in their pay envelopes. If Bill had received $50 less, he would have received exactly half of what Nikki received. And if Nicki had received one-third of what she received, she would have received $85 less than Bill. Thus, together Bill and Nikki received

(A) less than $200

(B) between $200 and $400

(C) between $400 and $600

(D) between $600 and $800

(E) more than $800

Directions for student-produced response questions 9–18: Solve the problem and then write your answer in the boxes on the answer sheet. Then mark the ovals corresponding to your answer as shown in the following examples. Note the fraction line and the decimal points.

Answer: $^7/_2$

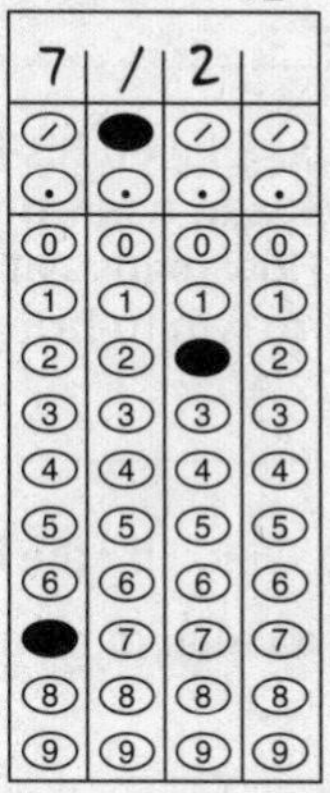

Answer: 3.25

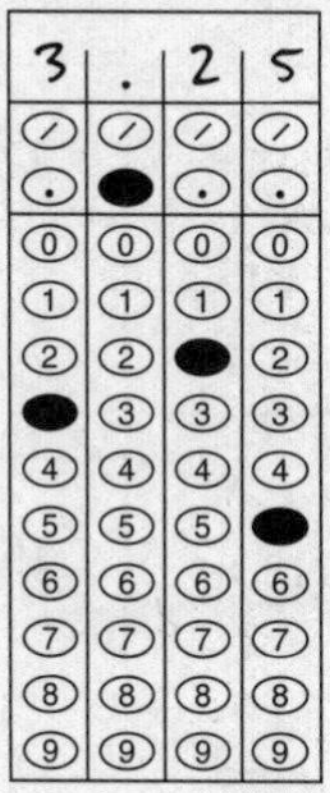

Answer: 853

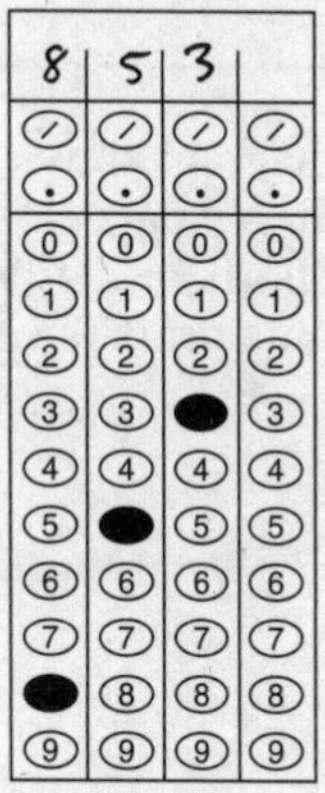

- Although you do not have to write the solutions in the boxes, you do have to blacken the corresponding ovals. You should fill in the boxes to avoid confusion. Only the blackened ovals will be scored. The numbers in the boxes will not be read.
- There are no negative answers.
- Mixed numbers, such as 3½, may be gridded in as a decimal (3.5) or as a fraction(7/2). Do not grid in 31/2; it will be read as $^{31}/_2$.
- Grid in a decimal as far as possible. You may round the last digit or simply cut off the decimal.
- A question may have more than one answer. Grid in one answer only.

Go on to next page

9. Sarah paid $74.40 for a digital camera that was marked down 40% from its original price. What was the original price of the camera, in dollars?

10. A pet store currently has a ratio of 3:4:10 of dogs, cats, and birds. If there were twice as many dogs and exactly 26 fewer cats, then the number of cats and birds combined would be exactly twice that number of dogs. What is the total number of cats, dogs, and birds currently in the store?

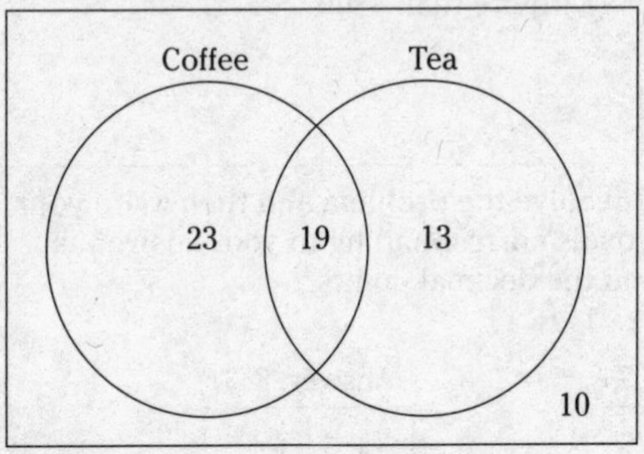

11. The Venn diagram above shows the distribution of survey participants who drink coffee, tea, both, or neither. What percent of participants drink tea only?

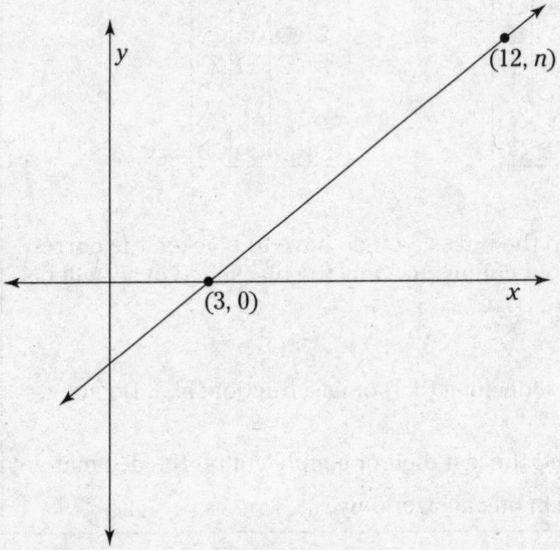

Note: Figure not drawn to scale.

12. The figure shows the graph of $y = \frac{2}{3}x + b$, passing through point (3, 0) and (12, *n*). What is the value of *n*?

13. Let $f(x) = x^2 - 3$ and $g(x) = x^2 + 5x$. What is the value of $f(4) + g(-2)$?

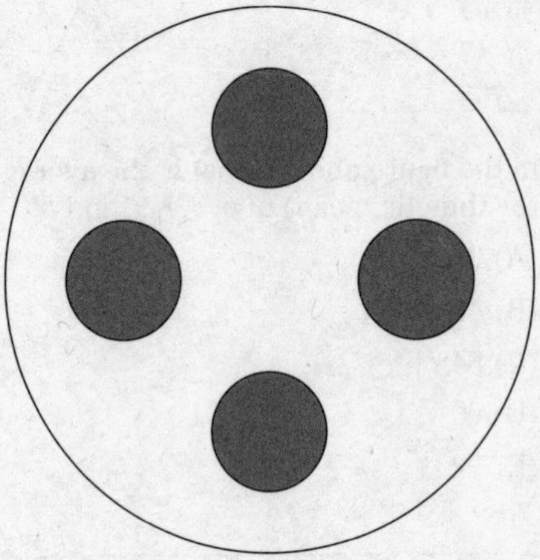

14. In the figure above, the radius of each of the small shaded circles is 1 and the radius of the large circle is 5. What is the probability that a dart that lands on the large circle will also land inside the shaded region?

15. Morey has played his favorite video game 310 times and has won 70% of all games played. How many games in a row does he need to win to bring his record up to 90%?

16. Let *f* be defined by the function $f(x) = \frac{x^2 + 9}{5}$. What is a value of *a* such that $f(3a) = 6a$?

Go on to next page

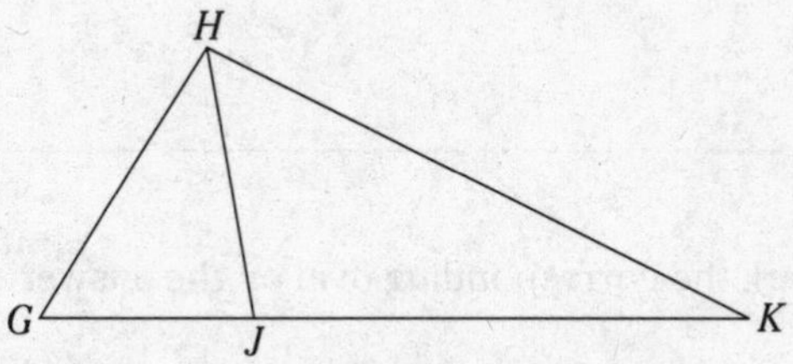

17. In $\triangle GHK$ above, J is a point on $\overline{GK}$ such that the ratio of GJ to JK is 1:2. If the area of $\triangle GHK$ is $\frac{4}{5}$, what is the area of $\triangle GHJ$?

18. A positive four-digit integer *abcd* has the following properties:

$$a > b > c > d$$
$$a = b + c$$
$$b = c + d$$

If M is the highest possible value for *abcd*, what is the value of M?

STOP DO NOT TURN THE PAGE UNTIL TOLD TO DO SO. DO NOT RETURN TO A PREVIOUS TEST.

Section 3

Time: 20 minutes for 16 questions

Directions: Choose the *best* answer to each question. Mark the corresponding oval on the answer sheet.

Notes:

- You may use a calculator.
- All numbers used in this exam are real numbers.
- All figures lie in a plane.
- All figures may be assumed to be to scale unless the problem specifically indicates otherwise.

Reference Information:

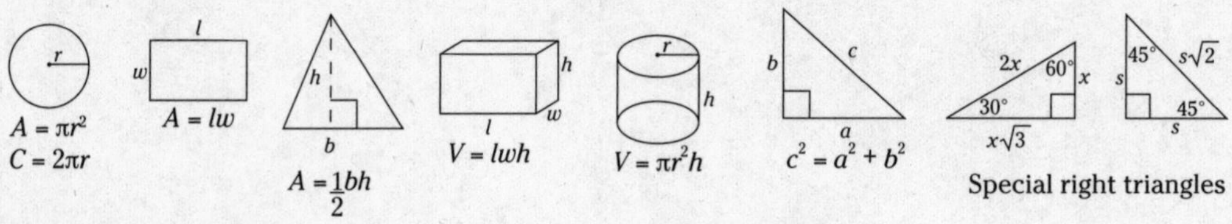

There are 360 degrees of arc in a circle.

There are 180 degrees in the sum of the interior angles of a triangle.

1. If $x + 4 = y - 3$, what is the value of $x - 2$ in terms of y?

   (A) $y + 5$

   (B) $y - 1$

   (C) $y - 6$

   (D) $y - 7$

   (E) $y - 9$

6, 7, 7, 7, 11, 13, 13, 24

2. For the above list of numbers, which of the following is also a number that is included in the list itself?

   I. The average (arithmetic mean)

   II. The median

   III. The mode

   (A) I only

   (B) III only

   (C) I and III only

   (D) II and III only

   (E) I, II, and III

Go on to next page

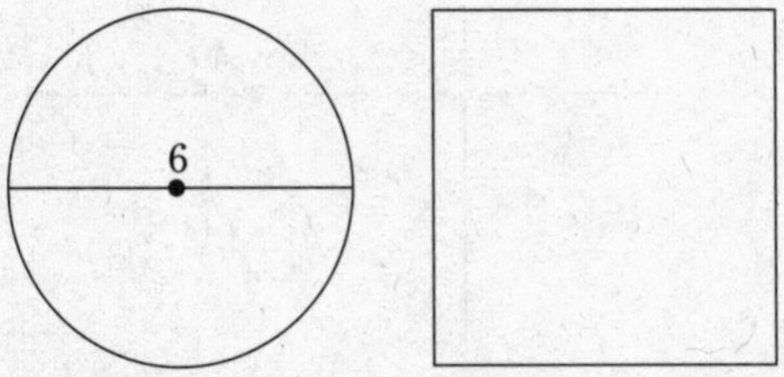

Note: Figure not drawn to scale.

3. In the figure above, the circle and the square have the same area. If the diameter of the circle is 6, what is the length of the side of the square?

(A) 3π

(B) 6π

(C) 9π

(D) $3\sqrt{\pi}$

(E) $6\sqrt{\pi}$

4. A die with 20 identically shaped sides has 5 faces painted red, 8 faces painted white, and 7 faces painted blue. What is the probability of rolling either a red or a blue face?

(A) $\frac{1}{4}$

(B) $\frac{3}{4}$

(C) $\frac{3}{5}$

(D) $\frac{5}{7}$

(E) $\frac{5}{8}$

5. Benita owns 3 jackets, 4 scarves, and 6 hats. What is the maximum number of days on which she can wear a different combination of jacket, scarf, and hat without duplicating a combination that she wore on a previous day?

(A) 13 days

(B) 24 days

(C) 48 days

(D) 72 days

(E) 95 days

6. If $|1 - 2x| > 4$, which of the following is a possible value of x?

(A) –2

(B) –1

(C) 0

(D) 1

(E) 2

Questions 7 and 8 refer to the following graph.

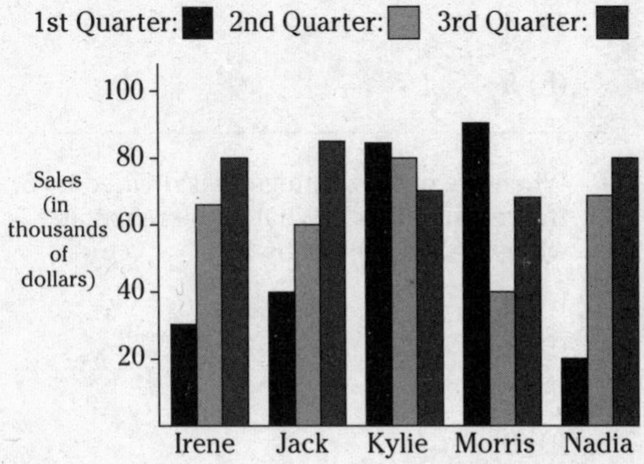

7. Which salesperson showed the greatest increase in sales from the first quarter to the second?

(A) Irene

(B) Jack

(C) Kylie

(D) Morris

(E) Nadia

8. Which of the following pairs of people had combined first-quarter sales closest to $120,000?

(A) Irene and Jack

(B) Jack and Kylie

(C) Jack and Morris

(D) Jack and Nadia

(E) Kylie and Morris

Go on to next page

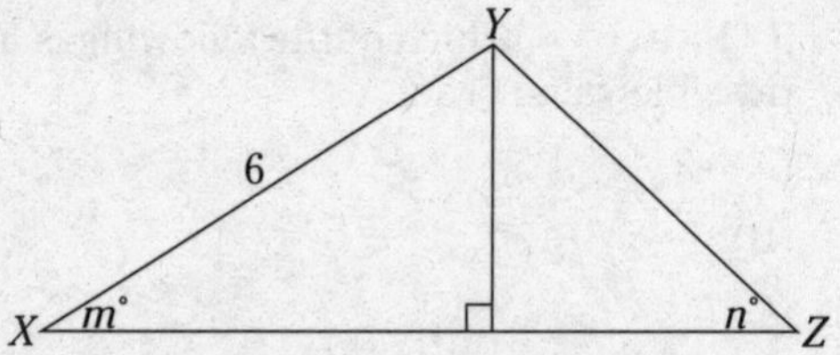

9. In $\triangle XYZ$ above, $XY = 6$ and angle XYZ is 105°. If m and n are in a ratio of 2:3, what is the height of the triangle from Y to $\overline{XZ}$?

(A) 1

(B) 2

(C) 3

(D) 4

(E) 5

10. When the positive integer v is divided by 5, the remainder is 2. What is the remainder when $v - 3$ is divided by 5?

(A) 0

(B) 1

(C) 2

(D) 3

(E) 4

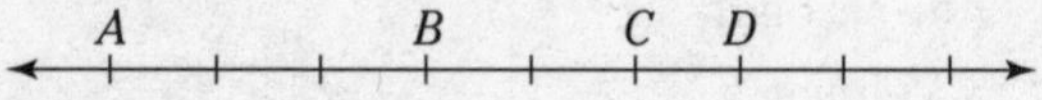

11. On the number line above, if $B = -1$ and $C - A = 0.25$, then $D =$

(A) 0.5

(B) –0.85

(C) –1.015

(D) –1.15

(E) –2.5

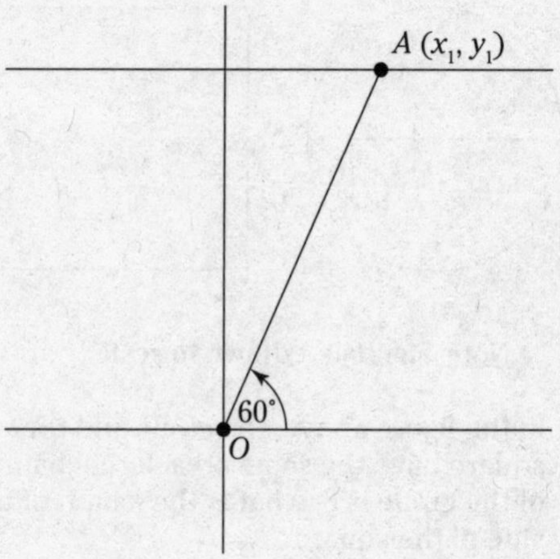

Note: Figure not drawn to scale.

12. In the graph above, line segment $\overline{OA}$ connects the origin O with point $A = (x_1, y_1)$ at a 60° angle with x-axis. If $OA = 4$, which of the following must be true?

(A) $x_1 = 1$

(B) $x_1 = 2$

(C) $y_1 = 2$

(D) $y_1 = 3$

(E) $y_1 = 4$

13. If $x(x - 2) = y(y - 2)$, then $x + y =$

(A) –2

(B) –1

(C) 0

(D) 1

(E) 2

Go on to next page

14. All full-time employees at the Metallious Company are members of the union. However, at least one Metallious employee is not a full-time employee. Which of the following must be true?

(A) All Metallious employees who are union members are full-time employees.

(B) Not all Metallious employees are union members.

(C) At least one Metallious employee is not a union member.

(D) No Metallious employee who is union member is not a full-time employee.

(E) Every Metallious employee is either a union member or is not a full-time employee.

x	0	1	2
$g(x)$	–1	1	15

15. The table above shows three values for the function g. If $g(x) = kx^3 + n$, what is the value of $k + n$?

(A) –1

(B) 0

(C) 1

(D) 2

(E) 3

16. The three sides of a rectangular solid have a ratio of 8:9:12. If the distance from one corner of the solid to the farthest corner is x, what is the length of the longest side of the box in terms of x?

(A) $\frac{4}{5}x$

(B) $\frac{5}{13}x$

(C) $\frac{9}{17}x$

(D) $\frac{12}{17}x$

(E) $\frac{24}{29}x$

STOP DO NOT TURN THE PAGE UNTIL TOLD TO DO SO.
DO NOT RETURN TO A PREVIOUS TEST.

Chapter 13

Answers and Explanations for Practice Test 2

In this chapter, you find the answers to the questions from Practice Test 2 in Chapter 12. Read through the detailed answer explanations to check your work and hone your skills. If you want to score yourself quickly, though, you can skip to the Answer Key at the end of this chapter.

Solutions to Section 1 Questions

1. **D.** Josh stocked one box with 9 packages of cookies and three boxes with 16 packages each: 9 + 3(16) = 9 + 48 = 57. Therefore, the right answer is (D).

2. **D.** Use the formula for the arithmetic mean:

$$39 = \frac{4+11+3x+7x+8x}{5}$$

$$39 = \frac{15+18x}{5}$$

Multiply both sides of the equation by 5 and solve for x: $195 = 15 + 18x$; $180 = 18x$; $10 = x$. So the right answer is (D).

3. **B.** The figure contains 24 squares and 8 triangles. Each square has an area of 1, and each triangle has an area of $\frac{1}{2}$, so multiply and add: $A = 24 + \frac{1}{2}(8) = 24 + 4 = 28$. Therefore, the right answer is (B).

4. **C.** The question asks you to find the "amount left," so use this concept to set up the problem: On Monday morning, Anthony washed 40% of his laundry, so the amount left after that was 60%. Then, on Monday afternoon, he did 60% of the amount that was left — that is, he did 60% of 60% — so the amount left was 40% of 60%:

40% of 60% = (0.4)(0.6) = 0.24 = 24%

Thus, Anthony had 24% left to do in the evening. Therefore, the right answer is (C).

5. **D.** After the first number, each subsequent number is produced by adding a different number:

	+2		+4		+8		+16	
1		**3**		**7**		**15**		**31**

Note that the number added doubles in each case. Thus, the sequence continues as follows:

	+2		+4		+8		+16		+32	
1		**3**		**7**		**15**		**31**		**63**

Therefore, the next number in the sequence is 63, so the right answer is (D).

6. **E.** The table shows commissions rising as sales rise, so you can rule out (A) and (D). The commission rises by $100 for every $2,000 of sales, so when sales are $0, the commission is $250 (find $350 – $100). Thus, the intercept at the vertical axis (normally, the *y*-intercept) is at 250. This is a positive number, so you can rule out (B) and (C). Therefore, the right answer is (E).

7. **B.** In this linear function, the variable *b* is the value when $x = 0$ — that is, when sales are $0. In the previous question, you calculate this as $250, so the right answer is (B).

8. **E.** The apples were first divided among the teachers, so each teacher received *a*/*t* apples. Then this number was further divided among *s* students:

$$\frac{a}{t} \div s = \frac{a}{st}$$

Therefore, the right answer is (E).

9. **C.** First, use the distance formula to find *PQ*: $PQ = \sqrt{(x_2 - x_1)^2 + (y_2 - y_1)^2} = \sqrt{(-4-0)^2 + (-2-1)^2}$. Then evaluate the square root: $\sqrt{(-4)^2 + (-3)^2} = \sqrt{16+9} = \sqrt{25} = 5$.

Thus $PQ = 5$, so $RS = 5$. Therefore, *S* is located 5 below *R*, so the *y*-coordinate of *S* is 5 less than the *y*-coordinate of *R*: $k = 2 - 5 = -3$. The right answer is (C).

10. **E.** Angle *a*, angle *b*, and angle *c* are three angles in a triangle, so $a + b + c = 180$. Angle *d* and angle *e* are supplementary, so $d + e = 180$. Adding the two equations together gives you $a + b + c + d + e = 360$. Therefore, the right answer is (E).

11. **C.** The intersection of two sets are elements of both sets, so you're looking for all the prime numbers from 26 to 44.

If a number under 121 (11^2) isn't divisible by the prime numbers less than its square root (2, 3, 5, or 7), then it's prime (as I explain in Chapter 3). So test all the numbers from 26 to 44 for divisibility, ruling out non-prime numbers as you go. First, you can rule out the even numbers, which are divisible by 2. Write down all odd numbers between 26 and 44:

27, 29, 31, 33, 35, 37, 39, 41, 43

Next, rule out the remaining numbers that are divisible by 3. You can cut 27, 33, and 39, which leaves you with

29, 31, 35, 37, 41, 43

Now rule out the numbers that are divisible by 5. You can cut 35, so your list becomes

29, 31, 37, 41, 43

Finally, rule out the numbers that are divisible by 7. None of the remaining numbers are divisible by 7, so they're all prime (be sure to count them all!):

29, 31, 37, 41, 43

Therefore, there are exactly five numbers in both sets, so the right answer is (C).

12. **B.** You can save time on this problem by noticing that all five answers have a numerator of 1. Thus, let the fraction you're looking for equal $\frac{1}{x}$. Now, adding 1 to the numerator and subtracting 2 from the denominator gives you the same result as subtracting 4 from the denominator, so

$$\frac{2}{x-2} = \frac{1}{x-4}$$

Cross-multiply and solve for x:

$$2(x-4) = x-2$$
$$2x-8 = x-2$$
$$2x = x+6$$
$$x = 6$$

Thus, $x = 6$, so the original fraction is $\frac{1}{6}$. The right answer is (B).

13. **B.** Let x be the number, and then translate the property into the following equation:

$$x^2 - 6 = x + 6$$

Put this equation into the standard quadratic form and factor:

$$x^2 - x - 12 = 0$$
$$(x+3)(x-4) = 0$$

Split into two equations and solve each for x:

$$x + 3 = 0 \quad \text{or} \quad x - 4 = 0$$
$$x = -3 \qquad\qquad x = 4$$

Thus, the two integers with this property are –3 and 4, so find their sum to get the answer:

$$-3 + 4 = 1$$

Therefore, the sum of these two numbers is 1, so the right answer is (B).

14. **D.** Let x be the total expenses. Advertising costs are 15% of expenses, so 15% of x is \$825:

$$0.15x = 825$$
$$\frac{0.15x}{0.15} = \frac{825}{0.15}$$
$$x = 5{,}500$$

So the total expenses are \$5,500. And 55% of this amount goes to payroll:

Payroll = 55% of 5,500 = (0.55)(5,500) = 3,025

Therefore, payroll costs \$3,025 per month, so the right answer is (D).

15. **C.** The chart shows 15 grades. If he gets five 10s on the next five quizzes, he will have 20 grades. Thus, take a weighted average:

$$\text{Weighted average} = \frac{10(3)+9(6)+8(4)+7(2)+10(5)}{20}$$

Evaluate as follows:

$$= \frac{30+54+32+14+50}{20} = \frac{180}{20} = 9$$

Thus, the right answer is (C).

16. **A.** The y-intercept (where $x = 0$) is –2, so $c = -2$. The function is concave down, so a is negative. And the function is shifted to the left, so a and b have the same sign; therefore, b is also negative. Thus, a, b, and c are all negative, with $c = -2$, so $a + b + c < -2$. Therefore, $a + b + c$ could only equal –3, so the right answer is (A).

17. **D.** To solve for x, a good choice is to make the base 5 on both sides. Note that $25 = 5^2$ and $\sqrt{5} = 5^{1/2}$, so you can make the following substitution:

$$25^{x-3} = \left(\sqrt{5}\right)^{2x}$$
$$\left(5^2\right)^{x-3} = \left(5^{1/2}\right)^{2x}$$

Next, shift the parentheses to the exponents:

$$5^{2(x-3)} = 5^{(1/2)(2x)}$$

Now, because the bases are equal, the exponents are also equal, so you can remove the bases:

$$2(x-3) = \frac{1}{2}(2x)$$

Simplify and solve for x: $2x - 6 = x$; $x - 6 = 0$; $x = 6$. Therefore, the right answer is (D).

18. **E.** The key to this problem is recalling that a line drawn from the center of a circle to any point on it is perpendicular to a tangent line at that point. So begin by labeling the three tangent points D, E, and F; then draw lines from O to each of these points. Then, $\overline{OD}$, $\overline{OE}$, and $\overline{OF}$ are all radii of the circle, they meet the triangle at right angles, and $OD = OE = OF = 1$. Additionally, draw $\overline{OC}$. The following figure summarizes these steps:

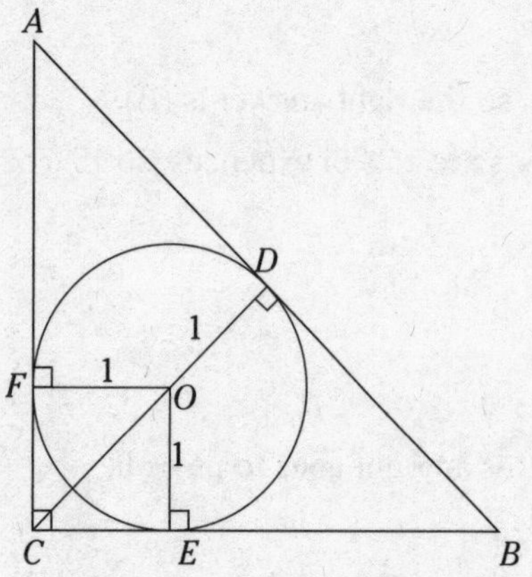

$FOEC$ is a square with a side of 1, so $OC = \sqrt{2}$. Thus, the height of $\triangle ADC$ is $CD = 1 + \sqrt{2}$. Triangle DBC is a 45-45-90 triangle, so $DB = 1 + \sqrt{2}$. $\overline{AB}$ is twice the length of $\overline{DB}$, so $AB = 2\left(1 + \sqrt{2}\right)$.

You can use the base of AB and the height of CD to find the area of $\triangle ABC$:

$$A = \frac{1}{2}bh = \frac{1}{2}2\left(1+\sqrt{2}\right)\left(1+\sqrt{2}\right)$$

Simplify:

$$= \left(1+\sqrt{2}\right)\left(1+\sqrt{2}\right) = 1 + 2\sqrt{2} + 2 = 3 + 2\sqrt{2}$$

Therefore, the right answer is (E).

19. **E.** Ms. D'Agostino has s seniors in her class, so she has $s - 5$ juniors. Therefore, altogether she has

Total = seniors + juniors = $s + s - 5 = 2s - 5$

Here's how you find the fraction of juniors in the class:

$$\frac{\text{Juniors}}{\text{Total}} = \frac{s-5}{2s-5}$$

To turn this fraction into a percent, multiply by 100:

$$= \frac{100(s-5)}{(2s-5)}\%$$

Therefore, the right answer is (E).

20. **A.** Let x equal the number of ounces of 70% solution to be used. Then, you'll need to add $32 - x$ ounces of the 95% solution to make a total of 32 ounces of an 80% solution. Organize this information in the following chart:

Solution	***% Alcohol***	***Ounces***	***Total***
70% solution	0.7	x	$0.7x$
95% solution	0.95	$32 - x$	$0.95(32 - x)$
80% solution	0.80	32	0.8(32)

Adding the first two results in the *Total* column gives you the final result, which you can turn into the following equation:

$$0.7x + 0.95(32 - x) = 0.8(32)$$

Simplify and solve for x:

$$\begin{aligned} 0.7x + 30.4 - 0.95x &= 25.6 \\ 30.4 - 0.25x &= 25.6 \\ -0.25x &= -4.8 \\ x &= 19.2 \end{aligned}$$

Thus, the right answer is (A).

Solutions to Section 2 Questions

1. **C.** The *triangle inequality* tells you that the third side of a triangle has to be greater than the difference and less than the sum of the other two sides. The triangle has sides of 7 and 4, so find the sum and difference: $7 + 4 = 11$ and $7 - 4 = 3$. Thus, the remaining side is greater than 3 and less than 11, so it could only be 10. Therefore, the right answer is (C).

2. **D.** For each combination of three types of fruit that she brings to work, Eleanor leaves two types of fruit out. To make the problem easier, count the combinations of fruit that she leaves out. To avoid counting a combination twice, start with apples and pair it with every type of fruit that appears later in the list. Then do the same with bananas, mangos, and so forth. (I use the initial of each type of fruit to save time and space.)

AB			
AM	BM		
AO	BO	MO	
AP	BP	MP	OP

There are ten pairs of fruit that she can leave out, so there are ten groups of three fruit that she can take to work. Therefore, the right answer is (D).

3. **C.** Let x be the lowest of the four integers. Then the remaining three are $x + 2$, $x + 4$, and $x + 6$. So you can set up the following equation:

   $$x + (x + 2) + (x + 4) + (x + 6) = 80$$

   Solve for x: $4x + 12 = 80$; $4x = 68$; $x = 17$. Thus, the four numbers are 17, 19, 21, and 23. So the product of the two lowest numbers is $17 \times 19 = 323$. Therefore, the right answer is (C).

4. **C.** The radius is $2x$ and the height is $5x$, so plug these numbers into the formula for the volume of a cylinder:

   $$V = \pi r^2 h = \pi(2x)^2(5x) = \pi(4x^2)(5x) = 20\pi x^3$$

   Thus, the right answer is (C).

5. **A.** Begin by translating the notation into standard math symbols: $x = 2$, $y = 0$, and $z = 4$

   $$2\$0\$4 = 5^2 - 3^0 - 2^4 = 25 - 1 - 16 = 8$$

   Thus, the right answer is (A).

6. **D.** The center square of the figure is spotted, so you can rule out Answer (E). The two small black triangles touch at one corner, so you can rule out Answer (C). The two large striped triangles touch at one corner, so you can rule out Answer (B). In the figure, the large spotted triangle is positioned clockwise from the large white triangle, so you can rule out (A). Therefore, the right answer is (D).

7. **E.** Angle p, angle q, and angle r are the three angles of a triangle, so $p + q + r = 180$. Angle s and angle t are supplementary, so $s + t = 180$. Plug these amounts into the formula for the mean average:

   $$\text{Mean} = \frac{p+q+r+s+t}{5} = \frac{180+180}{5} = \frac{360}{5} = 72$$

   Thus, the right answer is (E).

8. **B.** Let b equal what Bill received and let n equal what Nikki received. If Bill had received \$50 less, he would've received half of what Nikki received, so write the following equation:

   $$b - 50 = \frac{n}{2}$$

   You can multiply this equation by 2 to get rid of the fraction:

   $$2b - 100 = n$$

   If Nikki had received one-third of what she received, she would've received \$85 less than Bill, so you can write this equation:

   $$\frac{n}{3} = b - 85$$

   Multiply both sides of the equation by 3 to get rid of the fraction and isolate n:

   $$n = 3b - 255$$

   Substitute $3b - 255$ for n into the first equation: $2b - 100 = 3b - 255$. Solve for b to find how much Bill received: $-100 = b - 255$; $155 = b$.

   Substitute this value of b back into the first equation to find what Nikki received: $2(155) - 100 = n$. Then solve for n: $310 - 100 = n$; $210 = n$.

   Thus, Bill received \$155 and Nikki received \$210, so add them to find how much they received together: $155 + 210 = 365$. They received a total of \$365, so the right answer is (B).

9. **124**. Let x equal the original price of the camera in dollars. Then, the amount of the discount was 40% of x: $0.4x$. This discount was subtracted from the original price, resulting in a selling price of $74.40. So you can make the following equation:

$$x - 0.4x = 74.4$$

Simplify and solve for x: $0.6x = 74.4$; $x = 124$. Thus, the original price of the camera was $124, so the right answer is 124.

10. **221**. Let $3x$ equal the number of dogs, $4x$ equal the number of cats, and $10x$ equal the number of birds. The problem provides information about a hypothetical situation in which there are twice as many dogs and 26 fewer cats. Organize this information in a chart as follows:

Animal	***Currently***	***Hypothetically***
Dogs	$3x$	$6x$
Cats	$4x$	$4x - 26$
Birds	$10x$	$10x$

In the hypothetical case, there are twice as many cats and birds combined as there are dogs, so make the following equation:

$$\text{Cats} + \text{birds} = 2(\text{dogs})$$

$$(4x - 26) + 10x = 2(6x)$$

Simplify and solve for x: $14x - 26 = 12x$; $-26 = -2x$; $13 = x$. Thus, there are 39 dogs, 52 cats, and 130 birds: $39 + 52 + 130 = 221$. The store has 221 dogs, cats, and birds.

11. **20**. First find out how many people took the survey altogether: $23 + 19 + 13 + 10 = 65$. Of these, 13 people drink only tea, so divide to find the percentage: $\frac{13}{65} = 0.2 = 20\%$. Therefore, the right answer is 20.

12. **6**. The slope of the line is $\frac{2}{3}$, so starting at (3,0), go *up 2, over 3*, to (6,2), (9,4), and (12,6). Therefore, $n = 6$.

13. **7**. First, find the value of $f(4)$ by plugging in 4 for each x:

$$f(4) = 4^2 - 3 = 16 - 3 = 13$$

Next, find the value of $g(x) = x^2 + 2x$, plugging in -2 for the x's:

$$g(-2) = (-2)^2 + 5(-2) = 4 - 10 = -6$$

Add these two values to solve the problem: $f(4) + g(-2) = 13 - 6 = 7$. Therefore, the right answer is 7.

14. **4/25** or **.16**. Let x be the radius of a small circle. Use the area formula to find the area of each small circle:

$$A_{\text{small circle}} = \pi r^2 = \pi$$

The shaded region consists of four circles, so

$$\text{Shaded area} = 4\pi$$

The radius of the large circle is $5x$. Use the area formula to find the area of the large circle:

$$A_{\text{large circle}} = \pi r^2 = \pi(5)^2 = 25\pi$$

Calculate geometric probability using the following formula:

$$\text{Geometric probability} = \frac{\text{Target area}}{\text{Total area}}$$

Substitute the shaded area for the target area and the area of the large circle for the total area:

$$= \frac{4\pi}{25\pi} = \frac{4}{25}$$

Thus, the right answer is 4/25, or .16.

15. **620**. Morey has played 310 games and won 70% of them:

$$70\% \text{ of } 310 = (0.70)(310) = 217$$

Thus, Morey has won 217 games. Subtract this from his total games to find out how many games he's lost: 310 – 217 = 93. Thus, if he wants to have 90% wins, he must have 10% losses. So 10% of the total number of games he needs to play equals 93:

$$10\% \text{ of } x = 93$$

$$0.1x = 93$$

$$x = \frac{93}{0.1} = 930$$

So Morey needs to play 930 games altogether. Subtract the 310 games that he's already played: 930 – 310 = 620. To reach 90% wins, he needs to play 620 games without losing.

16. **3** or **1/3** or **.333**. To begin, substitute $3a$ for x in the function:

$$f(x) = \frac{x^2 + 9}{5}$$

$$f(3a) = \frac{(3a)^2 + 9}{5}$$

Now substitute $6a$ for $f(3a)$: $6a = \frac{(3a)^2 + 9}{5}$. Then simplify: $6a = \frac{9a^2 + 9}{5}$. Multiply both sides by 5 and put the function in standard quadratic form:

$$30a = 9a^2 + 9$$

$$0 = 9a^2 - 30a + 9$$

Divide both sides by 3:

$$0 = 3a^2 - 10a + 3$$

Then factor $3a^2 - 10a + 3$:

$$0 = (a - 3)(3a - 1)$$

Split into two separate equations:

$a - 3 = 0$ or $3a - 1 = 0$

$a = 3$ $\quad$ $3a = 1$

$a = \frac{1}{3}$

Thus, the right answer is either 3 or 1/3, which you can also write as .333 on the answer grid.

17. **4/15** or **.266** or **.267**. Begin by sketching the information from the problem:

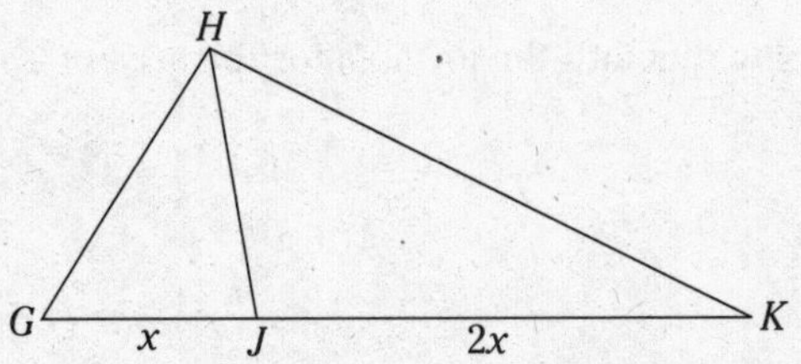

$$\text{Area of } \triangle GHK = \frac{1}{2}bh = \frac{1}{2}(3x)h = \frac{3}{2}xh$$

$$\text{Area of } \triangle GHJ = \frac{1}{2}bh = \frac{1}{2}xh$$

Compare the two triangles, and you can see that the area of $\triangle GHJ$ is $\frac{1}{3}$ the area of *GHK*, which is $\frac{4}{5}$:

$$\left(\frac{1}{3}\right)\left(\frac{4}{5}\right) = \frac{4}{15}$$

Therefore, the right answer is 4/15, which you can also give as a decimal, .266 or .267.

18. **9541**. *M* is the highest possible value of *abcd,* so assume that $a = 9$. Then, $b + c = 9$, with $b > c$, so there are only four possible combinations for *b* and *c:*

a	**b**	**c**	**d**
9	8	1	
9	7	2	
9	6	3	
9	5	4	1

For the first three rows, there is no value for *d* such that $c > d$ and $b = c + d$. However, in the last row, $d = 1$. So $M = 9{,}541$, which you enter into the grid as 9541.

Solutions to Section 3 Questions

1. **E.** First, solve for *x* in terms of *y:* $x + 4 = y - 3$; $x = y - 7$. Now subtract 2 from both sides: $x - 2 = y - 9$. Therefore, the right answer is (E).

2. **C.** Begin by calculating the arithmetic mean of the list of numbers:

$$\text{Mean} = \frac{6+7+7+7+11+13+13+24}{8} = \frac{88}{8} = 11$$

The median is the mean of the two middle numbers in the list (7 and 11):

$$\text{Median} = \frac{7+11}{2} = \frac{18}{2} = 9$$

The mode is the most often repeated number in the list, so it equals 7. Therefore, the mean and mode both appear in the list, but the median doesn't. The right answer is (C).

3. **D.** The diameter of the circle is 6, so its radius is 3. Use the area formula for a circle:

   $A = \pi r^2 = \pi(3)^2 = 9\pi$

   The area of the square is also 9π, so plug this into the formula for the area of a square to find the side:

   $$\begin{aligned} A &= s^2 \\ 9\pi &= s^2 \\ \sqrt{9\pi} &= s \\ 3\sqrt{\pi} &= s \end{aligned}$$

   Therefore, the right answer is (D).

4. **C.** There are a total of 20 possible outcomes. Of these, 12 are target outcomes (either red or blue). Plug these values into the formula for probability: $\text{Probability} = \frac{\text{Target outcome}}{\text{Total outcome}} = \frac{12}{20} = \frac{3}{5}$. Therefore, the right answer is (C).

5. **D.** Benita owns 3 jackets, 4 scarves, and 6 hats. She can choose any of these items independently, so multiply to find the number of combinations: $3 \times 4 \times 6 = 72$. Therefore, the right answer is (D).

6. **A.** Remove the absolute value bars by splitting the problem into two separate inequalities. Remember that with absolute value, you must change the inequality sign as you negate the opposite side of the inequality:

   $1 - 2x > 4 \qquad \text{or} \qquad 1 - 2x < -4$

   Solve the first inequality for *x:*

   $$\begin{aligned} 1 - 2x &> 4 \\ -2x &> 3 \\ \frac{-2x}{-2} &< \frac{3}{-2} \\ x &< -\frac{3}{2} \end{aligned}$$

   Now solve the second inequality for *x:*

   $$\begin{aligned} 1 - 2x &< -4 \\ -2x &< -5 \\ \frac{-2x}{-2} &> \frac{-5}{-2} \\ x &> \frac{5}{2} \end{aligned}$$

   Therefore, $x < -\frac{3}{2}$ or $x > \frac{5}{2}$. So of the five choices, only –2 could be a value of *x,* and the right answer is (A).

7. **E.** The first two bars over each person's name represent the first two quarters, respectively. Kylie and Morris both show decreases. Irene shows an increase of about $20,000, and Jack shows an increase of about $30,000. Nadia shows an increase of more than $40,000, so the right answer is (E).

8. **B.** In the first quarter, Jack had about $40,000 in sales and Kylie had about $80,000, so together they sold approximately $120,000 in merchandise. Therefore, the right answer is (B).

9. **C.** The three angles in the triangle add up to 180°, so $m + n + 105 = 180$; $m + n = 75$. The values m and n are in a 2:3 ratio, so let $m = 2x$ and $n = 3x$:

$$2x + 3x = 75$$
$$5x = 75$$
$$x = 15$$

Thus, m is 30°. So the height of the triangle from Y to $\overline{XZ}$ becomes the shortest leg of a 30-60-90 triangle. This triangle has a hypotenuse of 6, so the height is half the length of the hypotenuse, which is 3, as shown in the following figure.

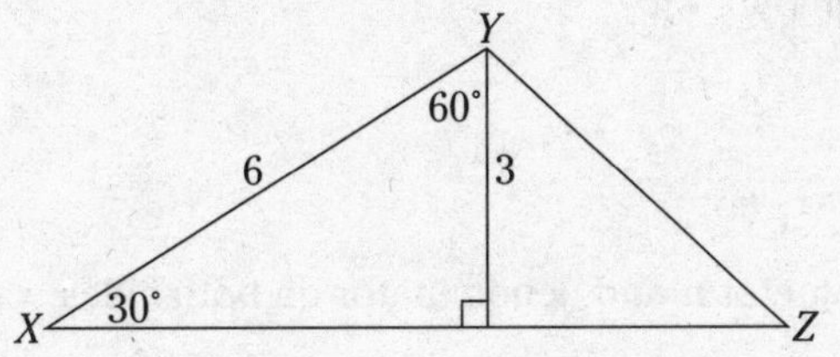

Therefore, the right answer is (C).

10. **E.** The only information that the problem gives you about v is that when it's divided by 5, the remainder is 2. Thus, you can choose any v that has this property. For example, let $v = 12$:

$12 \div 5 = 2 \text{ r } 2$

The question asks you about $v - 3 = 9$:

$9 \div 5 = 1 \text{ r } 4$

The remainder is 4, so the right answer is (E).

11. **B.** You know that $C - A = 0.25$. There are five intervals between A and C, so divide to find what each interval represents: $\frac{0.25}{5} = 0.05$. $B = -1$, and D is three intervals above B, so $D = -1 + 3(0.05) = -1 + 0.15 = -0.85$. The right answer is (B).

12. **B.** The x-axis and y-axis form a right angle, so the angle between $\overline{OA}$ and the y-axis is 30°. Therefore, the triangle shown in the figure is a 30-60-90 triangle:

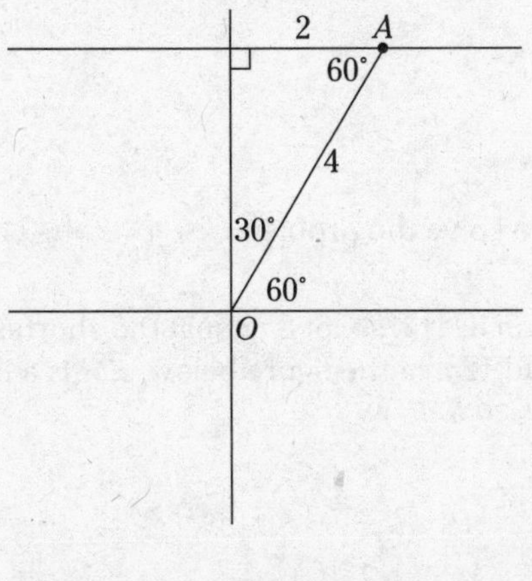

The hypotenuse is $\overline{OA}$, and this length is 4. Thus, the distance from A to the x-axis is half of the hypotenuse, so it's 2. Therefore, the x-coordinate of A is 2, so the right answer is (B).

13. **E.** To begin, distribute to remove the parentheses on both sides of the equation:

$$x(x-2) = y(y-2)$$
$$x^2 - 2x = y^2 - 2y$$

Now separate the two squared terms from the two nonsquared terms:

$$x^2 - y^2 = 2x - 2y$$

Factor the left as the difference of two squares, and factor out 2 on the right side:

$$(x+y)(x-y) = 2(x-y)$$

Now divide both sides of the equation by $x - y$:

$$\frac{(x+y)(x-y)}{(x-y)} = \frac{2(x-y)}{(x-y)}$$

Cancel out common factors in the numerator and denominator on both sides: $x + y = 2$. Therefore, the right answer is (E).

14. **E.** All full-time Metallious employees are in the union. Additionally, there's at least one part-time employee, who may or may not be in the union.

Suppose this part-time employee is in the union. Then you can rule out (A) and (D), because he is a part-time employee who is in the union.

Then, if you further suppose that he is the *only* part-time employee, you can rule out (B) and (C), because every Metallious employee would be a union member.

Thus, the right answer is (E): Every Metallious employee is either a union member (and, therefore, a full-time employee) or is not a full-time employee.

15. **C.** The table tells you that when $x = 0$, $g(x) = -1$. So plug both of these values into the function:

$$g(x) = kx^3 + n$$
$$-1 = k(0)^3 + n$$
$$-1 = n$$

Thus, $n = -1$. Also, according to the table, when $x = 1$, $g(x) = 1$. So substitute both of these values into the function, along with $n = -1$:

$$g(x) = kx^3 + n$$
$$1 = k(1)^3 + (-1)$$
$$1 = k - 1$$
$$2 = k$$

Thus, $k = 2$. Now add the values for k and n to solve the problem: $k + n = 2 + (-1) = 1$. Therefore, the right answer is (C).

16. **D.** The three sides of the box are in proportion 8:9:12, so let $8n$ equal the shortest side. Then the three sides are of lengths $8n$, $9n$, and $12n$. In the figure below, $\overline{KM}$ is a line from one corner of the box to the opposite corner, so $KM = x$.

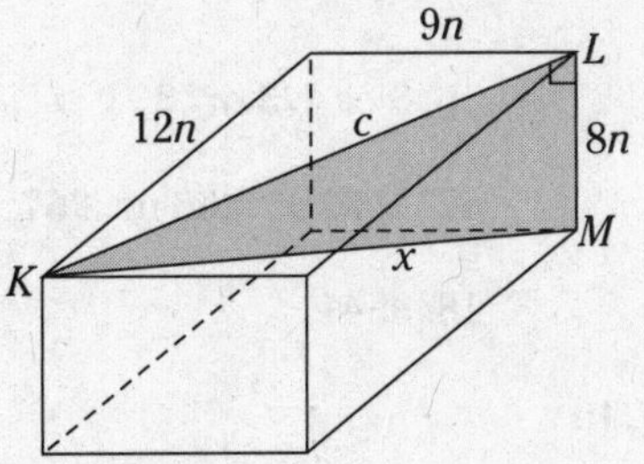

One side of the box has a length of $12n$ and a width of $9n$, so you can use the Pythagorean theorem to calculate its diagonal c ($\overline{KL}$ in the figure above) as follows:

$$a^2 + b^2 = c^2$$
$$(9n)^2 + (12n)^2 = c^2$$
$$81n^2 + 144n^2 = c^2$$
$$225n^2 = c^2$$
$$15n = c$$

Thus, the diagonal $\overline{KL}$ has a length of $15n$. This diagonal and the side that's $8n$ in length are the two legs of a right triangle whose hypotenuse ($\overline{KM}$ in the figure) is length x:

$$a^2 + b^2 = c^2$$
$$(15n)^2 + (8n)^2 = x^2$$
$$225n^2 + 64n^2 = x^2$$
$$289n^2 = x^2$$
$$17n = x$$

Thus, you can find n in terms of x:

$$n = \frac{x}{17}$$

The length of the longest side is $12n$. Therefore, in terms of x, the length of the longest side of the box is $12n = \frac{12}{17}x$. Therefore, the right answer is (D).

Answer Key

Section 1

1. **D**	6. **E**	11. **C**	16. **A**
2. **D**	7. **B**	12. **B**	17. **D**
3. **B**	8. **E**	13. **B**	18. **E**
4. **C**	9. **C**	14. **D**	19. **E**
5. **D**	10. **E**	15. **C**	20. **A**

Section 2

1. **C**	6. **D**	11. **20**	16. **3** or **1/3** or **.333**
2. **D**	7. **E**	12. **6**	17. **4/15** or **.266** or **.267**
3. **C**	8. **B**	13. **7**	18. **9541**
4. **C**	9. **124**	14. **4/25** or **.16**	
5. **A**	10. **221**	15. **620**	

Section 3

1. **E**	5. **D**	9. **C**	13. **E**
2. **C**	6. **A**	10. **E**	14. **E**
3. **D**	7. **E**	11. **B**	15. **C**
4. **C**	8. **B**	12. **B**	16. **D**

Chapter 14

Practice Test 3

Here's one more opportunity to test yourself. This test includes three sections of SAT math in the same basic form as the real test. To begin, tear out the answer sheet provided at the beginning of this chapter and use it to answer the questions. Set a timer as indicated at the top of each section. A calculator is permitted, as on the SAT.

When you're done, check your answers in Chapter 15, which provides both a quick list of answers for scoring, as well as detailed explanations to help you understand why the correct answer is correct.

Good luck!

Answer Sheet for Practice Test 3

Use the ovals and grid-ins provided with this practice exam to record your answers.

Section 1

1. Ⓐ Ⓑ Ⓒ Ⓓ Ⓔ
2. Ⓐ Ⓑ Ⓒ Ⓓ Ⓔ
3. Ⓐ Ⓑ Ⓒ Ⓓ Ⓔ
4. Ⓐ Ⓑ Ⓒ Ⓓ Ⓔ
5. Ⓐ Ⓑ Ⓒ Ⓓ Ⓔ
6. Ⓐ Ⓑ Ⓒ Ⓓ Ⓔ
7. Ⓐ Ⓑ Ⓒ Ⓓ Ⓔ
8. Ⓐ Ⓑ Ⓒ Ⓓ Ⓔ
9. Ⓐ Ⓑ Ⓒ Ⓓ Ⓔ
10. Ⓐ Ⓑ Ⓒ Ⓓ Ⓔ
11. Ⓐ Ⓑ Ⓒ Ⓓ Ⓔ
12. Ⓐ Ⓑ Ⓒ Ⓓ Ⓔ
13. Ⓐ Ⓑ Ⓒ Ⓓ Ⓔ
14. Ⓐ Ⓑ Ⓒ Ⓓ Ⓔ
15. Ⓐ Ⓑ Ⓒ Ⓓ Ⓔ
16. Ⓐ Ⓑ Ⓒ Ⓓ Ⓔ
17. Ⓐ Ⓑ Ⓒ Ⓓ Ⓔ
18. Ⓐ Ⓑ Ⓒ Ⓓ Ⓔ
19. Ⓐ Ⓑ Ⓒ Ⓓ Ⓔ
20. Ⓐ Ⓑ Ⓒ Ⓓ Ⓔ

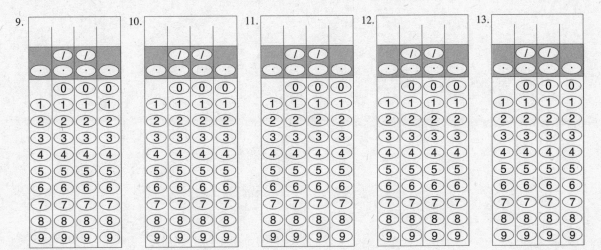

Section 2

1. Ⓐ Ⓑ Ⓒ Ⓓ Ⓔ
2. Ⓐ Ⓑ Ⓒ Ⓓ Ⓔ
3. Ⓐ Ⓑ Ⓒ Ⓓ Ⓔ
4. Ⓐ Ⓑ Ⓒ Ⓓ Ⓔ
5. Ⓐ Ⓑ Ⓒ Ⓓ Ⓔ
6. Ⓐ Ⓑ Ⓒ Ⓓ Ⓔ
7. Ⓐ Ⓑ Ⓒ Ⓓ Ⓔ
8. Ⓐ Ⓑ Ⓒ Ⓓ Ⓔ

9.

	/	/	
.	.	.	.
	0	0	0
1	1	1	1
2	2	2	2
3	3	3	3
4	4	4	4
5	5	5	5
6	6	6	6
7	7	7	7
8	8	8	8
9	9	9	9

10.

	/	/	
.	.	.	.
	0	0	0
1	1	1	1
2	2	2	2
3	3	3	3
4	4	4	4
5	5	5	5
6	6	6	6
7	7	7	7
8	8	8	8
9	9	9	9

11.

	/	/	
.	.	.	.
	0	0	0
1	1	1	1
2	2	2	2
3	3	3	3
4	4	4	4
5	5	5	5
6	6	6	6
7	7	7	7
8	8	8	8
9	9	9	9

12.

	/	/	
.	.	.	.
	0	0	0
1	1	1	1
2	2	2	2
3	3	3	3
4	4	4	4
5	5	5	5
6	6	6	6
7	7	7	7
8	8	8	8
9	9	9	9

13.

	/	/	
.	.	.	.
	0	0	0
1	1	1	1
2	2	2	2
3	3	3	3
4	4	4	4
5	5	5	5
6	6	6	6
7	7	7	7
8	8	8	8
9	9	9	9

14.

	/	/	
.	.	.	.
	0	0	0
1	1	1	1
2	2	2	2
3	3	3	3
4	4	4	4
5	5	5	5
6	6	6	6
7	7	7	7
8	8	8	8
9	9	9	9

15.

	/	/	
.	.	.	.
	0	0	0
1	1	1	1
2	2	2	2
3	3	3	3
4	4	4	4
5	5	5	5
6	6	6	6
7	7	7	7
8	8	8	8
9	9	9	9

16.

	/	/	
.	.	.	.
	0	0	0
1	1	1	1
2	2	2	2
3	3	3	3
4	4	4	4
5	5	5	5
6	6	6	6
7	7	7	7
8	8	8	8
9	9	9	9

17.

	/	/	
.	.	.	.
	0	0	0
1	1	1	1
2	2	2	2
3	3	3	3
4	4	4	4
5	5	5	5
6	6	6	6
7	7	7	7
8	8	8	8
9	9	9	9

18.

	/	/	
.	.	.	.
	0	0	0
1	1	1	1
2	2	2	2
3	3	3	3
4	4	4	4
5	5	5	5
6	6	6	6
7	7	7	7
8	8	8	8
9	9	9	9

Section 3

1. Ⓐ Ⓑ Ⓒ Ⓓ Ⓔ	5. Ⓐ Ⓑ Ⓒ Ⓓ Ⓔ	9. Ⓐ Ⓑ Ⓒ Ⓓ Ⓔ	13. Ⓐ Ⓑ Ⓒ Ⓓ Ⓔ
2. Ⓐ Ⓑ Ⓒ Ⓓ Ⓔ	6. Ⓐ Ⓑ Ⓒ Ⓓ Ⓔ	10. Ⓐ Ⓑ Ⓒ Ⓓ Ⓔ	14. Ⓐ Ⓑ Ⓒ Ⓓ Ⓔ
3. Ⓐ Ⓑ Ⓒ Ⓓ Ⓔ	7. Ⓐ Ⓑ Ⓒ Ⓓ Ⓔ	11. Ⓐ Ⓑ Ⓒ Ⓓ Ⓔ	15. Ⓐ Ⓑ Ⓒ Ⓓ Ⓔ
4. Ⓐ Ⓑ Ⓒ Ⓓ Ⓔ	8. Ⓐ Ⓑ Ⓒ Ⓓ Ⓔ	12. Ⓐ Ⓑ Ⓒ Ⓓ Ⓔ	16. Ⓐ Ⓑ Ⓒ Ⓓ Ⓔ

Section 1

Time: 25 minutes for 20 questions

Directions: Choose the *best* answer to each question. Mark the corresponding oval on the answer sheet.

Notes:

- You may use a calculator.
- All numbers used in this exam are real numbers.
- All figures lie in a plane.
- All figures may be assumed to be to scale unless the problem specifically indicates otherwise.

Reference Information:

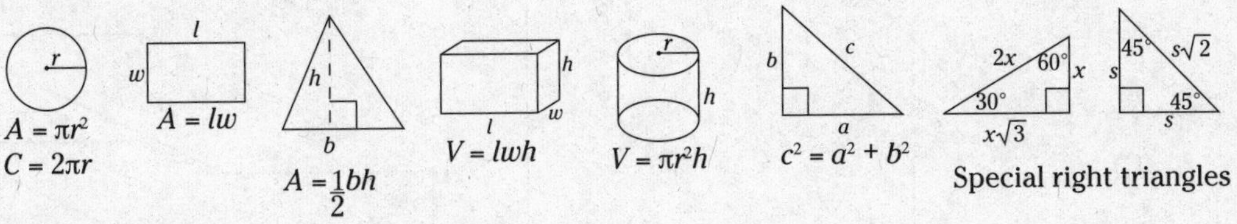

There are 360 degrees of arc in a circle.

There are 180 degrees in the sum of the interior angles of a triangle.

1. If $x + 4 = y$, then $2x - 2y =$

(A) 1

(B) –2

(C) 4

(D) –8

(E) 16

2. Over the summer, Megan saved twice as much money as Rita, and Rita saved $40 more than Kyra. If Kyra saved $200, how much money did Megan save?

(A) $60

(B) $240

(C) $320

(D) $400

(E) $480

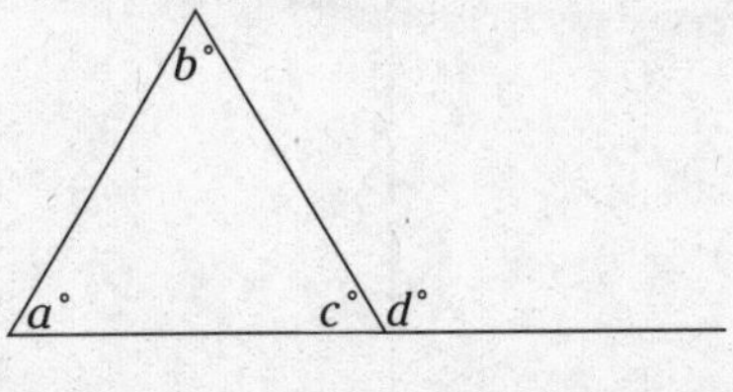

3. In the figure above, which of the following must be true?

(A) $a = b$

(B) $a + b = c$

(C) $a + b = d$

(D) $a + c = d$

(E) $b + c = d$

Go on to next page

4. Which of the following could be a graph of the equation $y = x - 3$?

(A)

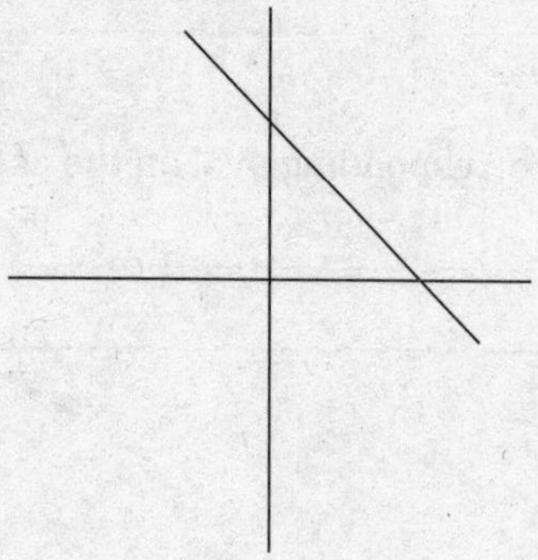

(B)

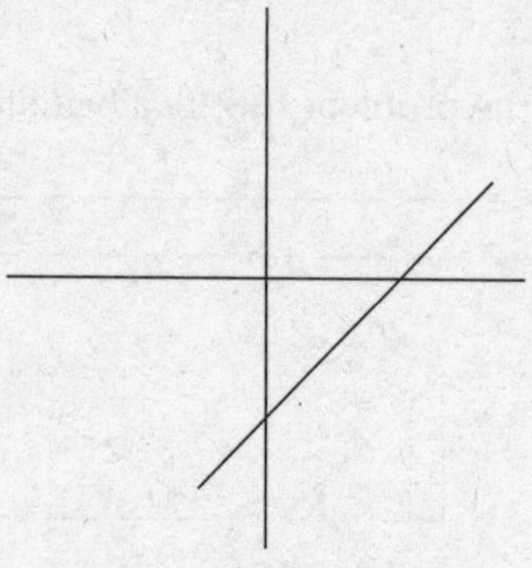

(C)

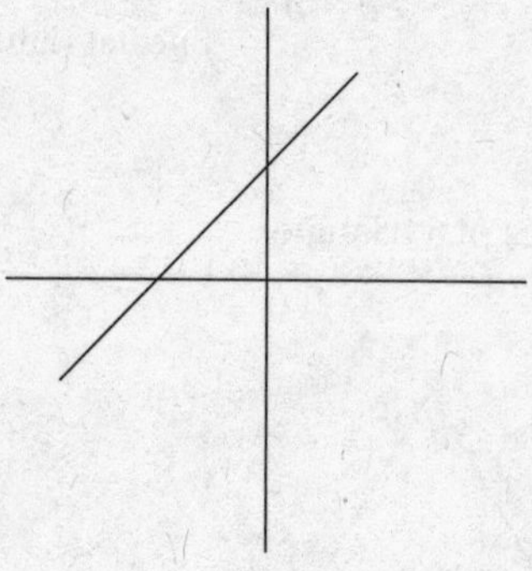

(D)

(E)

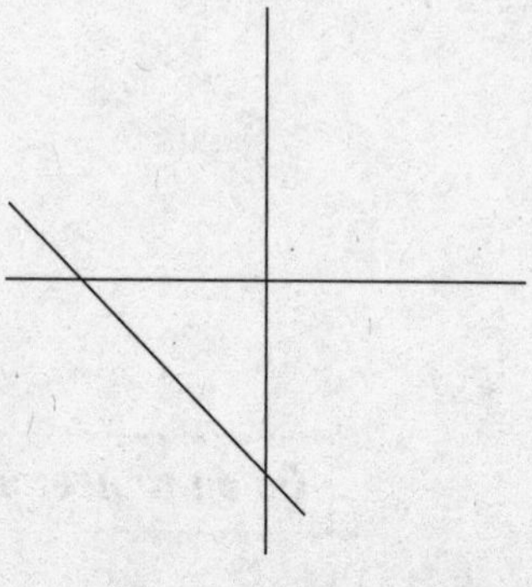

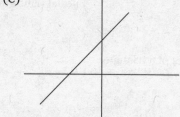

5. The first five numbers in a sequence are 2, 5, 11, 23, and 47. What is the next number?

(A) 87

(B) 89

(C) 91

(D) 93

(E) 95

6. If $3^{n+1} = 9^{n-1}$, then n =

(A) 1

(B) –1

(C) 2

(D) –2

(E) 3

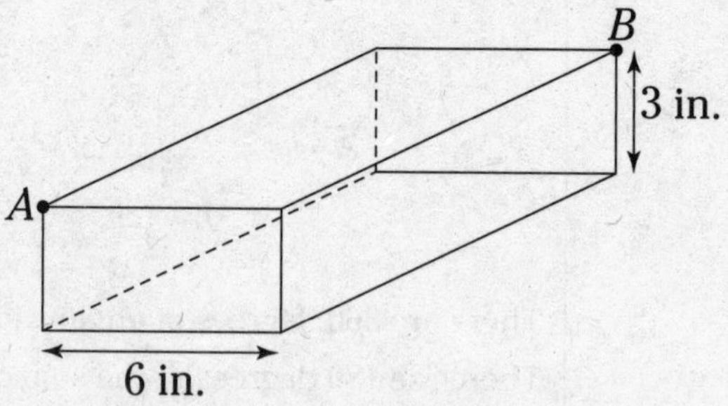

7. In the figure above, the box has a width of 6 inches, a height of 3 inches, and a volume of 144 cubic inches. What is the distance from corner *A* to corner *B?*

(A) 8 inches

(B) 9 inches

(C) 10 inches

(D) 12 inches

(E) 14 inches

Go on to next page

8. If $f(x) = x^2 + 3x - 2$, which of the following is equivalent to $f(a - 1)$?

(A) $a^2 + a$

(B) $a^2 + a - 4$

(C) $a^2 - 2a - 1$

(D) $a^2 + 4a - 1$

(E) $a^2 + 4a - 4$

9. Four women named Kaye, Lara, Mari, and Nola are married to four men named Ricky, Sammy, Tommy, and Vinny. Mari isn't married to Sammy, Sammy isn't married to Nola, Nola isn't married to Tommy, and Kaye is married to Vinny. Which of the following statements CANNOT be true?

(A) Kaye isn't married to Ricky.

(B) Lara isn't married to Ricky.

(C) Lara isn't married to Tommy.

(D) Mari isn't married to Tommy.

(E) Nola isn't married to Sammy.

10. If you roll a pair of six-sided dice, what is the probability that exactly one of the two numbers rolled is a 1?

(A) $\frac{1}{4}$

(B) $\frac{1}{6}$

(C) $\frac{5}{18}$

(D) $\frac{5}{36}$

(E) $\frac{11}{36}$

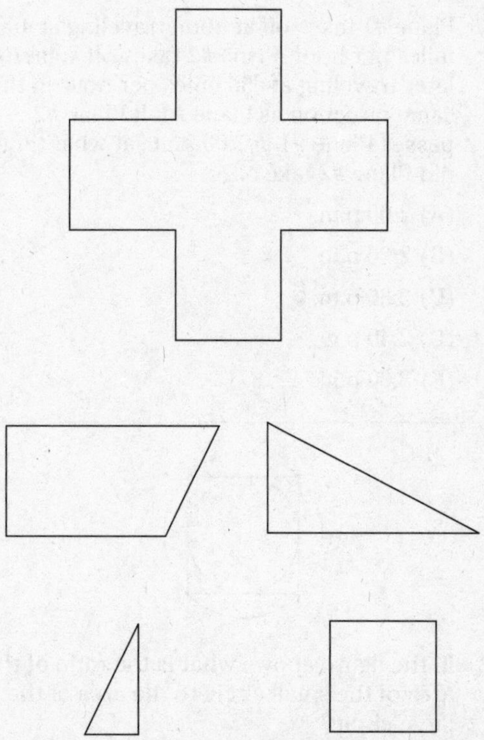

11. In the figure above, the cross is cut up into five pieces, four of which are shown. Which of the following is the missing piece?

(A) 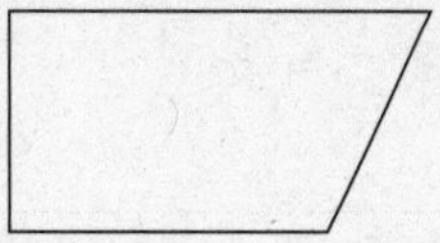

(B) 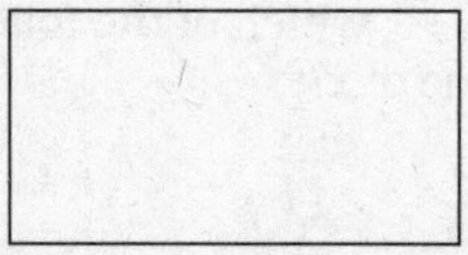

(C) 

(D) 

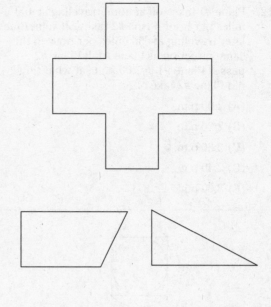

(E) 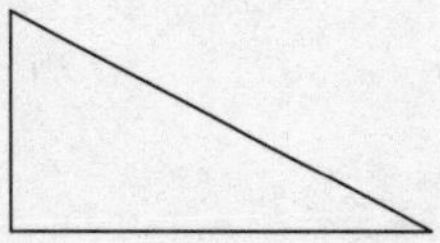

Go on to next page

12. Plane #1 takes off at noon traveling at 400 miles per hour. Plane #2 takes off sometime later traveling at 600 miles per hour in the same direction as Plane #1. If Plane #2 passes Plane #1 at 7:00 p.m., at what time did Plane #2 take off?

(A) 2:00 p.m.

(B) 2:20 p.m.

(C) 2:30 p.m.

(D) 2:40 p.m.

(E) 3:00 p.m.

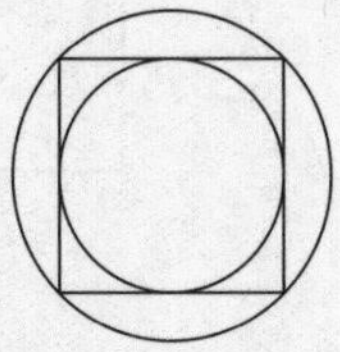

13. In the figure above, what is the ratio of the area of the small circle to the area of the large circle?

(A) 1:2

(B) 2:3

(C) 3:4

(D) $1:\sqrt{2}$

(E) $1:\sqrt{3}$

14. If $\sqrt{5x+24} = x+2$, which of the following is a positive value of x?

(A) 4

(B) 5

(C) 8

(D) 10

(E) 11

15. If p percent of n is z, then $\frac{p}{z} =$

(A) n

(B) $100n$

(C) $\frac{1}{n}$

(D) $\frac{100}{n}$

(E) $\frac{1}{100n}$

16. Let $y = f(x)$ be $y = ab^x$. If this function includes the two ordered pairs (0, 4) and (3, 4,000), what is the sum of a and b?

(A) 4

(B) 4.1

(C) 5

(D) 14

(E) 4,004

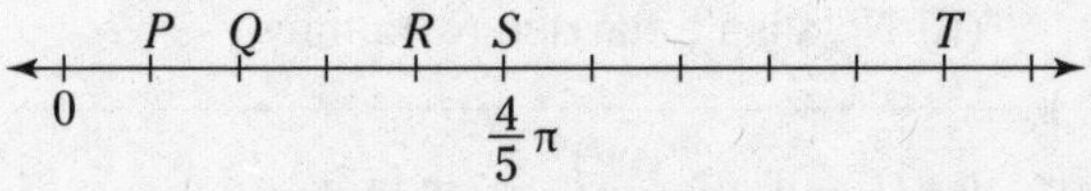

17. On number line above, which point represents the area of a circle with a diameter of $\frac{4}{5}$?

(A) P

(B) Q

(C) R

(D) S

(E) T

Go on to next page

18. For all numbers, let $x@y = xy - y^2$. Which of the following expressions is equivalent to pq?

I. $p@(p + q)$

II. $(p + q)@p$

III. $(p + q)@q$

(A) I only

(B) II only

(C) III only

(D) I and II only

(E) II and III only

19. What is the domain of the function $f(x) = \dfrac{1}{\sqrt{4 - x^2}}$?

(A) $x \neq 2$ and $x \neq -2$

(B) $x < -2$ or $x > 2$

(C) $x \leq -2$ or $x \geq 2$

(D) $-2 < x < 2$

(E) $-2 \leq x \leq 2$

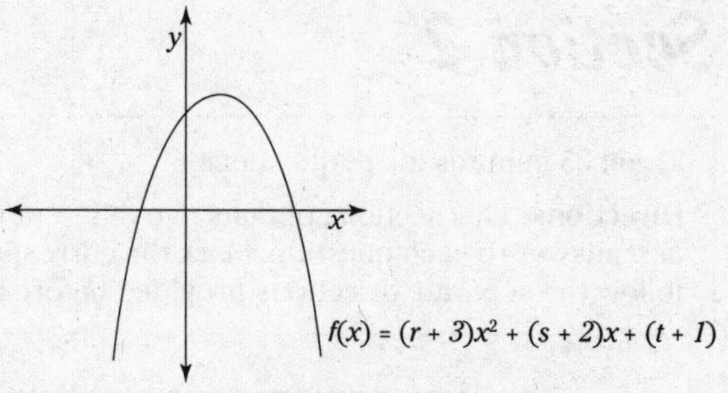

20. The figure above shows the graph of $f(x) = (r + 3)x^2 + (s + 2)x + (t + 1)$. Which of the following CANNOT be true?

(A) $r < 0$

(B) $s < 0$

(C) $t > 0$

(D) $r > s$

(E) $s > t$

STOP DO NOT TURN THE PAGE UNTIL TOLD TO DO SO. DO NOT RETURN TO A PREVIOUS TEST.

Section 2

Time: 25 minutes for 18 questions

Directions: This section contains two different types of questions. For questions 1–8, choose the *best* answer to each question. Mark the corresponding oval on the answer sheet. For questions 9–18, follow the separate directions provided before those questions.

Notes:

- You may use a calculator.
- All numbers used in this exam are real numbers.
- All figures lie in a plane.
- All figures may be assumed to be to scale unless the problem specifically indicates otherwise.

Reference Information:

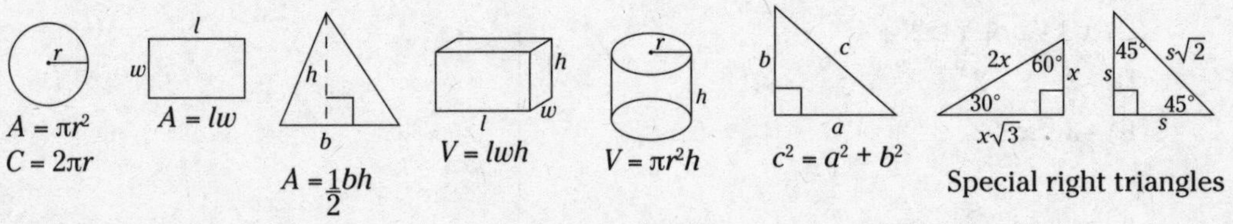

There are 360 degrees of arc in a circle.

There are 180 degrees in the sum of the interior angles of a triangle.

1. A recipe requires 8 ounces of chocolate chips to make 48 cookies. At this rate, how many ounces are needed to make 360 cookies?

   (A) 20

   (B) 30

   (C) 40

   (D) 48

   (E) 60

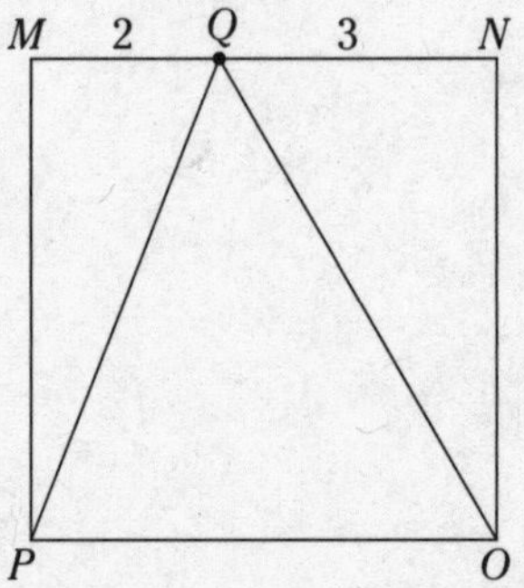

2. In the figure above, *MNOP* is a square, *MQ* = 2, and *QN* = 3. What is the area of $\triangle MQP$?

   (A) 2

   (B) 4

   (C) 5

   (D) 10

   (E) 20

Go on to next page

3. If $4a = \frac{b}{c}$, what is the value of c in terms of a and b?

(A) $4ab$

(B) $\frac{4a}{b}$

(C) $\frac{4b}{a}$

(D) $\frac{a}{4b}$

(E) $\frac{b}{4a}$

4. Which of the following shapes folds up to a cube in which all three pairs of faces that are opposite each other add up to 10?

(A)

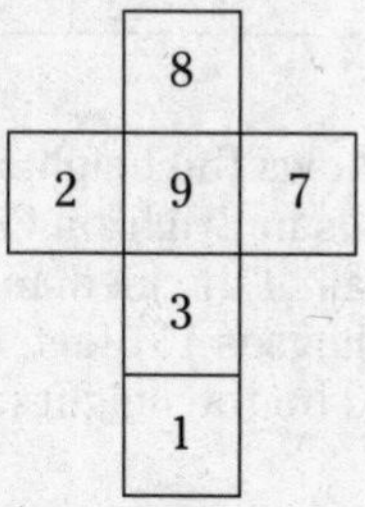

(B)

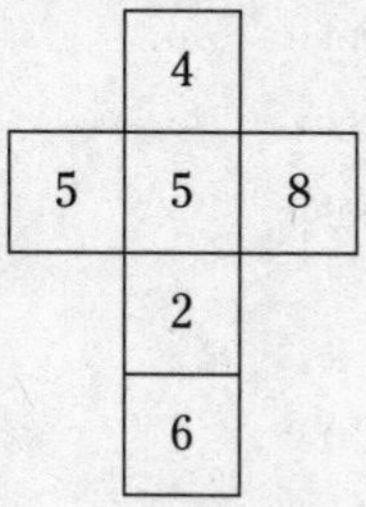

(C)

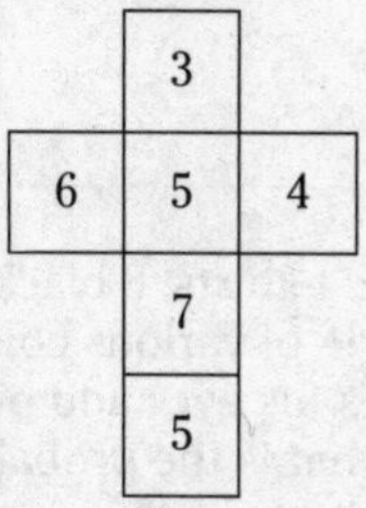

(D)

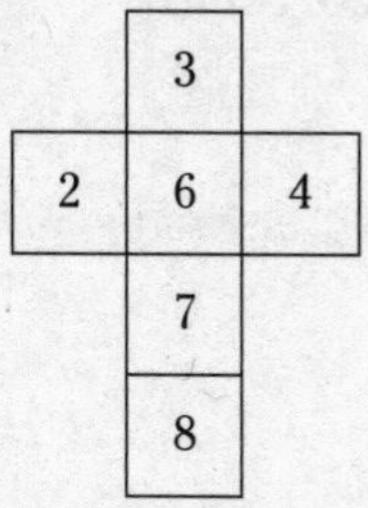

(E)

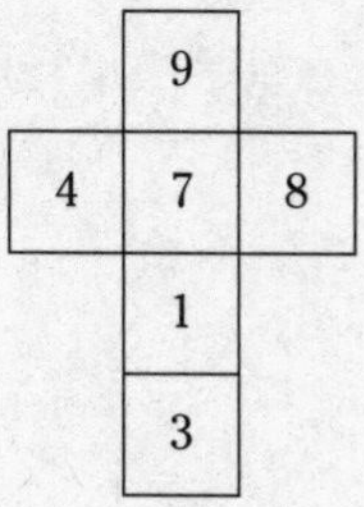

Go on to next page

Building	#1	#2	#3	#4	#5	#6	#7	#8	#9
Height	210	165	102	157	118	110	219	131	?

5. The table above shows the heights of eight of the nine buildings in Brighton City that are over 100 feet tall. If the median height of these nine buildings is 157 feet, which of the following could be the height of Building #9?

   I. 156 feet

   II. 157 feet

   III. 158 feet

   (A) I only
   (B) III only
   (C) I and II only
   (D) I and III only
   (E) II and III only

6. Aaron has 10 white t-shirts, 8 black t-shirts, and 17 other t-shirts of various colors in his drawer. If he closes his eyes and picks a shirt at random, what is the probability that it will be a white t-shirt?

   (A) $\frac{1}{3}$
   (B) $\frac{1}{5}$
   (C) $\frac{2}{5}$
   (D) $\frac{1}{7}$
   (E) $\frac{2}{7}$

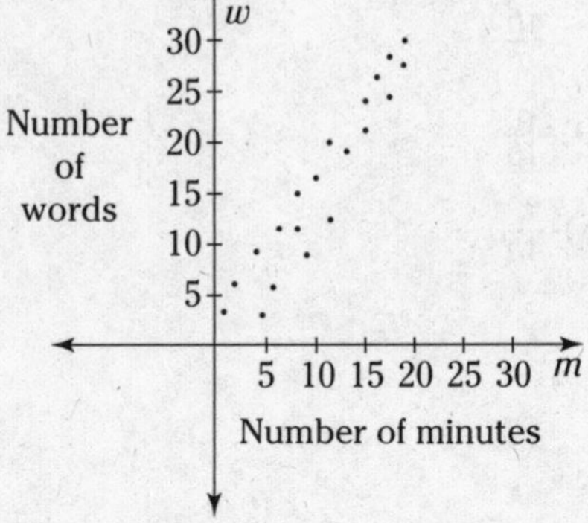

7. The figure above shows a scatterplot showing the relationship between the number of minutes *(m)* a set of students studied a list of vocabulary words and the number of words *(w)* that each was able to remember. Which of the following equations most accurately represents this relationship?

   (A) $w = \frac{5}{4}m - 20$
   (B) $w = \frac{4}{3}m + 10$
   (C) $w = \frac{2}{3}m - 5$
   (D) $w = \frac{3}{2}m$
   (E) $w = -\frac{3}{2}m - 5$

8. Set Q contains all the negative integers, set R contains all the odd integers, and set S contains all the integers that are divisible by 3. Which of the following numbers is NOT in any of these three sets?

   (A) –14
   (B) 18
   (C) 35
   (D) 44
   (E) 54

Go on to next page

Directions for student-produced response questions 9–18: Solve the problem and then write your answer in the boxes on the answer sheet. Then mark the ovals corresponding to your answer, as shown in the following example. Note the fraction line and the decimal points.

Answer: 7/2 Answer: 3.25 Answer: 853

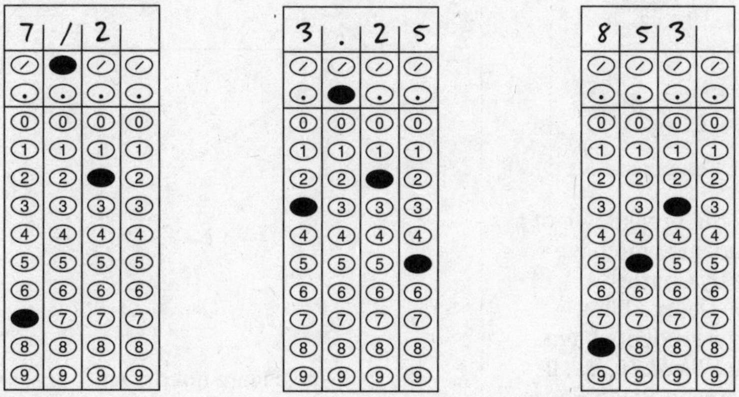

Write your answer in the box. You may start your answer in any column.

- Although you do not have to write the solutions in the boxes, you do have to blacken the corresponding ovals. You should fill in the boxes to avoid confusion. Only the blackened ovals will be scored. The numbers in the boxes will not be read.
- There are no negative answers.
- Mixed numbers, such as 3½, may be gridded in as a decimal (3.5) or as a fraction (7/2). Do not grid in 31/2; it will be read as $^{31}/_{2}$.
- Grid in a decimal as far as possible. You may round the last digit or cut off the decimal.
- A question may have more than one answer. Grid in one answer only.

9. Jeremy has taken 10 tests in math this semester, and his average score is 79. What does he need to score on his next test to bring his average up to 80?

10. When six is added to the product of a number and four, the result is the same as when one is subtracted from the product of the same number and six. What is the number?

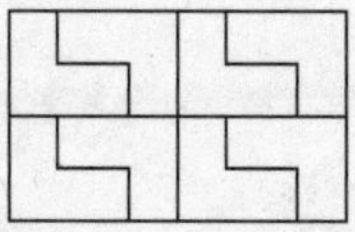

11. The figure above shows the placement of eight *L*-shaped tiles covering a rectangular area that is 4 inches by 6 inches. How many of these tiles will be needed to cover an area that is 60 inches by 72 inches?

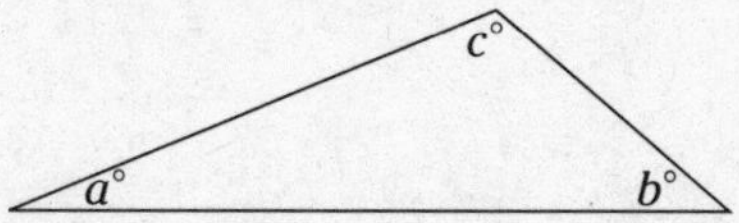

12. In the figure above, if *a*, *b*, and *c* are in a 1:2:5 ratio, what is the value of *a?*

Go on to next page

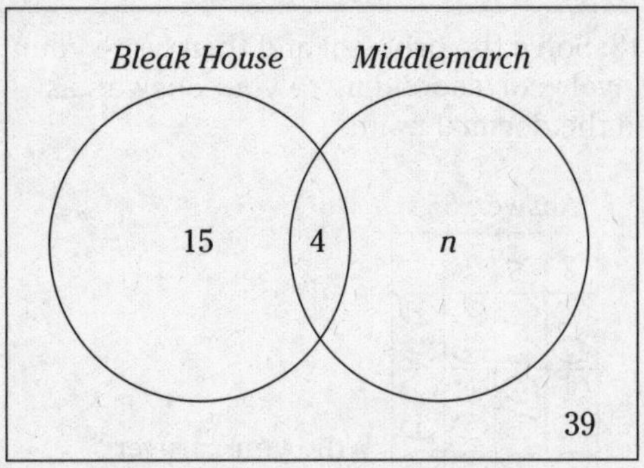

13. The figure above shows the breakdown of a classroom of college students who have read either *Bleak House* by Charles Dickens, *Middlemarch* by George Eliot, both, or neither. Exactly n students have read *Middlemarch* but not *Bleak House*. If 25% of the students have read *Bleak House*, how many have read *Middlemarch?*

14. When a number is a *palindrome,* it is the same whether its digits are read forward or backward. What is the lowest palindrome that is both greater than 1,000 and divisible by 9?

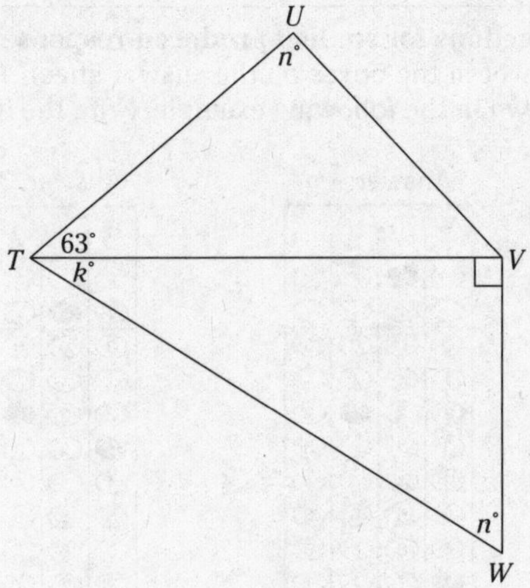

Note: Figure not drawn to scale.

15. In the figure above, $TU = UV$ with all angles labeled as shown. What is the value of k?

16. Alex ate $\frac{1}{3}$ of a box of cookies. Then Beth ate $\frac{1}{4}$ of what was left after Alex had finished. Finally, Carmine ate $\frac{1}{5}$ of what was left after Beth had finished. When Carmine was done, only 36 cookies were left. How many cookies were in the box originally?

17. Anjelica paid a discount price of \$107.25 for a coat that normally sells for \$165. If she pays \$61.75 for a pair of shoes that have the same percent discount as the coat, what is the regular price of the shoes?

18. Let the function $f(t) = t^2 - 4t - 100$. If $f(10k) = 440k$, what is a positive value of k?

STOP DO NOT TURN THE PAGE UNTIL TOLD TO DO SO. DO NOT RETURN TO A PREVIOUS TEST.

Section 3

Time: 20 minutes for 16 questions

Directions: Choose the *best* answer to each question. Mark the corresponding oval on the answer sheet.

Notes:

- You may use a calculator.
- All numbers used in this exam are real numbers.
- All figures lie in a plane.
- All figures may be assumed to be to scale unless the problem specifically indicates otherwise.

Reference Information:

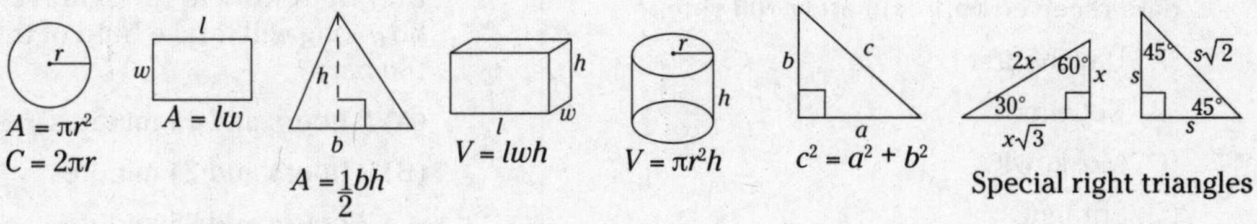

There are 360 degrees of arc in a circle.

There are 180 degrees in the sum of the interior angles of a triangle.

1. How many positive integers are factors of 60?

(A) 6

(B) 8

(C) 9

(D) 12

(E) 14

Go on to next page

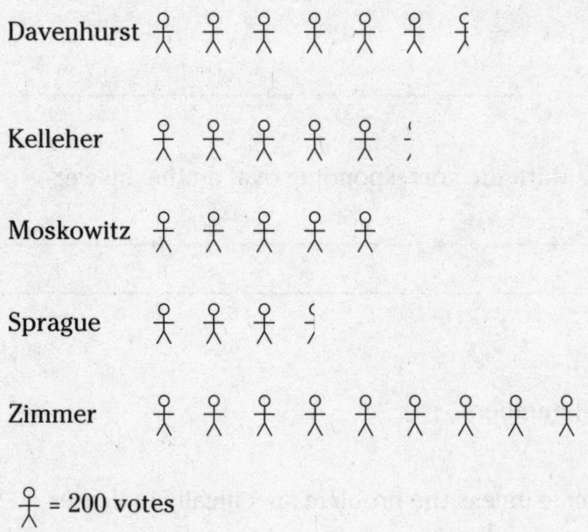

2. The pictogram above shows the number of votes each of five candidates received in a recent small-town election. Which candidate received approximately 700 votes?

(A) Davenhurst

(B) Kelleher

(C) Moskowitz

(D) Sprague

(E) Zimmer

3. If $3xy - x + 2y^2 = 22$ when $y = -2$, what is the value of x?

(A) 1

(B) 2

(C) –2

(D) 3

(E) –3

4. If k% of 85 is 17, what is k% of 400?

(A) 20

(B) 40

(C) 80

(D) 800

(E) 2,000

x	3	5	7	9
y	3	–2	–7	–12

5. The table above shows x and y values for an equation $y = mx + b$. What is the value of m?

(A) $\frac{3}{5}$

(B) $-\frac{3}{2}$

(C) $-\frac{3}{5}$

(D) $-\frac{5}{2}$

(E) $-\frac{5}{3}$

6. Bill can paint a small barn in 6 hours, and Jake can paint it in 4 hours. Assuming that they both work at the same rate as before, how long will it take both of them to paint the barn?

(A) 2 hours and 15 minutes

(B) 2 hours and 24 minutes

(C) 2 hours and 25 minutes

(D) 2 hours and 36 minutes

(E) 2 hours and 40 minutes

7. How many degrees of an arc are in $\frac{3}{5}$ of a circle?

(A) 200°

(B) 212°

(C) 216°

(D) 225°

(E) 240°

Go on to next page

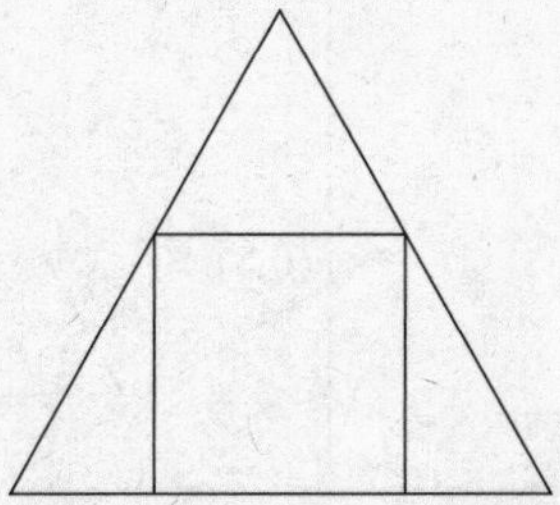

8. The figure above shows a square embedded in an equilateral triangle. If the area of the square is 3, what is the length of a side of the triangle?

(A) $\sqrt{2}$

(B) $2\sqrt{3}$

(C) $1+\sqrt{3}$

(D) $2+\sqrt{3}$

(E) $1+2\sqrt{2}$

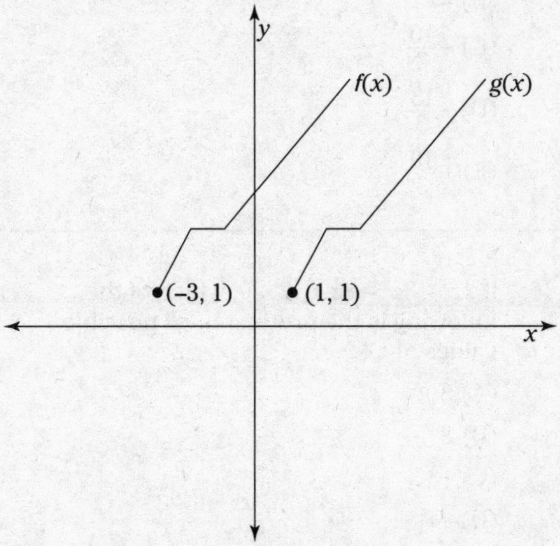

9. The figure above shows the functions $f(x)$ and $g(x)$. If $g(x)$ is a transformation of $f(x)$, then $g(x) =$

(A) $f(x + 4)$

(B) $f(x - 4)$

(C) $f(x) + 4$

(D) $f(x) - 4$

(E) $4f(x)$

10. What is the sum of the two possible x values for the equation $|3x - 4| = x$?

(A) 1

(B) 2

(C) 3

(D) 4

(E) 5

11. If $\dfrac{p^2 - q^2}{p^3 + p^2q} = 3$, what is the value of q in terms of p?

(A) $3p^2$

(B) $p + 3p^2$

(C) $p - 3p^2$

(D) $3p + 3p^2$

(E) $3p^3 + 3p^2$

12. Altogether, Sondra, Tenique, and Ursula have a total of \$60. If Ursula and Tenique each had three times as much money and Sondra had an additional \$10, they would have a total of \$110. How much money does Sondra have?

(A) \$20

(B) \$25

(C) \$30

(D) \$35

(E) \$40

13. Let p be a prime number. How many factors does p^5 have?

(A) 4

(B) 5

(C) 6

(D) 7

(E) 8

Go on to next page

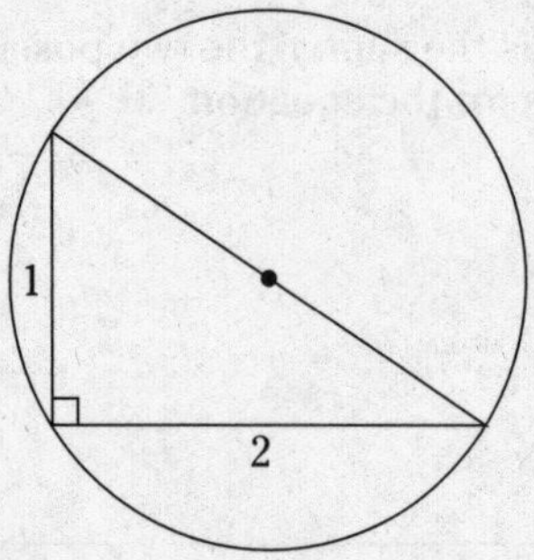

14. In the figure above, what is the probability that a randomly chosen point in the circle is also inside the triangle?

(A) $\frac{2}{5\pi}$

(B) $\frac{4}{5\pi}$

(C) $\frac{8}{5\pi}$

(D) $\frac{2\sqrt{5}}{5\pi}$

(E) $\frac{4\sqrt{5}}{5\pi}$

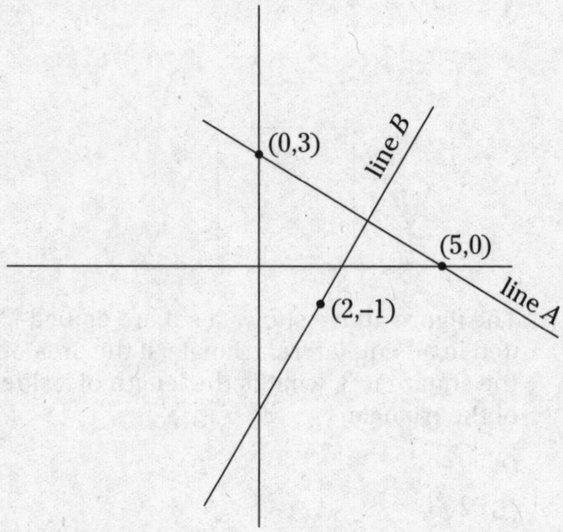

15. In the figure above, line *A* and line *B* are perpendicular to each other. What is the *y*-intercept of line *B*?

(A) –6

(B) –7

(C) $-\frac{10}{3}$

(D) $-\frac{13}{3}$

(E) $-\frac{16}{3}$

16. If $2z^3 - 3z^2 - 8z + 12 = 0$, which of the following is the product of all possible values of *z*?

(A) 3

(B) 8

(C) –3

(D) –4

(E) –6

STOP DO NOT TURN THE PAGE UNTIL TOLD TO DO SO.
DO NOT RETURN TO A PREVIOUS TEST.

Chapter 15

Answers and Explanations for Practice Test 3

This chapter contains the answers to the Practice Test 3 questions from Chapter 14. The bulk of this chapter contains detailed explanations to each of the 54 questions, which I recommend you read to further strengthen your math skills. If you simply want to score your test, you can skip to the Answer Key at the end of the chapter.

Solutions to Section 1 Questions

1. **D.** This problem gives you $x + 4 = y$ and asks you to find $2x - 2y$. A good way to solve this problem is to turn one side of the equation, $x + 4 = y$, into $2x - 2y$. Begin by rearranging the equation to isolate x and y on one side: $x + 4 = y$; $x = y - 4$; $x - y = -4$.

   Multiply both sides by 2 and simplify: $2(x - y) = 2(-4)$; $2x - 2y = -8$. So the right answer is (D).

2. **E.** First find how much Rita saved. Kyra saved \$200, and Rita saved \$40 more than Kyra, so Rita saved \$200 + \$40 = \$240. Megan saved twice as much as Rita, so Megan saved \$240 × 2 = \$480. Therefore, the right answer is (E).

3. **C.** The three angles in a triangle add up to 180 degrees, so $a + b + c = 180$. Angle c and angle d are supplementary, so they also add up to 180: $c + d = 180$. You can set the left sides of these two equations equal to each other and simplify: $a + b + c = c + d$; $a + b = d$. Therefore, the right answer is (C).

4. **B.** The slope of the equation is 1, so the graph slopes upward. Thus, you can rule out answers (A), (D), and (E). The y-intercept is –3, so the graph crosses the y-axis below the origin. Thus, you can rule out answer (C), so the right answer is (B).

5. **E.** To begin, figure out how much is being added to each number to generate the next number in the sequence:

	+ 3		**+ 6**		**+ 12**		**+ 24**	
2		5		11		23		47

   Each time, the number being added doubles from 3, to 6, to 12, to 24. So the next number in the sequence is the result of adding double 24, which is 48, to the preceding number: $47 + 48 = 95$. So the right answer is (E).

6. **E.** The problem tells you that $3^{n+1} = 9^{n-1}$. To solve it, you need to get the bases equal; with the bases equal, you can set the exponents equal to each other and solve. The easiest way to get equal bases is to express 9 as a power of 3:

   $3^{n+1} = 9^{n-1}$

   $3^{n+1} = (3^2)^{n-1}$

Now rearrange the power:

$$3^{n+1} = 3^{2(n-1)}$$

Because the bases are equal, the exponents are also equal:

$$n + 1 = 2(n - 1)$$

Now solve for n: $n + 1 = 2n - 2$; $n + 3 = 2n$; $3 = n$. Therefore, the right answer is (E).

7. **C.** The distance from A to B is the hypotenuse of a right triangle whose legs are the width and length of the box. You know that the width is 6 inches, but you don't know the length. So use the formula for the volume of a box to find the length: $V = lwh$. Plug in the values for the volume, length, and width: $144 = l(6)(3)$; $144 = 18l$; $8 = l$.

   Now use the Pythagorean theorem to find the triangle's hypotenuse, the distance from A to B:

   $$a^2 + b^2 = c^2$$
   $$6^2 + 8^2 = c^2$$
   $$36 + 64 = c^2$$
   $$100 = c^2$$
   $$10 = c$$

   So the right answer is (C).

8. **B.** You know that $f(x) = x^2 + 3x - 2$, and you want to find $f(a - 1)$. Substitute $a - 1$ for x into the equation:

   $$f(x) = x^2 + 3x - 2$$
   $$f(a-1) = (a-1)^2 + 3(a-1) - 2$$

   Now simplify the right side of the equation:

   $$= (a-1)(a-1) + 3(a-1) - 2$$
   $$= a^2 - 2a + 1 + 3a - 3 - 2$$
   $$= a^2 + a - 4$$

   Therefore, the right answer is (B).

9. **D.** Kaye is married to Vinny. Nola isn't married to Sammy or Tommy, so she's married to Ricky. Mari isn't married to Sammy, so she's married to Tommy. Therefore, the statement that Mari isn't married to Tommy CANNOT be true, so the right answer is (D).

10. **C.** To find probability, you need to count the number of target outcomes and total outcomes — that is, how many ways you can roll 1 on only one die and how many total combinations are possible. First, list the number of ways that you can roll 1 only on the first die:

    1-2 1-3 1-4 1-5 1-6

    Next, list the number of ways that you can roll 1 only on the second die:

    2-1 3-1 4-1 5-1 6-1

    So there are 10 ways to for the target outcome of a single 1 on a pair of dice to be rolled, and there are 36 total possible outcomes. Plug these numbers into the formula for probability:

    $$\text{Probability} = \frac{\text{Target outcomes}}{\text{Total outcomes}} = \frac{10}{36} = \frac{5}{18}$$

    Therefore, the right answer is (C).

11. **D.** A good strategy here is to start with the biggest piece (the trapezoid) and then see whether you can also get the second biggest piece (the large triangle) into the cross as well. In almost any position, the trapezoid blocks the big triangle from fitting. The only way to fit it in is by pushing the squared off part of the trapezoid all the way into one of the extreme parts of the cross. From there, the big triangle fits in only one way. With these two large pieces in place, the small square and triangle are forced into place, and the final piece is also determined. The four pieces fit into the cross as follows:

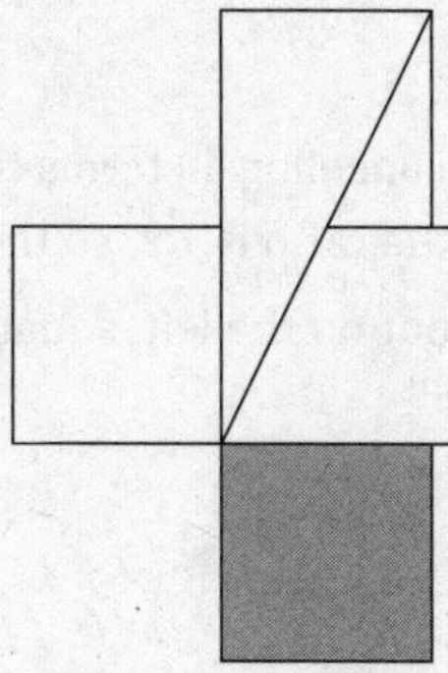

The shaded region matches the missing piece, so the right answer is (D).

12. **B.** When Plane #1 reaches Plane #2, the two planes have flown the same distance. If you determine how far the planes have traveled when they cross, you can use that info and Plane #2's speed to figure out how long Plane #2 has been in the air.

Let x equal the number of hours that Plane #2 is in the air. The first plane took off at noon and was passed by the second plane at 7 p.m., so Plane #1 has been flying for 7 hours. Using the given speeds, you can make the following chart:

	Rate	***Time in the Air***	***Distance***
Plane #1	400	7	2,800
Plane #2	600	x	$600x$

Now make the following equation, setting the distances equal, and solve for x: $600x = 2{,}800$; $x = 4\frac{2}{3}$. Thus, Plane #2 flies for $4\frac{2}{3}$ hours, which is 4 hours and 40 minutes. Thus, it takes off 4 hours and 40 minutes before 7:00, so it takes off at 2:20 p.m. Therefore, the right answer is (B).

13. **A.** You don't know the radius of either circle, so let the radius of the small circle equal x. You can make a 45-45-90 triangle as shown in the following figure:

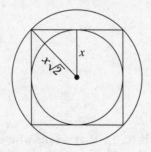

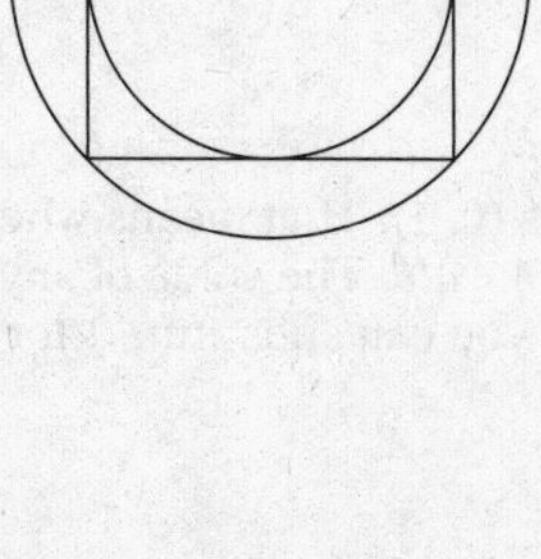

Thus, the radius of the large circle is $x\sqrt{2}$. Now use the area formula to find the areas of both circles:

Area small circle $= \pi r^2 = \pi x^2$

Area large circle $= \pi r^2 = \pi(x\sqrt{2})^2 = 2\pi x^2$

Make a fraction using these two areas:

$$\frac{\pi x^2}{2\pi x^2}$$

Now reduce the fraction by canceling all terms that appear in both the numerator and denominator: $\frac{1}{2}$. Therefore, the ratio is 1:2, so the right answer is (A).

14. **B.** To get rid of the square root on the left, square both sides of the equation. Then distribute and simplify the equation:

$5x + 24 = (x + 2)^2$

$5x + 24 = (x + 2)(x + 2)$

$5x + 24 = x^2 + 4x + 4$

Put the equation into standard quadratic form (set it equal to zero) and factor:

$0 = x^2 - x - 20$

$0 = (x + 4)(x - 5)$

Split into two equations, with the contents of each set of parentheses set equal to zero:

$0 = x + 4$ or $0 = x - 5$

$-4 = x$ $5 = x$

Thus, the only positive value of x is 5, so the right answer is (B).

15. **D.** Remember that *percent* means *out of 100* — that is, either $\frac{1}{100}$ or 0.01. The answers are fractions, so use $\frac{1}{100}$. Translate "p percent of n is z" into the following equation: $p\left(\frac{1}{100}\right)n = z$. Simplifying gives you $\frac{pn}{100} = z$. Then multiply both sides by 100 to get rid of the decimal: $pn = 100z$.

Now isolate p/z on one side of the equation. First divide both sides by z:

$$\frac{pn}{z} = \frac{100z}{z}$$

$$\frac{pn}{z} = 100$$

Now divide both sides by n:

$$\frac{pn}{zn} = \frac{100}{n}$$

$$\frac{p}{z} = \frac{100}{n}$$

The right answer is (D).

16. **D.** One ordered pair is (0, 4). That means where $x = 0$, $y = 4$, so plug these two numbers into the equation: $y = ab^x$; $4 = ab^0$. The value of any number raised to the power of zero equals 1, so $b^0 = 1$. That means you can substitute 1 for b^0 into the equation: $4 = a(1)$; $4 = a$.

You can plug the value $a = 4$ into the original equation, along with the values for the second ordered pair, $x = 3$, $y = 4{,}000$: $y = ab^x$; $4{,}000 = 4b^3$.

Solve for b: $1{,}000 = b^3$; $10 = b$. Thus, $a + b = 4 + 10 = 14$, so the right answer is (D).

17. **A.** A circle with a diameter of $\frac{4}{5}$ has a radius of $\frac{2}{5}$, so plug this value into the area formula for a circle:

$$A = \pi r^2 = \pi\left(\frac{2}{5}\right)^2 = \frac{4}{25}\pi$$

The number line shows five intervals between 0 and $\frac{4}{5}\pi$. So to find the value of each interval, divide $\frac{4}{5}\pi$ by 5:

$$\frac{4}{5}\pi \div 5 = \frac{4}{5}\pi \times \frac{1}{5} = \frac{4}{25}\pi$$

Thus, each interval is $\frac{4}{25}\pi$, so the distance from 0 to P is $\frac{4}{25}\pi$. Therefore, the right answer is (A).

18. **E.** The problem tells you that $x@y = xy - y^2$. First, find the value of option I, which says $p@(p + q)$. There, $x = p$ and $y = (p + q)$, so plug in the values and do the math:

$= p(p + q) - (p + q)^2$

$= p^2 + pq - p^2 - 2pq - q^2$

$= -pq - q^2$

Thus, option I doesn't equal pq. Next, find the value of option II, which says $(p + q)@p$. Then, $x = (p + q)$ and $y = p$:

$= (p + q)p - p^2$

$= p^2 + pq - p^2$

$= pq$

Thus, option II equals pq. Now, finally the value of option III, which says $(p + q)@q$. There, $x = (p + q)$ and $y = q$:

$= (p + q)q - q^2$

$= pq + q^2 - q^2$

$= pq$

Thus, option III also equals pq, so the right answer is (E).

19. **D.** A value of x can be excluded from the domain for either of two reasons: because it results in a denominator of zero or because it results in a negative value inside a square root. The quickest way to answer this question is to test some key values of x. The five answers depend heavily on whether 2 is in or out of the domain, so substitute 2 for x.

$$f(x) = \frac{1}{\sqrt{4 - 2^2}} = \frac{1}{\sqrt{4 - 4}} = \frac{1}{0}$$

A denominator of 0 isn't allowed, so 2 isn't in the domain, so you can rule out (C) and (E). At this point, you may notice that a larger value of x will be a problem. Test this out by substituting 3 for x:

$$f(x) = \frac{1}{\sqrt{4 - 3^2}} = \frac{1}{\sqrt{4 - 9}} = \frac{1}{\sqrt{-5}}$$

A negative square root is also forbidden, so 3 isn't in the domain. Thus, (A) and (B) are both ruled out. Therefore, the right answer is (D).

20. **D.** To change the function $f(x) = (r + 3)x^2 + (s + 2)x + (t + 1)$ into the more typical form $f(x) = ax^2 + bx + c$, set $(r + 3)$ equal to a, $(s + 2)$ equal to b, and $(t + 1)$ equal to c. Then solve the equations for a, b, and c. The following equations must be true:

- ***a* and *r*:** $r + 3 = a$, so $r = a - 3$
- ***b* and *s*:** $s + 2 = b$, so $s = b - 2$
- ***c* and *t*:** $t + 1 = c$, so $t = c - 1$

The graph of the function is concave down, so a is negative. It's shifted to the right, so a and b have different signs; therefore, b is positive. And it crosses the y-intercept above the origin, so c is positive (for info on why these statements are true, see Chapter 6). Thus,

- ***a*:** $a < 0$, so $a - 3 < -3$
- ***b*:** $b > 0$, so $b - 2 > -2$
- ***c*:** $c > 0$, so $c - 1 > -1$

Putting the second versions of each equation and inequality together gives you

- $r = a - 3 < -3$
- $s = b - 2 > -2$
- $t = c - 1 > -1$

You can simplify this as follows:

- $r < -3$
- $s > -2$
- $t > -1$

Thus, because r is less than –3 and s is greater than –2, r must be less than s. Therefore, $r > s$ CANNOT be true, so the right answer is (D).

Solutions to Section 2 Questions

1. **E.** To begin, set up a proportion of ounces to cookies: $\frac{\text{Ounces}}{\text{Cookies}} = \frac{8}{48}$. Plug in 360 for *Cookies* and x for *Ounces*:

$$\frac{x}{360} = \frac{8}{48}$$

Cross-multiply and solve for x:

$$2{,}880 = 48x$$
$$\frac{2{,}880}{48} = \frac{48x}{48}$$
$$60 = x$$

The recipe requires 60 ounces, so the right answer is (E).

2. **C.** *MNOP* is a square, so every side has the same length of 5. Thus, the height of $\triangle MQP$ is 5, and its base is 2. Plug these numbers into the area formula for a triangle: $A = \frac{1}{2}bh = \frac{1}{2}(2)(5) = 5$. The right answer is (C).

3. **E.** You need to use some algebra to solve the equation for *c*. Begin by multiplying both sides by *c* to remove the fraction:

$$4a = \frac{b}{c}$$

$$4ac = b$$

Now divide both sides by $4a$ to isolate the variable *c*:

$$\frac{4ac}{4a} = \frac{b}{4a}$$

$$c = \frac{b}{4a}$$

So the right answer is (E).

4. **C.** No pair of opposite faces share an edge. The figure below shows the three pairs of opposite sides, labeled *X*, *Y*, and *Z*:

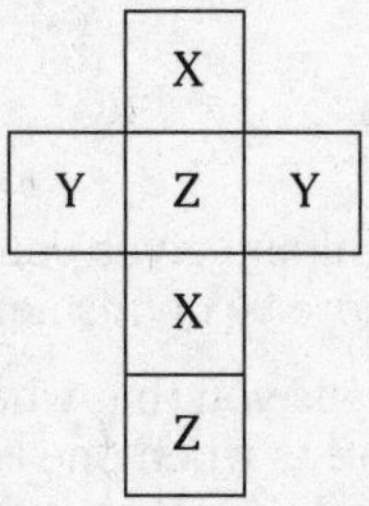

In Choice (A), the two *X* sides are 8 + 3 = 11, so this is wrong. In Choice (B), the two *X* sides are 4 + 2 = 6, so this is wrong. In Choice (D), the two *Y* sides are 2 + 4 = 6, so this is wrong. In Choice (E), the two *Y* sides are 4 + 8 = 12, so this is wrong. Therefore, the right answer is (C).

5. **E.** The median is the center value when you arrange the list from least to greatest. To begin, arrange the eight building heights in order from least to greatest:

102 110 118 131 157 165 210 219

Now insert each of the three possible values (underlined) and find the median in each case (in boldface):

I:	102	110	118	131	**<u>156</u>**	157	165	210	219
II:	102	110	118	131	**157**	<u>157</u>	165	210	219
III:	102	110	118	131	**157**	<u>158</u>	165	210	219

In case I, the median is 156, so this is incorrect. However, in cases II and III, the median is 157, so these are correct. Therefore, the right answer is (E).

6. **E.** The drawer contains 10 white t-shirts and a total of 35 shirts (10 white + 8 black + 17 other). To find the likelihood of pulling out a white shirt, plug these numbers into the formula for probability:

$$\text{Probability} = \frac{\text{Target outcomes}}{\text{Total outcomes}} = \frac{10}{35} = \frac{2}{7}$$

Thus, the right answer is (E).

7. **D.** Finding an equation from a scatterplot is an inexact science, but you can rule out answers that are clearly wrong. The slope is positive, so (E) is wrong. The slope goes up faster than it goes to the right, so it's greater than 1; therefore, (C) is wrong. The y-intercept is clearly below 10, so (B) is wrong. And the y-intercept is clearly above –20, so (A) is wrong. Thus, the right answer is (D).

8. **D.** The number –14 is negative, so it's in set Q; thus, you can rule out Choice (A). The number 35 is odd, so it's in set R; thus, you can rule out (C). The numbers 18 and 54 are both divisible by 3, so they're both in set S; thus, you can rule out answers (B) and (E). The number 44 isn't in any of these three sets; therefore, the right answer is (D).

9. **90**. Jeremy has received a mean score of 79 on 10 tests. Let x equal the score he needs to receive on 1 test in order to bring his total mean score on all 11 tests up to 80. Organize the information from the problem into a table:

	Mean Score	***Number of Tests***	***Total***
	79	10	790
	x	1	x
Total	**80**	**11**	**880**

Adding down in the last column gives you the following equation: $790 + x = 880$; $x = 90$. Thus, Jeremy needs to score 90 on his next test.

10. **3.5** or **7/2**. The problem tells you that when six is added to the product of a number and four, the result is the same as when one is subtracted from the product of the same number and six. Let x equal the number. Now translate the problem into the following equation:

$$4x + 6 = 6x - 1$$

Solve for x: $4x + 7 = 6x$; $7 = 2x$; $3.5 = x$. Therefore, the right answer is 3.5, which you can also grid in as 7/2.

11. **1440**. The figure shows a 4-by-6 block that contains 8 tiles. First, calculate how many blocks you need to tile the floor, and then multiply this number by 8 to find out the number of tiles. The floor is 60 by 72 inches:

Room width: $60 \div 4 = 15$ blocks

Room length: $72 \div 6 = 12$ blocks

Thus, you need 15 blocks along the 60-inch width of the room and 12 blocks along the 72-inch length. Multiply to calculate the number of blocks needed: $15 \times 12 = 180$.

Now multiply this number by 8 to discover the number of tiles needed: $180 \times 8 = 1{,}440$. The right answer is 1440.

12. **22.5** or **45/2**. The values of a, b, and c are in a 1:2:5 ratio, so let $a = x$, $b = 2x$, and $c = 5x$. These three angles add up to 180 degrees, so $x + 2x + 5x = 180$. Solve for x: $8x = 180$; $x = 22.5$. Thus, the right answer is 22.5, which you can also write as 45/2.

13. **22**. The Venn diagram shows that a total of $15 + 4 = 19$ students have read *Bleak House* (15 read *Bleak House* only, and 4 read *Middlemarch* as well). The problem tells you that this is 25% of the class, so the class has a total of 76 students: $0.25x = 19$; $x = 76$.

Thus, add the students and find n, the number of students who've read only *Middlemarch*: $15 + 4 + n + 39 = 76$; $58 + n = 76$; $n = 18$. So the number of students who have read *Middlemarch* is $4 + 18 = 22$.

14. **1881**. The number is a palindrome, so the first and last digits are the same and the two middle digits are the same: *XYYX*. You're looking for the lowest number, so try $X = 1$: $1YY1$.

A number is divisible by nine if and only if its digits add up to 9. (If you don't remember that rule, fill in the middle two numbers, beginning with 2, then 3, then 4, and so on, testing each number for divisibility on your calculator.) The only value that works for *Y* is 8. Thus, the right answer is 1881.

15. **36**. You know that $TU = UV$, so $\triangle TUV$ is isosceles. Therefore, angle UVT = angle $UTV = 63°$. The sum of the three angles in $\triangle TUV$ is 180°, so set up the following equation: $63 + 63 + n = 180$; $126 + n = 180$; $n = 54$. The sum of the three angles in $\triangle TVW$ is likewise 180°, so you can plug in 54 for *n* and solve the equation:

$$90 + n + k = 180$$
$$90 + 54 + k = 180$$
$$144 + k = 180$$
$$k = 36$$

Thus, the right answer is 36.

16. **90**. One way to approach this problem is to focus on what fraction of the cookies each person left. Alex ate $\frac{1}{3}$ of the box, so he left behind $\frac{2}{3}$ of the box. Then, Beth ate $\frac{1}{4}$ of what Alex left, so she left $\frac{3}{4}$ of the $\frac{2}{3}$ that Alex left:

$$\left(\frac{3}{4}\right)\left(\frac{2}{3}\right) = \frac{1}{2}$$

So Beth left behind $\frac{1}{2}$ of the box. Finally, Carmine ate $\frac{1}{5}$ of what Beth left, so he left $\frac{4}{5}$ of the $\frac{1}{2}$ that Beth left:

$$\left(\frac{4}{5}\right)\left(\frac{1}{2}\right) = \frac{2}{5}$$

Thus, Carmine left $\frac{2}{5}$ of the box, which equals 36 cookies. Let *x* equal the number of cookies originally in the box:

$$\frac{2}{5}x = 36$$
$$\frac{2x}{5} = 36$$

Multiply both sides by 5 and solve for *x*: $2x = 180$; $x = 90$. So originally, the box contained 90 cookies.

17. **95**. To begin, use the formula for percent decrease: $\text{Percent decrease} = \frac{\text{Amount of decrease}}{\text{Original amount}}$. The amount of the decrease is the difference between the original price of \$165 and the discount price \$107.25:

$$\frac{165 - 107.25}{165} = \frac{57.75}{165} = 0.35 = 35\%$$

The discount on the coat was 35%, so this is also the discount on the shoes. Let *x* equal the original price of the shoes. This price minus the discount equals the price that Anjelica paid, which was \$61.75:

$$x - 35\% \text{ of } x = 61.75$$
$$x - 0.35x = 61.75$$

Solve for x:

$$0.65x = 61.75$$
$$\frac{0.65x}{0.65} = \frac{61.75}{0.65}$$
$$x = 95$$

Therefore, the original price of the shoes was $95.

18. **5.** The problem tells you that $f(t) = t^2 - 4t - 100$ and $f(10k) = 440k$. Plug in $10k$ for the t's in the original function:

$$f(t) = t^2 - 4t - 100$$
$$f(10k) = (10k)^2 - 4(10k) - 100$$

Simplify:

$$f(10k) = 100k^2 - 40k - 100$$

Now, because $f(10k) = 440k$, set this value equal to $440k$. Simplify and put the equation in standard quadratic form by setting the equation equal to zero:

$$100k^2 - 40k - 100 = 440k$$
$$5k^2 - 2k - 5 = 22k$$
$$5k^2 - 24k - 5 = 0$$

Factor to solve:

$$(5k + 1)(k - 5) = 0$$

Split into two equations:

$$5k + 1 = 0 \quad \text{or} \quad k - 5 = 0$$

The first equation solves to a negative number:

$$5k = -1$$
$$k = -\frac{1}{5}$$

The second equation solves to a positive number: $k = 5$. So the positive value of k is 5.

Solutions to Section 3 Questions

1. **D.** The problem asks you how many positive integers are factors of 60. Begin by listing 1 and 60 as factors of 60, leaving space between them:

1 60

The number 60 is even ($60 \div 2 = 30$), so both 2 and 30 are factors:

1 2 30 60

The number 60 is also divisible by 3 ($60 \div 3 = 20$), so both 3 and 20 are factors:

1 2 3 20 30 60

Continue testing the numbers 4, 5, and 6, all of which are factors of 60:

1 2 3 4 5 6 10 12 15 20 30 60

The numbers 7, 8, and 9 aren't factors of 60, so you've listed all 12 factors of 60. Therefore, the right answer is (D).

2. **D.** According to the key, each icon equals 200 votes. Thus, the candidate who received 700 votes must have about $3\frac{1}{2}$ icons, so this candidate is Sprague. Therefore, the right answer is (D).

3. **C.** Substitute –2 for y into the equation $3xy - x + 2y^2 = 22$:

$$3xy - x + 2y^2 = 22$$
$$3x(-2) - x + 2(-2)^2 = 22$$

Simplify: $-6x - x + 8 = 22$; $-7x + 8 = 22$; $-7x = 14$; $x = -2$. Therefore, the right answer is (C).

4. **C.** To begin, turn "k% of 85 is 17" into an equation: $k(0.01)(85) = 17$. Simplify and solve for k:

$$0.85k = 17$$
$$k = \frac{17}{0.85} = 20$$

So $k = 20$. Now find 20% of 400: $(0.2)(400) = 80$. Therefore, the right answer is (C).

5. **D.** Use the two-point formula for slope: Slope $= \frac{y_2 - y_1}{x_2 - x_1}$. Substitute any corresponding values for x and y. Here, I use the values from the first and second columns of the chart. The two points are (3, 3) and (5, –2):

$$= \frac{-2-3}{5-3} = \frac{-5}{2} = -\frac{5}{2}$$

Therefore, the right answer is (D).

6. **B.** Let x equal the number of hours it takes the two men to paint the entire barn. Bill can paint the barn in 6 hours, so he can paint $\frac{1}{6}$ of the barn in an hour. Jake can paint it in 4 hours, so he can paint $\frac{1}{4}$ of the barn in an hour. Thus, in one hour, the two of them can paint the following:

$$\frac{1}{6} + \frac{1}{4} = \frac{2}{12} + \frac{3}{12} = \frac{5}{12}$$

Together, the two men can paint $\frac{5}{12}$ of the barn in one hour, so

$$\frac{5}{12}x = 1$$

Solve for x:

$$\frac{5x}{12} = 1$$
$$5x = 12$$
$$x = \frac{12}{5} = 2\frac{2}{5}$$

Thus, together they take $2\frac{2}{5}$ of an hour, which is 2 hours and 24 minutes ($\frac{2}{5} \times 60$ minutes = 24 minutes), so the right answer is (B).

7. **C.** Let x equal the number of degrees of arc in $\frac{3}{5}$ of a circle. A circle contains a total of 360° of arc, so you can make the following proportion:

$$\frac{3}{5} = \frac{x}{360}$$

Cross-multiply and solve for x: $3(360) = 5x$; $1{,}080 = 5x$; $216 = x$. So the right answer is (C).

8. **D.** The area of the square is 3, so the side of the square is $\sqrt{3}$ (because for a square, $A = s^2$). Each angle in the equilateral triangle is 60°, so the two right triangles flanking the square are 30-60-90 triangles. The sides of the square are also the long legs of these triangles. Thus, the short legs of these triangles are 1 and the hypotenuses are 2, as in the following figure:

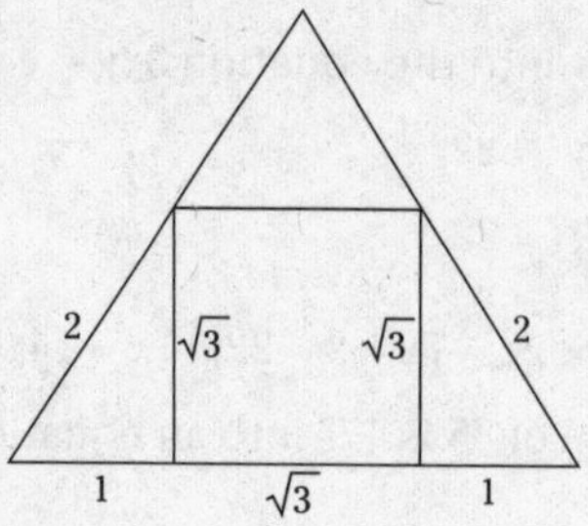

Thus, the side of the large equilateral triangle is $1+\sqrt{3}+1=2+\sqrt{3}$. Therefore, the right answer is (D).

9. **B.** The function $g(x)$ is a transformation that shifts $f(x)$ four units to the right — that is, in the positive direction. The transformation that causes this change to happen is $f(x-4)$, so the right answer is (B). (For info on transformations, flip to Chapter 6.)

10. **C.** Begin by removing the absolute value bars in the equation $|3x-4| = x$. To do this, split the equation into two versions: one with the positive value of the expression inside the bars and the other with the negative value of this expression:

$3x - 4 = x$ or $3x - 4 = -x$

Solve the first equation for x: $3x - 4 = x$; $-4 = -2x$; $2 = x$. Thus, 2 is a possible value for x. Now solve the second equation for x: $3x - 4 = -x$; $-4 = -4x$; $1 = x$. So 1 is the other possible value for x. Therefore, the sum of the two x values is 3, so the right answer is (C).

11. **C.** To answer this question, you need to solve the equation for q. To start, factor both the numerator and the denominator:

$$\frac{p^2-q^2}{p^3+p^2q}=3$$

$$\frac{(p+q)(p-q)}{p^2(p+q)}=3$$

Cancel out the factor $p + q$:

$$\frac{(p-q)}{p^2}=3$$

Multiply both sides by p^2 to remove the fraction from the equation :

$p - q = 3p^2$

Isolate q:

$p = 3p^2 + q$

$p - 3p^2 = q$

Therefore, the right answer is (C).

12. **E.** Let s, t, and u equal the amounts of money that Sondra, Tenique, and Ursula have, respectively. Then you can make the following two equations:

$$s + t + u = 60$$

$$(s + 10) + 3t + 3u = 110$$

Subtract the first equation from the second:

$$10 + 2t + 2u = 50$$

Simplify and solve for $t + u$:

$$2t + 2u = 40$$

$$t + u = 20$$

Now substitute 20 for $t + u$ in the first equation; then solve for s: $s + 20 = 60$; $s = 40$. Therefore, Sondra has $40, so the right answer is (E).

13. **C.** The question asks about a property of the fifth power of an unspecified prime number, so this property must be true for the fifth power of *any* prime number. Thus, you can choose an easy prime number to work with, so let $p = 2$. Then find p^5:

$$p^5 = 2^5 = 32$$

Now find out how many factors 32 has. Begin by listing 1 and 32, leaving space for more factors between these two numbers:

1 32

The number 2 is also a factor of 32 (because $2 \times 16 = 32$), so both 2 and 16 are factors of 32:

1 2 16 32

The number 3 isn't a factor of 32, but 4 is (because $4 \times 8 = 32$). Thus, both 4 and 8 are factors of 32:

1 2 4 8 16 32

The numbers 5, 6, and 7 are all not factors 32, so 32 has exactly 6 factors. Therefore, this property must be true of all prime numbers, so the right answer is (C).

14. **B.** The triangle is a right triangle, so the two legs are the base and height. Therefore, plug these values into the area formula for a triangle:

$$\text{Area of triangle} = \frac{1}{2}bh = \frac{1}{2}(1)(2) = 1$$

The diameter of the circle is the hypotenuse of the triangle, so use the Pythagorean theorem to find this length:

$$a^2 + b^2 = c^2$$
$$1^2 + 2^2 = c^2$$
$$1 + 4 = c^2$$
$$5 = c^2$$
$$\sqrt{5} = c$$

Therefore, the diameter of the circle is $\sqrt{5}$, so the radius is $\frac{\sqrt{5}}{2}$. Plug this into the formula for the area of a circle:

$$\text{Area of circle} = \pi r^2 = \pi\left(\frac{\sqrt{5}}{2}\right)^2 = \frac{5}{4}\pi = \frac{5\pi}{4}$$

The formula for geometric probability is Geometric probability $= \frac{\text{Target area}}{\text{Total area}}$. In this case, the target area is the triangle and the total area is the circle:

$$= \frac{\text{Area of triangle}}{\text{Area of circle}} = \frac{1}{\left(\frac{5\pi}{4}\right)} = \frac{4}{5\pi}$$

Therefore, the right answer is (B).

15. **D.** To solve this problem, you need to find the equation for line *B* in slope-intercept form. Because lines *A* and *B* are perpendicular, knowing the slope of *A* will allow you to find the slope of *B*. So first, find the slope of line *A* using the two-point formula for slope:

$$\text{Slope} = \frac{y_2 - y_1}{x_2 - x_1} = \frac{3-0}{0-5} = -\frac{3}{5}$$

Line *B* is perpendicular to line *A*, so its slope is the negative reciprocal of line *A*. Thus, the slope of line *B* is $\frac{5}{3}$. A point on line *B* is (2, –1), so use the point-slope form to find the equation for line *B*:

$$y - y_1 = m(x - x_1)$$
$$y - (-1) = m(x - 2)$$

Now put this equation into the slope-intercept form:

$$y + 1 = \frac{5}{3}x - \frac{10}{3}$$
$$y = \frac{5}{3}x - \frac{10}{3} - 1$$
$$y = \frac{5}{3}x - \frac{13}{3}$$

Therefore, the *y*-intercept of this line is $-\frac{13}{3}$, so the right answer is (D). (For more on line equations, flip to Chapter 6.)

16. **E.** Begin by factoring the first two terms and the last two terms on the left side of the equation:

$$2z^3 - 3z^2 - 8z + 12 = 0$$
$$z^2(2z - 3) - 4(2z - 3) = 0$$

Notice that the terms inside the parentheses match. That means you can use the distributive property:

$$(z^2 - 4)(2z - 3) = 0$$

Factor $z^2 - 4$ as the difference of two squares:

$$(z + 2)(z - 2)(2z - 3) = 0$$

Now, split the equation into three separate equations:

$$z + 2 = 0 \qquad z - 2 = 0 \qquad 2z - 3 = 0$$

Solve each equation in turn:

$$z = -2 \quad \text{or} \quad z = 2 \quad \text{or} \quad 2z = 3$$
$$z = \frac{3}{2}$$

The three values of z are –2, 2, and $\frac{3}{2}$, so multiply these together:

$$(-2)(2)\left(\frac{3}{2}\right) = -6$$

Thus, the right answer is (E). Note that if you're good with your graphing calculator, an alternative approach to this problem is to enter the equation and graph it. The three points where the graph crosses the x-axis are the three values of z. Then just multiply them together for the right answer of –6.

Answer Key

Section 1

1. **D**	6. **E**	11. **D**	16. **D**
2. **E**	7. **C**	12. **B**	17. **A**
3. **C**	8. **B**	13. **A**	18. **E**
4. **B**	9. **D**	14. **B**	19. **D**
5. **E**	10. **C**	15. **D**	20. **D**

Section 2

1. **E**	6. **E**	11. **1440**	16. **90**
2. **C**	7. **D**	12. **22.5** or **45/2**	17. **95**
3. **E**	8. **D**	13. **22**	18. **5**
4. **C**	9. **90**	14. **1881**	
5. **E**	10. **3.5** or **7/2**	15. **36**	

Section 3

1. **D**	5. **D**	9. **B**	13. **C**
2. **D**	6. **B**	10. **C**	14. **B**
3. **C**	7. **C**	11. **C**	15. **D**
4. **C**	8. **D**	12. **E**	16. **E**

Part V
The Part of Tens

The 5th Wave By Rich Tennant

In this part . . .

Just for fun, Part V includes a few top-ten lists related to SAT math. The first list gives you ten tips telling you how to make the most of your study time between now and your SAT and how to boost your score on the actual test. And in Chapter 17, I discuss ten ways to help you feel calm and comfortable on test day.

Chapter 16

Ten Tips to Improve Your SAT Math Score

In This Chapter

- Using your current math class to your best advantage
- Doing calculations in your head and with a calculator
- Focusing on math and problem-solving skills that are SAT-specific
- Taking and retaking timed tests

What are the best uses of your precious time while studying for the math sections of the SAT? In this chapter, I list what I consider to be the ten most important practices you can implement to garner the skills you need most.

Study Diligently in Your Math Classes

Getting a good score on the SAT isn't a trick. The SAT does a very good job of testing what you really know about math. No amount of "guessing (B) or (D)" is going to get you a good score if your math skills are nonexistent.

Fortunately, your current math class is the one place that you can go where, for no money out of your pocket, you can build these skills. Even if the curriculum in your current class is beyond what's tested on the SAT I — for example, if you're studying trigonometry, pre-calculus, or calculus — staying current is going to help you. (And blowing it off isn't going to help your SAT score, your grades, or your readiness for college.)

Look at it this way: If you're looking to get into college, you need both a good SAT score *and* good grades. Studying hard in your math classes will pay off on both fronts.

Get Good at Doing Basic Calculations in Your Head

There's a big difference between knowing something and knowing it cold. Chances are, you know what 2 + 2 equals without even thinking about it. But do you get thrown by $-8 - (-6)$? How quickly can you find the common denominator of $\frac{5}{6}$ and $\frac{7}{8}$? Do you feel confident about your ability to factor $6x^2 - 4xy$ without stress?

In Chapter 2, I list types of calculations that you should be able to do in your head quickly and without much thought. These include performing operations on negative numbers and fractions, doing simple percent problems, decomposing small numbers into their prime factors, finding common denominators, and doing some basic algebraic manipulations.

Get Good at Using Your Calculator

Calculators — including graphing calculators and scientific calculators — are allowed on the SAT, providing you with a great opportunity to save time and avoid mistakes. Although you don't want to use your calculator for simple calculations that you could do more quickly in your head, I encourage you to use it whenever it may be really helpful.

In Chapter 2, I provide a list of the calculator skills I believe are most helpful on the SAT. These include working with fractions, calculating powers and square roots, solving and graphing equations, and generating input-output tables.

Study SAT-Specific Math Skills

The SAT tests a relatively limited set of skills, such as arithmetic, algebra, geometry, functions and coordinate geometry, and a smattering of additional topics. (You don't need trigonometry, for instance, to do well on the SAT.) And inside each of these broad skills is a related set of subskills. For example, in geometry, you need to know how to find the area of a triangle, but you can safely avoid just about everything you know about doing geometric proofs.

You can think of these as the basic toolset that you need to answer most SAT questions. In Chapters 3 through 7, I break down these skills and subskills. Focusing on strengthening these SAT-specific math skills is time well spent as you prepare for the test.

Study SAT-Specific Problem-Solving Skills

SAT questions are usually quick to solve after you see the "way in" — the math principle or formula that's being tested. Some problems are tough because they rely on putting together two unrelated math ideas together in a novel way.

After you know the basic math skills necessary to succeed, the next skill to attain is becoming quick at identifying which tools are most likely to help you answer a specific question. In Chapter 9, I focus on these problem-solving skills, such as determining what a question is asking and which skills you need to answer it, making diagrams and charts, identifying useful formulas, and finding a path from the facts you're given to what the question is asking for.

Get Comfortable Turning Words into Numbers

In a sense, word problems are a very specific type of reading comprehension question. You need to become good at the careful type of reading that allows you to turn information in a word problem into numbers, symbols, and equations. In many cases, you may find that after turning words into numbers, the rest of a word problem is a lot easier than it looks, and you can solve it easily in your head or with a calculator. Check out Chapter 8 for some tips on translating between math and English.

Take Timed Practice Tests

No matter how good your math skills are, you should practice for the SAT with timed tests. Time pressure adds a dimension to a test that isn't normally present when you're studying. It also forces you to make trade-offs, such as skipping over a problem that looks difficult or time-consuming.

This book contains hundreds of questions to practice on without the clock running. But it also includes three full timed practice tests with a total of 162 questions. I highly recommend saving these questions for when you're ready to practice under the timed conditions stated at the top of each test. You can also visit `sat.collegeboard.com` to get a free, official SAT practice test from the College Board.

Study from Your Timed Practice Tests

After you take a practice test, go over the answers you got wrong and find out why. Use the test to fill in gaps in your knowledge that may be useful on the next test.

Remember, any math skill that showed up on one question is likely to show up on a later SAT — possibly yours. Furthermore, as you spend time examining SAT questions in depth, you'll begin to get a sense of how they're put together, giving you an advantage in answering questions you haven't seen.

Retake Your Timed Practice Tests

In studying from the practice tests you've already taken, did you really absorb new material? One way to find out is to take the test again. My advice is to wait a few weeks so that you forget the specifics of each question. In the meantime, take a few more practice tests and study those, too. Then go back and retake a test. Your score will almost certainly be better than your score the first time you took it. But take a good, hard look at the questions you miss the second time around to be sure you know what you need to know on your SAT date.

Take the SAT More Than Once

No matter how prepared you are for your SAT, you're bound to be a little nervous and uncertain your first time. But if you take the test more than once, you'll begin to know what to expect and be able to plan ahead for it.

I recommend taking the test for the first time as early as you can, just for practice. That way, you know that your first time taking the test doesn't have to count, so you can relax and (dare I say?) have fun with it — or at least minimize your anxiety throughout the process.

Chapter 17

Ten Tips to Be at Your Best on the SAT

In This Chapter

- Making sure you're relaxed
- Limiting your study time

The SAT is a big deal, right? So for the 24 hours before the test, you're entitled to do whatever it is you do to gain peace, focus, and self-empowerment. If that sounds a bit selfish, so be it. It's only for one day, so your friends and family should understand, provided you don't act like a complete heel. Here are my top ten recommendations for the day and night leading up to the SAT.

Do Something Fun the Day Before the Test

The day before your SAT is *your day* to do whatever you like to feel good: go out to dinner, order a pizza, spend time with friends, spend time alone, watch a romantic comedy, watch a scary movie, go swimming, go roller skating, play with the dog, go out to the mall — whatever makes you happy and glad to be alive.

This includes taking the day before the test off from work. I mean it. Your job is important, but the SAT is more important than any single day of work. Given proper notice (at least two weeks if possible), any employer should be ready, willing, and able to accommodate you.

Don't Study for More Than 20 Minutes the Night Before the Test

A common piece of advice is not to study the night before the SAT. I recommend this, too, and if it works for you, then definitely use it. I understand, however, that some students simply won't be able to put the books and the notes away and not look at them.

So if you're convinced that *not* studying the night before the test will make you more nervous than studying, here's a compromise: Study no more than 20 minutes the night before. Don't take a practice test or try to cram in any new information. Instead, just look over a few notes and reread what you already know to reinforce it.

Pack Everything You Need the Night Before

REMEMBER

I recommend that you make a checklist of everything you want to bring to the test, pack these items the night before, and place them by the door so you won't forget them. Here are some must-have items for the SAT:

- Admission ticket
- Photo ID
- Calculator with fresh batteries
- Extra batteries
- Lots of sharp number 2 pencils

Additionally, here are a few extra items you may consider:

- Water bottle
- Convenient snacks (energy bars or trail mix is perfect)
- Pocket pencil sharpener
- Tissues

Also, if you have any special-needs items, consider these as well. For example, if you wear contact lenses, you may want to bring an extra pair or a pair of glasses just in case.

Do Something Relaxing before Bed

The night before your SAT is a good time to just take it easy and wind down so you can get to bed early. It's natural to be nervous, so do whatever you can to quiet yourself before bed so that you sleep better. I recommend soft lighting, a cup of hot milk or chamomile tea, and something really boring on TV, like a documentary on the history of the paper clip.

Get a Good Night's Sleep

TIP

Get to bed early and, if you have trouble sleeping, try this trick: Put your pillow at the foot of the bed and sleep in a different direction from your usual position. Sounds goofy, but it works every time!

Wear Several Layers of Clothing

Nothing is worse in my experience than being too hot or too cold. So wear enough layers of clothing that you can remove or add to them depending upon the temperature of the room.

Arrive at the Test Site Extra Early

The last thing you want is to get a late start or run into an unexpected delay and arrive at the test site stressed and out of breath. So plan to get to the test site especially early.

By the way, be sure to check the date of your test. I have a friend who had some really tense moments when she arrived and the test administrators for a *different* test told her the SAT wasn't being given that day. She discovered that she was one week early for her test!

Spend Your Time Just before the Test However You Please

Between your arrival at the test site and the start of the test, do whatever works for you. Be alone if you want to be alone, talk to a friend if you feel like it, and excuse yourself from talking to anyone you don't care for or about anything you don't want to talk about. After the test is over, you can resume the normal give-and-take of social living. But until the test is over, give yourself full permission to take care of yourself the way *you* need instead of worrying about anybody else.

Remember to Breathe

Breathing is so important. I do it every day, and so should you. Seriously, though, if you find yourself getting nervous as the test approaches or while you're taking it, stop and take a couple of slow, deep breaths. Whether you believe it or not, a bit of oxygen is very calming, provided you don't overdo it. And it's free, while supplies last. While you breathe, repeat to yourself the words "I'm doing my best." You can do no better.

Skip Over Any Questions That Throw You

Read each question, but give yourself the liberty of skipping over any questions that you're really not sure what to do with. All the questions are scored equally, so you might as well start out by answering as many of the easy ones as you can.

As the questions start to get tough toward the end of a section, feel free to circle back to the beginning and start working on the first question you jumped over. Compared to the tougher questions, an earlier question may not look quite as difficult as it did when you first encountered it.

Index

• Q •

• R •

• S •

Notes

Notes